THE CROW AND THE EAGLE

THE CROW AND THE EAGLE

A TRIBAL HISTORY FROM
LEWIS AND CLARK TO CUSTER

KEITH ALGIER

Cover Artwork by Larry Milligan

The CAXTON PRINTERS, Ltd.

Caldwell, Idaho

1993

Library of Congress Cataloging-in-Publication Data

Algier, Keith W.
    The Crow and the Eagle : a tribal history from
Lewis and Clark to Custer / Keith Algier.
        p.   cm.
    Includes bibliographical references and index.
    ISBN 0-87004-357-9 (pbk) : $14.95
    1. Crow Indians--History.   2. Crow Indians--
Government relations.
    I. Title.
E99.C92A44   1993
973'.04975--dc20   93-8008

Lithographed and bound in the United States of America by
The CAXTON PRINTERS, Ltd.
Caldwell, ID 83605
156486

FOR ANN AND JO

CONTENTS

LIST OF ILLUSTRATIONS

ABBREVIATIONS

DRNR   *Documents Relating to the Negotiations of Ratified and Unratified Treaties with Various Tribes of Indians, 1801–69.* National Archives Microfilm Publications, Microcopy T-494, reel 4.

HSML   Historical Society of Montana.

ISHL   Illinois State Historical Library.

LRMS   *Letters Received by the Office of Indian Affairs, Montana Superintendency, 1864–1880.* National Archives Microfilm Publications, Microcopy 234.

LRUM   *Letters Received by the Office of Indian Affairs, 1824–1881, Upper Missouri Agency.* National Archives Microfilm Publications, Microcopy 234.

LRUP   *Letters Received by the Office of Indian Affairs, 1824–1881, Upper Platte Agency.* National Archives Microfilm Publications, Microcopy 234.

MHS   Missouri Historical Society

RCFS   *Returns from U.S. Military Posts, 1800–1916, Fort C.F. Smith, Montana, August 1866-July 1868.* National Archives Microfilm Publications, Microcopy 617, reel 1190.

RCIA   Annual Report of the Commissioner of Indian Affairs.

ROLS   *Records of the Office of Indian Affairs: Letters Sent.* National Archives Microfilm Publications, Microcopy, M21.

RPFE   *Returns from U.S. Military Posts 1800–1916, Fort Ellis, Montana, August, 1867-December, 1876.* National Archives Microfilm Publications, Microcopy 617, reel 347.

RMSI   *Records of the Montana Superintendency of Indian Affairs, 1867–73.* National Archives Microfilm Publications, Microcopy M883.

RWDS   *Records of the War Department Army Commands: Fort C.F. Smith, Montana: General and Special Orders, March, 1867-July, 1868.* Microcopy, Wyoming State Archives.

RWLR   *Records of the War Department Army Commands: Department of the Platte, Selected Letters Received, 1867–68.* Microcopy, Wyoming State Archives.

TCG   *The Congressional Globe,* University Microfilms, Ann Arbor, Michigan, 1957. Microform.

TCR   *The Congressional Record,* University Microfilms, Ann Arbor, Michigan, 1956. Microform.

PREFACE

History is replete with instances of aggression. Certainly the story of relations between the several European states and the aboriginal peoples of the Americas during the sixteenth and seventeenth centuries could serve as a primer on the subject. By far the most spectacular example of conquest in the New World was prosecuted in the name of Spain. Within little more than a generation, Spanish *conquistadores* not only conquered the advanced Aztec and Inca civilizations, they, by defeating a congeries of smaller and weaker tribes, extended Spanish sovereignty over additional regions of the Western Hemisphere as well. Spain consolidated her conquests in the New World and elsewhere into an enormous overseas empire which contributed to the country's emergence as a world power during the sixteenth century.

The English conquest of the Americas followed a less dramatic, more gradual course. Generally, English colonists displaced Indians only as their lands appeared to have value. As in the Spanish instance, however, they didn't hesitate to use force when it suited their purposes. The United States, as heir to the English colonial system, followed the English model in its relations with Indian neighbors. This book is dedicated to an examination and analysis of the United States government's displacement of a small tribe of Indians, the Crow, from their homeland on the western extremities of the Northern Plains.

The conquest of Crow domain was complicated by the persistence of intertribal warfare for most of the nineteenth century. The Crow found it necessary, not always successfully, to protect their lands against the territorial aspirations of one or another of their larger and more powerful neighbors. It is ironic, then, that when the tribe eventually lost most of its traditional homeland, it was to an entity with which it enjoyed generally peaceful relations. The United States employed tactics far more subtle than warfare to displace the Crow from their lands. Taking advantage of an ever-increasing dependency on whites for manufactured goods, representatives of Great Father, perhaps unwittingly, found it a simple matter to establish and maintain a presence in the tribe's homeland until such time as the government of the United States was ready to absorb it.

THE CROW AND THE EAGLE

ONE

EXACTLY IN THE RIGHT PLACE

The nineteenth century, notable for so many profound changes in so many areas of life, was appropriately ushered in by two cataclysmic political upheavals. The American Revolution launched a bold political experiment based on radical ideas about the business of governing which would eventually change the face of politics throughout the world. The French Revolution followed hard on the heels of the American movement to serve as a model for violent political change for generations to come. It also unleashed forces which kept not only France in a state of turmoil for at least a generation but most of the rest of Europe as well. Two heirs of these movements, Thomas Jefferson and Napoleon Bonaparte, negotiated an agreement early in the new century which would prove to have convulsive consequences for a small tribe of American Indians, the Crow or Absaroka. In 1803 the two rulers signed the Louisiana Purchase for their respective nation states. It is unlikely that either man was aware of the existence of the Crow, and certainly no member of that tribe had ever heard of either Jefferson or Bonaparte. The Louisiana Purchase, nonetheless, set in motion a train of events that in time would irrevocably change most circumstances of Crow life.

The Crow homeland during the first half of the nineteenth century conformed generally to the drainage basin of the Yellowstone (Elk)[1] River, embracing something less than the southern quarter of the state of Montana and most of the northern two-thirds of Wyoming. The Yellowstone River flows northward out of Yellowstone Lake through north-western Wyoming into Montana, where, near Livingston, it disgorges from steep canyon walls to abruptly change course to the east. From the Big Bend the river courses through a valley bordered on the north by sandstone hills and on the south by the Absaroka Mountains. Yellowstone Valley gradually widens after it leaves the Absarokas, and, in the vicinity of Miles City, veers in a northeasterly direction to join the Missouri River near the Montana-North Dakota border.

Wind River is the Yellowstone's major affluent. It rises in the Wind River Range to flow in an easterly direction to a point near Riverton, Wyoming where it makes juncture with the Popo Agie River. Here the combined streams turn sharply north to flow through Wind River Canyon where it emerges with a new identity. The Big Horn River runs in a northerly direction to receive waters from the Greybull and Shoshone (Stinking Water) Rivers on the west and from Nowood and Shell Creeks from the east before reaching Big Horn Canyon. From the mouth of the canyon it flows north by east to its confluence with the Little Big Horn River and eventual union with Yellowstone River some fifty miles east of Billings, Montana. Tributaries which enter the Yellowstone on its south bank are Clark's Fork (Rotten Sun Dance Lodge) and Stillwater River (Buffalo Jumps Over the Bank). East of the mouth of the Big Horn, the Rosebud, Tongue and Powder Rivers empty into the Yellowstone from its south side. No streams of any consequence enter the river from the north.

The Crow and their neighbors seem not to have recognized precise territorial boundaries in the same sense that modern nation states do. Generally, however, the Crow tribe regarded the Yellowstone and North Platte Rivers as its north and south boundaries, respectively. The Absaroka Mountains constituted its west boundary and a nebulous line running in a north-south direction someplace between the Missouri and Powder Rivers served as its eastern border. Crow territory encompassed a vast plain which ranges in elevation fro 3,500 to 6,000 feet. Its landscape, much of it harsh and forbidding in appearance, is dominated by lonely buttes, sharp escarpments, low mesas, and rolling hills. Its surface is scarred by hundreds of arroyos or ravines sculpted by the region's many intermittent streams.

Several major mountain chains relieve the monotony of this immense tableland. The Absaroka Range forms a massive barrier on the west with its elevated volcanic plateau capped by peaks ranging in elevation from 12,000 to 13,000 feet. In the vicinity of Togowatee Pass, the Absarokas bifurcate to form the Owl Creek and Wind River Mountains. The magnificent Wind Rivers rise abruptly out of the prairie to create a serrated wall which at its highest point, Gannett Peak, attains an elevation of 13,785 feet and which forms the southern rim of the cornucopia-shaped Wind River Valley. The Owl Creek Mountains, significantly less impressive, form the northern rim of the valley.

Wind River Canyon separates the Owl Creek Range from the Bridger Mountains which bend gently east by north to meld with the much larger Big Horn Range. These mountains run generally north for fifty miles or so at a width varying from thirty to fifty miles. The majestic Big Horns are capped by Cloud Peak, which, at an altitude of 13,615 feet, straddles the range much like a squat sentinel searching the horizon in every direction for enemies of the Crow. In the vicinity of Cloud Peak, near Buffalo, Wyoming,

the Big Horns arc to the northwest, terminating at Big
Horn Canyon. A convenient way of looking at this
particular part of Crow territory is to visualize the
Absaroka/Owl Creek and Bridger/Big Horn Mountain
Ranges as lofty, craggy parentheses marks enclosing
the Big Horn River, and, in the process, forming the
Big Horn Basin. The area on both sides of the T
traced by the Big Horn River from the mouth of Big
Horn Canyon to its confluence with the Yellowstone
constituted the heart of Crow domain. This region of
gently-rolling and grass-covered hills, bounded by the
Rosebud River on the east and by Stillwater River on
the west, served as a focus for tribal ceremonies and
buffalo hunts.

The sharp contrasts which characterize the
topography of the Crow homeland are mirrored in a
climate which ranges from frigid alpine to searing
desert. Lowland regions are dry, varying from semi-
arid to arid. The paucity of precipitation is due in
part to the great distances which separate this region
from the nearest bodies of ocean waters but also to
topographic configuration. The Absaroka and Wind
River Mountains milk moisture-laden clouds of their
precious cargo, creating a rain shadow over the Big
Horn Basin. The Big Horn Range is responsible for
creating a similar situation on its leeward side. As a
consequence, mountainous regions average as much as
forty inches per year while some lowland areas receive
as little as six inches per annum. Most precipitation
falls in the summer months, usually during late
afternoon or early evening, and is often in the form of
cloudbursts accompanied by spectacular displays of
lightning and thunder.

The oblique angles at which the sun's rays strike
the earth's surface at this latitude dictate sharply
defined seasons. Winter is the time that tries men's
souls in Crow country. Frigid Canadian air can seep

through mountain passes to chill the land and collide with warmer air to produce snow as early as the month of September. Sub-zero temperatures are likely in mid-winter, even at lower elevations, bringing raw days and bitterly cold nights. Occasional relief is afforded inhabitants of the region by sudden intrusions of warm air, called chinooks, which sweep down from surrounding mountains to unexpectedly cause temperature rises of from thirty to forty degrees within a matter of minutes.

Winter gives way only grudgingly and tentatively to spring. Killing frosts and snow storms can occur as late as the month of June, even in the lowlands. July is the hottest month. Daytime temperatures of 100 degrees are not at all uncommon on the plains, but temperatures fall dramatically during the evening hours making summer nights passably cool. Autumn is by far the most pleasant and comfortable season of the year. Fall days are marked by bright sunshine but are, for the most part, crisp and cool. During late fall, although warm winds from the Gulf of Mexico intermittently delay the onset of cold weather, there are unmistakable signs in the air that the dreaded winter months are not far off.

A spare, muscular kind of land, the desert-like plains of Crow territory are treeless except for the valleys of permanent streams and rivers. The region's mountain ranges perform the critical function of storing precious water reserves in the form of deep snow packs and glaciers until needed by parched lowland areas. Runoffs feed a ribbon-like network of stream and river bottoms which support stands of cottonwood, willow, ash, and box-elder trees as well as a variety of shrubs and bushes. All of this is not to say that lands at lower elevations are otherwise devoid of vegetation. The prairie is, in fact, covered with an olive-drab carpet of xerophytic grasses which assume various hues of brighter green during the spring months and which turn a tawny color in winter. It is, moreover, studded with sagebrush and other xerophytic shrubs, lending texture to an otherwise rather barren landscape.

Given its sparse vegetation, Crow domain supported a surprisingly wide variety of wild life in surprisingly large numbers throughout most of the nineteenth century. Game animals included bear, bison or buffalo, elk, pronghorn or antelope, deer, and big horn sheep. Smaller animals such as coyotes, wolves, beaver, and otter were also found there in abundance. Water fowl in the form of ducks, geese, and cranes were present during certain seasons. Land-based birds, including magpies, sage-cocks, hawks, and eagles, could be found there throughout the year. The area's waterways literally teemed with trout, carp, and other fish. The Crow homeland was, in fact, widely regarded by those most intimate with the American West, as prime hunting grounds. Most nineteenth century visitors to the region who have left written accounts of their travels commented not only on the wide variety of wild life to be found there but on the large quantities of game as well.[2]

For the Crow, buffalo was the game animal of choice, constituting, in fact, a migratory natural resource which provided the tribe with virtually all raw materials necessary to satisfy its material needs. Not only did buffalo constitute a rich natural resource, they were also relatively easy to harvest. Although almost constantly moving in search of sustenance, they travel with deliberate slowness, and because they have strong herd instincts, migrate in large bodies. Meat from cows was preferred by the Crow. Tongue, brains, and liver were routinely consumed raw. Other edible parts were either boiled or broiled; cuts from the hump were considered to be

TAKING THE HUMP RIB
Buffalo were the game animals of choice for not only the Crow and other Plains
Indians but for trappers as well.
Courtesy Walters Art Gallery, Baltimore   *A. Jacob Miller*

a particular delicacy. Meat not immediately consumed was processed into pemmican for future consumption.[3] So completely did buffalo flesh satisfy their food needs and wants and so fond were they of buffalo meat that the Crow only infrequently ate meat from other game animals found in such abundance in their homeland. And, unlike some neighboring tribes, they never resorted to the eating of dogs, nor did they normally consume fish or fowl.[4]

Until late in the nineteenth century, the Crow used buffalo skins to cover their tipis. They preferred hides without hair for this purpose, and, because bison shed their winter coats as the weather warms, the tribe conducted hunts for new lodge coverings during the late spring and early summer months. From twelve to twenty skins were needed for each lodge, depending on the size desired. Skins taken from other animals were utilized for some articles of clothing, but robes designed to provide warmth invariably were taken from buffalo. Hides from females killed during autumn and early winter when coats were new, shiny, and thick made ideal robes, and special hunts for suitable specimens were made during this season.[5] Bull hides were too thick to be used for this purpose but could be made into straps, saddles, bridles, shields, and boats. The hides of young bulls were suitable for making parfleche bags. Actually, little of this utilitarian animal was allowed to go to waste. Horns could be fashioned into bowls, cups, and spoons; tails could be made into whips; bladders were suitable for use as receptacles to hold liquids and buffalo droppings sometimes served as a substitute for firewood.[6]

A natural resource not highly valued by the Crow was responsible for first attracting citizens of the United States to the tribe's homeland. Prior to intrusion by whites, beaver were little more than objects of curiosity to the Indians; certainly they weren't valued for economic reasons. The Crow believed that of all the animals known to them, beaver were the most closely akin to humans. In fact, according to one of their myths, the first Crow were offspring of beaver.[7] The attribute of the animals which most interested outsiders, forerunners of those who would eventually displace the tribe from most of its lands, was their thick fur. Beaver fur is made up of two distinct layers: a dense and woolly growth close to the skin and a more luxuriant growth of longer, silky hairs. European and American hat makers found this combination ideal as the main ingredient in the manufacture of formal headwear. As in the case of bison and other game animals, visitors were struck by the number and size of beaver colonies to be found in the region's waterways.[8]

In addition to supporting a plethora of wild life, Crow domain also hosted a variety of mythic beings. One such was a wolf-man who inhabited the lower reaches of Big Horn Canyon. He customarily hid in water falls, waiting to pounce upon and devour unsuspecting human beings.[9] Actually, all large bodies of water contained frightening creatures of one kind or another. What they all had in common was an insatiable appetite for human flesh. It was thought by some Crow that bright colors painted on the body would ward off the area's water creatures, but the more prudent cast food upon the waters before attempting to cross streams or rivers as a means of assuaging the creatures' hunger.

More benign from the Crow perspective were the Spectre Horsemen. These often appeared on either flank of battlefields to aid Crow fighting contingents which found themselves in difficult straits. Spectre Horsemen were invisible to Crow warriors, but their presence was all too apparent to their enemies, according to tribal mythology.[10] Other unworldly inhabitants of Crow territory included the dwarf people, a tribe of tiny people possessed of extraordinary physical strength. Stone arrowheads, quite different from any ever used by the Crow, were to be found in various parts of the tribe's territory, and conventional wisdom had it that these were made and used by the dwarfs.[11]

Crow domain was a magical land in yet another

sense. It was an article of faith among tribal members that almost anything found in nature had the ability to confer *maxpe*, the Crow version of "medicine," on human beings. The idea here was that the Great Spirit, or First Worker as he was known to most Crow, routinely assigned a "helper" to each individual at birth. A helper could be in almost any form. It might be the wind, the sun, the moon, or one of the more prominent stars. Or it could be an animal or a plant. It might even be a combination of two or more of the above. The problem with this arrangement from the standpoint of the individual was that First Worker assigned helpers without bothering to identify them to recipients. The trick, then, was to somehow persuade or induce one's helper to reveal and identify itself. Tribal custom dictated that this would be most likely achieved by retiring to a secluded mountain top in search of revelation.[12]

Mountain vigils began with a sweat bath to purify the body so that it would be acceptable to the helper if and when it should appear. Supplicants then entered into a rigorous fast and stretched out, feet pointing to the east, in the hope that the supernatural partisan, whatever it might turn out to be, would take pity and reveal itself in a vision. If a vision had not been received by sunrise, those truly dedicated to the enterprise placed an index finger on a log and lopped it off at the first joint. The severed flesh was immediately proffered on a buffalo chip. At this point the aspirant threw himself on the ground to grovel and wail in supplication.[13]

Visions, if and when received, included the appearance of an apparition representing the supplicant's assigned helper, usually in surrealistic form. In most instances the apparition foretold the seeker's future, identified taboos to be observed and revealed a chant which could be used to summon aid when needed. Because most visions had an enigmatic quality about them, recipients in almost all cases found it convenient to seek interpretations for their visions from tribal leaders known to possess strong *maxpe*. Once identified, helpers were expected to provide aid in prevailing against one's enemies, garnering respect from fellow tribesmen, acquiring horses and attracting good-looking women. Fetishes representing helpers were fashioned so that the embodiment of one's access to supernatural power might be kept close at hand at all times. Vigils might last four days and nights, although not every seeker of revelation possessed the stamina and fortitude to persist for that length of time. Nor did all those who endured for the prescribed time receive revelations. Many found it necessary to hold more than one vigil to achieve success in this regard, and some were never successful in persuading helpers to reveal themselves.[14]

The Crow homeland was, then, an enchanted, game-rich oasis tucked away in the northern reaches of the Great American Desert. Crow attitudes and general sentiments about their domain were probably accurately expressed by a tribal leader named Rotten Belly (Arapooish) in the early 1830s when he described his country in the following terms to Robert Campbell, a prominent fur trapper and trader:

> The Crow country is a good country. The Great Spirit has put it exactly in the right place; while you are in it you fare well; whenever you go out of it, whichever way you travel, you fare worse. If you go to the south, you have to wander over great barren plains; the water is warm and bad, and you meet the fever and ague. To the north it is cold; the winters are long and bitter with no grass; you cannot keep horses there, but must travel with dogs. What is a country without horses? On the Columbia they are poor and dirty, paddle about in a canoe and eat fish. Their

teeth are worn out; they are always taking fish bones out of their mouths. Fish is poor food. To the east, they dwell in villages; they live well, but they drink the muddy water of the Missouri—that is bad. A Crow dog would not drink such water. About the forks of the Missouri is a fine country; good water, good grass, plenty of buffalo. In summer it is almost as good as the Crow country; but in winter it is cold; the grass is gone; and there is no salt weed for horses. The Crow country is exactly in the right place. It has snowy mountains and sunny plains, all kinds of climate and good things for every season. When the summer heats scorch the prairies, you can draw up under the mountains where the air is sweet and cool, the grass fresh, and the bright streams come tumbling out of the snow banks. There you can hunt the elk, the deer, and the antelope, when their skins are fit for dressing; there you will find plenty of white bears and mountain sheep. In the autumn, when your horses are fit and strong from the mountain pasture, you can go down into the plains and hunt the buffalo, or trap beaver on the streams. And when winter comes on, you can take shelter in the woody bottoms along the rivers; there you will find buffalo meat for yourselves, and cottonwood bark for your horses; or you may winter in the Wind River Valley where there is salt weed in abundance. The Crow country is exactly in the right place. Everything good is to be found there. There is no country like the Crow country.[15]

Advantages to be found in Rotten Belly's homeland as cited by the chief, especially the variety of game there, would prove to be a mixed blessing for the tribe during the nineteenth century. On the one hand, the presence of so many buffalo in Crow domain assured a plentiful food supply, but, on the other hand, their numbers excited the envy of neighboring tribes whose lands were less generously endowed with game animals. During the second half of the century, a gradual decline in the numbers of buffalo to be found on lands to the south and particularly on lands to the east would increase the attractiveness of Crow domain in the eyes of the inhabitants of those areas. The Crow tribe, with a population which probably did not exceed sixty-five hundred at any time during the century, enjoyed numerical superiority over few of its neighbors. The tribe, in fact, was overwhelmingly outnumbered by at least two tribes on or near its borders and would consequently find itself hard pressed at times to maintain its territorial integrity.

The Crow seem to have had rough numerical parity with the Cheyenne tribe, living proximately east of Crow territory on lands lying between the Powder and Missouri Rivers.[16] Three tribes living east of the Cheyenne had smaller populations than the Crow. The Arikara, Mandan, and Hidatsa were horticulturists who inhabited semi-permanent villages situated on or near the banks of the Missouri. Farming supplemented both trade and the chase in all three tribes. At the turn of the century, the Arikara villages were located near the mouth of Grand River; the Mandan and Hidatsa lived in close proximity to one another in five villages clustered around the confluence of Knife River with the Missouri. All three tribes had known better times in that by the year 1800 they found themselves in greatly diminished circumstances as compared with earlier days in terms of power, wealth, prestige, and total numbers. What influence they still enjoyed among the inhabitants of the area had to do with a trading monopoly they had earlier established with European firms.[17]

Immediately behind these sedentary tribes, the powerful Sioux or Dakota nation was poised to continue a westward thrust which by 1800 had already displaced the Cheyenne from their lands along the eastern banks of the Missouri. Nomadic and bellicose, the Dakota made up the most populous family of Indians in the West. The Teton division of the nation was in the vanguard of this particular wave of expansion. Once the Cheyenne had been pushed across the river, the Tetons, occasionally joined by the Yankton and Yanktonai tribes who comprised a second division of the Dakota, turned their attention to the Arikara, Mandan, and Hidatsa villages. Prior to 1800 the aggressors seem to have been content to limit their attacks to small raids and general harassment. Large scale assaults were mounted only infrequently, perhaps because the Dakota tribes found the presence of the villages a convenience in acquiring European manufactured goods. A third Dakota division, the Santee, inhabited lands lying to the east of the Missouri River.[18]

Another nomadic tribe, the Assiniboine, occupied lands north of the confluence of the Yellowstone and Missouri Rivers. Originally part of the Dakota nation, they were every bit as bellicose as their former brethren. Although probably not much larger than the Crow, they, along with their allies, the Cree, constituted a definite threat to Crow security. However, most Assiniboine hostility was directed toward an alliance of four tribes which occupied lands west of and bordering on Assiniboine hunting grounds. The Blackfoot Alliance, which enjoyed at least a two-to-one numerical advantage over the Crow, was made up of the Blackfoot or Siksika, Blood, Piegan, and Atsina or Gros Ventre of the Prairie tribes. With the exception of the Atsina, they shared a common culture and historical background. Atsina culture more closely approximated that of the Arapaho, suggesting a common heritage with that tribe.[19]

Alliance tribes ranged over lands in that part of

present-day Montana lying east of the Rocky
Mountains, north of the Yellowstone and west of
Milk River. Atsina lands bordered those of the Crow
on its southern border, extended west to Judith River
and abutted Assiniboine lands on the east. Alliance
relations with the Assiniboine at the turn of the
century were characterized by vicious if intermittent
warfare, and it can therefore be reasonably concluded
that the Atsina had joined the Alliance as a strategy to
enhance their security against a larger and more
powerful enemy. The Piegan tribe occupied lands
lying between Atsina territory and the Rocky
Mountains, making them the Crow's closest neighbors
to the northwest. The Blackfoot and Blood tribes
occasionally wandered into Montana but spent the
majority of any given year in present-day Canada.
British traders from Canada had forged strong trade
relationships with all four Alliance tribes by 1800.[20]

The country west of Crow domain was inhabited by
a congeries of peoples. Most of these tribes, namely
the Nez Perce, Flatheads, Pend d'Oreille, Coeur
d'Alene, and Kalispell Indians, were too small and
weak to represent a security threat. A much larger
tribe, the Snake or Shoshone, was scattered along the
western flank of the Rocky Mountains, stretching
from Salt Lake on the south all the way to the present
border between the United States and Canada on the
north. Unconsolidated in character, some Shoshone
hadn't progressed beyond the gathering stage of civilization by the turn of the nineteenth century; others
subsisted on buffalo and participated in the nomadic
existence typical of Plains Indian life. During the early
years of the nineteenth century, the most aggressive of
the latter could generally be found on the prairies of
what is today southwestern Wyoming, southeastern
Idaho, and northern Utah.[21]

The point should be made here that the Crow and

their neighbors violated each other's territorial sovereignty with impunity. Plains tribes, extraordinarily mobile, were on the move almost continuously except during the winter season. The vagaries of buffalo migration patterns sometimes inadvertently led tribes onto neighboring lands. Or the necessity of conducting trade might entail the crossing of another tribe's domain to reach trading partners. Intertribal marriages, even among members of traditionally antagonistic peoples, were not uncommon, and trips to visit relatives often involved intrusions into the territory of neighboring tribes.

The major dynamic for boundary violations, however, was the practice of horse-stealing. Plains Indian societies were organized around the horse in much the same sense that industrial societies are organized around the automobile. Horses were regarded as not only being essential for survival but also as an important source of status, particularly if stolen from an enemy. Raiding expeditions conducted for the purpose of acquiring horses belonging to neighboring peoples were therefore everyday occurrences. For whatever reason, representatives of any one of the many Plains tribes might be found in the territory of any other at any given time, sometimes provoking violent responses, sometimes not.

Tribal boundaries, as recognized by the interested parties in 1800, would be rendered moot by a powerful external force which gradually extended its influence and power over the Northern Plains during the course of the first three quarters of the century. The young and dynamic republic created by the American Revolution came to view the addition of this region to its national territory as simply another step in its westward stretch for continental status. Its rambunctious citizenry would prove to be only too willing to act as instruments of expansion as the new nation set out to fulfill what it believed was manifestly its destiny: to become a continental power.

NOTES

1. In those instances in which Crow names differed from modern usage, the Crow name will follow in parenthesis.
2. For reference to wild life to be found in Crow territory during the nineteenth century see RCIA, 1854, Senate Document No. 1 (Serial 746), p. 294; W.F. Raynolds, *Report on the Exploration of the Yellowstone River* (Washington Government Printing Office, 1868), p. 11; L.J. Burpee, ed., *Journal of Larocque from the Assiniboine to the Yellowstone, 1805,* Publications of the Canadian Archives, No. 3 (Ottawa Government Printing Bureau, 1910), p. 30; Edwin Thompson Denig, *Of the Crow Nation* (New York: AMS Press, 1980), p. 21; Hiram Martin Chittenden and Alfred Talbert Richardson, eds., *Life, Letters and Travels of Father De Smet* (New York: Arno Press & New York Times, 1969), I, 239, 243; W.T. Hamilton, *My Sixty Years on the Plains* (Norman: University of Oklahoma Press, 1960), p. 33; F.V. Hayden, *On the Ethnography and Philology of the Indian Tribes of the Missouri Valley,* Transactions of the American Philosophical Society (Philadelphia: Blanchard and Lea, 1862), II, 392.
3. Thomas B. Marquis, *Memoirs of a White Crow Indian* (Lincoln: University of Nebraska Press, 1974), p. 156.
4. A.M. Quivey, ed., "Bradley Manuscript: Book F," *Contributions to the Historical Society of Montana,* VIII (1917), 200; Thomas B. Marquis, *Custer, Cavalry & Crows* (Fort Collins: The Old Army Press, 1975), p. 127.
5. Frank B. Linderman, *Pretty Shield* (Lincoln: University of Nebraska Press, 1972), p. 127.
6. Nicholas Point, *Wilderness Kingdom* (New York, Chicago, San Francisco: Holt, Rinehart and Wilson, 1967), p. 120.
7. Chittenden and Richardson, *op. cit.,* IV, 1375.
8. F.G. Young, *The Correspondence and Journals of Captain Nathaniel J. Wyeth* (New York: Arno Press, 1973), p. 209; Richard E. Jensen, ed., "A Description of the Fur Trade in 1831 by John Dougherty," *Nebraska History,* LVI, No. 1 (Spring, 1975), 116.
9. Burpee, *op. cit.,* p. 42.
10. James H. Bradley, "Indian Traditions," *Contributions to the Historical Society of Montana,* IX (1923), 294.
11. Frank B. Linderman, *Plenty Coups: Chief of the Crows* (Lincoln: University of Nebraska Press, 1962), p. 40.
12. Robert H. Lowie, *The Crow Indians* (New York: Farrar and Rinehart, Incorporated, 1935), pp. 237-51; Peter Nabokov, *Two Leggings: The Making of a Crow Warrior* (New York: Thomas Y. Crowell Publishers, 1967), pp. 23-26.
13. For first-hand accounts of vigils, see *Ibid,* pp. 56-60, 62-65; Linderman, *Plenty Coups,* pp. 34-43, 58-67.
14. Lowie, *op. cit.,* p. 248.

15. Washington Irving, *The Adventures of Captain Bonneville, U.S.A.* in *The Rocky Mountains and Far West,* ed. Edgeley Todd (Norman: University of Oklahoma Press, 1961), pp. 164–65.
16. John H. Moore, *The Cheyenne Nation* (Lincoln and London: University of Nebraska Press, 1987), pp. 82–85.
17. Roy W. Meyer, *The Village Indians of the Upper Missouri* (Lincoln and London: University of Nebraska Press, 1977), pp. 37–43.
18. *Ibid,* p. 40; George E. Hyde, *Spotted Tail's Folk* (Norman: University of Oklahoma Press, 1974), p. 4.
19. John C. Ewers, *Blackfeet Indians* (New York and London: Garland Publishing, Inc., 1974), pp. 34–37.
20. *Ibid,* pp. 51–53.
21. Chittenden and Richardson, *op. cit.,* III, 990–7.

TWO

THROUGH A GLASS SEEN DARKLY

In the beginning there was only water. And there were water creatures. But First Worker[1] was unhappy because there was no place suitable for sitting or standing. He therefore ordered a huge duck to dive into the water to look for something of substance. After several unsuccessful attempts, the duck broke the water's surface with its bill full of sand and clay. First Worker thereupon compressed the sand into a cake and cast it upon the waters to create plains and mountains, crowding the waters into lakes and streams. Then he caused the mountains and stream courses to be covered with trees or shrubs and the plains to be covered with grasses. Buffalo and other land animals were fashioned out of clay and given permission to roam the mountains, plains, and valleys. And it was good, but First Worker was lonely. So he used what was left of the clay to create the first human couple. As humans multiplied, they became divided into tribes. At first all spoke the same tongue, but one day, for no apparent reason, First Worker assigned a different language to each tribe so that none could understand the others. At the same time he granted to each tribe its own lands and distributed bows and arrows so that tribal domains could be defended. The Crow, because their hearts were strong, found themselves inhabiting lands surrounded by jealous enemies. Thus did tradition describe the creation of the Crow world, and thus did the Crow, from the perspective of their limited universe, interpret the human condition.[2]

Actually, of course, Crow territory had been inhabited for a very long time before the tribe established itself there. Perhaps as early as 10,000 B.C., small bands of Clovis peoples foraged for edible plants and hunted mammoths and smaller animals in Yellowstone Valley. As mammoths died out, they were replaced by bison as the major source of protein for those later cultures which inhabited the valley. Beginning in about 2,500 B.C., the buffalo population began to increase, attracting new immigrants into the area. One of the new groups, the Avonlea, made a major contribution to the hunting and warfare capabilities of the area's inhabitants through introduction of the bow and arrow. The typical bison-hunting, nomadic way of life followed by the Crow and other Plains Indians, prior to the acquisition of horses and guns, evolved out of these early cultural influences. It is likely that most of the tribes which had become neighbors of the Crow by 1800 had at one time or another occupied, or had at least hunted in, what by that date had become Crow territory.[3]

Most of what passes for Crow history before 1800 is based on oral tradition, a source of doubtful validity at best. One of the few things about the tribe's history that most authorities on the subject agree upon is that sometime prior to taking over the Yellowstone Valley, they had lived along the banks of the Missouri River as part of the Hidatsa tribe. A common origin is reflected in the oral traditions of both, similarities in customs and habits as described by nineteenth-century observers, and, most compelling of all, similarities in the two languages. In fact, the two tongues were virtually interchangeable at the time of first contact with the Europeans.[4]

On the other hand there is great confusion concerning the whereabouts of the Hidatsa/Crow prior to their arrival at the Missouri River. In 1876,

Lieutenant James Bradley was told by Little Face, a member of the Crow tribe acting as a scout for a cavalry detachment commanded by Bradley in the ill-fated campaign waged against the Dakota and their allies by the United States Army in that year, that he had been told as a boy that the tribe had at one time lived on the shores of a large body of water someplace to the south and east of Crow territory. At some undetermined point in time, according to Little Face, it migrated first to the Arkansas River and then on to the Platte before taking up residence along the Missouri. Bradley was told by an unidentified informant that The Poorest, a female centenarian who had died in 1875, remembered living on Blue Water River in Kansas. She had also recalled being told as a child that the Hidatsa/Crow had previously lived someplace to the south and east of that area. The Poorest claimed to remember having moved from the Blue Water River to the Platte River before settling in along the banks of the Missouri as part of the Hidatsa tribe.[5]

Joe Medicine Crow, for many years the tribe's official historian, contrarily places the tribe's ancestral home someplace in the Great Lakes region. His version has the Hidatsa/Crow leaving that area at some point in time in the distant past to migrate westward in search of buffalo. They settled down for a time someplace in the northern part of present-day Minnesota. Then, in about 1550, a shortage of buffalo there or perhaps the intrusion of a stronger foe, prompted another westward migration. Following a layover at Devil's Lake in South Dakota, they continued on to the banks of the Missouri where they established their presence at about the turn of the seventeenth century.[6]

Accounts of the circumstance surrounding the break-up of the Hidatsa/Crow are likewise contradictory. Most authorities attribute the separation to a tiff over buffalo meat. It seems that soon after taking up residence along the Missouri, a series of minor disputes created a rift within the original tribe, resulting in the emergence of two factions. Each built its own village, but moderately peaceful relations prevailed between them until a temporary shortage of buffalo created famine conditions. One village was lucky enough to eventually bag a buffalo but when asked by the chief of the other village, No Vitals, to share the kill with his people, offered him only the paunch. Incensed, No Vitals and his followers abandoned their village and migrated westward to settle in the Rocky Mountains where they became the nucleus for a new tribe, the Crow.[7]

Another version explains the separation into distinct tribes in terms of difficulties which arose among three sons of a legendary Hidatsa woman. One son established a village in the general vicinity of the early nineteenth-century Hidatsa villages and another moved his people down the Missouri River never to be heard from again. The third led his followers away from the river toward the Rocky Mountains to form the Crow tribe.[8] Yet another rendering of the event has two brothers of the Hidatsa tribe murdering some relatives and subsequently fleeing for their lives to the security of the Rocky Mountains. Here they married women of the Flathead tribe to father the first generation of Crow.[9]

Joe Medicine Crow's reconstruction of the separation, based on his understanding of twentieth-century oral tradition, differs substantially from most other versions. During the Hidatsa/Crow layover at Devil's Lake, according to this interpretation, First Worker appeared before No Vitals and another tribal leader, Red Scout. He gave Red Scout an ear of corn with instructions to settle his people along the banks of the

Missouri River where they were to raise corn for sustenance. No Vitals was given a pod of tobacco seeds and told to lead his followers to the Rocky Mountains where the seeds were to be planted in an appropriate spot. After stopping for a time along the banks of the Missouri with Red Scout and his people, No Vitals, early in the seventeenth century, left the river with four hundred of his followers in conformance with First Worker's revelation. The first phase of the migration led them to Canada in the vicinity of Cardston, Alberta, where the new tribe began to refer to itself as One Side. Finding their new homeland to be far too cold, they headed for more southerly climes after only a short stay. This leg of the migration took them to Great Salt Lake where they took up residence for a time. However, they found the climate here too arid for their liking and eventually left. Moving in a southeasterly direction, they happened onto a large crater which they called "Where There Is Fire." Lingering here for only a short time, the migrants made their way eastward to the Canadian River in Oklahoma and eventually trekked even further east to settle down in a heavily forested country. Unhappy because the trees gave them a closed-in feeling, they packed up again and journeyed westward to the North Platte River. The final leg of the migration took them to the valley of the Yellowstone, about 100 years after setting out on their quest for the promised land.[10]

This account dates the arrival of the tribe in its homeland sometime in the early 1700s. Robert H. Lowie, father of Crow ethnological studies, estimated that, based on differences he found in the Crow and Hidatsa languages, separation from the Hidatsa occurred in about 1400.[11] Data from other sources, however, suggest a later arrival. According to The Poorest, the Crow took up residence in Yellowstone

Valley sometime after her birth. If true, Crow occupation of the valley could not have occurred much before 1770. Little Face recollected in 1876, at the time in his early sixties, that his grandfather could recall the tribe's arrival in the valley. Assuming that Little Face was conceived before his father's fortieth birthday and that his father's conception didn't occur after Little Face's grandfather turned forty, the Crow could not have reached their homeland until, at the very earliest, 1746.[12]

Crow oral tradition is unanimous in recounting an absence of both horses and guns until sometime after the arrival of the tribe in Yellowstone Valley. Robert Meldrum, a trapper and trader who spent much of his adult life with the tribe, recalled in 1862 that when he first went among the tribe in 1828, some older Crow claimed to have been alive when horses were introduced, suggesting that they were without the animals until sometime after 1750.[13] Little Face was told by his grandfather that horses were first obtained from the Nez Perce shortly after the tribe took up residence along the banks of the Yellowstone.[14] This dating conforms generally with that provided by Meldrum. Assuming that horses were not in fact introduced until after the tribe's arrival in Yellowstone Valley, The Poorest's migration chronology would place introduction of animals at roughly this same time.

Probably the area of life most radically changed by acquisition of horses was the chase. Mounted hunters could range over a much wider territorial expanse in search of buffalo than could hunters on foot. Moreover, because horses could outrun buffalo, their adoption by hunters assured greater success in hunting, substantially increasing the number of kills. An improved mobility on the part of hunters made possible by the horse, therefore, undoubtedly reduced

RUNNING BUFFALO
Small groups of hunters approached herds quietly before dashing in to kill as
many as possible before the animals stampeded.
Courtesy Walters Art Gallery, Baltimore   *A. Jacob Miller*

the amount of time required to ensure adequate food
supplies. The tribe employed a variety of strategies in
conducting buffalo hunts. A method commonly used
was the surround. This required the presence of a
large number of hunters; in most instances as many as
200 participated. Riders were assigned to stations,
positioned in a large circle surrounding prospective

A SURROUND OF BUFFALO BY INDIANS

The surround was a hunting strategy often employed by the Crow. It involved the presence of a large number of hunters positioned in a large circle around a herd. Participants converged toward the center on a prearranged signal, concentrating the animals for easy killing.

Courtesy Walters Art Gallery, Baltimore   *A. Jacob Miller*

hunting grounds. On a pre-arranged signal, hunters converged toward the center of the circle, driving all buffalo before them. Once a sufficient number of animals had been concentrated within the constricted circle, the killing began.[15]

Alternatively, riders might stampede a buffalo herd over a nearby cliff to certain death, or they might drive them into a box canyon. A fence constructed across the open end of the enclosure created a holding pen where animals could be killed and butchered as needed. Smaller groups of hunters or, in some cases, individuals, simply approached herds quietly before dashing in among the animals to kill as many as possible before their presence created a stampede.[16] Buffalo carcasses were not necessarily the property of those who killed them. If another person asked for a share in a freshly-killed buffalo, the hunter was expected to give up one-half of his kill to the supplicant. If more than one person requested a share, the successful hunter had to be satisfied with keeping only one-third of the carcass, the remainder to be divided equally among all supplicants.[17]

Horses not only increased the efficiency of the chase, they also provided more effective means of transporting surplus cuts of meat for future consump-

HUNTING BUFFALO
The most efficacious method of killing buffalo was simply to stampede a herd over a cliff.
Courtesy of Walters Art Gallery, Baltimore   *A. Jacob Miller*

tion. In fact, next to the chase, the aspect of Crow existence most improved by adoption of the horse had to do with transportation capabilities. Dogs had been the only beasts of burden available to the tribe before the horse was introduced, and the utility of dogs in this respect was limited by their size and strength. Horses, so much stronger and larger, greatly increased the weight and size of articles which could be transported form one camp site to the next. They furthermore lengthened the distance which could be traversed in any given time period, and this, of course, shortened the time needed to move from one location to another.

Improved mobility had its darker side. Acquisition of the horse broadened the range over which raiding parties could operate, increasing possibilities for casual contact with enemy warriors and thus increasing the incidence of warfare. Furthermore, the ability to mount a cavalry charge undoubtedly increased mortality rates. On the other hand acquisition of horses also admitted of a freer play of humanitarian instincts than had been possible when dogs provided the only means of transportation. Those unable to maintain the pace of migrating bands, the infirm and the elderly mainly, of necessity had been left behind to die. With the availability of horses as a mode of conveyance, it was possible to transport anyone with the ability to ride.[18]

The horse, then, was a valued possession, probably the most highly prized for most members of the tribe. Ownership of as many as 200 was not unusual for males of middle age. Any who owned fewer than twenty were thought to be poor. Some nineteenth-century observers were of the opinion that the Crow, of all the Indians on the Northern Plains, were the richest in horses. As animals of great utility and value, they were, of course, closely guarded. When in friendly territory, horses were allowed to graze some distance from camp under the guardianship of young men posted as sentinels against theft by neighboring tribes. When in or near enemy territory, an owner's best horses were kept in camp, securely tethered to his lodge.[19] Children were taught to ride at an early age. As infants their cradle boards were slung from saddles during migrations, and as soon as they could sit up, youngsters were strapped into saddles of horses led by one parent or another. By age four children of both sexes were expected to ride unassisted. Virtually born to the saddle, most Crow became expert horsemen at a very early age.[20]

Surviving oral tradition, beyond establishing the absence of guns prior to the settling in of the Crow along the banks of the Yellowstone, has little to say on the subject and nothing about the date of acquisition. Little Face could recall only that he had been told by his ancestors that the first guns ever seen by the tribe had been brought into a camp by two white men. Impressed with the power and accuracy of the new weapon, some tribal members later acquired them from the Hidatsa. The dynamics of this process can be reasonably reconstructed. Once firearms were introduced into the area, there must have been irresistible pressures placed on the tribe to acquire them. Given the high incidence of tribal warfare, any tribe which failed to acquire this deadly new form of weaponry did so at the risk of extinction. Surprisingly, guns played only a minor role in hunting. Mounted hunters found it impossible to reload muzzle-loaders, the only type of firearm available until after mid-century, when at the gallop. Accordingly, buffalo continued to be killed by bow and arrow until the introduction of breech-loading rifles in the 1860s. Consequently, until well after mid-century the use of firearms in killing animals was limited to hunts conducted on foot.[21]

Both guns and horses had become integral com-
ponents in the region's intertribal commerce by 1800.
Trade between tribes on the Northern Plains, of
course, existed long before the introduction of the
horse and European trade goods. Prehistoric trade
involved the barter of products derived from the
chase for agricultural products between nomadic
tribes such as the Crow and the semi-sedentary tribes
living along the banks of the Missouri River. Horses
and mules, obtained from the Spanish settlements
through Indian intermediaries, entered the trade from
the south. European trade goods introduced from the
north, perhaps as early as 1732 by British, French,
and Spanish traders, were also integrated into prehistoric trade patterns. By the beginning of the
nineteenth century, Hudson's Bay Company and the
North West Company had established trading relations with the Mandan, Hidatsa, and Arikara tribes,
giving to these people a virtual monopoly on the
distribution of European trade goods to the nomadic
tribes of the Northern Plains, including the Crow.[22]
The Crow role in this network was to act as an
intermediary in the exchange of manufactured goods
for horses. The tribe made an annual trading expedition to the Mandan and Hidatsa villages, usually in
early June, carrying products derived from the chase
and driving horses and mules to barter for corn,
tobacco, and manufactured goods. Horses and mules
to replace animals bartered on the Missouri River
were obtained from the Shoshone, Flathead, and Nez
Perce tribes to the south and west in return for
furnishing these tribes with manufactured goods.[23]
    The earliest documented instance of direct trade
between the Crow and white traders dates from 1795
when an employee of the North West Company, one
Menard, made a trip to the Crow homeland. He was
hospitably received and was successful in bartering

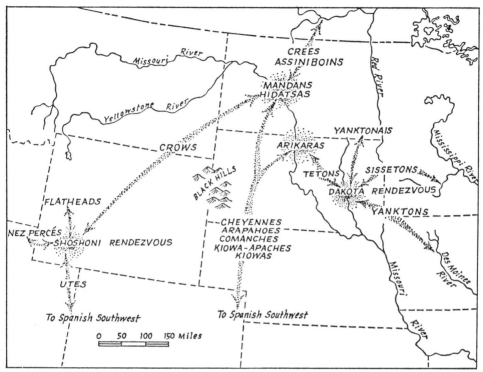

ROUTES AND CENTERS OF INTERTRIBAL TRADE IN 1805
From *Indian Life on the Upper Missouri*, by John C. Ewers. Copyright © 1968 by
the University of Oklahoma Press.

manufactured goods for some horses and a few beaver
pelts. On the return trip, however, he was dogged by
a band of young Crow warriors who relieved him, not
only of the peltries and horses he had just acquired
from the tribe, but of his equipment and clothing as
well. Although apparently never in serious danger of
losing his life, when Menard finally arrived at the
Mandan villages, he was in a pitiful state.[24]

The North West Company seems to have had in
mind eventually bypassing the Mandan and Hidatsa

villages as intermediaries between itself and the Crow. The first serious attempt made by the firm to form a permanent trading relationship with the tribe occurred in 1805. Francois Larocque, whose account of his trip to Crow domain provides the first reliable data on the tribe, left the North West Company's post on the Assiniboine River in early June of that year.[25] He was destined for the Hidatsa village where he hoped to intercept the Crow tribe on its annual trading expedition to the Missouri River and secure permission from its leaders to accompany them back to their homeland.[26] He had spent some time trading along the Missouri during the previous year where he encountered two Crow warriors who had informed him that their homeland abounded in both beaver and buffalo. The trader's intent was to confirm the area's peltry potential and, if encouraging, enlist the tribe's trapping and hunting talents. Larocque was accompanied by two colleagues, Charles MacKenzie and a Mr. Lafrance, who were going only as far as the Hidatsa villages. Two unidentified voyageurs were also included in the party. The latter would accompany Larocque all the way to the Crow homeland.

The small party arrived at the village on June 12 to find that the Crow had not yet arrived. Larocque observed that the Hidatsa became, to his discomfort, less than enthusiastic about his presence when they learned what he had in mind. The trader was warned by Hidatsa leaders that if he persisted in his venture he would undoubtedly have to spend the ensuing winter with the Crow because of the long distances involved. He was also told that the Crow were unreliable, and, as proof, was given an account of the misfortunes experienced by Menard when among them. Furthermore, according to the Hidatsa, the Crow probably wouldn't make it to the Missouri this year anyway because it was common knowledge that the Assiniboine planned to attack their trade caravan. Larocque interpreted Hidatsa opposition as an expression of concern that the trade goods he carried were intended for the Crow rather than for them. It seems more likely that Missouri River Indians correctly sensed that a trading relationship between Larocque's firm and their brethren to the west would put a crimp in their own lucrative trade with the tribe. In any event he made it a point to visit the Hidatsa leader, Le Borgne, to secure his blessing for the proposed trip.

A small vanguard of the Crow caravan reached the village on June 22. The main body arrived three days later. To make their presence known, the visitors formed a huge circle on a nearby hill where they were addressed for a short time by their leaders. Suddenly, warriors dressed in full war regalia dashed through the village at full gallop. MacKenzie, for one, was astonished at their horsemanship, observing that in his experience they were the most expert horsemen of the region. Following this display of equine proficiency, the visitors dismounted to set up camp in close proximity to the village. Le Borgne escorted Larocque and his companions into the recently-established camp where he introduced them to Red Calf, one of two head men of the tribe and, incidentally, an adopted son of one of the Hidatsa chiefs. The other tribal leader, Red Fish, was not at the time in camp. When Larocque extended his hand for the traditional handshake, Red Calf seemed confused and had to be instructed by Le Borgne how to respond to the gesture. The latter explained to Larocque that the Crow were unaccustomed to white ways.[27]

Preliminary formalities completed, Le Borgne smoked the pipe of peace with Crow elders and presented them with presents consisting of 200 guns, ammunition, 100 bushels of corn, kettles, axes, and various articles of European cotton goods. The recipients responded by offering their hosts 250 horses, many bundles of buffalo robes, and numerous items of clothing made from animal skins. This phase of the proceedings was ended with ceremonial dancing performed by the Crow. There then ensued a general trading session during the course of which MacKenzie bartered for a quantity of beaver pelts. He noted that those accquired from the Crow were faultily dressed, having been split down the back rather than the belly as required by the company. He drew the obvious conclusion that the tribe was unaccustomed to preparing beaver pelts for the European market.[28]

Several days later, on June 27, Larocque held a council with a number of the more important head men of the tribe. He began by offering them gifts of ammunition, tools, knives, tobacco, and articles of personal adornment. He then produced and lit a peace pipe which he informed them belonged to the chief of the whites and went on to say that the white chief felt sorry for them because they lacked sufficient arms with which to defend themselves. He therefore was extending an invitation for them to become his children for protective purposes. Larocque, as his agent, had been dispatched not only to visit their land but also to instruct them in proper hunting, trapping, and dressing techniques in order that they might procure enough weaponry for a proper defense of their homeland. At this point Red Calf was presented a ceremonial uniform, sash, and flag, with an apology to Red Fish, clearly miffed, for not having a set of ceremoniial clothing for him, too. The reason, explained Larocque, was that the white chief was unaware that the tribe had two leaders.[29]

There followed a lively, at times acrimonious, discussion on the merits of Larocque's request to visit

Crow domain. One speaker voiced concern about the danger some of the more hot-headed young men of the tribe might pose for the outsiders during the journey. Yet another raised the spectre of the bad *maxpe* which would inevitably follow from the presence of strangers. Le Borgne came to Larocque's rescue by pointing out that only three whites were asking to accompany them, and that, furthermore, only whites were foolish enough to trade arms and ammunition for worthless beaver pelts. The Hidatsa leader performed one more service for the North West Company representative. He staved off a last-ditch effort on the part of his people to prevent the trader from fulfilling his mission. Just as Larocque and his two voyageurs were preparing to join the Crow caravan, a delegation of Hidatsa crowded into the trader's hut to demand that he forego his projected trip. Le Borgne then made a dramatic entrance, clutching his battleaxe, to tell his followers that it was really none of their business if the whites were foolish enough to risk their lives in making the trip to a strange land. The Hidatsa thereupon departed in a huff, leaving Larocque and his party free to join the Crow caravan as it set out for the Yellowstone River on June 29.[30]

The procession wended its deliberate way toward the Big Horn Mountains in a general southwesterly direction. In the vicinity of present-day Sheridan, Wyoming, its course was altered in a northerly direction to skirt the mountains and then resumed a westerly course to the Big Horn River. From here the column followed the river to its confluence with the Yellowstone, ending the long journey near present Billings, Montana on September 10. The journey consumed seventy-three days. The caravan's slow progress was due in part to irregular patterns of march. Daily travel time varied from less than one to

never more than seven hours. On some days the
travelers struck camp at dawn and on others not until
late afternoon. Sometimes they traveled until dusk,
but on several occasions camp was made as early as
eleven o'clock in the morning. The chief reason for its
slow progress, though, was that the column was so
frequently distracted from the march.

It halted to conduct buffalo hunts on well over a
dozen occasions, for example. Successful hunts in
turn called for additional delays while meat was
processed and dried. Inclement weather forced the
wayfarers to remain in camp on two occasions, and
temporary halts were occasionally called to await
reports from scouts sent out to sweep neighboring
areas for signs of enemy warriors. And the tribe's
leaders delayed the march periodically to go into
council for the purpose of discussing future lines of
march. When the Big Horn Mountains were reached,
for instance, progress was delayed for two days while
they argued about the route to take from that point to
the Yellowstone River. What precipitated this dis-
agreement was that, as the column had approached
the mountains, a few women had deserted their mates
to join lovers they knew were waiting for them on the
other side of the mountains. The problem was that
the husbands of those women who had slipped away
wanted to proceed directly across the Big Horns to
recover their fickle spouses. In the end it was decided
to follow the usual route around the mountains.

The most interesting of the distractions from
Larocque's point of view was a skirmish with an
unidentified band of enemy warriors which occurred
on the morning of September 4 while the column was
camped near the Little Big Horn River. Scouts
reported the discovery of thirty-five strangers moving
on foot toward the Big Horn River. Camp was
immediately emptied of all but a few old men,

women, and children. The intruders hurriedly dispersed as the Crow converged on them at the gallop.
Two enemy warriors, probably scouts, were unable to
get away, however, and were immediately surrounded
and killed. By the time Larocque arrived at the scene,
they had been scalped and the fingers of their right
hands severed. The trader watched with revulsion as
men and women alike crowded in to furiously strike
the corpses and hack away at the bodies to obtain
pieces of flesh as personal trophies. In celebration of
the victory, that entire night was devoted to a scalp
dance. All remained in camp the next day to continue
the festivities. These mainly took the form of
informal parades in which those who had arrived on
the battle ground soon enough to acquire body parts
of the victims displayed their grisly trophies. All told,
for one reason or another, no traveling was done at
all on sixteen days. Minor distractions which delayed
progress for shorter periods of time included berry
picking, bear baiting, beaver trapping, and quarrels
over women.

Larocque was able to maintain good relations with
his hosts throughout the trip, but at about the
halfway point, they began to pester him with
questions about his return plans. As they became ever
more insistent, he patiently tried to explain to them
that he hadn't as yet gathered enough data about their
homeland for his purposes and that he absolutely
needed to examine the Yellowstone Valley. Apparently in the hope of assuaging his curiosity about
their homeland, he was given a map which someone
had drawn on deerskin and which identified major
landmarks and located the tribe's seasonal camp-
grounds. The trader was adamant, however, and they
reluctantly agreed that he could complete the trip.
Larocque was at first puzzled about the disparity in
cordial hospitality afforded him and the obvious

desire of his hosts to be rid of him. He eventually concluded that they wanted him to leave simply because they were anxious to receive gifts he had promised to distribute to them at the conclusion of the journey.

The trader didn't tarry long once the caravan reached its destination. On September 14 he convened his new friends in a formal council, and after distributing the long-awaited gifts, informed them that he was satisfied with their conduct toward him and that the peltry potential of their homeland warranted his return. After asking them to trap beaver in his absence so that they might satisfy their needs for trade goods, he worked out a system of signal fires to be used for recognition purposes when he returned to trade with them sometime during the following autumn. Larocque then took his leave from the tribe, bearing 122 beaver pelts, 4 bear robes and two otter skins. After an arduous but uneventful trip, he arrived at his home base in Canada on October 22.

The North West Company failed to follow up on its representative's attempt to open up a direct trading relationship with the Crow partly because Larocque's report was less than enthusiastic about trade possibilities with the tribe and partly because, in late 1805, the company's management decided to de-emphasize trade in the Missouri River area. However, at about the time Larocque had promised to return, representatives of a far more powerful entity paid a visit to the Crow homeland. Crow leaders undoubtedly would have been puzzled to learn in 1803 that their domain was the subject of negotiations on the part of strangers who lived half a world away. France had reacquired Louisiana Territory, which included Crow domain, from Spain in 1800. Napoleon Bonaparte assumed control over France in 1803, and his program for the nation included plans to re-establish its overseas empire in the New World along with an effort to expand French suzerainty over all of Europe. It soon became painfully apparent to Bonaparte that he couldn't do both. Faced with making a choice, he opted for the latter and subsequently decided to sell what was left of France's possessions in the western hemisphere to help finance his European adventures.

He found an eager buyer in the brash young nation state his country had only recently helped achieve independence from England. The United States, almost from its inception, had evinced an interest in lands west of the Mississippi River. President Thomas Jefferson asked for and got funds from Congress in early 1803 to finance an expedition to the Pacific Ocean. Therefore, when the opportunity arose to purchase the vast expanse of Louisiana Territory from France for fifteen million dollars in that year, Jefferson accepted. Questions about the legality of the transaction were raised in both countries. France had an agreement with Spain that the lands in question would never be transferred to a third party, and there were constitutional issues involved in the purchase from the United States' perspective. Nevertheless, on December 10, 1803, an agreement transferring Louisiana Territory to the United States was signed by the two leaders.

Meriwether Lewis, Jefferson's private secretary, had already been chosen to lead an expedition to the Pacific Ocean.[31] Lewis had recruited thirty-one men for the adventure, including Captain William Clark, brother of George Rogers Clark. By the time the expedition began its ascent of the Missouri River on May 13, 1804, Clark had been named co-commander by Lewis. Progress of the small band of explorers was interrupted to winter at the Mandan and Hidatsa villages where the two leaders gathered and compiled data from both traders and Indians not only about the territory they intended to traverse but about the region's aboriginal inhabitants as well. Toussaint Charbonneau, a veteran trader and sometime employee of the North West Company, signed on here to act as guide and interpreter. His Shoshone wife, Sacajawea, was granted permission to tag along.

The expedition resumed its march on April 17, 1805 to follow the Missouri almost to its sources, thus missing the Crow homeland altogether. From the Three Forks area, Lewis and Clark led their intrepid band westward to the shores of the Pacific, arriving at their destination on November 7, 1805. On its return trip the party divided itself at Three Forks; Lewis and nine others followed the outbound route along the Missouri River. He interrupted his contingent's line of march in mid-July to explore the Marias River system. This excursion resulted in the only serious problem with the Indian inhabitants of the region encountered by the expedition. On July 26, 1806, eight mounted warriors, who claimed to be of the Atsina tribe but who seem rather to have been members of the Piegan tribe, approached the small party of whites. Lewis conversed with their leader through the medium of sign language, and, although suspicious of the Indians' motives, agreed to an overnight stay with them. As it turned out the explorer was right to have been wary. He and his companions were awakened early the next morning to find their hosts pilfering the small party's store of firearms. In the scuffle which ensued, one of the Piegans was fatally stabbed, but the survivors were able to make off with several of their guests' horses. Lewis and one of his men pursued them, wounding one in the stomach and eventually recovering the stolen horses. Following this encounter, the Piegans dispersed, abandoning their lodges, horses, and weapons. Lewis and party then returned to the mouth of Marias River to resume their return trip down the Missouri River to the Mandan and Hidatsa villages.

Meanwhile William Clark and the remainder of the party, which included Sacajawea and her infant son, born on February 11, 1805, followed a route which took them through the heart of Crow country.[32] They reached the Yellowstone River on July 15, and several days later fashioned two pirogues out of large cottonwood trees. Clark and the majority of his contingent used the newly constructed vessels to float down the Yellowstone while certain of his men herded the party's horses down Yellowstone Valley. On July 18, near the mouth of Stillwater River, puffs of smoke were observed coming from mountains near the river. Clark assumed that the Crow had mistaken his party for a band of Shoshone whom they were attempting to signal to come in to trade. It is likely that the smoke signals had indeed been made by the Crow but that rather than being mistaken for Shoshone, Clark's party had been taken for one led by Larocque returning with trade goods as promised.

Additional evidence of a Crow presence in the vicinity was provided on the morning of July 21. The camp awoke to find twenty-four of their fifty horses missing. Two days later signs were discovered which indicated that their camp site had been visited again sometime during the previous night. A hurried investigation revealed that no horses were missing. Nonetheless, fearful that what remained of the party's herd was at risk, Clark dispatched four men ahead to drive the horses out of Crow territory as soon as possible. His precautions came to naught, however; Clark later learned that Indians, presumably Crow, had made off with the herd soon after the advance party departed.

The explorer never did come face-to-face with even a single member of the tribe during the course of his journey. Had he come across the Crow, though, Clark had prepared remarks for the occasion. He would have told them that he was visiting their lands at the behest of Great Father who wanted to know what his children, the Crow, most needed. He would have gone on to inform them that Great Father intended to build a house in their territory which would contain a store of useful goods which could be exchanged for peltries. The proposed speech would have closed with an admonition against stealing horses and a promise that two of their leaders would soon be invited to visit with Great Father.

The forces of Lewis and Clark were reunited on August 12 at the mouth of Little Knife River and thereafter continued down the Missouri River to St. Louis. Their journals, first published in 1814, contain a marvelously detailed description of the area traversed by the two men and their companions. The journals also include an abundance of data on the region's aboriginal inhabitants. The section devoted to the Crow noted that the tribe had a population of thirty-five hundred and depended on the hunt for sustenance. It correctly identified the Yellowstone Valley as its main territory. The Hidatsa and Mandan tribes were cited not only as the Crow's primary source of manufactured goods but also as their most constant allies. The Dakota, Assiniboine, and Arikara Indians were identified as their most formidable enemies.

With regard to the economic potential of Crow domain, the journals pointed out that the Yellowstone River was navigable, at least by pirogue, from the Big Bend to its confluence with the Missouri. The mouth of Clark's Fork was identified as an appropriate site for a trading post. From this location, it could, according to the explorers, service not only the Crow but the Shoshone and other tribes to the west as well.

Addressing themselves to the area's potential for international trade, the authors reported they had been told that the headwaters of the Yellowstone lay a relatively short distance from the closest Spanish settlement to the south. They also pointed out that they had encountered nothing on their route to the Pacific Ocean that would constitute a serious barrier to transportation. They went on to postulate that furs collected in the area could be shipped more quickly and economically directly across the Pacific to China than from Montreal through England to the Orient as routed by the British trading companies. The explorers were of the opinion that beaver were present in sufficient numbers to warrant exploitation. A caveat was added that because the formidable North West Company had in mind expanding its operations into the Upper Missouri region, immediate action was essential if the United States seriously intended to exploit the peltry resources of the land recently acquired from France.

NOTES

1. The Crow also used the terms Great Spirit, Old Man Coyote, and The One Who Made All Things to describe their creator god.
2. The most complete version of the Crow creation myth is found in Robert H. Lowie, *The Crow Indians* (New York: Farrar and Rinehart, Incorporated, 1935), pp. 122–31. For other versions, see A.M. Quivey, ed., "Bradley Manuscript: Book F," *Contributions to the Historical Society of Montana,* VIII (1917), 211; James H. Bradley, "Indian Traditions," *Contributions to the Historical Society of Montana,* IX (1923), 288–91; Peter Nabokov, *Two Leggings: The Making of a Crow Warrior* (New York: Thomas Y. Crowell Publishers, 1967), pp. 22–23; S.C. Simms, "Traditions of the Crows," *Field Columbian Museum Publication No. 85, Anthropological Series,* II, No. 6, 281–2.
3. C. Adrian Heidenreich, "The Native American Yellowstone," *Montana: The Magazine of Western History,* XXXV (October, 1985), 3–4.
4. For early white, or Alien Culture, references to the Hidatsa-Crow relationship, consult Reuben Gold Thwaites, ed., *Original Journals of the Lewis and Clark Expedition, 1804–1806* (New York: Arno Press, 1969), V, 348;

Alexander Henry and David Thompson, *The Manuscript Journals of Alexander Henry and of David Thompson, 1799–1814,* ed. Elliott Coues (Minneapolis: Ross and Haines, Inc., 1897), I, 399; Annie Heloise Abel, ed., *Tabeau's Narrative of Loisel's Expedition to the Upper Missouri* (Norman: University of Oklahoma Press, 1939), p. 160.

5. Quivey, *op. cit.,* pp. 215-6, 218. Bradley was a native of Ohio who enlisted in the 14th Ohio Volunteers during the Civil War as a private. Discharged as a sergeant in 1865, he reenlisted as a second lieutenant in February of 1866. He served under General Gibbon in the 1876 campaign against the Dakota and under General Miles in his military action against Chief Joseph and the Nez Perce tribe. He was killed in the Battle of Big Hole on August 9, 1877.

6. Leslie B. Davis, ed., "Symposium on the Crow-Hidatsa Separations," *Archaeology in Montana,* XX, No. 3 (Sept.-Dec., 1979), 64-67.

7. For accounts of this phase of the tribe's history, see Edwin Thompson Denig, *Of the Crow Nation,* ed. John C. Ewers (New York: AMS Press, 1980), p. 19-20; Edward S. Curtis, *The North American Indian,* ed. Frederick Webb Hodge (New York and London: Johnson Reprint Corporation, 1970), IV, 38; Alexander Philip Maximilian, *Travels in the Interior of North America,* ed. Reuben G. Thwaites, 3 vols. (Cleveland: The Arthur H. Clark Company, 1905), II, 367; Quivey, *op. cit.,* p. 219.

8. Maximilian, *op. cit.,* II, 375.

9. Charles MacKenzie, "The Mississouri [sic] Indians: A Narrative of Four Trading Expeditions to the Mississouri [sic], 1804-1805-1806," in Louis Francois Rodrigue Masson, *Les Bourgeois de la Compagnie du Nord-Oest* (New York: Antiquarian Press, 1960), I, 349-50.

10. Davis, *op. cit.,* pp. 66-68.

11. Lowie, *op. cit.,* pp. 3-4.

12. Quivey, *op. cit.,* pp. 215-16, 219.

13. Lewis Henry Morgan, *The Indian Journals* (Ann Arbor: The University of Michigan Press, 1959), p. 197.

14. Bradley, *op. cit.,* p. 298.

15. Zenas Leonard, *Zenas Leonard, Fur Trader,* ed. John C. Ewers (Norman: University of Oklahoma Press, 1959), pp. 143-4.

16. Quivey, *op. cit.,* p. 201.

17. Osborne Russell, *Osborne Russell's Journal of a Trapper,* ed. Aubrey L. Haines (Lincoln: University of Nebraska Press, 1959), p. 147.

18. Frank B. Linderman, *Pretty Shield* (Lincoln: University of Nebraska Press, 1972), pp. 82-83; Denig, *op. cit.,* p. 38.

19. *Ibid,* p. 25; Maximilian, *op. cit.,* I, 352.

20. Letter, W. Gordon to L. Cass, October 3, 1831, published in Annie Heloise Abel, ed., *Chardon's Journal at Fort Clark: 1834-1839* (Freeport: Books for Libraries Press, 1932), p. 347.

21. Denig, *op. cit.,* p. 37; Frank B. Linderman, *Plenty Coups: Chief of the Crows* (Lincoln: University of Nebraska Press, 1962), pp. 17-18.

22. John C. Ewers, "The Indian Trade of the Upper Missouri before Lewis and Clark; An Interpretation," *Bulletin of the Missouri Historical Society,* X, No. 4, Part 1 (July, 1954), 429-31.

23. *Ibid,* pp. 432-40.

24. "Trudeau's (Truteau's) Description of the Upper Missouri," in A.P. Nasatir, ed., *Before Lewis and Clark: Documents Illustrating the History of the Missouri, 1785-1804* (St. Louis: Historical Documents Foundation, 1952), II, 381; L.J. Burpee, ed., *Journal of Larocque from the Assiniboine to the Yellowstone, 1805,* Publications of the Canadian Archives, No. 3 (Ottawa: Government Printing Bureau, 1910), p. 17.

25. Charles Le Raye may have preceded Larocque into the Crow homeland. Le Raye claimed to have visited the Big Horn and Yellowstone Rivers as a captive of the Dakota. However, his descriptions of Indian tribes encountered and of his itinerary give rise to doubts about the authenticity of his account. Readers are invited to draw their own conclusions by consulting "The Journal of Charles Le Raye," *South Dakota Historical Collections,* V (1905), 150–80.

26. Unless otherwise indicated, the following account of Larocque's journey to Crow territory is taken from Burpee, *op. cit.,* pp. 11–54.

27. MacKenzie, *op. cit.,* I, 345.

28. *Ibid,* I, 346.

29. *Ibid,* I, 343, 349.

30. *Ibid,* I, 346–8.

31. Unless otherwise indicated, the following account of the epochal Lewis and Clark Expedition is taken from Thwaites, *op. cit.,* I, II, III, IV and V.

32. The boy was named Jean Baptiste Charbonneau by his parents but was dubbed Pompey by William Clark. Later Sacajawea and Pompey lived for a time in Clark's St. Louis home. At age eighteen Pompey was taken to Europe by Prince Paul of Wurttenberg with Clark's consent. After six years on the prince's estate near Stuttgart, the young man returned to the United States where he spent the remainder of his life as a mountain man.

THREE

OF MEN AND BEAVER

Light shed on the economic potential of Louisiana Territory by the epochal Lewis and Clark expedition acted as a catalyst to focus American entrepreneurial energies on the newly acquired lands. There inevitably followed the evolution of a relationship between the Crow and those attracted to their homeland by its peltry resources. This turned out to be a union of peoples of wildly disparate cultures. So dissimilar in fact were the two peoples that relations between them, although generally free of violence, would be fraught with mutual distrust, misunderstandings, disagreements, and bitter acrimony. Moreover, the relationship would prove to be of a grossly unequal character. Citizens of the United States were heirs to several millennia of advances in technology, notably the power loom, the smelting of iron, and the manufacture of gun powder. The Crow, along with the rest of the New World's aboriginal population, remained isolated from these phenomena until the settlement of the Americas by Europeans. Technological superiority provided white entrepreneurs with the means to create a dependency on them for manufactured goods which, once introduced, were, more often than not, regarded as necessities by the Indian. Whites constituted a small minority in Crow country and in the general Northern Plains region for the first half of the nineteenth century, but during the second half of the century they gained an over-whelming numerical superiority over the Crow and their neighbors. This Alien Culture, then, enjoyed distinct advantages over the Indians with whom its members came into contact.

The first organized attempt to harvest the virgin beaver fields of Crow territory was a bold thrust into the very heart of the American wilderness by Manuel Lisa, a resident of St. Louis with many years of fur trade experience on the lower reaches of the Missouri River. He and a party of fifty men began an ascent of the Missouri River on April 17, 1807 to establish an American presence on the fur frontier. Difficulties in navigating the treacherous river coupled with less than friendly encounters with some obstreperous Assiniboine delayed the expedition; it didn't reach its destination, the confluence of the Big Horn and Yellowstone Rivers, until early November. Lisa immediately assigned some of his men to the task of constructing a trading post near the mouth of the Big Horn to serve as headquarters for the venture.[1]

While the installation was yet under construction, the St. Louis entrepreneur dispatched several of his charges out into neighboring areas to recruit clients for the enterprise. John Colter, who had served with Lewis and Clark, was sent westward to search out customers from among the Crow and any other tribes he might encounter. Colter was successful in persuading a band of about 500 Flatheads to return to the trading post with him, but his mission was thwarted by an attack of a large war party of Alliance Indians. It happened that a contingent of Crow warriors was also in the vicinity, and they joined the fray on the side of the Flatheads, turning the tide of battle in their favor. Colter took an active part in the battle and received a leg wound for his trouble.[2]

Another veteran of the Lewis and Clark expedition, George Drouillard, was sent out to visit any Crow winter camps he might find south of the Yellowstone

River, pressumably for the purpose of extolling the virtues of beaver trapping as a means of acquiring trade goods. Drouillard left the site of the post and ascended Yellowstone River to the mouth of Pryor Creek where he found a Crow camp of 150 lodges. The next day he moved farther up the river to Clark's Fork which he followed for several miles to another Crow winter camp. He spent the night here and the following morning continued his route up Clark's Fork to one of its tributaries, which he identified as Dry Branch Creek. He camped at the mouth of the small stream and when he continued his journey the following day, left the main stream to follow the tributary southward to its head. Here he spent the night. From his overnight camp Drouillard continued a southerly course to the Shoshone (Stinking) River which he struck a short distance below the junction of its two major forks. He ascended the north fork for several miles to a large encampment of Crow with whom he spent the night. From this camp he retraced his steps down the north fork to the main body of the river and continued downstream to its confluence with the Big Horn River. Here he encountered yet another large Crow camp. The explorer's return trip took him north to Pryor Creek which he followed to its confluence with the Yellowstone. From this point his itinerary followed the latter river back to the post.[3]

Other employees were sent out into neighboring areas with trade goods to be exchanged for beaver pelts. Edward Rose, a mulatto of obscure ancestry with no prior experience in trading among the Indians, was one such. He quickly learned that the distribution of gifts to potential customers, which was customary in the Indian trade, seemed to enhance Crow estimation of the giver. He ensconced himself in a winter camp and proceeded to judiciously exchange his goods for the esteem and admiration of the camp's leading men rather than for beaver pelts as instructed by Manuel Lisa. After spending the winter in comfortable and congenial circumstances, Rose returned to the now-completed post with no peltries to show for an entire winter's trade. Lisa sacked him in summary fashion, and Rose returned to the camp of his newly-found friends. He subsequently took up residence with the tribe, abandoning himself to the Crow style of life. Rose would maintain a close, if intermittent, association with them for the better part of the next three decades.[4]

Lisa, not long after his encounter with Rose, set out for St. Louis from the new fort, which he named Fort Raymond after his only son, with peltries garnered during the winter of 1807-08. Benito Vasquez, a long-time associate of the entrepreneur, was left in charge of the Fort Raymond operation to oversee trapping and trading parties which had been dispatched to the Three Forks, Green River, and Wind River areas. Back in St. Louis, Manuel Lisa was able to persuade a number of the city's prominent residents, including William Clark and Meriwether Lewis, to invest a total of forty thousand dollars in the Missouri Fur Company, a firm created to continue and expand the trading enterprise he had established the previous autumn. In June of 1809, having recruited two hundred or so new hands, Manuel Lisa once again set out for the fur trade frontier. En route he built a new post, Fort Mandan, located on the Missouri River about twelve miles above the mouth of Knife River.[5] Before construction on the trading house was completed, Andrew Henry, a partner in the newly-formed company, set out with forty men to reinforce the garrison at Fort Raymond. Pierre Menard, another partner, followed a short time later with an additional fifty-six men.[6] In early April of 1810, Henry and

Menard led fifty men, including Reuben Lewis, representing the interests of his famous brother and probably those of William Clark, from Fort Raymond to the Three Forks of the Missouri. After constructing a small stockade there, the party broke up into small contingents of trappers which spread out to work the many beaver-rich streams of the region. Trapping turned out to be spectacularly good, but attacks by Alliance warriors proved troublesome. By early May the hostile Indians had killed eight trappers, including George Drouillard, and had stolen horses, traps and most of the peltries collected.[7] At this point discretion won out over the acquisitive impulse. Some members of the party, including John Colter and Pierre Menard, retreated to the relative security of Fort Raymond. A few trappers deserted, and the remainder followed Andrew Henry westward into the less dangerous Flathead country to continue trapping operations. On a tributary of the Snake River, later named Henry's Fork, they built another stockade to serve as their headquarters.[8]

Lisa, meanwhile, had returned to St. Louis to purchase supplies and raise additional capital. But because returns for the 1808–09 season were less than had been anticipated by investors, he experienced resistance in his efforts to raise money for future operations. Finally, by the spring of 1811, he had secured enough capital to purchase supplies and hire reinforcements. On his way up the Missouri River, he encountered Benito Vasquez en route to St. Louis. Lisa learned from Vasquez that Alliance opposition to the company's trapping operations had ruined the 1809–10 trapping season and forced its employees to abandon Fort Raymond. Lisa was understandably relieved, then, to find Andrew Henry waiting for him at Fort Mandan with a sizeable quantity of beaver pelts when he arrived there in June, 1811.[9]

Despite the insecurity of Crow territory created by the implacable hostility displayed by tribes of the Alliance against American trappers, the company continued its operations in the region for several more years. Louis Lorimer, a West Point graduate turned trapper, can be placed on the upper Big Horn River with four men during early spring of 1812. Reuben Lewis and several company employees trapped the Little Big Horn River from September of 1812 until January of 1813.[10] Edward Rose, apparently back in the good graces of Lisa, was a member of Lewis' brigade for a time. En route to the Little Big Horn, Rose informed Lewis that when last with the Crow, he had left a large quantity of beaver skins with them and therefore needed some trade goods to be used in retrieving them. Goods in hand, Rose forthwith made his way to a Crow camp where he settled in again for the good life, Crow style. Rose's deceptive practices notwithstanding, Lewis enjoyed a successful season of trapping and trading; word was received at Fort Manuel in December, 1812, that the brigade leader would be in soon with sizeable returns.[11]

The days of the Missouri Fur Company's operations in Crow territory were numbered, however. By the first months of 1813, a sharp drop in prices for beaver pelts caused by the outbreak of the War of 1812, coupled with the increased frequency of hostilities with Alliance Indians and a general increase in antagonism against whites displayed by other tribes, prompted Lisa to withdraw all his forces from the area. There followed a hiatus of eight years during which no beaver pelts from Crow country were received in St. Louis. It can therefore be reasonably concluded that few if any Americans were in Crow domain during these years. Even the redoubtable Edward Rose found it convenient to return to St. Louis in 1813.[12]

By the year 1820, fur prices were once again at a reasonable level, and general economic conditions in St. Louis made fur trade operations once again attractive to investors. Manuel Lisa died that year, but Joshua Pilcher, a partner in the Missouri Fur Company, reorganized the firm in preparation for another assault on the Northern Rockies. The company enjoyed a modicum of success in what would turn out to be its last venture in Crow country. Robert Jones and Michael Immell were selected by Pilcher to command a trapping and trading party to work the lower Big Horn River region. Jones was a newcomer to the fur trade, but Immell was a veteran who had served with Andrew Henry at Fort Raymond. After constructing a new trading post, Fort Benton, at the mouth of the Big Horn sometime during the fall of 1821, the leaders dispatched trapping parties out onto neighboring streams and rivers. There followed almost a year and a half of successful trapping and trading without serious interference from the Alliance tribes.[13]

In February of 1823, Jones and Immell decided to press their luck by leading a contingent of their trappers into Three Forks country. They were able to evade hostile warriors long enough to conduct a successful hunt, but their luck ran out along the Yellowstone River on the return trip to Fort Benton. As they approached the mouth of Pryor Creek on May 31, a band of several hundred Blood Indians appeared out of nowhere to block their progress. In the ensuing battle seven Americans were killed, including both Immell and Jones. Moreover, the attacking warriors made off with the party's horses, equipment, and all the furs they had accumulated.[14] Their leaders dead, the survivors were left to fend for themselves. Some were able to make their way safely back to the fort, and others found refuge in Crow camps. Losses sustained in the battle were so substantial that Pilcher withdrew the company from Crow territory, and after a year of inconclusive trading along the Missouri, dissolved the firm.[15]

Meanwhile, in 1822, another St. Louis businessman, William Ashley, had entered into an informal partnership with Andrew Henry, and they too would make an abortive attempt to establish trading and trapping operations among the Crow. Henry assumed responsibility for field operations and by late September of 1822, had completed construction of a small stockade near the mouth of the Yellowstone to serve as a depot for furs being collected by members of his party who were working tributaries of the Missouri River.[16] The succeeding September, Henry moved to the mouth of the Big Horn with thirteen men and either occupied Fort Benton or constructed a new trading post.[17] Jedediah Smith, a Bible-thumping newcomer to the mountains, led another group of Ashley men across the Big Horn Mountains to the Big Horn River that same year. Here, their numbers augmented by several survivors of the Jones-Immell party, they trapped until late November. Smith then moved his men across the Owl Creek Mountains into Wind River Valley to spend the winter with a band of Crow Indians camped there.[18]

James Clyman, a member of Smith's band of trappers, recorded his impressions of life in a Crow winter camp. He was particularly impressed by the tolerance of tribal members to cold weather, reporting that even on the coldest days males stripped off to the waist for buffalo hunts and that members of both sexes customarily took morning plunges. On occasion surface ice had to be broken to do so. Clyman was surprised to see that at any given time, even during the winter months, at least one-third of the camp's young men were absent on horse-stealing raids. In late

February of 1824, Smith and his party left Crow territory to trap along the upper reaches of Green River.[19]

After a disappointing season of trapping, Andrew Henry abandoned his post at the mouth of the Big Horn and returned to St. Louis in August of 1824. He subsequently dissolved his partnership with William Ashley and retired from active participation in the fur business. Ashley continued in the trade but shifted his locus of operations to the more lucrative confines of the Green River region. At the same time he abandoned the trading post concept in favor of holding an annual rendezvous at which trappers could barter pelts for trade goods. Among other things, this new mode of operating deprived the Crow of easy access to manufactured goods. Ashley didn't ignore the Crow homeland entirely, however. In 1825, he availed himself of its river systems to transport furs collected elsewhere in an extraordinarily successful season. These were transported by pack train from Green River to the head of navigation on the Big Horn and thence down that river to St. Louis via the Yellowstone and the Missouri Rivers.[20]

In 1826, Ashley sold out his trapping and trading operations to three of his employees who formed a new company which they named Smith, Jackson, and Sublette. Beginning in 1828, the new firm began to send trapping parties into Crow territory where they enjoyed two successful seasons. In 1830, the company was reorganized under the name of Rocky Mountain Fur Company, which counted Jim Bridger among its partners and which continued to exploit Crow beaver resources. Like Smith, Jackson, and Sublette, the new firm utilized Ashley's rendezvous system which, for one thing, did little or nothing to satisfy the Crow tribe's appetite for manufactured goods. There was waiting in the wings, however, a powerful aggressive company, the American Fur Company, which was prepared to do just that. Commonly referred to as simply the "Company" on the fur frontier, it constructed a trading post near the confluence of the Yellowstone and Missouri Rivers under the supervision of Kenneth McKenzie.[21] Named Fort Union, it was located some distance from Crow country, but it nonetheless offered trade goods to the tribe at little more inconvenience than did their traditional trading expeditions to the Mandan and Hidatsa villages. Furthermore, the Company assigned certain individuals to various tribes, including the Crow, to trade with the Indians in their camps and encourage them to trap beaver.[22]

Several years later the Company took an action which would make its trade goods even more conveniently available to the tribe. In the autumn of 1832, a small detachment of Crow warriors came upon a number of keelboats near the mouth of Rosebud River which were being cordelled up the Yellowstone by whites positioned along either bank. The Indians returned to their village to report what they had seen, and horses were immediately driven to the area to serve as pack animals for the cargo contained in the boats. Rather than utilizing the horses for this purpose, though, they were used to replace the men who had been pulling the boats against the river's current. Samuel Tulloch, a veteran employee of the Company, was in charge of the operation. He halted the boats at the mouth of the Big Horn, unloaded their cargo and distributed mirrors to those Crow who had lent their horses to the enterprise. Tulloch subsequently convened a small council to inform the Crow that a trading post would be constructed during the coming winter to serve the tribe. And sure enough, when a band of warriors returned the following spring, they found a fortified post situated in a pleasant, wooded valley on the right bank of the Yellowstone about two miles below the mouth of the Big Horn.[23] Fort Cass, named in honor of Secretary of War Lewis Cass, was designed to survive in a hostile environment. A stockade of cottonwood logs sunk vertically in the earth enclosed an area of one hundred thirty feet on each side. Living quarters, storehouses, stables, and a trading house lined the interior walls at a height which permitted utilization of the flat roofs as parapets. Additional protection was afforded by two block-houses set at opposite corners of the stockade.[24]

Fort Union and Fort Cass, along with a third Company post, Fort McKenzie, which was located at the mouth of Marias River to serve tribes of the Alliance, constituted an attempt by the Company to monopolize the fur trade in the region. The dynamics of the peltry trade were additionally altered by the entry of new players into the business during the early 1830s. Most notable among these was Captain Benjamin E.L.B. Bonneville, at the time on temporary leave from the U.S. Army. He added his contingent of 110 trappers to those already working Crow water-ways while he gathered data about the West for the Secretary of War. Oddly enough, just at the time the beaver trade began to attract new participants, it was entering a state of decline. In addition to an increase in the number of trappers working the region's beaver streams, production costs increased, productive trapping areas became more and more difficult to locate and, beginning in 1830, the price of beaver pelts in both domestic and overseas markets began to decline in the face of competition from hats made of silk.[25]

Relations between the tribe and representatives of the Alien Culture who came to Crow domain for the purpose of exploiting its beaver resources were characterized by amity for almost two decades, despite the circumstance that there was no love lost between the two peoples. Americans generally thought the Crow to be a barbaric, larcenous, and superstitious people. For their part the Crow held most trappers and traders in contempt because it was the Indians' opinion that whites who came west did so only because they had been failures at home.[26] A general harmony between individuals of these disparate cultures prevailed, then, despite ill feelings on both sides. Differences which arose between the two groups were for the most part vitiated by self-interest. The Crow found the presence of trappers and traders to be convenient for several reasons. For one thing, Americans almost immediately came into conflict with Alliance tribes, creating a community of interest with the Crow who regarded their larger and more powerful neighbors to the north as a threat to their security.

That the tribe regarded Americans as a military ally in its struggle with the Alliance is suggested by an incident which occurred in 1811. Early in that year a contingent of Crow warriors happened to be joined in battle someplace in Yellowstone Valley with some Atsina braves. The engagement turned out to be indecisive, and as the Crow departed they taunted their traditional enemies with the threat that, reinforced by American trappers, they would meet the Atsina on the Saskatchewan River in a few months to continue the battle.[27] From the trappers' perspective, Crow territory served as a haven in a hostile wilderness. It not only provided them with a relatively safe environment in which trapping operations could be conducted, it served as a base of operations from which they could make occasional forays into neighboring trapping grounds controlled by Alliance Indians as well.

Apart from the mutual security aspect of the relationship, the two groups enjoyed a symbiotic economic relationship. The presence of American traders on Crow soil assured the tribe of access to manufactured goods without having to make the time-consuming and sometimes dangerous trek to the Mandan and Hidatsa villages. For their part the Crow furnished not only rich trapping grounds, but, increasingly as time passed, beaver pelts for the trade. On an individual level, trappers and traders could expect to be hospitably received in most Crow camps. Daniel Potts, a member of a contingent of trappers which camped with a Crow band in Wind River Valley for part of the 1823-24 winter season, was afforded what he considered singularly generous treatment by the camp's chief. Potts had experienced severe frost bite on the trip into the valley and had been forced to amputate two toes. The chief took it upon himself to look in on the trapper at least twice a day to check on his wounds.[28] Renegades like Edward Rose who adopted Crow ways could be reasonably certain that they would be accommodated with one or more Crow women and eventually offered member-ship in the tribe. Such individuals adopted Indian dress and customs, learned the Crow tongue and generally assumed the appearance and demeanor of a Crow warrior.

Beginning in about 1825, however, relations between whites and the tribe began to sour. In the fall of that year, one of William Ashley's trappers killed two Crow warriors who were attempting to steal supplies from him on the last night of the rendezvous held that year in the Green River region. Then, while the entrepreneur's caravan was en route to the head of navigation on the Big Horn River, a small band of Crow stole some of his horses. A few days later, while camped in the Big Horn Basin, Ashley and his men were alarmed to discover that they had suddenly been surrounded by Crow warriors with guns at the ready. One of Ashley's party, Caleb Greenwood, had served with Manuel Lisa and was therefore acquainted with many tribal members. He identified himself to the Indians and explained to their leader that the caravan was simply passing through Crow territory en route to St. Louis. The chief responded by accusing the whites of killing two Crow warriors and went on to demand gifts for relatives of the deceased. Ashley complied but recognizing horses recently stolen from him, asked the chief why his warriors had taken them. The Indian candidly replied that he and his men had lost their horses and were tired of walking. The Indian leader did, though, arrange for the stolen horses to be returned and ordered that the trappers be allowed to pass through Crow country unmolested.[29]

It appears that there were few if any American trappers or traders in Crow territory from 1825 until the autumn of 1828, when Smith, Jackson, and Sublette changed the locus of their operations from Green River to the Yellowstone River drainage basin. By this time the tribe's attitude toward white trappers seems to have hardened into one of implacable hostility. Familiar with trappers' travel patterns and daily routines, it was a simple matter for bands of warriors to waylay intruders as they went about their business of trapping beaver. The result was intermittent harassment of working parties often involving thefts of horses, equipment, and beaver pelts.[30]

Captain Bonneville's introduction to frontier life included a mild form of Crow harassment. In late May, 1832, as his caravan was approaching Laramie River, a large band of Crow warriors in full war raiment charged menacingly at the gallop. At the last moment, the column divided itself to wheel in a wide circle on either side of the caravan. Following their display of horsemanship, the visitors dismounted in friendly fashion, and the leader offered his peace pipe to Bonneville. In the council which followed, it was decided that the two parties would camp together. Nothing untoward occurred that night, but the Americans were mildly surprised at the nature of the farewell given them the next morning. The Crow braves assumed a familiarity which proved embarrassing to the whites. As it turned out, though, their unwelcome embraces and caressing gestures had more to do with the acquisitive impulse than with affection. Once the Indians had completed their effusive farewells and departed, many of Bonneville's men found that their pockets had been expertly picked.[31]

The major focus of Crow hostility during the following year was a large trade caravan which moved through Crow territory following the Rocky Mountain Fur Company's fur rendezvous, again held in the Green River area. The caravan was led by Robert Campbell, who, with William Sublette had formed a partnership to supply trade goods for the rendezvous system. Accompanying Campbell was Thomas Fitzpatrick, a partner in the Rocky Mountain Fur Company, who commanded a detachment of twenty trappers headed for Crow country. Fitzpatrick's contingent included Dr. Benjamin Harrison and Sir William Drummond Stewart. Harrison was a physician by training and a hell-raiser by inclination. He had come west at the insistence of his father, William Henry Harrison, hero of the Battle of Tippecanoe and future president of the United States. The elder Harrison, obviously ignorant of rendezvous dynamics, had persuaded himself that a trip to the fur frontier would cure his son's dipsomania. Stewart, a native of Scotland, was a war hero in his own right, having been decorated for valor at the Battle of Waterloo.

CARAVAN EN ROUTE

Some American entrepreneurs employed the rendezvous system to acquire beaver pelts. Annual trade fairs, supplied by large trade caravans, were central to this strategy.

Courtesy Walters Art Gallery, Baltimore   *A. Jacob Miller*

He had subsequently retired from the British army and after several years seeking adventure in Turkey and Russia, returned to Scotland where he married a laundress from a neighboring estate. The social consequences of this rash act may have had something to do with his decision to visit the United States in 1832. Bonneville and his brigade of trappers also

accompanied Campbell as did Nathaniel Wyeth, a
sophisticated and urbane ice merchant from
Massachusetts. The latter had come west the previous
year with what turned out to be a flawed plan to link
the fur trade with Asian markets. He was now
returning to Massachusetts with a few beaver peltry
and a multitude of shattered dreams.[32]

Campbell's pack train carried beaver pelts obtained
by the Rocky Mountain Fur Company at the
rendezvous which that year had been held in the
verdant triangle formed by the confluence of Horse
Creek and Green River. Campbell followed a route
which generally retraced the route followed by
William Ashley in 1825. Once the column reached
the head of navigation on the Big Horn, Campbell
ordered the construction of bull boats which were
used to float both cargo and men downstream to the
Yellowstone River. En route they were hailed by a
large band of Crow who made it clear through
threatening gestures that they wanted the whites to
debark. The river was too narrow at this point to
safely elude the Indians, so the whites reluctantly
landed to make camp with their insistent hosts.
Harassment of the visitors turned out to be minimal,
involving only isolated instances of theft; otherwise
the party was allowed to resume its trip unscathed the
following morning. At Fort Cass the Wyeth and
Campbell contingents continued to take advantage of
the area's waterways by floating down the Yellowstone, headed for St. Louis via the Missouri River.[33]

Bonneville and his men reversed course at the
mouth of the Big Horn to trap the western half of the
Big Horn Basin. Fitzpatrick marched his trappers
south by east to Tongue River with the intent of
spending the fall trapping season in that general area.
Before he and his men could settle in for a proper
round of trapping, however, they found themselves

ATTACK BY CROW INDIANS

Relations between the Crow and white trappers were generally amicable during the early years of the fur trade, but beginning in about 1825, some tribesmen became increasingly hostile as they came to regard whites as competitors for peltries. This painting depicts a confrontation between a small party of Crow warriors and a detachment of trappers headed by William Drummond Stewart.

Courtesy Walters Art Gallery, Baltimore   *A. Jacob Miller*

squarely in harm's way. After establishing a camp on the river in early September, Fitzpatrick learned that a large Crow band was camped only several miles distant. Wishing to pay its chief the customary courtesy call prior to trapping tribal lands, he designated William Drummond Stewart as camp commander in his absence. Not long after the veteran mountain man's departure, a Crow war party of eighty men charged into camp. They immediately dismounted and, brandishing their weapons, proceeded to threaten the trappers with insults and menacing gestures. The veteran of Waterloo, taken by surprise and outnumbered four-to-one, ordered his charges to stand fast. The cheeky braves eventually left without inflicting bodily harm on any of the trappers but not until they had relieved them of everything of value, including Stewart's watch. Fitzpatrick, after receiving the Scottish aristocrat's account of the incident, hastily broke camp and headed his men in the direction of the friendlier confines of Green River.[34]

Bonneville and his men fared little better. Small trapping parties were subjected to various forms of harassment including outright attacks and horse thefts. On the lighter side, some harassment took the form of pure devilment. The most notable instance occurred in Wind River Valley. Happening upon a solitary trapper, a small band of Crow warriors took him prisoner. After amusing themselves for a time with mock attempts on the unfortunate man's life, they forced him to strip, took his horses as well as all of his equipment and left him to make his way back to Bonneville's camp as best he could.[35]

Changes in the Crow attitude toward trappers during the late 1820s and early 1830s undoubtedly had something to do with the Indians' increased estimation of the worth of beaver. William Gordon, a survivor of the Jones-Immell massacre, was persuaded that Crow hostility during this period stemmed from their unhappiness over the loss of this valuable natural resource without appropriate compensation. During the late 1820s, he explained, the tribe began to set beaver traps on a much larger scale than had been the case in past years. They therefore came to regard white trappers as competitors for what the tribe had come to regard as an important form of trade currency. Moreover, unlike earlier exploiters of Crow beaver resources, the new generation of trappers did little trading and therefore played only a minor role in satisfying the tribe's need for manufactured goods. Crow hostility, Gordon believed, stopped short of killing trappers because they didn't really want Americans to abandon tribal lands; their presence offered too many opportunities to rob and loot trapping parties.[36]

American trappers and traders with whom the Crow had contact during the early years of the nineteenth century were unwittingly acting as agents for the Alien Culture's political system. The War Department originally assumed responsibility for managing relations between the government of the United States and the various tribes which inhabited lands within its borders. More specifically such matters were handled by what was commonly referred to as the Indian Department, a loose grouping of War Department clerks and officials assigned to Indian matters by the secretary. The management of Indian affairs was institutionalized in 1824 with creation of the Bureau of Indian Affairs as a separate department within the War Department. In 1832 Congress passed legislation which authorized the position of commissioner of Indian affairs to supervise operation of the new bureau.[37]

With specific reference to the Crow tribe and its neighbors, the Upper Missouri Indian Agency was created by Congress in 1819 for the dual purpose of promoting peaceful relations among the tribes under its jurisdiction and assisting in the development of the fur trade. William Clark, serving as superintendent of Indian affairs at St. Louis, appointed his nephew,

James O'Fallon, as the region's first agent. Two sub-agents were authorized by Congress in 1824. The small number of officials designated to cover the entire Northern Plain's region effectively left it to American traders and trappers to promote peace and develop trade in the area.[38] In fact the only contact of record between the Bureau of Indian Affairs and the Crow tribe during the first quarter of the nineteenth century didn't occur until 1825. In that year Indian intransigence along the Missouri River prompted the government to dispatch a joint military-Bureau of Indian Affairs expedition to the area in an effort to restore peace to the fur frontier. Specifically, O'Fallon was instructed to negotiate treaties of amity with all tribes living along or near the river. Colonel Henry Atkinson was detailed to support the agent with a military force sufficient in size to impress the Indians with the might and power of the system represented by the agent.[39]

O'Fallon and his military escort boarded nine keel boats to begin their journey up the Missouri River on May 16, 1825. In late July, having negotiated treaties with most of the tribes living along the river, the commission arrived at the Mandan and Hidatsa villages where they were to negotiate treaties with those tribes and with the Crow as well. On July 27, eight members of the tribe came in to inform O'Fallon that the main body was about thirty miles behind them. The eight were given gifts and told to return to their people with word that the commission was anxiously awaiting their arrival. The following day Toussaint Charbonneau, apparently dispatched earlier by O'Fallon to find the Crow, arrived with word that they would arrive in three or four days. Actually, the tribe's representatives didn't come in until the afternoon of August 3.

A council was convened the following day with a

chief named Long Hair (Red Feather at the Temple)
representing the tribe and with the peripatetic Edward
Rose serving as interpreter. During the course of
negotiations, a number of Crow participants became
violently exercised over O'Fallon's demand that they
release some prisoners they were holding. Others
resented the agent's insistence that promised gifts not
be distributed until treaty negotiations had been
completed. In the confusion which ensued, O'Fallon
lost his temper and pistol whipped several of the
Crow participants. Only the presence of armed troops
prevented an open outbreak of hostilities.[40] In the
end, though, the tribe accepted and signed the treaty
which in effect placed the Crow under the political
jurisdiction of the United States government in return
for protection by that entity. The Crow also agreed,
under certain provisions of the treaty, that they
would trade only with authorized American citizens at
locations designated by the president and, further,
that they would not trade arms and ammunition to
enemies of the United States government. Other
provisions of the treaty provided that any tribal
members who might commit crimes against Americans
were to be remanded to the United States' judicial
system for trial.[41]

The treaty seems to have done little to cement
friendly relations between the Alien Culture's
political system and the Crow. To the contrary it is
likely that the pistol whipping administered by
O'Fallon contributed to the hostility displayed by the
tribe toward whites after 1825. Certainly the incident
created a lasting negative impression among tribal
members. At a council held with government representatives in 1867, a Crow leader complaining about
past treatment received by the tribe from the
government, buttressed his case by citing this
incident.[42]

The first quarter century of contact with the Alien Culture resulted in a number of basic and fundamental changes in Crow life. Not the least of these was the creation of a market for a natural resource virtually ignored in the past by the tribe: beaver pelts. On the one hand this meant that the tribe had access to an almost limitless supply of trade currency. On the other hand acquisition of the new currency called for substantial changes in daily patterns of life for both sexes. Those males who wishes to avail themselves of this new form of wealth found it necessary to devote some part of their time to trapping; their wives were required to set aside even longer periods of time to prepare the peltries for market.

The presence of white traders in Crow domain was undoubtedly a convenience to the tribe, but it also served to increase the tribe's dependence on the Alien Culture. White trading establishments along with the new form of trade currency made manufactured goods available to more and more tribal members. As ever larger numbers of Indians became accustomed to using these goods, dependence upon outsiders and their sophisticated technologies inevitably increased. Arms and ammunition were far and away the manufactured items most avidly sought by Crow males because it made them more formidable foes in battle and made them more successful hunters of small animals.[43] Dependency extended to all manner of goods. Metal knives, axes, and the like were found to be much more efficient tools than those made of stone. Likewise, kettles and other receptacles made of metal proved more durable than those made of materials readily available to the tribe. Clever males learned how to fashion items of utility, especially arrowheads, from scrap metal obtainable from white traders. Non-metal goods which many Crow came to regard as essentials included saddles, sugar, coffee, and woolen blankets.[44]

The importance attached to having traders in their territory is suggested by an incident experienced by Robert Campbell while spending the winter of 1828-29 as a resident of Long Hair's camp in Wind River Valley. Campbell suffered a loss of beaver pelts during his stay. When Long Hair learned of the theft, he assembled the entire camp to berate his followers for their lack of hospitality. During the course of his harangue, the chief reminded his fellow tribesmen that they had been without traders for several years and warned them that they needed to end their thieving ways if they expected American trappers and traders to once again take up residence among them. Most of the skins were surreptitiously returned to Long Hair's lodge that same night.[45]

The Crow largely avoided dependence on a trade item which wreaked havoc on many neighboring tribes. Liquor was rejected by tribal leaders and apparently by most tribal members. Referred to as "white man's fool water" and "bad water," there seems to have been a consensus among the Crow that it induced quarrelsome behavior, illness, and a foolishness that caused humans to behave as animals.[46] For whatever reason the use of liquor was limited to a small minority. Charles Larpenteur, a trapper and trader who travelled through Crow country in 1833 with Robert Campbell's caravan, observed in his diary that the Crow dressed better, were cleaner, and owned more horses than any of their neighbors. He attributed their superiority in these matters to their rejection of alcohol.[47]

The basic social unit of the Crow tribe was the matrilineal clan.[48] Each clan had its own leader, or chief. The clans, in turn, were grouped into two major divisions, each of which also had its own chief. Unusually strong and successful clan chiefs might be recognized as chief of the entire tribe. The record is silent on the fates of Red Calf and Red Fish, each of whom headed a major division of the tribe at the time Larocque accompanied them to their homeland in 1805, but it is known that both had been replaced as leaders by 1825. At the treaty council held in that year, Long Hair was identified as the chief of one of the tribe's major divisions and Rotten Belly as chief of the other. Long Hair also seems to have enjoyed the status of serving as chief of the entire tribe at that time because Rotten Belly did not sign the treaty. He was reportedly in the vicinity with his followers at the time but refused to participate in the proceedings.[49] Long Hair's name was descriptive. As a young man he had received a vision that his reputation within the tribe would be commensurate with the length of his hair. He thereafter allowed his hair to grow without ever cutting it, and its length eventually served as his *maxpe*. Contemporary estimates of its length ranged from nine to thirty feet. Whatever its actual length, it was long enough that he had to roll it into two balls which he hooked to the front of his saddle when riding. When afoot he carried it in an antelope bag slung over one shoulder.[50] There were, it should be noted, those in the trapping fraternity who suspected that the length of the chief's hair owed more to pine gum than to either natural growth or supernatural intervention of some sort.[51]

Rotten Belly's name was not descriptive insofar as is known. His *maxpe* was the thunderbird which he claimed unerringly guided him directly to enemy forces and ensured his invincibility in warfare. He became a chief at the relatively young age of thirty despite a generally disagreeable personality. Contemporary accounts portray him as being abrupt, surly, and a man of few words. He was also, though, a superb physical specimen and an effective organizer. Rotten Belly is credited with establishing a tradition of posting camp sentinels on an around-the-clock basis and with encouraging his warriors to improve their weaponry. He tended to be popular with Americans because he was a leading exponent of maintaining peaceful and friendly relations with them. By the early 1830s, he had supplanted Long Hair as chief of the entire tribe.[52]

The two major tribal divisions sometimes traveled together but more often separately. They always came together in early spring and again in late summer for the tobacco planting ceremony. Legendary Chief No Vitals was thought by the Crow to have given the first tobacco seed to the tribe and to have introduced the planting ceremony at the same time.[53] The ceremony was customarily held either in Wind River Valley or someplace in the vicinity of the mouth of the Little Big Horn River. The tribe returned to harvest the sacred crop in late August. Seeds were preserved for the following year's planting ceremony and tobacco leaves were stored in sacks to be used for both medicinal and ceremonial purposes. The operative belief connected with the ceremony was that only so long as the Crow were able to reproduce seed for planting each year could they expect to survive as a people. Tobacco seed, then, was regarded as the tribe's *maxpe*, essential to ensuring the tribe's well being and, indeed, its very survival.[54]

As a practical matter the major source of insecurity for the Crow was not the possibility that they might sometime be unsuccessful in reproducing tobacco seed but rather that they might be overwhelmed by one or another of their larger and more powerful neighbors. Warfare was a fact of life on the Northern Plains long before the arrival of white trappers and traders, and the frequency of intertribal conflict prompted most of the tribes inhabiting the region to form alliances as one approach to ensuring survival. To the north of the Crow homeland, the Blackfoot Alliance included the Blackfoot, Blood, Piegan, and Atsina tribes. Taking advantage of their combined power, they harassed, raided, and robbed the Shoshone, Flathead, and other small tribes living in or situated west of the Rocky Mountains. They also conducted raids on the Crow and on the Assiniboine. The Assiniboine, for their part, were allied with the Cree who occupied lands to their north and east. Along the Missouri River the Mandan, Hidatsa, and the Arikara had formed an alliance, mainly as a means of trying to protect themselves from the obstreperous Dakota nation.[55]

The various Dakota tribes seem to have been at least informally aligned with each other for military purposes. The Teton division, at the turn of the century, was made up of the Saones, Oglala, Uncpapa, and Broken Arrow tribes and, together with the Yankton and Yanktonai tribes, which made up the Yankton division of the nation, constituted by far the largest military alliance in the region. The Crow, on the other hand, were virtually bereft of allies; their only permanent alliance was with the Hidatsa. This arrangement can't have provided them much comfort. Their relatives were much too weak and too far removed from the Crow homeland to provide effective resistance in times of difficulty. It was probably the absence of reliable Indian allies which brought about the uneasy alliance between the Crow tribe and white trappers during the early 1800s.[56]

Tribes of the Blackfoot Alliance posed the most immediate threat to Crow security during the first half of the nineteenth century. In fact, throughout this period there existed an almost constant, if intermittent, state of warfare between the tribe and those Indians who made up the Alliance. It is an open question as to whether or not the presence of

THE BLACKFEET
Blackfeet, or Alliance, warriors constituted the most serious threat to Crow
security during the fur trade years.
Courtesy Walters Art Gallery, Baltimore   *A. Jacob Miller*

American trappers and traders in the Crow homeland
actually enhanced Crow security. During the first
three decades of the century, Alliance tribes occupied
northern Montana and southern Canada, venturing
south to the Three Forks and Yellowstone Valley
areas only on hunting and marauding parties.[57] It
seems likely that raids conducted to convince

Americans that Alliance hostility was too high a price to pay for the privilege of trading with the Crow, coupled with opportunities to steal horses, equipment, and peltries provided by the presence of American traders increased the incidence of violent confrontations between the Crow and the Alliance.

Another source of conflict between the two groups was the Atsina practice of periodically traveling south to the Arkansas River for the purpose of visiting their Arapaho relatives. This activity often took the Atsina through Crow territory, adding to the probability of hostile encounters between traditional enemies. In 1832, for example, returning from an extended visit with the Arapaho, a large band of Atsina was ambushed by Crow warriors in or near Wind River Valley. In the ensuing battle sixty-five Atsina males were killed and more than one hundred women and children were taken captive. In fairness to the Atsina, it should be noted that they were in a weakened condition at the time because they had only recently fought a major engagement with a large contingent of American trappers at Pierre's Hole, losing perhaps sixty warriors in that fray.[58] The heavy casualties taken in the two battles may have created a sense of insecurity among the Atsina, and it was perhaps for this reason that they negotiated a peace with the Crow later that same year.[59] Despite the frequency of warfare between the Crow and tribes of the Alliance during the first several decades of the nineteenth century, no territory was lost by the Crow to them. The struggle took its toll in other ways, though. Losses of males to warfare during these years created a pronounced demographic imbalance in favor of females.[60]

Another large and powerful neighbor, the Dakota nation, also exchanged raids with the Crow during the early decades of the nineteenth century. For the most part these took the form of horse-stealing raids or expeditions mounted by small war parties.[61] However, encounters between the two occasionally were of a more serious nature, resulting in heavy casualties on both sides. During the winter of 1801–02, for instance, a large Dakota war party made a surprise attack on a Crow village of thirty lodges. In the battle which followed, all male inhabitants of the camp were killed and surviving women and children were taken captive.[62] An even more catastrophic engagement from the Crow point of view occurred in the early 1820s. A joint war party of Dakota and Cheyenne warriors ventured into Crow country to exact revenge for an ambush of a Cheyenne raiding party perpetrated by a band of Crow warriors. Someplace along Powder River, the intruders happened on a Crow camp from which a number of warriors were at the time absent. There followed a complete rout in which most of the males present in camp were killed and large numbers of women and children were taken prisoner. The catastrophic character of the defeat suffered by the Crow on this occasion is suggested by the fact that it was still remembered by some tribal members more than fifty years after the event.[63] Despite the generally violent tenor of relations between them, the Crow and Dakota did enjoy at least one short period of peaceful relations during the winter of 1816–17.[64]

As the foregoing suggests, Crow relations with the Cheyenne tribe were also generally hostile. If the Cheyenne ever did represent a threat to Crow security, though, the magnitude of the threat lessened after 1830. In that year part of the Cheyennes abandoned the Missouri River region to join the Arapaho in the Arkansas River region. Thereafter, those who remained in the vicinity of the Missouri were referred to as the Northern Cheyenne while those who migrated to the Arkansas were referred to as the Southern Cheyenne.[65] This change, however, didn't entirely remove the migrants from contact with the Crow. In 1833, Rotten Belly led a contingent of warriors south to the Arkansas River to punish a Southern Cheyenne band which had recently harassed and killed the inhabitants of a small Crow camp. Rotten Belly's party made a surprise attack on a Cheyenne village, killing more than a hundred men, taking several hundred women and children captive and making off with almost a thousand horses.[66]

Crow relations with both the Assiniboine and Arikara tribes were uniformly hostile.[67] Crow-Shoshone relations were more irregular and complicated. Individual members of the Shoshone tribe could sometimes be found living with the Crow. Larocque, for example, mentioned that twenty lodges accompanied the Crow to the Mandan and Hidatsa villages in 1805.[68] On the other hand, Crow raiding parties occasionally attacked Shoshone camps and conducted raids on their horse herds. It seems to have been the case that at times the two tribes enjoyed amicable relations and at other times they found themselves at loggerheads.[69]

By all accounts, horse-stealing raids were the most frequent causes of intertribal warfare, and the Crow had the reputation for being the most accomplished horse thieves in the Northern Plains.[70] James Beckwourth, who lived among the tribe for almost a decade, compared their appetite for horses to a miser's greed for gold. So common were horse raids, in fact, that tribal leaders, fearful that camp security would be compromised by the absence of warriors, found it necessary to limit the practice with threats of severe punishment.[71] Although horse thefts by their very nature were conducted in secrecy, thieves were sometimes detected and occasionally killed. In cases of deaths resulting from a horse-raiding party, a war party was inevitably formed to exact revenge. This, if successful, invited retaliation from their enemies, *ad nauseam.*[72]

Revenge, then, also contributed to the frequency of intertribal warfare. Every death of a tribesman at the hands of an enemy, whether as a consequence of horse theft or any other type of raid or form of warfare, called for retribution. So strong was the revenge motive that it was institutionalized in tribal custom. Relatives of slain warriors were expected to go into a state of mourning. This involved hacking off hair, slashing arms and legs, cutting off one or more fingers at the first joint and temporarily living apart from the main body of the clan to which one belonged. Blood from wounds of self-mutilation was allowed to dry on the body and remained there until the mourning period ended, and mourning ended only with the death of a warrior from the offending tribe.[73] Another expression of institutionalized revenge was the Sun Dance as performed by the Crow. Their version of this ceremony was purely and simply an appeal for supernatural assistance in wreaking vengeance on the tribe's enemies. Unlike Sun Dances held by neighboring tribes, Crow Sun Dances were sponsored and organized by individuals rather than by the tribe. Moreover, they were held at irregular intervals; no ceremonies of this type were held during some years and, by the same token, more than one might be held during any given year.[74]

Yet another cause of Crow participation in intertribal wars was institutionalized in the sense that doing battle with an enemy had its own social imperatives. Being a warrior was the *raison d'etre* of a male's existence. If a male was unsuccessful in his role of warrior, he was nothing in the eyes of his contemporaries. On the other hand society generously rewarded those who performed specified valorous acts. These were four in number: counting coup, i.e., touching an armed enemy with a coup stick, wresting away an enemy's weapon in the heat of battle, leading a successful war party, and stealing a horse found tethered to an enemy tipi. The title of *batse tse*, or valiant man, was conferred upon all who performed at least one prescribed exploit. Not only was this an honor that allowed recipients to symbolically represent valorous deeds on wearing apparel, it also carried eligibility for certain tribal offices and the right to marry. Those who failed to achieve the rank of valiant man had to postpone marriage until the age of twenty-five. The larger the number of valorous exploits performed by a warrior, the more respect and status he could expect to enjoy during his lifetime. And at celebrations honoring victorious war parties, any who had achieved the rank of *batse tse* had the right to stand before the tribe and recount those acts for which he had received recognition.[75]

Traditional tribal animosities and contests over territory also contributed to intertribal warfare. Ethnocentrism prompted Plains tribes to look upon one another with distrust, thus increasing the possibility that casual contacts between individuals or groups of different tribes would lead to violent confrontations.[76] That tribal antagonisms were passed on from one generation to another is suggested by the persistence of hostile relations between the Crow and Alliance tribes as well as with those of the Dakota nation. To appreciate competition over territory as a cause of warfare, one need only consider the many territorial displacements of one tribe by another during prehistoric times.[77] This phenomenon would become all too real to the Crow tribe during the second half of the nineteenth century as it was forced to defend its homeland against the territorial aspirations of its neighbors.

Warfare as waged by the Crow and its neighbors was quite different from the warfare waged by the Alien Culture. Perhaps the way in which it differed most substantially was in the matter of organizing for war. The Crow system had no official body with responsibility for waging war; it lacked even the concept of war chief. War parties were organized by individuals who had received a calling in the form of a vision. Called "pipe holder" or "he who carries the pipe," the leader of a war party attracted followers to his enterprise by recounting particulars of his revelation. These included the precise objective of the projected campaign, strategies to be employed, the course of the battle or battles to be fought and the outcome of the venture. Participation was voluntary and the number of warriors which made up any given war party depended on the pipe holder's power of persuasion and, more to the point, the reputation of his *maxpe*. Military engagements therefore tended to have a random quality with little or no reference to tribal security considerations. In fact, the notion of prolonged, sustained campaigns executed for specific strategic purposes seems to have been foreign to the Crow mind set.[78]

The concept, fairly common in Alien Culture military tradition, of fighting against overwhelming odds for an ideal was also foreign to the Crow. Discretion was definitely the better part of valor for Crow warriors in most circumstances. Superior forces were rarely attacked nor was it usual for a Crow war party to remain on the field of battle if an engagement suddenly turned to their disadvantage; it was an article of faith that the lives of warriors should never be needlessly risked. In fact victory over a foe, no matter the number of casualties inflicted, was not considered a victory if attended by the loss of even one of their own. Pipe holders whose expeditions took casualties found their reputations as war leaders accordingly diminished. On the other hand it wasn't at all unusual for a Crow warrior to make a fearless charge in the heat of battle if he believed that his *maxpe* was particularly strong that day. By the same token an entire war party might fight like demons against all odds if its members believed that their pipe holder's *maxpe* was strong. Conversely, if for some reason a war party lost faith in their leader's *maxpe*, they most likely would refuse to fight even if they enjoyed a clear advantage.[79]

The major focus of intertribal warfare for the Crow tribe during the early decades of the nineteenth century was with its neighbors to the north, but the Dakota nation also had to be reckoned with in this regard. Although fighting seems to have occupied inordinate amounts of the tribe's time and energies during these years, its territorial integrity was never seriously compromised. Crow relations with white trappers were for the most part peaceable, probably because they were grounded on a community of interest involving both economic and security considerations. After 1825, however, relations grew increasingly bitter as some tribal members came to regard trappers as competitors for beaver pelts. Ashley's decision to replace the trading post system with his rendezvous system deprived the Crow of convenient access to trade goods and therefore undoubtedly added to their disaffection. It was mostly this growing dependency for manufactured goods which obliged the Indians to accept the Alien Culture's presence, and, in the process, allowed its representatives to establish a toehold in this part of the Northern Plains.

NOTES

1. Henry Marie Brackenridge, *Views of Louisiana: Together with a Journal of a Voyage up the Missouri River, in 1811* (Chicago: Quadrangle Books, Inc., 1962), pp. 90–92.

2. Thomas James, *Three Years Among the Indians and the Mexicans* (New York: The Citadel Press, 1966), pp. 52–54.

3. Drouillard's itinerary can be reconstructed with some precision because he later provided William Clark with details of his travels. These were incorporated into a map of the lower Big Horn River area drawn by Clark in 1809. See "Map and Notes by William Clark based on Information Furnished to him by George Drouillard, 1809," MHS. The map has been reproduced in M.O. Skarsten, *George Drouillard: Hunter and Interpreter for Lewis and Clark and Fur Trader, 1807–1810* (Glendale: The Arthur H. Clark Company, 1964), p. 339.

4. Reuben Holmes, "Five Scalps," *Glimpses of the Past,* V, Nos. 1–3 (January–March), 8–11.

5. James, *op. cit.,* p. 29.

6. Letter, Manual Lisa to Mrs. Pierre Menard, November 20, 1809, Pierre Menard Collection, ISHL; Letter Pierre Menard to Adrien Langlois, October 7, 1809, Kaskaskia Papers, MHS. Pierre Menard was not related to the Menard who visited the Crow tribe in 1795.

7. Letter, Reuben Lewis to Meriwether Lewis, April 21, 1810, Meriwether Lewis Collection, MHS; Letter, Pierre Menard to Sweetpea (Mrs. Pierre Menard), April 21, 1810, ISHL.

8. "Trade and Intercourse," *Annals of Wyoming,* XV (April, 1943), 135–6; James, *op. cit.,* p. 87; "Joshua Pilcher's Report," *Senate Document No. 90* (Serial 213), p. 12.

9. Brackenridge, *op. cit.,* p. 93.

10. John C. Luttig, *Journals of a Fur-Trading Expedition on the Upper Missouri, 1812–1813,* ed. Stella M. Drummond (New York: Argosy-Antiquarian, Ltd., 1964), pp. 76–77.

11. Holmes, *op. cit.,* pp. 26–27.

12. *Ibid,* p. 39; Charles E. Peterson, "Manuel Lisa's Warehouse," *Bulletin, Missouri Historical Society,* IV, No. 2 (January, 1948), 79.

13. "Investigations as to Causes of Indian Hostilities West of the Missouri River, 1824," *Annals of Wyoming,* XV, No. 3 (July, 1943), 207.

14. Letter, W. Gordon to J. Pilcher, June 15, 1823, published in Abraham P. Nasatir, "Notes and Documents: The International Significance of the Jones and Immell Massacre and of the Aricara Outbreak of 1823," *Pacific Northwest Quarterly,* XXX (1939), 100–101.

15. "Mr. Pilcher's Answers to Questions Put to Him by the Committee of the Senate on Indian Affairs," Senate Document No. 56 (Serial 89), pp. 11–13.

16. Maurice S. Sullivan, *The Travels of Jedediah Smith: A Documentary Outline, Including the Journal of the Great American Pathfinder* (Santa Ana: The Fine Arts Press, 1934), pp. 8–10.

17. Letter, Daniel T. Potts to Robert Tower Potts, July 16, 1826, in Charles L. Camp, ed., *Essays for Henry Raup Warner* (San Francisco: California Historical Society, 1947), p. 6; Letter, Daniel Potts to Thomas Cochran, July 27, 1824, in Dale L. Morgan, ed., *The West of William Ashley* (Denver: The Old West Publishing Company, 1964), pp. 79–80.

18. Morgan, Dale L., *Jedediah Smith and the Opening of the West* (Indianapolis and New York: The Bobbs-Merrill Company, Inc., 1953), pp. 80–87.

19. Charles L. Camp, ed., *James Clyman; Frontiersman: The Adventures of a Trapper and Covered-wagon Emigrant as Told in His Own Reminiscences and Diaries* (Portland: Champoeg Press, 1960), p. 21-25.

20. Morgan, *The West*, pp. 129-30; James P. Beckwourth, *The Life and Adventures of James P. Beckwourth*, ed. Delmont R. Oswald (Lincoln: University of Nebraska Press, 1972), pp. 77-81.

21. David J. Wishart, *The Fur Trade of the American West, 1807-1840: A Geographical Synthesis* (Lincoln and London: University of Nebraska Press, 1979), pp. 53-54, 126, 138-40. The Western Department of the American Fur Company was sold to the St. Louis firm of Pratte and Chouteau in 1836. The name of the company was changed to Pierre Chouteau, Jr. and Company in 1838. It was commonly referred to on the fur frontier as simply the Company.

22. Richard Jensen, ed., "A Description of the Fur Trade in 1831 by John Dougherty," *Nebraska History*, LVI (Spring, 1975), 111-12.

23. James H. Bradley, *The March of the Montana Column: A Prelude to the Custer Diaster*, ed. Edgar I. Stewart (Norman: University of Oklahoma Press, 1961), pp. 114-15.

24. F.G. Young, ed., *The Correspondence and Journals of Captain Nathaniel J. Wyeth* (New York: Arno Press, 1973), p. 211.

25. Wishart, *op. cit.*, pp. 61, 141, 152.

26. Rudolph Friederich Kurz, *Journal of Rudolph Friederich Kurz*, ed. J.N.B. Hewitt, Bureau of American Ethnology, Bulletin 115 (Washington: Government Printing Office, 1937), p. 144; Alexander Philip Maximilian, *Travels in the Interior of North America, 1832-1835*, ed. Reuben Gold Thwaites (Cleveland: The Arthur H. Clark Co., 1906), I, 353.

27. Alexander Henry and David Thompson, *The Manuscript Journals of Alexander Henry and of David Thompson, 1799-1814*, ed. Elliott Coues (Minneapolis: Ross and Haines, Inc., 1965), II, 720.

28. Letter, Potts, July 16, 1826, *op. cit.*, p. 7.

29. Beckwourth, *op. cit.*, pp. 52-53, 76-79.

30. Washington Irving, *The Adventures of Captain Bonneville, U.S.A. in the Rocky Mountains and the Far West*, ed. Edgeley W. Todd (Norman: University of Oklahoma Press, 1961), pp. 9-10.

31. *Ibid*, pp. 33-36.

32. Mae Reed Porter, *Scotsman in Buckskin; Sir William Drummond Stewart and the Rocky Mountain Fur Trade* (New York: Hastings House, 1963), pp. 70-71.

33. For first-hand accounts of the trip, see Young, *op. cit.*, pp. 206-10; Charles Larpenteur, *Forty Years a Fur Trader on the Upper Missouri: The Personal Narrative of Charles Larpenteur, 1833-1872*, ed. Elliott Coues (Minneapolis: Ross and Haines, Inc., 1962), pp. 38-46.

34. Letter, T. Fitzpatrick to W.L. Sublette, November 13, 1833, Sublette Family Papers, MHS.

35. Irving, *op. cit.*, pp. 205-6.

36. Letter, W. Gordon to L. Cass, October 13, 1831, in Annie Heloise Abel, ed., *Chardon's Journal at Fort Clark, 1834-39* (Freeport: Books for Libraries Press, 1970), pp. 345-7.

37. Francis Paul Prucha, *The Great Father: The United States Government and the American Indians* (Lincoln and London: University of Nebraska Press, 1984), I, 159, 164-5.

38. Ernest L. Schusky, "The Upper Missouri Indian Agency, 1819-1868," *Missouri Historical Review*, LXV, No. 3 (April, 1971), 249-51.

39. Unless otherwise indicated, the following account of the treaty negotiations of 1825 was taken from Russell Reid and Clell G. Gannon, eds., "Journal of the Atkinson-O'Fallon Expedition," *North Dakota Historical Quarterly*, IV (October, 1929), 5-56.
40. For slightly different versions of the incident, consult Holmes, *op. cit.*, pp. 53-54; Beckwourth, *op. cit.*, pp. 83-84.
41. The treaty has been reproduced in Charles J. Kappler, ed., *Indian Affairs; Laws and Treaties* (2nd ed: Washington: Government Printing Office, 1904), II, 244-6.
42. Louis L. Simonin, *The Rocky Mountain West in 1867* (Lincoln: University of Nebraska Press, 1966), p. 108.
43. Beckwourth, *op. cit.*, p. 165; Irving, *op. cit.*, p. 9.
44. John C. Ewers, "The Influence of the Fur Trade upon the Indians of the Northern Plains," in Malvina Bolus, ed., *People and Pelts: Selected Papers of the Second North American Fur Trade Conference* (Winnipeg: Peguis Publishers, 1972), p. 11; Kurz, *op. cit.*, p. 149.
45. Robert Campbell, *Col. Robert Campbell's Narrative*, Bancroft Library, MS P-W 22, p. 16.
46. Osborne Russell, *Osborne Russell's Journal of a Trapper*, ed. Aubrey L. Haines (Lincoln: University of Nebraska Press, 1959), p. 149; A.M. Quivey, ed., "Bradley Manuscript: Book F," *Contributions to the Historical Society of Montana*, VIII (1917), 228.
47. Larpenteur, *op. cit.*, p. 45.
48. Thaddeus Culbertson spent part of the year 1850 at Fort Union gathering data and artifacts on various aspects of the frontier. He lists twelve clans for the Crow. Thaddeus A. Culbertson, *Journal of an Expedition to the Mauvaises Terres and the Upper Missouri in 1850*, ed. John Frances McDermott, Bureau of American Ethnology, Bulletin 147 (Washington: United States Printing Office, 1952), p. 137. Robert Meldrum was of the opinion that the tribe was made up of thirteen clans. Lewis Henry Morgan, *The Indian Journals* (Ann Arbor: The University Press, 1959), p. 167. Robert H. Lowie also believed that there were thirteen clans or, depending upon how one interprets clan nomenclature, only eleven. Robert H. Lowie, *The Crow Indians* (New York: Farrar & Rinehart, Incorporated, 1935), p. 9.
49. Reid and Gannon, *op. cit.*, pp. 36-37; There exists great confusion regarding the internal structure of the tribe during the early years of the nineteenth century. Lewis and Clark, apparently drawing upon data obtained at their winter camp, reported that it was made up of four bands. Reuben Gold Thwaites, ed., *Original Journals of the Lewis and Clark Expedition, 1804-1806* (New York: Arno Press, 1969), VI, 103. Larocque was under the impression that the tribe was divided into three major units while his colleague, Charles MacKenzie, believed that it had only two major subdivisions. L.J. Burpee, ed., *Journal of Larocque from the Assiniboine to the Yellowstone, 1805*, Publications of the Canadian Archives, No. 3 (Ottawa: Government Printing Bureau, 1910), p. 55; Charles MacKenzie, "The Mississouri [sic] Indians: A Narrative of Four Trading Expeditions to the Mississouri [sic], 1804-1805-1806," in Louis Francois Rodrique Masson, ed., *Les Bourgeois de la Compagnie du Nord-Oest* (New York: Antiquarian Press, Ltd., 1960), I, 345. Whatever the situation was in this regard during the first two decades of the century, it seems to have been the case that the tribe had only two major subdivions during the 1830s. Trappers James Beckwourth, Leonard Zenas, and W.A. Ferris were all under

the impression that the tribe was divided into two basic units. Beckwourth, *op. cit.*, pp. 268, 270; Zenas Leonard, *Zenas Leonard, Fur Trader*, ed. John C. Ewers (Norman: University of Oklahoma Press, 1959), p. 140; W.A. Ferris, *Life in the Rocky Mountains* (Denver: Fred A. Rosenstock, The Old West Publishing Company, 1940), p. 305. Thaddeus Culbertson lists only two subdivisions. Culbertson, *Ibid.* And in a treaty the government negotiated with the tribe in 1851, only two chiefs were signatory to the document. The treaty can be found in Charles J. Kappler, ed., *Indian Affairs: Laws and Treaties* (Washington: Government Printing Office, 1904), II, 594-6; and in George E. Fay, ed., *Treaties, Land Cessions, and other U.S. Documents Relative to American Indian Tribes: The Crow 1825-1912* (Greeley: Museum of Anthropology, 1982), pp. 5-8.

50. Edwin Thompson Denig, *Of the Crow Nation*, ed. John C. Ewers (New York: AMS Press, 1980), p. 63; Edward S. Curtis, *The North American Indian*, ed. Frederick Webb Hodge (New York and London: Johnson Reprint Corporation, 1970), IV, 47; Quivey, *op. cit.*, pp. 224-5.

51. Edward F. Corson, "A Final Note about Long Hair," *Archives of Dermatology*, LXXXIII, No. 2 (May, 1961), 852-3. Dr. Corson examined the chief's hair, which had been preserved by the tribe as a relic, in 1958 and found a cement-like substance holding the hair together at intervals of three to five inches.

52. Irving, *op. cit.*, pp. 168-9; Denig, *op. cit.*, pp. 38-56; James H. Bradley, "Indian Traditions," *Contributions to the Historical Society of Montana*, IX (1923), 299-304; all carry accounts of Rotten Belly's career as chief of the tribe.

53. Curtis, *op. cit.*, IV, 44.

54. Denig, *op. cit.*, pp. 59-63; Lowie, *op. cit.*, pp. 287-95; Beckwourth, *op. cit.*, pp. 259, 325.

55. John C. Ewers, "Intertribal Warfare as the Precursor of Indian-White Warfare on the Northern Great Plains," *Western Historical Quarterly*, VI, No. 4 (October, 1975), 398-400, 403-5.

56. *Ibid*, pp. 406-7.

57. John C. Ewers, *Blackfeet Indians* (New York and London: Garland Publishing, Inc., 1974), pp. 66-68.

58. Irving, *op. cit.*, pp. 51-55; Ferris, *op. cit.*, p. 202.

59. Young, *op. cit.*, p. 210.

60. George Catlin, *North American Indians: Being Letters and Notes on Their Manners, Customs, and Conditions Written During Eight Years Travel Among the Wildest Tribes of Indians* (Edinburgh: John Grant, 1926), I, 49.

61. Garrick Mallery, *Picture Writing of the American Indians*, Tenth Annual Report of the Bureau of Ethnology, 1888-89 (Washington: Government Printing Office, 1893), p. 273; Garrick Mallery, *Pictographs of the North American Indians: A Preliminary Paper*, Fourth Annual Report of the Bureau of Ethnology, 1882-83 (Washington: Government Printing Office, 1886), pp. 104, 107, 135-137.

62. *Ibid*, p. 134.

63. Bradley, *March*, pp. 77-79.

64. Mallery, *Pictographs*, p. 136.

65. Joseph Jablow, *The Cheyenne in Plains Indian Trade Relations*, Monographs of the American Ethnological Society, XIX (New York: J.J. Augustin, 1951), 63-64.

66. Denig, *op. cit.*, pp. 40-44.

67. For accounts of hostilities between the Crow and these tribes, see Quivey, *op. cit.,* pp. 236-8; Beckwourth, *op. cit.,* pp. 270, 401; Hiram Martin Chittenden and Alfred Talbot Richardson, eds., *Life, Letters and Travels of Father De Smet* (New York: Arno Press, 1969), III, 1183.
68. Burpee, *op. cit.,* p. 22.
69. Beckwourth, *op. cit.,* p. 139.
70. Chittenden and Richardson, *op. cit.,* I, 238; Henry A. Boller, *Among the Indians: Four Years on the Upper Missouri, 1858-1862* (Lincoln and London: University of Nebraska Press, 1973), p. 243.
71. Beckwourth, *op. cit.,* pp. 199, 367.
72. Denig, *op. cit.,* p. 25.
73. Quivey, *op. cit.,* p. 211; Morgan, *Indian Journals,* pp. 171-2; Beckwourth, *op. cit.,* pp. 163, 201; Lowie, *op. cit.,* p. 223.
74. Beckwourth, *op. cit.,* pp. 292-6; Morgan, *Indian Journals,* pp. 183-8 both contain contemporary, eye-witness accounts of the ceremony.
75. Ferris, *op. cit.,* pp. 304-5; Lowie, *op. cit.,* pp. 5, 215-18; Beckwourth, *op. cit.,* p. 161.
76. Ewers, "Intertribal Warfare," pp. 397-8.
77. Thomas Biolisi, "Ecological and Cultural Factors in Plains Indian Warfare," in R. Brian Ferguson, ed., *Warfare, Culture and Environment* (San Diego: Academic Press, 1984), pp. 143-5.
78. Lowie, *op. cit.,* p. 219; Earl of Dunraven, *The Great Divide: Travels in the Upper Yellowstone in the Summer of 1874* (Lincoln: University of Nebraska Press, 1967), p. 88.
79. Lowie, *op. cit.,* p. 227; John F. Finerty, *War Path and Bivouac or The Conquest of the Sioux* (Norman: University of Oklahoma Press, 1961), p. 262; Thomas B. Marquis, *Memoirs of a White Crow Indian* (Lincoln: University of Nebraska Press, 1974), pp. 215-16; Leonard, *op. cit.,* p. 140.

FOUR

OF MEN AND BUFFALO

The construction of Fort Cass in 1832 constituted a rejection of the rendezvous system inaugurated by William Ashley and a return to the trading post system first brought to Crow country by Manuel Lisa in 1807. The Crow tribe undoubtedly found the latter type of operation more to its liking if for no other reason than that it afforded them convenient access to trade goods. The trading post as operated by the Company provided a market for not only beaver pelts but also for a commodity which had been produced by the tribe since time immemorial but never before marketed: buffalo robes. Fort Cass served the tribe as a trading center until 1835 when it was replaced by Fort Van Buren, located near the mouth of the Rosebud River.[1] This post was, in turn, supplanted by Fort Alexander, which was constructed in 1842 near the mouth of Emmels Creek, situated about halfway between the deltas of the Big Horn and the Rosebud Rivers.[2]

Trading procedures at company posts were accompanied by considerable pomp and ceremony. Approaching bands of Indians were greeted by cannon volleys and appearance of the bourgeoisie decked out in a uniform designed expressly for this purpose. Once assembled within the confines of the fort, a welcoming speech was delivered by the bourgeoisie to his clients, and this greeting was answered in kind by one or more of the visiting band's leading men. The distribution of trinkets as gifts was completed before the actual bartering of peltries for manufactured goods commenced. Business was conducted in the post's trading center where merchandise was exchanged for skins through a rectangular opening in a wall which separated an anteroom from the storeroom.[3]

In addition to personnel which staffed its posts located in Crow territory, the Company also hired individuals to promote the firm's economic interests on a more personal basis. The idea here was to assign employees to the tribe's various bands for the purpose of trading with the Indians in their own camps and, additionally, to encourage them to trap beaver. In some cases Company employees lodged with the leader of the band to which assigned. In these instances the chief's lodge served as a storage depot for goods to be traded. Other employees built crude log structures to be used as temporary living, storage, and trading centers.[4] Still others simply joined the tribe, taking Crow wives and assuming the trappings of Crow life.

The most notorious of the firm's employees to use this approach was James Beckwourth. Born in Virginia of a white father and a black or mulatto mother at about the turn of the century, he had come west with William Ashley in 1824. Beckwourth served with Ashley until the general sold out in 1826, and then with Smith, Jackson, and Sublette until 1828, when he assumed residence with the Crow. He took employment with the Company at a later undetermined date as one of its representatives with the tribe.[5]

Keeping the Crow on task at gathering beaver pelts turned out to be a more difficult assignment than anticipated. For example, to counter their natural proclivities for leaving camp on horse-stealing expeditions or participating in war parties, Beckwourth was forced to come up with ever more

JAMES BECKWOURTH

James Beckwourth worked for the Company as one of its representatives with the Crow during the 1830s.

Courtesy Nevada Historical Society

compelling arguments to focus their efforts on trapping. His strategies included injunctions against leaving camp in a weakened condition, warnings about displeasing First Worker, and suggestions that the arms and ammunition which might be acquired with peltries would strengthen the tribe against its enemies. The American work ethic he was trying to instill, however, seems to have been foreign to Crow nature because nothing he tried in this regard worked for very long.[6] Beckwourth, in short, found that his charges preferred almost any other activity to trapping.

Like others in his situation, Beckwourth discarded the externals of his own culture to slip easily into the Crow life style. In the early 1830s a fellow trapper named Zenas Leonard visited a Crow camp located near the mouth of Shoshone River in which Beckwourth was at the time living. Leonard's account of his own life in the mountains tells us that at the time of his visit to the camp, Beckwourth's needs and wants were being attended to by four wives and that the mulatto was indistinguishable in dress and manner from other males in camp. Leonard was of the opinion that Beckwourth enjoyed the status of chief.[7]

Robert Meldrum served the Company in the same capacity. He had likewise come west with Ashley but not until 1827. Known as Round Iron from his practice of distributing small iron medallions as gifts, Meldrum went to work for the firm as one of its representatives with the tribe in 1833.[8] Like his contemporary, James Beckwourth, he affected Crow dress, learned the Crow language and married into the tribe. Round Iron and his wife lived in the lodge of her parents, where his major responsibility was to tend the family's horses. After moving the animals to pasture early in the morning, he customarily returned to the family's tipi to take breakfast and thereafter

ROBERT MELDRUM
Robert Meldrum's relationship with the Crow tribe began in 1833.
Courtesy Montana Historical Society, Helena

INDIAN HOSPITALITY
The Company assigned employees to live with the Crow tribe during the 1830s
and 1840s to promote the firm's economic interests.
Courtesy Walters Art Gallery, Baltimore   *A. Jacob Miller*

gossip and smoke for an hour or so. Shortly before
noon Meldrum was expected to return to the horses
under his care to satisfy himself that they had
sufficient pasturage for the remainder of the day. If so
disposed he came back to the lodge for a midday
meal, after which he was free to spend the afternoon

as he pleased. At nightfall it was his duty to return the horses to the lodge where his wife and mother-in-law bedded them down for the night.[9]

Meldrum's only other regular duty was to supply meat for the family. On days when he chose to hunt, his father-in-law assumed responsibility for care of the horses. There were, of course, certain other obligations he assumed as a member of the tribe, most notably participation in warfare against Crow enemies. He counted coup on four different occasions and was credited with killing five Piegans. For these achievements, Round Iron was regarded as a warrior of some distinction and accorded the status of *batse tse*. His fellow warriors believed that he had the power to make himself invisible while engaged in battle because, despite his participation in numerous engagements, he had never received even a minor wound.[10]

In addition to Company employees assigned to the tribe, a number of free trappers could be found living among the Crow on a more or less permanent basis during the decade of the 1830s. Most were renegades or deserters from the various companies which had exploited the peltry resources of Crow lands over the years. Like Company agents who lived with the tribe, they generally took Crow mates and gave themselves over to Crow ways. For the most part they lounged around camp, did a bit of trapping now and then and occasionally conducted trade with their hosts. Periodically they repaired to Fort Union for a round of drinking, lying, and brawling. From sixty to eighty free trappers could be found living in one Crow camp or another at any given time during the 1830s.[11]

Edwin Denig, a Company official with decades of experience on the fur frontier and a keen observer of the area's aboriginal inhabitants, had little if any respect for the likes of Beckwourth and Meldrum. He

SIOUX INDIAN GUARD
Situated to the east of the Crow homeland, the Dakota, or Sioux, Nation
threatened the tribe's security.

Courtesy Walters Art Gallery, Baltimore   *A. Jacob Miller*

believed that those whites who abandoned their own culture in favor of Indian ways and manners were held in contempt by those whose behavior they aped. In his considered judgment the only whites admired by Indians were those who possessed and utilized skills and talents they themselves lacked. Meldrum came in for particular opprobrium from Denig who claimed that the trader's admitted popularity with the Crow had more to do with the prodigality of his trading practices than with their natural admiration for him.[12]

By the year 1840, free trappers had pretty much disappeared from Crow camps and, for that matter, from the Crow homeland. Streams, which in the past had literally teemed with beaver, had become nearly depleted by that date. At the same time the market for beaver peltry was declining as silk from China replaced beaver in the manufacture of hats. There naturally occurred a corresponding decrease in the price of beaver skins, bringing the market for this commodity to a state of near collapse. Veteran trappers had begun to complain about hard times in the late 1830s and most mountain men quit the mountains for more stable and lucrative enterprises elsewhere.[13] At about the same time that the beaver trade began to collapse, the Company turned its attention to another natural resource found in Crow territory, the buffalo. Although found in great numbers almost everywhere in the Northern Plains region during the early decades of the nineteenth century, traders had previously found buffalo to be of only slight commercial value. Buffalo robes were too bulky and heavy to be transported to market profitably with existing transportation facilities.[14]

Introduction of a new form of transportation, the steamboat, by the Company in 1832 made buffalo robes commercially viable for the first time. Robes

INTERIOR OF FORT LARAMIE

Trading posts operated by the American Fur Company replaced the rendezvous system during the 1830s. Company posts in Crow country were smaller than Fort Laramie but were similar in appearance and construction.

Courtesy Walters Art Gallery, Baltimore   *A. Jacob Miller*

collected at the firm's Crow posts could now be shipped by keel boat to Fort Union and then transhipped by steamer from that point to St. Louis. By the mid-1800s buffalo robes had replaced beaver pelts as the standard trade currency. One robe brought a pound of tobacco or twenty-five loads of ammunition, and ten robes could be exchanged for one rifle.[15] The transition from collecting beaver furs to buffalo robes called for changes in the dynamics of the Company's day-to-day operations. For one thing fewer employees were needed to live in Crow camps. Buffalo hunts were a traditional and popular activity and therefore required little or no encouragement on the part of outsiders as had been the case with beaver trapping. The robe trade did demand, however, large numbers of properly dressed hides. Employees assigned to Crow trading posts were therefore urged by Company officials to encourage the tribe to give up its traditional wintering grounds in Wind River Valley in favor of wintering in the vicinity of Company posts where employees could supervise and encourage the proper and timely dressing of robes.[16] A career change made by Robert Meldrum serves as a convenient marker for this shift in Company operations. In 1840 he gave up residence with the tribe to begin a period of service at one or another of the various Crow forts.[17]

The Crow hunted buffalo at all seasons but customarily held only two organized hunts in any given year. One was conducted during early summer and the other during late fall and early winter. Only those hides from cows and very young bulls killed in fall or winter, when coats were richly thick, were suitable for the robe trade. Hides obtained in the summer months were used mainly for lodge coverings. By mid-century, trading post environs were being utilized as wintering grounds by at least part of the tribe. Here hides killed during the winter hunt were dressed and subsequently used to purchase trade goods. The posts were abandoned by the tribe during the summer months to hunt and gather food from

edible plants. It was also during the summer months
that the tribe continued its time-honored practice of
visiting the Flathead, Nez Perce, and Shoshone tribes
for the purpose of bartering recently acquired manufactured goods for horses.[18]

As the foregoing suggests, the emphasis placed by
the Company after 1832 on collecting buffalo robes
modified traditional wintering patterns for some
Crow bands. The presence of Company posts on
tribal lands brought about other changes as well. For
one thing, trading forts served as social centers where
tribal members could congregate to gossip and renew
old friendships or establish new relationships. For
another thing the posts offered primitive banking
services to their clients. Most bourgeoisie could be
persuaded to extend credit for needed trade items
with the understanding that payment could be
deferred until the winter hunt was completed. Other
banking-type services provided by the posts included
the safekeeping of valuables along with purchase and
redemption of pawn articles.[19] The Crow posts
additionally served as a source of intoxicating
beverages on occasion. In 1837 a trapper named Joe
Meek witnessed what he called a drunken orgy
involving an entire Crow camp, adults and children
alike.[20] The tribe enjoyed a reputation for being one
of the most abstemious tribes in the region during the
first half of the nineteenth century, and this incident
would therefore appear to have been an exceptional
instance rather than an expression of the norm.[21]

Although never able to establish a complete
monopoly of the Northern Plains Indian trade, the
Company nonetheless consistently pursued this goal.
In the process, Fort McKenzie was successful in
breaking the monopoly on trade with Alliance tribes
enjoyed by British firms for more than a quarter
century.[22] The most serious competition for the Crow

trade during the 1830s came from successor companies to William Ashley's fur trade operations.
Robert Campbell and William Sublette, for example,
constructed a trading post, Fort William, at the
mouth of the Yellowstone in 1833 to compete with
Fort Union.[23] The interlopers dispatched traders to
Crow camps early that same autumn in an effort to
collect furs that might otherwise be traded at Fort
Cass. McKenzie responded by instructing Samuel
Tulloch, still serving as bourgeoisie at the post, that
he was to use any means at his disposal, including the
barter of goods at cost, to deprive the opposition of
trading opportunities.[24] Despite Tulloch's best efforts,
though, Sublette and Campbell traded for more pelts
that season than did Fort Cass.[25] McKenzie changed
tactics the following year and bought Fort William
from the partnership, ending competition from that
quarter. In 1835 the Company also bought out the
firm of Fontanelle, Fitzpatrick, and Co., successor
company to the Rocky Mountain Fur Company.[26]
This left only Antonio Montero, who, under the
auspices of Captain Bonneville, had built a trading
post along the upper reaches of Powder River to
service the Crow. But like Bonneville's other fur trade
enterprises, it came to naught and was abandoned
sometime prior to 1840.[27]

Two new firms challenged the Company's operations during the 1840s. In 1842 the New York firm of
Ebbetts, Cutting and Kelsey extended its trading area
from the Missouri River to the Yellowstone drainage
basin. Known as the Union Fur Company beginning
in 1843, it established a trading post near the mouth
of the Little Big Horn and began to offer liquor to
attract the tribe's trade. Inexperience, coupled with
the superior resources of the Company, forced Union
Fur Company's principals to sell out in May of
1845.[28] The only other opposition of any con-

sequence came from a firm organized by former employees of the Company in 1846. In that year Harvey, Primeau, and Company was granted a license to trade along the Missouri River. Two years later it constructed a trading post several hundred yards from Fort Alexander.[29] Despite repeated challenges to its dominant trading position in Crow territory and surrounding areas, the Company at mid-century still controlled at least four-fifths of all trade conducted with the Indians of the region. Competition did, however, have the effect of increasing prices paid for peltries, thus lowering the prices of trade goods to the Crow and their neighbors.[30]

With one notable exception the Company enjoyed peaceful relations with the Crow tribe throughout the decades of the 1830s and 1840s. The only breakdown in relations during these years stemmed from a dispute over the firm's operations in Alliance territory. The existence of Fort McKenzie was deeply resented by Crow leaders because they believed that it represented a threat to Crow security through its trade of arms and ammunition to their traditional enemies. Repeated remonstrances by tribal chiefs and requests that the post be abandoned were ignored by Company officials. In the summer of 1834, Rotten Belly decided to take matters into his own hands. At the head of 400 warriors, he approached the fort on June 25, and asked for permission to enter. The post bourgeoisie, Alexander Culbertson, had been forewarned by a recently-escaped Alliance captive from Rotten Belly's band that the Crow had in mind firing the fort.[31]

Culbertson consequently refused to grant them entry. Rotten Belly thereupon ordered his warriors to surround the fort, placing it under siege. The bourgeoisie responded by manning the stockade's parapets with armed employees, and, at the same time, sending word to the chief that Fort McKenzie would be defended to the last man. The following morning Rotten Belly again petitioned for entry and was again summarily refused. Twice rebuffed he returned to his warriors and ordered them to open fire on the post's defenders. Culbertson, his temper growing short, arranged for a cannon to be rolled into position, and, once in place, gave the order to fire. The shot slammed harmlessly into the earth, well short of the closest Crow skirmishers. It nonetheless had the intended effect. Rotten Belly and his followers quickly retreated to fold their tents and slip away into the wilderness.[32]

The vast majority of whites to whom the Crow were exposed prior to mid-century were, in a sense, kindred spirits. To successfully exploit the peltry resources of the tribe's homeland, trappers and traders had to acquire many of the same skills that allowed the Indians to survive in their native environment. Many mountain men, in fact, gave themselves over completely to Crow ways. They married Crow women, fathered children, and for all intents and purposes became, at least temporarily, tribal members. Occasionally white visitors to the area came out of curiosity rather than in satisfaction of the acquisitive impulse. Their published descriptions of Crow life provided views quite different from those found in accounts left by traders and trappers.

The first of these hardy, inquisitive souls to leave a written record of adventures among the Crow was George Catlin. Catlin was an attorney by education and training who deserted the law for art after only a few years at the bar. A self-taught painter, he made a lucrative new career for himself by painting portraits in Philadelphia. In 1830 he decided to combine an abiding interest in the American Indian with his artistic talent to capture and preserve what he feared was a rapidly disappearing way of life. To this end he moved to St. Louis where he spent more than a year doing portraits of the city's more prominent residents to support himself. He also painted portraits of Indians whenever the opportunity presented itself. In the spring of 1832, he eagerly accepted an invitation extended by the Company to ascend the Missouri River in its steamboat, the *Yellowstone*. When the vessel put in at Fort Union, Catlin was undoubtedly pleased to learn that two tribes from remote areas had recently arrived at the post; a band of Crow and a few warriors from one of the Alliance tribes were both camped in close proximity to the fort. Although he had come to fur country primarily to record his impressions in paint, the artist made it a point to record them in words as well. His observations on the Crow and other tribes he encountered on the trip appear in his *Manners, Customs and Conditions of the North American Indian* which was first published in 1841.[33]

In comparisons he made between the two visiting tribes, the Crow came off much the better. Crow males, Catlin thought, were both more neatly groomed and better favored by nature than their Alliance counterparts. Crow women, on the other hand, he thought undistinguished in appearance and interesting only for the streak of vermillion they applied along the hair's part line. Raiment of Crow males was not only lighter in color than that worn by Alliance warriors but was also more tastefully decorated, he reported. As for lodges, he thought those of the Crow more attractive than those of their traditional enemies. Catlin spent a month at Fort Union painting any Indians who would stand or sit still long enough for a portrait to be completed.

He thereafter descended the Missouri to another Company post, Fort Clark, which was located near the mouth of Knife River and not far from the Mandan and Hidatsa villages. Here he had an opportunity to observe another band of Crow. It had made the long trip eastward from the mountains to visit their Hidatsa relatives, and, at the time of the artist's arrival, were being appropriately welcomed by their hosts. The visitors reciprocated by staging a sham battle. Crow warriors, with shields and arrow quivers slung over one shoulder, assembled for the war games clad in buckskin breeches, eagle head dresses, and shirts fringed with scalp locks. Mounted on spirited, prancing horses, they divided themselves into two squads and squared off at opposite ends of a level plain. As the tableau unfolded the two contingents charged one another at full gallop, each warrior chanting his particular *maxpe* song, to engage in mock combat. All in all the visitor from Philadelphia thought it an exciting and thoroughly entertaining spectacle.[34]

George Catlin returned to St. Louis in August with more than one hundred paintings and many pages of his impressions of the fur frontier and its inhabitants. His writings reflect a genuine admiration for the Crow. Before making the trip he had heard trappers' tales of thievery and harassment of whites on the part of the tribe. Catlin passed these on to his readers but went on to explain that, actually, theft was abhorrent to the Crow and most other tribes. Crow appropriation of horses, equipment, and trade goods from whites, he contended, was in way of meting out justice to trespassers on tribal lands. In support of his defense of Crow actions in this regard, he cited statements made by both Kenneth McKenzie and Samuel Tulloch. Both men, he averred, attested to the basic honesty and goodness of the Crow.[35] However, it must be said that Catlin's writings reflect a highly romanticized picture of all the tribes with whom he visited and an overly enthusiastic appreciation of Indian life generally. A more realistic, hard-headed appraisal of Indians and their ways was made the following year by an experienced natural scientist, Prince Alexander Phillip Maximilian of the tiny Germanic state of Wied-Neuwied.

Like William Drummond Stewart, Maximilian was a decorated veteran of the Napoleonic Wars. He seems, however, to have found military service less appealing than science. Shortly after the final defeat of Napoleon, he set out for South America to study the flora, fauna, and aborigines of Brazil. Published accounts of his findings there were well received by the European scientific community. He consequently already enjoyed a considerable reputation as a natural scientist at the time of his visit to the American West in 1833. The major focus of his investigations on this trip was to be the American Indian with whom he hoped to make comparisons with their Brazilian counterparts. Prince Maximilian had rendered his own illustrations for the Brazilian study but had been disappointed with the results. He had consequently engaged a Swiss artist named Karl Bodmer to accompany him as illustrator for his North American expedition.

Traveling under the alias of Baron Braunsberg, the fifty-year-old gentleman/naturalist boarded the *Yellowstone* at St. Louis in April, 1833, for his rendezvous with aboriginal America. Maximilian, as had been the case with Catlin, did not visit the Crow homeland but was nonetheless afforded an opportunity to study the tribe. When he debarked at Fort Clark, he found that Rotten Belly's band was camped nearby, and, as it turned out, the naturalist was able to visit the camp twice. On the first occasion, he was introduced to the Crow leader and then taken on a tour of the camp. The prince was puzzled to see that

Rotten Belly was dressed in rags until told that the chief's less than majestic appearance was in keeping with the tribe's customary practice for mourning relatives recently killed in warfare. Clothing notwithstanding, the prince thought the Crow leader a fine, tall man of pleasing countenance. As for the camp it seemed to the German aristocrat that it lacked order and form. He could discern no pattern to the placement of lodges, and, worse, five hundred to six hundred surly, wolf-like dogs roamed the premises, making life precarious for visitors. As he was leaving, an invitation was extended and accepted to return that same evening for a visit to Rotten Belly's lodge.[36]

Accompanied by Toussaint Charbonneau as interpreter, the visitor found that most of the dogs had disappeared but that they had been replaced by horses, each tethered to its owner's tipi. When he entered Rotten Belly's lodge, he found the chief seated directly opposite the entrance, flanked by officials of lesser rank. After sharing a ceremonial pipe, the two aristocrats chatted about various matters, the nature of which Maximilian failed to record. He did, however, later record some of his impressions about the tribe. Like Catlin, he commented on the skill of Crow women in dressing skins and was laudatory of their ingenuity in decorating clothing with shells and porcupine quills. Crow males received his praise for their craftsmanship in constructing bows and for their extraordinarily skillful horsemanship. On the other hand he appears to have been looking down his German nose at the tribe's sexual mores when he observed that Crow women had the reputation for being the most dissolute of all the Indian women in the region. In support of this allegation, he noted that the Mandans believed the Crow were responsible for the introduction of venereal disease along the Missouri River. In the same vein he reported that, appallingly, the tribe tolerated hermaphrodites.[37]

A view of the tribe from a Christian missionary's perspective can be found in the writings of Father Pierre de Smet. A member of the Jesuit Order who had left his native Belgium to minister to the spiritual needs of North America's aboriginal inhabitants, his first encounter with the Crow occurred in 1840. At the time, he was traveling down Yellowstone Valley with an escort of Flathead warriors. De Smet had just completed a visit to that tribe preparatory to founding a permanent mission to serve its members and was returning to St. Louis to report on the feasibility of the project to his superiors. Near Clark's Fork his escorts became highly exercised when they discovered signs that a large body of Indians was nearby. A few moments later the small party came upon a pile of rocks spattered with fresh blood. The missionary was surprised to see that this grisly discovery had a calming effect on the Flatheads. They quickly explained that the blood-stained rocks told them that the Indians responsible for the fresh tracks had been made by the Crow, with whom they were, at time, at peace. De Smet was informed that the Crow made it a point to return to areas where large numbers of casualties had been sustained for the purpose of commemorating the bravery of fallen tribesmen by letting blood upon the field of battle.[38]

As it turned out, the Flatheads had accurately interpreted the signs left by the recently-departed Indians. The missionary and his small party sub-sequently came upon and entered a Crow camp where they learned that the band had indeed just completed a blood-letting ceremony to honor forty warriors killed in a battle fought with Alliance warriors on that site two years earlier. The visitors were cordially received and spent several days with the Crow as they

made their way down the Yellowstone. At one stop
the priest witnessed a trading session involving one of
his escorts whose horse had caught the eye of a Crow
warrior. The latter led his own horse to the Flathead,
placing the reins at his feet. Receiving absolutely no
reaction to this overture, the Crow added his gun,
then his other accoutrements, one-by-one, until only
his clothing remained. Not until his moccasins and
leggings had been added to the pile did the Flathead
relent by taking the reins of the proffered horse. Thus
was the trade completed, all without the exchange of a
single word or hand sign.[39]

On the final day of his stay with the tribe, de Smet
was feted at so many banquets that he found it
convenient, indeed necessary, to have at his side a
Flathead to eat in his stead. Utilizing each banquet as
an opportunity to proselytize, he tried to explain the
nature of the Christian God along with some of the
major precepts of Christian morality. After listening
to the evangelist's disquisition on the Ten
Commandments and the consequences of failure to
obey same, the host of one feast rose to observe that
in his experience there were only two creatures in all
of Crow territory that might reasonably expect to
escape the horrors of the Christian hell. These, he
declared, were the weasel and the otter, but went on
to say he wasn't all that certain that even they would
qualify for the Christian heaven.[40]

The Jesuit's second encounter with the tribe
occurred two years later when he was once again
descending the Yellowstone River en route to St.
Louis. On this occasion he was astonished at the
warmth and enthusiasm with which he was received.
Warriors pressed in upon him shouting, "Black Robe!
Black Robe!" each jostling for position to make a case
for serving as the cleric's host. To end the clamor and
confusion, he agreed to stay in the lodge of a

supplicant who, by his bearing and dress, seemed to be an individual of some importance in the tribal hierarchy. De Smet later arranged with his host to have the village assemble for a religious service. The evangelist was gratified to see that virtually the entire camp turned out and was most pleased with the rapt attention paid by the Indians to his sermon.[41]

At a feast held by the priest's host following completion of the service, one of the guests inadvertently revealed the reason for the hearty reception that had marked de Smet's arrival as well as for the respect accorded his sermon. At some point in the festivities, the Indian deferentially thanked the cleric for providing the *maxpe* which had seen him safely through many military engagements and which was therefore mainly responsible for his reputation as one of the tribe's most renowned warriors. Puzzled, the priest watched as the Crow opened his medicine bag to reveal that it contained some matches that de Smet had left with the tribe on his first visit. The grateful warrior explained that before engaging the enemy in battle, he made it a point to strike a match to determine if fire appeared on the first rubbing. If so he charged the enemy with great abandon, secure in the knowledge that he had immunity from danger and that he was assured of a victorious outcome. Clearly, then, the missionary's popularity with the tribe was due less to his skills as an evangelist than to his reputation as a purveyor of magic.[42]

The following day it was learned that two of the tribe's most distinguished warriors had been killed in a skirmish with a band of Alliance intruders. As the bad tidings spread, an oppressive pall descended over the camp, punctuated by the anguished screams and moans of mourners. De Smet was appalled as he watched relatives of the deceased, blood dripping from self-inflicted gashes on the upper body, go from warrior to warrior demanding immediate retribution.[43]

Contacts between the tribe and the Indian Service prior to mid-century were minimal. Preoccupied with internal politics, hampered by frequent changes in both personnel as well as jurisdictional boundaries and distracted by concern over the liquor traffic, the department's bureaucrats seem to have had neither the inclination nor the time to concern themselves with tribes remote from the Missouri River. John Dougherty was appointed agent of the Upper Missouri in 1830. Dougherty brought a world of experience to the job, dating back to 1810 when he had signed on with Manuel Lisa as a trapper. As one of his responsibilities as agent, he supervised the Mandan sub-agency which theoretically administered relations between the Crow tribe and Great Father. Headquartered at the Mandan and Hidatsa villages, its first administrator was John F.A. Sanford. Better known to history as the defendant in the Dred Scott case some three decades later, Sanford seems to have devoted an inordinate amount of time and energy trying to undermine John Dougherty's reputation with officials in Washington. Unable to convince his superiors that he should replace Dougherty, Sanford resigned in 1834.[44]

William A. Fulkerson, who replaced Sanford, resigned in March of 1838 under pressure from his brother-in-law, Superintendent William Clark. The difficulty was that Fulkerson spent so little time at his post that Clark found it necessary to sack him. He was never replaced. Joshua Pilcher replaced Dougherty as agent that same year and served in that post until September of 1838 when he was named to succeed William Clark as superintendent in St. Louis.[45] Because Pilcher failed to name a replacement for himself as Upper Missouri Agency agent, the Crow, along with other tribes of the Upper Missouri region, were without an agent until 1842 when Andrew Drips, a former Company employee, was named to the post. Drips served as agent until March 31, 1846, when he was replaced by Thomas P. Moore. Moore served for less than a year to be in turn replaced by Gideon C. Matlock, who served for only a year or so to be succeeded by William S. Hatton in 1849. In that same year, the Upper Missouri Agency was reduced to the status of sub-agency and placed under the jurisdiction of the Salt Lake Agency.[46]

Given this state of affairs, it is not surprising that only one piece of business between the Indian Service and the Crow tribe during the 1830s and 1840s can be documented. John F.A. Sanford met with Rotten Belly in council during the early summer of 1833 near Fort Clark in what appears to have been a *pro forma* attempt to cement peaceful relations with the tribe. Sanford hung a medal around the chief's neck and presented him with several gifts, all in the name of Great Father. Prince Maximilian, who witnessed the ceremony, noted that the presents were received by Rotten Belly without the slightest sign of gratitude. The aristocratic observer concluded that the goods were accepted as tribute payments from Great Father rather than as gifts.[47]

Relations between the Crow and their neighbors during the 1830s and 1840s continued in much the same violent mode that had characterized earlier decades of the century. The major change in inter-tribal relations during these years was a shift in the balance of power among the tribes of the Northern Plains caused by invisible invaders. On June 19, 1837 the Company steamship, *St. Peters*, put in at Fort Clark with some most unwelcome visitors in the form of smallpox viruses. The steamer subsequently made its way upstream to also infect the denizens of Fort Union. The disease raged up and down the Missouri

River for the next several months with appallingly high mortality rates. Unable to stem the virulence with traditional medications or incantations, the region's aboriginal inhabitants not only suffered disastrously high mortality rates but experienced, in the process, profound demoralization as well.[48]

Tribes were affected in uneven fashion; some were devastated by the disease while others escaped virtually unscathed. As might be expected those closest to the loci of infection suffered the most severely. In fact the smallpox epidemic of 1837 constituted a disaster of cataclysmic dimensions for the semi-sedentary tribes living along the banks of the Missouri. Smallpox took virtually all the Mandans, leaving only twenty-three adult males, about forty women and perhaps seventy children.[49] The Hidatsa and Arikara tribes fared better, but, still, both tribes lost approximately one-half of their numbers to the disease.[50] The effects of the epidemic, coupled with harassment from neighboring Dakota tribes, prompted most of the Arikara tribe to abandon their villages and move to the mouth of Knife River where they consolidated with survivors of the Hidatsa and Mandan tribes. Then, beginning in 1845, elements from all three tribes began migrating to a location some fifty miles upriver to found Like-A-Fishhook village.[51]

The Assiniboine tribe, occupying lands adjacent to Fort Union, likewise suffered a fifty percent mortality rate from the infection. Actually no Assiniboine were present at the post when the St. Peters docked, and the tribe might therefore have avoided the infection. When the first band of Assiniboine approached the fort after the virulence broke out, employees were dispatched to intercept and warn the Indians not to enter the trading post. They refused to heed the warning, however, and of those subsequently exposed to the disease on that occasion, only a few survived. Other bands of Assiniboine were later exposed and infected.[52] Their relatives to the south, the populous Dakota nation, largely escaped the ravages of the epidemic. Some had been previously inoculated against smallpox; most simply happened to find themselves out of harm's way at the time the disease was running its course. A few bands of the Teton division were in fact infected, but the number of casualties only marginally decreased the Dakota nation's total numbers.[53]

Tribes which inhabited the area situated to the west of the Rocky Mountains, including the Shoshone, Flathead, and Nez Perce Indians, seem to have escaped the consequences of the epidemic altogether. For their part the Crow suffered only minimally from the disease. It did reach Fort Van Buren during the summer of 1837, but, typically, there were few members of the tribe present at the post in that season. As word of the virulence reached camps of the various bands, however, they scattered to the four winds.[54] Trapper Robert Newell happened to be visiting a large village camped along the banks of the Little Big Horn when news was received that Company employees at Fort Van Buren had contracted the illness. Lodges were immediately struck and the camp's inhabitants scurried southward as fast as their mounts would carry them. The headlong retreat ended only when they reached Wind River Valley.[55]

Alliance tribes frequented neither Fort Union nor Fort Clark on a regular basis and should therefore have also been spared. That they were not was due to the presence of one of their number on board the *St. Peters*. This unfortunate debarked at Fort Union to catch a Company keel boat bound for Fort McKenzie. He got off there to infect large numbers of Piegans

and Bloods who were impatiently waiting at the post
for trade items expected on the keel boat. When the
disease had finally run its course, it had taken well
over one-half of the Piegan, Blackfoot, and Blood
tribes. Of the Alliance tribes only the Atsina escaped
devastating losses; they suffered only two hundred
deaths from the disease.[56] A trapping party which
included Kit Carson among its numbers was working
the Yellowstone and Musselshell areas in the fall of
1837. They were puzzled by the absence of customary
harassment by Alliance Indians until informed by a
band of Crow that what remained of their traditional
enemies had scattered to areas north of the Missouri
River to escape the ravages of the smallpox
epidemic.[57]

During the decade preceding the outbreak of smallpox, the Piegan tribe had gradually shifted its
activities southward to the Three Forks region. By the
early 1830s, the greater part of the tribe was spending
the summer months there and some occasionally
wintered in that area as well. This placed the tribe in
closer proximity to Fort McKenzie, thus affording its
members more convenient access to trading facilities.
It also brought the tribe closer to the Crow homeland,
increasing the likelihood of casual contact between
two antagonistic tribes and thus also increasing the
likelihood of violent encounters between traditional
enemies.[58]

One of the major engagements fought by the two
tribes during these years took place in the Big Horn
Basin during the month of November, 1834. A large
village of a thousand or more Crow was conducting
its winter hunt there under Long Hair when a party of
one hundred or more Piegan was spotted nearby.
Doing battle with an outnumbered enemy was one of
the few distractions capable of diverting the Crow
from the chase. Warrior after warrior broke away

from the buffalo herd they had been pursuing to converge on the enemy, only to find that the Piegan had entrenched themselves in a natural fortification of rocks. The attackers first mounted a frontal assault on foot but were driven back by withering rifle fire. Long Hair regrouped his forces to send mounted horsemen, one at a time, to ride at breakneck speed across the front of the fortification. After firing at the enemy, riders stretched out behind their mounts, leaving only an arm and a leg exposed to enemy fire. This exercise may have given participants an opportunity to display their horsemanship and daring but did absolutely nothing to dislodge the intruders from their rocky refuge.[59]

Long Hair then held a council in an attempt to devise a more efficacious strategy, but the best he could come up was another frontal attack. With enthusiasm for the enterprise waning, it seemed at this point that the Crow were on the verge of abandoning the field of battle to the enemy. That they did not was due to James Beckwourth. The veteran mountain man stepped forward to appeal to the Crow sense of honor by contemptuously referring to those present as squaws unfit to bear the title of warrior. He warned that if they retreated in the face of a greatly outnumbered enemy, the Crow would ever thereafter be held in contempt by Indians and whites alike. Beckwourth concluded his harangue with a loud war whoop and then charged the fortification. Immediately joined by a host of his adopted brothers-in-arms, the mountain man's assault completely overwhelmed the enemy, and when the dust had settled, not a single defender of the fortification was left standing.[60]

At least one successful attempt was made by the Piegans to end the mutually destructive and seemingly interminable warfare between the two tribes. During the summer of 1836, Piegan leaders petitioned the Crow for a truce and their overtures were favorably received. There followed a period of peace during which both parties refrained from making horse-stealing expeditions and during which friendly visits were exchanged in lieu of raiding parties, but the peace turned out to be only temporary in character. Sometime during the autumn of that same year, five Crow warriors, on their way to a Piegan camp for a friendly visit, encountered two Piegan hunters. Old habits die hard; unable to resist the temptation, the visitors killed and scalped their erstwhile enemies. The Crow warriors nonetheless proceeded on to their destination where they received a reception befitting newly-acquired allies. That night, however, as the guests slept, a Piegan woman rifled through their baggage and found the two Piegan scalps. Putting the two scalps together with two missing hunters, the Piegan hosts summarily executed their guests, ending the short-lived peace.[61]

One of the major battles fought between the Piegans and the Crow after the abortive peace and before mid-century occurred in 1845. In early October of that year, the Small Robes band of the Piegan tribe was en route from the Judith River to the valley of the Musselshell when they were surprised by a war party of Crow. Unable to organize themselves for an adequate defense, the Small Robes suffered a disastrous defeat at the hands of their long-time enemy. They lost at least a hundred warriors in the battle; in excess of one hundred women and children were taken captive to be subsequently absorbed into the Crow tribe.[62]

Crow warfare with the Alliance was by no means limited to the Piegan tribe. Raiding parties from both the Blood and Blackfeet tribes made occasional forays into Crow territory on horse-stealing expeditions, but

Crow-Atsina conflicts were much more frequent. The close proximity of the Atsina coupled with their practice of crossing Crow lands to visit the Arapaho increased changes of casual contact between the two tribes. The Crow and Atsina did enjoy a brief period of amity in 1830, however. The Atsina took the initiative in negotiating a treaty with the Crow, but peaceful relations lasted for only a few months. The status quo was restored after three Crow warriors were attacked while making a friendly visit to an Atsina camp.[63] A year later an Atsina hunting party had the good fortune to be in the right place at the right time to deliver a devastating blow to Crow military power, and the bad fortune to pay the ultimate price for the opportunity to do so. Rotten Belly, following his abortive attempt to close down Fort McKenzie in 1834, was returning to Crow territory with his followers when he sighted a small band of Atsina making its way up the valley of the Musselshell River. The Crow chief, undoubtedly smarting from his inability to prevail in the face-off with Alexander Culbertson, rashly charged the enemy and was promptly killed. His warriors avenged the loss of their leader by slaying the entire party of Atsina, but the Crow, in the meantime, had lost their most effective war leader.[64]

By mid-century, Alliance tribes had recovered from the disastrous consequences of the smallpox epidemic to a remarkable degree. Edwin Denig estimated in 1856 that their numbers had increased to the point that total Alliance population was only about one-third less than it had been before the disease struck. In any event, they were still the major adversary of the Crow at mid-century. Alliance truculence was directed not only at the Crow but at trading posts located in the tribe's territory as well. These were resented for the same reason that Rotten Belly resented Fort McKenzie; they furnished arms and ammunition to an enemy. So dangerous did employees regard service at the posts located on the Yellowstone River that the Company found it difficult to keep them adequately staffed during the decade of the 1840s.[65]

If tribes of the Alliance still constituted a threat to Crow security in 1850, the Assiniboine tribe did not. The Assiniboine enjoyed a reputation as good fighters, and in addition to their enmity of the Crow, were also implacably inimical to both the Dakota and the Alliance tribes. The epidemic of 1837 had seriously compromised their ability to defend themselves against traditional enemies, and, probably for this reason, they subsequently approached the Crow with a proposal that the two tribes cease fighting and make common cause against common enemies. The Crow at first refused, but in 1844, perhaps because they were feeling increased pressures from the Dakota on the east along with continued pressure by Alliance tribes from the north, reopened and satisfactorily concluded peace negotiations with the Assiniboine.[66]

The smallpox contagion of 1837 undoubtedly increased the relative strength of the Dakota nation on the Northern Plains. It suffered only minimally from the disease, while its closest neighbors (the Mandan, Hidatsa, and Arikara) all experienced fatalities of a magnitude that rendered them virtually helpless in the face of Dakota truculence. The migration of these tribes to Like-A-Fishhook village in 1846 removed the final barrier to Dakota expansion into Crow territory. No less dependent on the buffalo for subsistence and trade currency than other Plains tribes, a gradual decline in herds to be found along the lower Missouri River greatly increased the attractiveness of better-stocked lands lying to the west of their own territory.

As early as 1830, the Yankton Dakota were suffering from the diminution of buffalo in their hunting groups according to Agent Dougherty.[67] By 1844 few could be found on lands south of the headwaters of the Little Cheyenne River, forcing inhabitants of that area to abandon their usual haunts in search of better hunting grounds.[68] Father de Smet summarized the situation in a letter written to the commissioner of Indian affairs in 1848. According to de Smet, buffalo could still be found at one time or another in all parts of the Northern Plains but he also reported that areas which still supported large numbers of the animals were becoming ever more circumscribed. He went on to note that shortages on Dakota lands had already prompted the tribes of that nation to regularly encroach on the lands of its neighbors.[69]

A Dakota migration in search of more reliable hunting grounds began during the early 1830s, and this movement had the effect of increasing the threat that nation posed to Crow security. Parts of the Oglala and Brule tribes extended their buffalo hunting grounds south and west to the valley of the North Platte River during these years. In 1834 William Sublette and Robert Campbell, having sold out their trading interests on the Upper Missouri River to the Company, built a trading post at the mouth of Laramie River to service the recently-arrived Dakota tribes. Fort William for some years thereafter functioned as a commercial and social center for Oglala and Brule inhabitants of that area. In the process these elements of the largest and most powerful of Crow adversaries were obtaining a foothold on the tribe's southern border.[70]

Of all the Dakota tribes, the Oglala seem to have been the Crow's most active antagonist during the 1840s. The typical Oglala raid took the form of horse-stealing expeditions. They were almost always short of mounts, and Crow camps offered convenient opportunities to replenish the tribe's herds. In these encounters the Dakota raiders often made off with large numbers of the animals, but in most cases, suffered a loss of warriors to Crow pursuers. One of the more satisfying encounters between the two tribes from the Crow perspective occurred in 1844 when a band of their warriors caught up with an Oglala raiding party and killed twenty-six of the malefactors, driving the survivors off with only whips and bows. Flogging a fleeing enemy was meant to convey utter contempt for an opponent, and was widely regarded as the ultimate insult among Plains Indians.[71]

Other tribes of the Dakota's Teton division continued to roam on lands situated to the west of the Missouri River. The Two Kettle tribe claimed lands bordering the Cheyenne River, and the Minneconjou occupied adjoining lands as far north as Grand River. The area between the Grand and Heart Rivers was home to the Blackfoot Sioux, the Sans Arc, and the Uncpapa. By mid-century, warriors from the latter three tribes were making a nuisance of themselves by mounting attacks on Fort Union and the Company's Crow posts. Those bands of the Brule and Oglala tribes which had not made the migration with their fellow tribesmen to the North Platte River occupied the areas drained by the White and Teton Rivers, respectively. Generally, the Teton division of the Dakota nation extended its hunting grounds as far west as Powder River during the 1840s, displacing the Crow as it advanced westward toward the Big Horn Mountains.[72]

By 1842 the North Platte River Valley was becoming less attractive to its Oglala and Brule inhabitants. Not only were the Indians experiencing periodic shortages of buffalo by this date, it was also becoming increasingly apparent to them that the valley was serving as a thoroughfare for Americans headed for the Pacific coast. By 1847, upwards of five thousand Americans were annually using what was commonly referred to as the Oregon Trail to reach both Oregon and California. The acquisition of California by the United States in 1847 and the discovery of gold there in 1848 had, in fact, increased the number of migrants using the road by a factor of ten by mid-century. The influx of travelers not only hastened the diminution of buffalo herds along the Oregon Trail but also introduced infectious diseases to the aboriginal inhabitants of the region. The major consequence of these changes was, of course, to force the Oglala and Brule to cast about for a more hospitable environment. The rich Crow hunting grounds, not only full of game but also seemingly isolated from intrusion on the part of whites, must have seemed to offer the best possibilities for an alternative homeland. To assure themselves of successful displacement of that area's inhabitants, the two Dakota tribes forged a confederation with the Northern Cheyenne and Arapaho tribes for the express purpose of taking over the Crow homeland.[73]

Unlike most of their neighbors, Dakota tribes living west of the Missouri experienced significant population growth during the first half of the nineteenth century. Some estimates place their numbers as low as five thousand at the turn of the century and as high as twenty-five thousand in 1850.[74] As the largest Indian entity on the Northern Plains, they by this date had come to constitute a problem not only for their Indian neighbors but for the United States government as well. As the trickle of travelers over the Oregon Trail became a virtual flood, for example, the Brule and Oglala tribes came to be viewed more and more as obstacles to safe passage for American citizens. In 1845, Col. S.W Kearny, at the head of five companies of dragoons, met with upwards of a thousand Dakota at Fort Laramie, successor trading post to Fort William. Kearny first conveyed greetings from Great Father to those assembled, and then went on to inform them that the government was determined to keep the emigrant road open at all costs. At the instigation of Thomas Fitzpatrick, who was serving at the time as Indian agent for the Upper Platte region, Great Father bought Fort Laramie in 1849 and converted it into an army post to provide protection for migrants against Dakota depredations. In that same year, Fitzpatrick, fearful that the paucity of buffalo in the region might provoke intertribal wars over hunting grounds and thus place the lives of migrants in jeopardy, recommended to his superiors that a peace council be convened to include all the Northern Plains tribes.[75]

Diminishing buffalo herds were also a matter of critical concern for tribes which inhabited lands west of Crow territory. As early as 1830, in fact, the Nez Perce, Flatheads, and Shoshone, as well as tribes living further to the west like the Kootenai, Pend d'Oreille, and Kalispell, were experiencing shortages of buffalo. By mid-century their lands had become bereft of that utilitarian animal. The nearest well-stocked lands for these people were those controlled by the Crow and Alliance tribes.[76] That tribes west of the mountains utilized Crow domain as hunting grounds is indicated by the fact that Father de Smet, in 1842, visited a large camp near the mouth of Shields River, made up of Flathead, Kalispell, Nez Perce, and Shoshone hunters.[77]

Of the western tribes, the Shoshone was the most numerous and powerful. It seems that its relations with the Crow tribe were generally peaceful during the 1840s. By the early part of that decade, a branch of the Shoshone led by Chief Washakie customarily spent the summer months in Wind River Valley. A contingent of trappers, including William Hamilton, spent several weeks there with Washakie and his band during early spring of 1842. That the Shoshone chief believed he and his people had a proprietary interest in the valley is suggested by his reaction to the discovery of a band of Piegan in the vicinity. The chief immediately organized a war party to punish the intruders. Several years later Hamilton found the same band of Shoshone conducting a buffalo hunt near Stinking River. It happened that a party of Crow came to visit Washakie's camp while the trapper was present. Hamilton was told by the visitors that the Shoshone were their friends and that they had come from their camp on Clark's Fork for a friendly visit. Obviously, then, the Shoshone were using the Big Horn Basin as a hunting ground with Crow forbearance. Washakie and his band can be placed in the Greybull River area in 1848.[78]

It seems probable that the Crow accepted a Shoshone presence on such a large portion of their traditional homeland for security reasons. The two tribes shared a common enemy, the Alliance, during the 1830s, and found themselves fighting another enemy in common, the Dakota, during the 1840s. The Shoshone seem to have had at least as much trouble with the Oglala and Brule tribes during these years as did the Crow. Sometime during the winter of 1839-40, for instance, the Oglala attacked and killed all the inhabitants of a Shoshone village. Shortly thereafter the Crow and Shoshone broadened their alliance to mount joint expeditions against Dakota tribes.[79]

The Crow tribe at mid-century was clearly in a weakened state when compared with its condition during the 1830s. For one thing, the quality of the tribe's leadership had diminished. Rotten Belly had died in 1834 to be replaced by another warrior,

Grizzly Bear.[80] However, the new chief proved to be a much less effective leader than had been his predecessor.[81] For another thing, the tribe had not only lost exclusive control over Wind River Valley and the Big Horn Basin by that date, it has also experienced a contraction of its territory to Powder River on the east as well. The most dramatic expression of the tribe's declining circumstances, however, had to do with changes in its population. Although the smallpox epidemic of 1837 had had only slight impact on them, the Crow took more serious losses from subsequent epidemics. In 1845 they suffered from an outbreak of scarlet fever, in 1848 from another smallpox epidemic, and in 1849 from an outbreak of influenza. Edwin Denig estimated that a combination of deaths from disease and casualties taken in warfare had reduced Crow population from about sixty-four hundred in the 1830s to thirty-seven hundred at mid-century.[82]

Losses sustained in combat were a significant component in the tribe's population decline. In fact, it seems to have been the case that the incidence of warfare increased during the 1840s. Conflict with Alliance tribes continued virtually unabated despite their losses to smallpox in 1837, and, furthermore, warfare between the Crow and their Dakota neighbors undoubtedly increased during that same decade. The decision by the Brule and Oglala tribes to wrest away from the Crow their rich hunting grounds could only have increased violent confrontations between old enemies. It also undoubtedly added warriors of the Northern Cheyenne and Arapaho tribes to the forces arrayed against the Crow. Furthermore, the Uncpapa and other Dakota tribes were, by mid-century, challenging the Crow for possession of the Yellowstone Valley. So common was warfare in the valley, in fact, that Father de Smet regarded it as the bloodiest battleground in the entire region.[83]

This is not to say that the tribe abandoned any part of Yellowstone Valley to its enemies. In 1847, a large band made a trip to Like-A-Fishhook Village to visit the Hidatsa. Nor did the Crow allow Alliance depredations to go unanswered. In addition to the previously mentioned rout of the Small Robes band in 1845, they, on at least three other occasions during the 1840s, mounted attacks against Alliance tribes. And that the tribe continued to roam lands inhabited by the Shoshone is made evident by a trip made to Wind River Valley by a band of Crow in 1846.[84]

The decline of Alliance power, coupled with the relative increase of Dakota power brought about by the smallpox epidemic of 1837, constituted a major shift in the balance of power on the Northern Plains. Although the Crow still regarded the tribes of the Alliance as the most immediate threat to their security, the Dakota clearly represented a more menacing force than had been the case in the early 1830s. The presence of the Brule and Oglala tribes on the southern extremities of Crow domain augured ill for the tribe's security as the lands of these two tribes became less and less attractive to them. Moreover, growing shortages of buffalo herds on Dakota lands west of the Missouri River increased the appeal of Crow hunting grounds to the tribes which inhabited this area. By mid-century these Indians had already displaced the Crow on their lands which lay to the east of Powder River. Concern about the Dakota threat had prompted the tribe to give up exclusive control over the Big Horn Basin and Wind River valley so as to permit joint occupation of these areas with the Shoshone tribe. Relations with representatives of the Alien Culture improved during the 1830s and 1840s. Except for Rotten Belly's quixotic attempt to close down Fort McKenzie in 1834, relations with the Company and its employees appear to have been uniformly peaceful. Introduction of the buffalo robe trade increased dependence upon Americans for manufactured goods, and the reintroduction of the trading post system had the effect of altering some types of Crow behavior, including wintering patterns, social activities, trading practices, and, perhaps, liquor consumption.

NOTES

1. Letter, K. McKenzie to Pratte, Chouteau & Co., December 10, 1835, published in Annie Heloise Abel, ed., *Chardon's Journal at Fort Clark: 1834-1839* (Freeport: Books for Libraries Press, 1970), pp. 377-8.
2. Charles Larpenteur, *Forty Years a Fur Trader on the Upper Missouri: The Personal Narrative of Charles Larpenteur, 1833-1872,* ed. Elliott Coues (Minneapolis: Ross & Haines, Inc., 1962), pp. 170-5.
3. David J. Wishart, *The Fur Trade of the American West, 1807-1840: A Geographical Synthesis* (Lincoln and London: University of Nebraska Press, 1979), p. 98.
4. Richard E. Jensen, ed., "A Description of the Fur Trade in 1831 by John Dougherty," *Nebraska History,* LVI, No. 1 (Spring, 1975), 111-12.
5. Elinor Wilson, *Jim Beckwourth: Black Mountain Man and War Chief of the Crows* (Norman: University of Oklahoma Press, 1972), pp. 30, 46-48.
6. James P. Beckwourth, *The Life and Adventures of James P. Beckwourth,* ed. Delmont R. Oswald (Lincoln: University of Nebraska Press, 1972), pp. 220, 343.
7. Zenas Leonard, *Zenas Leonard, Fur Trader,* ed. John C. Ewers (Norman: University of Oklahoma Press, 1959), pp. 51-52.
8. Keith Algier, "Robert Meldrum and the Crow Peltry Trade," *Montana: the Magazine of Western History,* XXXVI, No. 3 (Summer, 1986), 39-40.
9. Lewis Henry Morgan, *The Indian Journals, 1859-62* (Ann Arbor: The University of Michigan Press, 1959), p. 175.
10. *Ibid,* pp. 175, 191-2.
11. James H. Bradley, "Affairs at Fort Benton from 1831 to 1869," *Contributions to the Historical Society of Montana,* III (1900), 261-2.
12. Rudolph Friederich Kurz, *Journal of Rudolph Friederich Kurz,* ed. J.N.B. Hewitt, Bureau of American Ethnology, Bulletin 115 (Washington: Government Printing Office, 1937), p. 205.
13. Dorothy O. Johansen, ed., *Robert Newell's Memoranda* (Portland: Champoeg Press, 1959), pp. 236-8; Osborne Russell, *Osborne Russell's Journal of a Trapper,* ed. Aubrey L. Haines (Lincoln: University of Nebraska Press, 1959), p. 123; Frances Fuller Victor, *The River of the West* (Oakland: Brooks-Sterling Company, 1974), p. 237.
14. Edwin Thompson Denig, *Of the Crow Nation,* ed. John C. Ewers (New York: AMS Press, 1980), p. 56; Robert Campbell, *Col. Robert Campbell's Narrative,* Bancroft Library, MS PW-22, pp. 6, 8.

15. Morgan, *op. cit.*, p. 179; Wishart, *op. cit.*, pp. 59, 66, 161-2.
16. Letter, K. McKenzie to S. Tulloch, January 8, 1834, Pierre Chouteau Collection, Ft. Union Letterbook, MHS.
17. Morgan, *op. cit.*, p. 192.
18. Denig, *op. cit.*, pp. 56-70.
19. John C. Ewers, "The Influence of the Fur Trade upon the Indians of the Northern Plains," in Malvina Bolus, ed., *People and Pelts: Selected Papers of the Second North American Fur Trade Conference* (Winnipeg: Peguis Publishers, 1972), pp. 6-7.
20. Victor, *op. cit.*, pp. 225-6.
21. RCIA, 1847, Senate Executive Document No. 1 (Serial 503), p. 851; Hiram Martin Chittenden and Alfred Talbot Richardson, eds., *Life, Letters and Travels of Father de Smet* (New York: Arno Press, 1969), I, 397.
22. John C. Ewers, *The Blackfeet: Raiders on the Northwestern Plains* (Norman: University of Oklahoma Press, 1958), pp. 63-64.
23. Campbell, *op. cit.*, p. 21.
24. McKenzie to Tulloch, *op. cit.*
25. Letter, K. McKenzie to S. Tulloch, March 11, 1834, Pierre Chouteau Collection, Fort Union Letterbook, MHS.
26. Wishart, *op. cit.*, pp. 150-2.
27. Russell, *op. cit.*, p. 81; W.F. Raynolds, *Report on the Exploration of the Yellowstone River* (Washington: Government Printing Office, 1868), p. 65. Captain Raynolds report can also be found in Senate Executive Document No. 77 (Serial 1317), pp. 1-137.
28. John E. Sunder, *The Fur Trade on the Upper Missouri, 1840-1865* (Norman: University of Oklahoma Press, 1965), pp. 52-55, 81.
29. "Biographical Sketches of North Dakota Pioneers," *Collections of the State Historical Society of North Dakota,* VII (1924), 83-84.
30. RCIA, 1850, Senate Executive Document No. 1 (Serial 587), pp. 62-63.
31. Sunder, *op. cit.*, pp. 62-63. Culbertson entered the Upper Missouri fur trade in 1833. After serving for a time at Fort McKenzie, he was promoted to the office of bourgeoisie at Fort Union. He eventually became a partner in the Company and went on to become a leading figure in the region's fur trade.
32. Alexander Culbertson, "Extracts from Mr. Culbertson's Journal," in Maria R. Audubon, *Audubon and His Journals,* ed. Elliott Coues (New York: Dover Publications, 1960), II, 178-80; Denig, *op. cit.*, pp. 50-53.
33. George Catlin, *North American Indians: Being Letters and Notes on Their Manners, Customs, and Conditions Written During Eight Years Travel Amongst the Wildest Tribes of Indians in North America, 1832-39* (Edinburgh: John Grant, 1926), I, 48.
34. *Ibid,* I, 52-53, 58, 215-16.
35. *Ibid,* I, 53-55.
36. Alexander Philip Maximilian, *Travels in the Interior of North America, 1832-1835,* ed. Reuben Gold Thwaites (Cleveland: The Authur H. Clark Co., 1906), I, 349.
37. *Ibid,* I, 351-4.
38. Chittenden and Richardson, *op. cit.*, I, 236-7.
39. *Ibid,* I, 237-8.
40. *Ibid,* I, 239-40.
41. *Ibid,* I, 393-6.
42. *Ibid,* III, 1035-6.
43. *Ibid,* I, 398-9.

44. Letter, J.F.A. Sanford to J.H. Eaton, December 24, 1830, LRUM, reel 883; J.F.A. Sanford to Commissioner of Indian Affairs, December 31, 1834, *ibid;* Ernest L. Schusky, "The Upper Missouri Indian Agency," *Missouri Historical Review,* LXV, No. 3 (April, 1971), 252.
45. Chester L. Guthrie and Leo L. Gerald, "Upper Missouri Agency: An Account of the Indian Administration on the Frontier," *Pacific Historical Review,* X, No. 1 (March, 1941), 52; Letter, W. Clark to C.A. Harris, February 21, 1838, LRUM, reel 884; Letter, W. Fulkerson to W. Clark, March 1, 1838, *ibid.*
46. Guthrie, *op. cit.,* p. 53; Letter, T. Moore to W. Medill, March 6, 1847, LRUM, reel 884; Letter, T. Ewing to Commissioner of Indian Affairs, April 11, 1849, *ibid;* Proclamation to the Senate, March 1, 1846, *ibid;* Sunder, *op. cit.,* pp. 97, 112.
47. Maximilian, *op. cit.,* I, 351.
48. Letter, J. Pilcher to W. Clark, February 27, 1838, LRUM, reel 884; Letter, W. Fulkerson to W. Clark, September 20, 1837, *ibid;* Chittenden and Richardson, *op. cit.,* II, 42–46.
49. Roy W. Meyer, *The Village Indians of the Upper Missouri: The Mandans, Hidatsa, and Arikara* (Lincoln and London: University of Nebraska Press, 1977), pp. 95–96.
50. Letter, J. Pilcher to W. Clark, February 27, 1838, LRUM, reel 884.
51. Meyer, *op. cit.,* pp. 85–86, 90, 99–100.
52. Edwin Thompson Denig, *Five Indian Tribes of the Upper Missouri* (Norman: University of Oklahoma Press, 1961), pp. 71–72.
53. Richard White, "The Winning of the West: The Expansion of the Western Sioux in the Eighteenth and Nineteenth Centuries," *The Journal of American History,* LXV, No. 2 (September, 1978), 328–9.
54. Letter, J. Halsey to Pratte, Chouteau and Co., November 2, 1837, published in Abel, *op. cit.,* pp. 394–6.
55. Johansen, *op. cit.,* p. 34.
56. Ewers, *Blackfeet, Raiders,* p. 65; Bradley, *op. cit.,* pp. 225–6.
57. Harvey Lewis Carter, *Dear Old Kit: The Historical Christopher Carson* (Norman: University of Oklahoma Press, 1968), pp. 67–68.
58. John E. Ewers, *Blackfeet Indians* (New York and London: Garland Publishing, Inc., 1974), pp. 70, 72–74.
59. Beckwourth, *op. cit.,* pp. 190–5.
60. *Ibid,* Beckwourth's accounts of his adventures on the fur frontier tend to exaggerate his own importance in events described, but in this instance Zenas Leonard witnessed the battle and his account of the fray agrees in almost every detail with Beckwourth's rendering of the event. See Leonard, *op. cit.,* pp. 145–9.
61. Bradley, *Fort Benton,* p. 218; Chittenden and Richardson, *op. cit.,* III, 1036–43.
62. *Ibid,* II, 524; *Ewers, Blackfeet Indians,* p. 75; Denton R. Bradford, "The Fight at the Mountain on Both Sides," *Indian Historian,* VIII, No. 2 (Fall, 1975), 20.
63. F.G. Young, ed., *The Correspondence and Journals of Captain Nathaniel J. Wyeth* (New York: Arno Press, 1973), p. 210.
64. Denig, *Crow Nation,* pp. 54–55; Bradley, *op. cit.,* p. 216.
65. *Ibid,* p. 261; Denig, *Crow Nation,* p. 69.
66. Denig, *Five Tribes,* p. 89; Beckwourth, *op. cit.,* p. 358; Kurz, *op. cit.,* p. 51.
67. Letter, J. Dougherty to T.L. McKinney, June 30, 1830, LRUM, reel 883.
68. Denig, *Five Tribes,* p. 30.

69. Letter, P.J. de Smet to T.L. Harvey, December 4, 1848, LRUM, reel 884.
70. White, *op. cit.,* pp. 333–5.
71. Denig, *Five Tribes,* p. 21. For other references to Crow-Oglala encounters during this period, see Garrick Mallery, *Pictographs of the North American Indians: A Preliminary Paper,* Fourth Annual Report of the Bureau of Ethnology, 1882–83 (Washington: Government Printing Office, 1886), p. 142; Garrick Mallery, *Picture Writing of the American Indians,* Tenth Annual Report of the Bureau of Ethnology, 1888–89 (Washington: Government Printing Office, 1893), pp. 280, 322–3.
72. Denig, *Five Tribes,* pp. 16, 19, 22–27.
73. Wesley R. Hurt, *Dakota Sioux Indians* (New York and London: Garland Publishing, Inc., 1974), p. 224; George E. Hyde, *Red Cloud's Folk: A History of the Oglala Sioux* (Norman: University of Oklahoma Press, 1957), pp. 62–64; John Charles Fremont, *The Expeditions of John Charles Fremont,* eds. Donald Jackson and Mary Lee Spence (Urbana, Chicago and London: University of Illinois Press, 1970), I, 493.
74. White, *op. cit.,* pp. 329–30.
75. *Ibid,* p. 340; RCIA, 1844, House Document No. 1 (Serial 463), pp. 433–4; James C. Olson, *Red Cloud and the Sioux Problem* (Lincoln: University of Nebraska Press, 1965), pp. 4–6.
76. Letter, P.J. de Smet to T.H. Harvey, December 4, 1848, LRUM, reel 885.
77. Chittenden and Richardson, *op. cit.,* I, 393.
78. W.T. Hamilton, *My Sixty Years on the Plains: Trapping, Trading, and Indian Fighting* (Norman: University of Oklahoma Press, 1960), pp. 31, 49–53.
79. George Frederick Ruxton, *Life in the Far West* (Norman: University of Oklahoma Press, 1964), p. 76; Mallery, *Pictographs,* p. 141.
80. Leonard, *op. cit.,* p. 140.
81. James B. Marsh, *Four years in the Rockies: Or the Adventures of James P. Rose* (New Castle: W.B. Thomas, 1884), pp. 188–9. The only extant reference to Long Hair's death is found in Denig, *Crow Nation,* p. 63. Written in 1856, this source notes that he died "a few years since."
82. Chittenden and Richardson, *op. cit.,* II, 524; Denig, *Crow Nation,* pp. 24, 44, 57. Estimates of Indian populations made during the nineteenth century are notoriously unrealiable. The method most commonly employed involved counting or estimating the total number of lodges and then multiplying that number by the average number of persons thought to live in each lodge. In the case of the Crow, the numbers customarily used were eight, ten, or twelve, depending on the person doing the estimating. Denig used a factor of eight in this instance.
83. Chittenden and Richardson, *op. cit.,* I, 399.
84. *Ibid,* II, 584; Beckwourth, *op. cit.,* p. 300; Bradley, *Fort Benton,* pp. 214, 242.

FIVE

GREAT FATHER INTRUDES

Shortly after Joshua Pilcher assumed the post of Indian Agent for the Upper Missouri Agency in 1838, he suggested to William Clark that the day-to-day conduct of Indians affairs on the Northern Plains be left in the hands of the fur trade, as in the past.[1] What Pilcher, a man of vast experience on the fur frontier, seems to have been saying was the jurisdiction to which he had just been assigned was far too large and included far too many Indians to be effectively administered with the resources at his disposal. Fur traders, and to an even greater degree, the Company, had, he was suggesting, served as surrogates for Great Father since the inception of the trade and had not only maintained a modicum of stability among the unruly and obstreperous Indians, but had, in addition, effectively secured the entire region against British territorial designs. During the second half of the century, however, the Company would fall upon hard times. A gradual disintegration of the firm's power and vigor would culminate in 1865 with its dissolution. Concurrent with the Company's decline, there would occur a gradual increase in Great Father's interest and influence in the region. By 1870 the Alien Culture's political system would have taken upon itself total responsibility for administering the affairs of the nation's aborigine population, including, of course, those of the Crow tribe, replacing the Company as the dominant outside force in their lives.

In the meantime, if only intermittently, the Company maintained trading posts in Crow territory. Fort Alexander was abandoned in 1849 but was replaced sometime during the following year by Fort Sarpy. Robert Meldrum supervised construction of the new post, located five miles below the mouth of the Rosebud, and then stayed on as bourgeoisie.[2] Meldrum's clerk, James Chambers, kept a journal which provides a rare glimpse into daily life in a Crow post. The diary opens with an entry for New Year's day of 1855 and continues up to the point in time, some five months later, when the post was closed. Chambers' entries reflect the generally disagreeable character of service in a frontier trading post. There was the cold blustery winter weather coupled with a deadly ennui, interrupted only by an occasional Crow scalp dance or unpleasant chores, such as gathering firewood or stripping bark from cottonwood trees for use as horse fodder. Less onerous tasks included hunting buffalo for the post commissary and packing peltries for storage.[3]

A number of Crow bands wintered in close proximity to the fort and, consequently, security was not a problem until the last of them departed in late April. Once the post's informal guard left, parties of both Alliance and Dakota warriors could occasionally be spotted skulking about. On May 4 a war party from one of the Alliance tribes commenced firing on the fort from a distance. The only casualty was a Crow woman who had ventured outside the stockade to fetch water from the river. A week later a band of Indians made up of two hundred Uncpapa and Blackfoot Sioux warriors appeared out of nowhere to completely surround the fort.[4] It appeared as though Fort Sarpy's personnel would be called upon to fend off an attack, or at best, withstand a siege. As it turned out, though, the intruders were content with frightening the Americans, and after an hour or so, they left peaceably. Despite the obvious security advantages afforded by the presence of the Crow, Chambers was hardly an admirer of the tribe. His journal contains frequent complaints about their exasperating habit of crowding uninvited into the fort to pester employees for food and gifts. He was also annoyed by their penchant for pilfering articles belonging to the Company or its employees. He was particularly irritated by their seeming inability to desist from indulging themselves in their favorite pastime of buffalo hunting, thereby scattering animals that otherwise might wander close enough to the fort to be killed for meat by post hunters.

Chambers' most caustic comments, however, were reserved for Robert Meldrum. The bourgeoisie's pampering of certain of the post's clientele by feeding them free of charge and allowing them to sleep inside the stockade Chambers believed to be contemptible ploys to curry favor with the Indians. Meldrum's prodigality in trading for peltries scandalized the clerk to the point that he seriously considered blowing the whistle on his boss. Whether he ever filed the complaint is doubtful, but if so, he need not have bothered. Meldrum's trading practices were already common knowledge among his superiors at Fort Union. In 1851 Edwin Denig confided to an employee at the post that the trader's prodigality had increased the esteem with which he was held by some Crow, as calculated, but that it had militated against his success as a trader. The problem, according to Denig, was that Meldrum's trading practices fostered jealousies among those tribal members less favored by his generosity, causing them to trade with the opposition.[5]

On March 11 the bourgeoisie took an action which suggests that he sometimes took his professional responsibilities less seriously than circumstances dictated. On that date he left Chambers in charge of the fort to go on a bison hunt with some Crow friends. This placed the clerk in a difficult position; the trading season was not yet over but the post's supply of trade goods had been virtually depleted. Not only did this create dissatisfaction among those Crow who came in to trade, it also opened the Crow trade to some opposition traders who happened to be in the vicinity. Chambers' problems in this regard were resolved in early May when he received instructions from Fort Union to abandon the Crow post. Meldrum returned barely in time to supervise the burning of the installation on May 19. Personnel, equipment, and peltries were subsequently floated down the Yellowstone to Fort Union. After nearly a quarter century of being serviced by the Company, the Crow were once again faced with the prospect of making the long, dangerous journey to the Missouri River to conduct trade.

As it turned out, however, alternative trading opportunities presented themselves almost immediately. One came from a most unlikely source: an eccentric Irish aristocrat named George Gore. After a season of hunting in the Platte River region, Sir George diverted his sporting instincts northward into Crow country. In what must have been the most lavishly appointed expeditions yet mounted in the West, it took six wagons and twenty-one carts to carry the sportsman's hunting equipment and personal effects across the prairie to the lower reaches of Tongue River. His party arrived at its destination in late summer of 1855. A retinue of fifty men, including Jim Bridger, assured the immediate satisfaction of the aristocrat's every want. Gore first supervised construction of a stockade on Tongue River, approximately eight miles above the mouth of the river, to serve as his headquarters. The fort doubled as a trading post from which a lively trade was conducted with the Crow for the better part of a year. Gore hadn't come to the Yellowstone Valley to trade, of course. He had come to hunt, and hunt he did. By his own account, he and his party killed 2,500 buffalo, 1,600 elk and deer, as well as countless antelope and small game, all in less than a year. His sporting lust apparently sated, the Irish aristocrat abandoned his stockade in June of 1856 and led his hunting companions to Fort Union.[6]

The Crow had undoubtedly been gratified to discover Gore's trading post, but they became increasingly disenchanted with his presence as they witnessed his indiscriminate slaughter of their chief means of subsistence. In retaliation, they staged horse raids on the hunting party's herd and registered complaints with the Upper Missouri Indian Agency about the expedition's wanton destruction of game.[7] Agent Alfred Vaughan passed these along to the Superintendent of Indian Affairs in St. Louis along with his own charge that Gore had illegally engaged in trade while in Crow country. Superintendent Cumming considered filing charges against Sir George on these counts but was dissuaded from doing so by his superiors in Washington on the grounds that expenses involved in bringing the action would be prohibitively high.[8]

When Gore arrived at Fort Union, he entered into negotiations with Alexander Culbertson for the purchase of his wagons and carts. Unable to reach agreement on price, the choleric Irishman burned his vehicles at the gates of the post and stomped off with what remained of his entourage. On November 9 Agent Vaughan wrote Alfred Cumming to report a rumor that Gore had been killed by Indians, but this turned out to be only wishful thinking on the part of the agent.[9] The Irish aristocrat and his party did indeed have a confrontation with a band of Dakota at about this time, but the intruders were eventually allowed to proceed unharmed after being relieved of most of their possessions.[10] Gore spent the winter near Fort Berthold in an Indian encampment. Here he dedicated most of his time lodging endless complaints with post officials about this and that.[11] This strange man seems to have antagonized nearly everyone on the Northern Plains. Indians and whites alike must have heaved a collective sigh of relief when he finally quit the country in the spring of 1857.

Other less frustrating opportunities to trade were made available to the Crow by North Platte traders. At any given time during the winter months, one or more could be found in Crow camps during the decade of the 1850s, and it wasn't at all unusual for Crow bands to journey south to the North Platte River when in need of trade goods. Others still made the long, difficult, and dangerous trek to Fort Union to conduct trade. However, during the middle years of the 1850s, two-thirds of all Crow trade was, in one way or another, going to North Platte River posts.[12]

Perhaps to staunch a larger than expected flow of trade to opposition firms and individuals, the Company re-established its presence in Crow territory in late 1857 or early 1858. It constructed a new post called Fort Sarpy II situated on the south bank of the Yellowstone at the mouth of Emmels Creek, about twenty miles down river from the mouth of the Big Horn.[13] Robert Meldrum was named bourgeoisie and served in that capacity until the fort was abandoned sometime between August of 1859 and July of 1860.[14] The Crow probably should have considered themselves fortunate to have been serviced by the Company for so many years. The Crow trade was never particularly profitable and not nearly so profitable, for example, as trade with tribes of the Alliance. Furthermore, the Yellowstone posts were by far the most dangerous of any operated by the firm. As many as fifteen men annually fell to attacks made by both Alliance and Dakota warriors during the decade of the 1850s. As a consequence, reluctance on the part of employees to serve in Crow domain left these posts chronically understaffed. Only the Company's determination to deprive the competition of trading opportunities made the Crow posts viable.[15]

In any event, the days of the Company, itself, were numbered. A combination of factors, including disruption of markets by the Civil War, lax discipline among employees, Indian problems, competition from other firms, and the movement of white settlers into the fur frontier, prompted the Chouteau family in 1865 to sell out to a group of investors headed by James Boyd Hubbell of Mankato, Minnesota.[16] After more than three decades of dominance on the Northern Plains, the embodiment of the Alien Culture in that region simply ceased to exist. Robert Meldrum died that same year; to serve as a convenient personification, temporal and otherwise, for the close relationship which existed between the Company and the Crow tribe for all those many years.[17]

As the presence of the Company in Crow territory diminished, that of Great Father increased. The first step in this process occurred in 1851. Agent Thomas Fitzpatrick's recommendation, made in 1849, that a general peace council be held was endorsed and sent on to Washington by David D. Mitchell, superintendent of Indian affairs in St. Louis. Congress finally got around to acting on the matter in early 1851 by authorizing a hundred thousand dollars for that purpose. On May 26 of that year, the commissioner of Indian affairs notified subordinates to make arrangements for a council, to be held in the vicinity of Fort Laramie. Mitchell charged Fitzpatrick with responsibility for notifying those tribes under his jurisdiction, and asked Alexander Culbertson to notify and escort the Crow, Assiniboine, and Alliance tribes to Fort Laramie in time for deliberations scheduled to begin on September 1. Mitchell was almost late for his own meeting. He delayed departure from St. Louis, awaiting arrival of goods purchased in the east intended to be used as gifts for participating tribes. Although the merchandise hadn't arrived in St. Louis by July 24, he nonetheless set out for Fort Laramie on that date after making arrangements for the goods to follow him as soon as they arrived. As it turned out, the superintendent hadn't left a day too soon; he didn't arrive at the fort until August 31.[18]

Mitchell found ten thousand or more Indians impatiently awaiting his arrival. However, the Crow, Assiniboine, and Alliance tribes had not yet appeared. Finding that pasturage was fast disappearing, and perhaps hoping to distract the Indians from their almost incessant questions about promised gifts, Mitchell, on September 4, moved the council site approximately forty miles east to Horse Creek. Assuming that those tribes which had not arrived were not coming, he opened negotiations on September 8 with assistance from Thomas Fitzpatrick and Robert Campbell. Two days later the Crow and Assiniboine delegations unexpectedly entered the encampment in two mounted columns, prominently displaying weapons and chanting *maxpe* songs. Once settled in, they entered into deliberations already in progress.[19]

The tardy arrival of the two tribes was due partly to a late start. Culbertson later complained that he had received notification about the council barely in time to round up a few Assiniboine and Crow. Actually, he had dispatched Robert Meldrum from Fort Sarpy to bring in as many Crow as he could muster, but the best Meldrum could do was persuade about forty warriors to accompany him back to the post where Culbertson, de Smet, and the Assiniboine delegation were awaiting their arrival. Culbertson had been unable to find and organize a suitable Alliance delegation, and these tribes consequently played no role in the proceedings.[20] Father de Smet accompanied Culbertson as an observer, and Robert Meldrum made the trip as interpreter for the Crow. The other reason the two delegations were late was that they were given faulty directions. Striking a southerly course from Fort Sarpy, the party encountered three Crow warriors returning from a horse-stealing expedition against the Dakota. The three assured the travelers that they would reach the fort if they but maintained their present course. When Red Butte came into view several weeks later, they realized that their course had taken them to a site at least a hundred and sixty miles west and north of their intended destination.[21]

Council deliberations were completed on September 17, and a treaty was signed by representatives of all tribes present, except for the Shoshone delegation. Mitchell excluded them because their tribe was administratively attached to the Utah Superintendency rather than to his own Central Superintendency. The caravan carrying the participants' gifts finally arrived on September 20, and the next day a howitzer salvo summoned the various delegations to assemble for distribution of the long-awaited presents from Great Father. Delegation leaders were "dressed" for the proceedings, that is, they were clad in army uniforms complete with red sashes and ceremonial swords furnished by the treaty commission. Apportionment of goods consumed the better part of two days. Not long after the last gift was dispensed, word circulated among the Indians that a large herd of buffalo had been spotted at some distance south of the council grounds. The news hastened dispersal of those assembled, and the Treaty Council of 1851 ended on that happy note.[22]

The Treaty of 1851 was mainly designed to reduce intertribal warfare and thus facilitate safe passage for the torrent of American citizens coursing through the Oregon Trail. Article I called for signatory tribes to maintain peaceful relations with each other, and to reduce the possibility of conflict arising from disputes over land, tribal boundaries were delineated in Article V. Crow lands were identified as those lying west of Powder River, north of Rattlesnake Hills, east of the Wind River and Absaroka Mountains, and south of Musselshell River. In what may have been an error in wording, Crow lands were described as also including a small triangular-shaped tract situated along Big Dry Creek between the Missouri and Musselshell Rivers. By accepting and signing the treaty, the tribe gave up any legal claim it might have had on lands between Powder River and the Black Hills. On the other hand the treaty did set up a legal foundation for the inclusion into tribal territory of lands lying between the Musselshell and Yellowstone Rivers.[23]

Dakota territory was identified as beginning at the mouth of White River, thence running southwestward to the forks of Platte River where the boundary line then followed the North Platte to Red Butte and from there extended in a northerly direction to the head-waters of Heart River. From here the line ran to the mouth of that river, and then down the Missouri River to the beginning. Thus, lands lying between the Black Hills and Powder River were treated as vacant territory by the treaty. Cheyenne and Arapaho territories were designated as those lands lying between the North Platte and Arkansas Rivers. The Mandan, Hidatsa, and Arikara tribes, according to the treaty, controlled lands bounded on the east by the Missouri River and on the north and west by the Yellowstone River to its confluence with Powder River. Heart River was designated as their southern boundary. The northern border of Assiniboine lands was described by the treaty as a line extending north and west along the Missouri River from the mouth of the Yellowstone to the mouth of the Musselshell. That tribe's western border was described as being coterminous with the eastern border of Crow territory, and its southern and western borders were defined by the Yellowstone River from its confluence with the Powder River to its mouth. Although none of the Alliance tribes was represented at the treaty council, their collective domain was nonetheless described. As delineated by the treaty, Alliance territory included lands lying east of the Rocky Mountains, north of Crow domain, south of the Missouri River and west of the Musselshell River. The final paragraph of Article V would appear to have been at cross purposes with the treaty's overall aims and goals. It specifically sanctioned hunting by all signatory tribes on any of the lands described in the treaty. Given the rapidly diminishing buffalo population of the region, this would seem to have been a prescription for fomenting intertribal discord and conflict over hunting grounds.[24]

Article VII must have been the provision which most interested the Indians. It obligated Great Father to furnish them, collectively, with $50,000 worth of provisions, merchandise, domestic animals, and agricultural implements annually for a period of fifty years. Mitchell apparently had lacked authorization to make a commitment of this magnitude. In the report of the treaty council which he made to the commissioner of Indian affairs, he tried to justify the annuities provision on both humanitarian and pragmatic considerations. The superintendent pointed out that the Indians were faced with eventual loss of their chief means of subsistence, the buffalo, and that annuities promised by the treaty were therefore essential if they were to make a successful transition from hunting and gathering to an economic system based on agriculture. Otherwise, he warned, the United States government would sooner or later be faced with the prospect of protracted and expensive warfare on the Northern Plains.[25]

The commissioner of Indian affairs probably made these same arguments when he submitted the treaty to the senate for ratification. When ratified in 1852, however, an amendment was added to the approved treaty which shortened the annuity payment period from fifty to ten years with the option to continue them for another five years at the government's discretion. Agent Alfred Vaughan met with representatives of the Crow tribe on September 18, 1854 and the amendment was duly accepted by them on that occasion.[26]

Superintendent Mitchell came away from the council with high expectations for the treaty as did Father de Smet.[27] De Smet's optimism stemmed from the amity which had reigned during the three weeks that the various tribes, many mutually antagonistic, were camped together. Many white inhabitants of the region were less sanguine about the treaty's likely consequences. Charles Larpenteur, a veteran frontiersman with twenty years of experience in the Indian trade, probably spoke for most of his colleagues when he opined that the Indians had signed the treaty only to receive promised gifts. He went on to predict that intertribal warfare would diminish not at all.[28] Larpenteur's pessimistic assessment proved to be closer to the mark than those of the missionary and the Indian Service official. One can forgive Father de Smet for his overly enthusiastic expectations. After all he was in the business of being optimistic about the human condition. Mitchell should have known better. His background included almost thirty years as a trapper and trader among the Indians.

If the treaty of 1851 did nothing else, it enormously complicated the lives of officials who administered the Upper Missouri Indian Agency. Agents were given ultimate responsibility for distributing all annuities destined for tribes in their respective jurisdictions. This turned out to be a particularly difficult and frustrating task in the case of Crow annuities because the tribe's home ground was so far removed from the closest steamship port. When Agent Vaughan arrived at Fort Union with the 1853 annuities, he learned that the tribe had made the long trek from their homeland to the trading post to receive the promised annuities. But, short of provisions, they had decided to return home a week or so prior to the agent's arrival with their goods. While at Fort Union, various members of the tribe had vehemently complained about being forced by Great Father to travel through lands inhabited by their enemies to pick up annuities he had promised to deliver to them. Vaughan sent runners out to bring the Crow back, but the search was fruitless. Distribution of the first year's annuities consequently had to be postponed.[29] The Crow may have had a point. Article III reads in part: "The United States bind themselves to deliver the said Indians the sum of . . . ."[30]

The tribe refused to make the trip to Fort Union for their annuities the following year. Agent Vaughan therefore contracted with the Company to transport both the 1853 and 1854 annuities to Fort Sarpy for distribution. When the keel boats arrived at the trading post on August 15, Vaughan, who had accompanied the goods, was dismayed to learn that no Crow were present. Three runners were subsequently dispatched to bring the tribe in. The messengers were out for almost a month. But when they finally did return they had enough head men in tow to satisfy the agent, and distribution of the annuities for both years was effected.[31]

Examination of the invoice for the 1854 annuities reveals that they included a wide variety of goods. Foodstuffs included 2,500 pounds of flour, 250 pounds of rice, 1,000 pounds of coffee, 2,300 pounds of sugar, 40 pounds of hard bread, and 48 pounds of corn. Merchandise intended for the distaff side of the tribe consisted of 8,697 yards of cloth, 1,156 yards of bed ticking, 28 shawls, and various quantities of buttons, scissors, thread, and cooking utensils. Goods obviously meant for Crow males were muskets, lead balls and powder, hasp iron suitable for making horseshoes, knives, and, of all things, 30 silk cravats.[32] Vaughan made arrangements for the Company to transport the 1855 annuity goods up the Yellowstone to their intended recipients, but an attack by Dakota warriors prompted a hasty return to Fort Union. It is known that a partial distribution was made on November 7 to some Crow who happened to visit the post, but disposition of the remainder of the merchandise is not revealed by the record. There was no Crow trading post in operation anytime during the year 1856, so the agent, escorted by James Chambers, journeyed up the Yellowstone to notify the Crow that they must proceed to Fort Union if they intended to collect their annuities for that year. He found most of the tribe camped along the banks of the Little Big Horn in early August, and here learned that the remainder of the tribe was hunting in the Rosebud

River area. The head men in both camps, after receiving gifts, agreed to make the trip.[33]

Alfred Vaughan was transferred to the Blackfoot Agency in 1857 and was replaced by A.H. Redfield.[34] The new agent found seventy lodges of Crow waiting for their annuities when he arrived at Fort Union on July 5. Assured by Robert Meldrum, at the time serving at the post, that most of the tribe was expected to some in sometime during the coming autumn, he distributed a few gifts to those Crow present and suggested that they return with their tribesmen later in the year to receive their share of the 1857 annuities. The tribe did not make an appearance that fall, and the goods were placed in storage for distribution in 1858.[35]

The Crow, however, refused to come to Fort Union to pick up their 1858 annuities. Agent Redfield therefore negotiated a contract with the Company to carry both the 1857 and 1858 annuity goods to Fort Sarpy II in keel boats.[36] The agent intended to accompany the goods to the fort, but he took sick at the mouth of Powder River. After arranging with a Henry Beeson to continue on down the river to distribute the merchandise at the Crow post, Redfield returned to Fort Union. Two German missionaries headed for Crow country were among the passengers making the trip. Moritz Braeuninger and Johann Schmidt were being sponsored by the Lutheran Synod of Iowa to establish a Crow mission somewhere in the tribe's homeland. Agent Redfield had tried to dissuade them from the enterprise, pointing out that language problems, a generally hostile environment, and dietary considerations all made the likelihood of a successful missionary effort minimal at best. The Germans refused to be deterred, and Redfield reluctantly issued them a license to remain in Crow territory for a year. He refused to approve their application for a trading license, however.[37]

Braeuninger and Schmidt were appalled by the coarse language and boorish behavior of the crew, but presumably they were pleased that the voyage was completed with few delays and without serious incident. Distribution of the annuities was begun soon after arrival of the boats at the post and was completed on August 14.[38] Beeson asked the missionaries to sign a statement attesting to proper distribution of annuity goods for both years. They refused, citing the circumstance that only one-third of the goods transported up the river had actually been distributed. Beeson then asked them to distribute the remainder of the merchandise to absent tribal members when and if they came in. The missionaries likewise declined this request, probably because they wanted absolutely nothing to do with what they believed to be a fraudulent enterprise. They had been told at Fort Union that at least one-half of the 1857 annuities had been sold to the Company by Redfield. It is possible, of course, that the agent's refusal to issue them a trading license may have contributed to their uncooperative attitude.[39]

The frustrated German missionaries left the fort on August 17 with a band of Crow headed for the North Platte River. Despite having been denied the means for supporting their missionary efforts among the tribe by Redfield's refusal to issue them a trading license, they had persuaded themselves that a Crow mission should nonetheless be established. The mouth of the Little Big Horn was chosen as the site for the installation, but they had to first return to Synod headquarters in Iowa to raise money and recruit additional missionaries for their venture. They did make it safely back to Iowa from the North Platte River, but neither ever got back to the Little Big Horn. Braeuninger eventually returned to Crow country and in May of 1860 was successful in establishing a mission on the headwaters of Powder River, but it all ended badly. Following a visit by a band of Oglala warriors some two months later, the missionary disappeared without a trace. The mission was shortly thereafter abandoned, ending the first Protestant attempt to convert the Crow tribe to Christianity.[40]

Meanwhile, the difficult and frustrating business of implementing the Treaty of 1851's annuity provisions continued. Responsibility for distributing the 1859 goods fell to Bernard S. Schoonover, who replaced Redfield as agent in March of that year. The Crow apparently failed to come into Fort Union to pick up their annuities for that year because Robert Meldrum, accompanied by the new agent, transported the consignment of supplies for 1859 from Fort Union to Fort Sarpy II where they were apportioned in late August.[41]

Delivery of the 1860 annuities was complicated by an administrative decision to transfer jurisdiction over the tribe to the Upper Platte Agency. Thomas Twiss, an eccentric ex-army officer, had been appointed agent there in 1857 and had begun to agitate for inclusion of the tribe into those under his administration soon after assuming the post.[42] He did trading on the side and perhaps wanted to increase his clientele, but his arguments in favor of the transfer were based on the desirability of providing the Crow with more convenient access to their annuity goods.[43] The recommended change was approved in February of 1860, and Crow annuities for that year were subsequently delivered to Twiss at his agency head-quarters located on Deer Creek near present Douglas, Wyoming. As luck would have it, a large contingent of Crow was on hand to meet the steamship which should have been carrying their annuities when it docked at Fort Union. They of course were furious to learn that they would have to pick their goods up at Deer Creek.[44] The ultimate disposition of the annuities is not reflected by extant documentation, but it is known that the goods were still in storage at Twiss's agency headquarters in December of 1860.[45]

Administration of Crow affairs was returned to the Upper Missouri Agency in 1861, but when the annuities for that year arrived at Fort Union, there were no Crow present. Disposition of the goods is shrouded in controversy. Agent Schoonover maintained that they had never been unloaded at the fort and had later been destroyed when the steamer *Chippewa* exploded and burned on its journey from Fort Union to Fort Benton. Samuel Latta, who replaced Schoonover as agent in September of the following year, gathered evidence that the Crow annuities had in fact been unloaded at Fort Union before the steamship left for Fort Benton. The goods, according to Latta, were turned over to the Company by his predecessor after destruction of the *Chippewa* to replace goods the firm had lost in the accident.[46]

Jurisdictional and administrative changes make it virtually impossible to trace disposition of the Crow annuities after 1861. Creation of Dakota Territory in that year placed responsibility for administering the Upper Missouri agency in the hands of the territorial governor. In 1864 Montana Territory was created, giving its chief executive officer administrative control over all Indians within its borders. This meant, among other things, that administration of Crow affairs was transferred from the Upper Missouri Agency to the appropriate governor's office. About all that can be said with any certainty about Crow annuities during this confusing period of changing jurisdictions is that partial distributions of merchandise were made at Fort Union in 1863 and again in 1865.[47]

It was probably the case that the annuity provision

of the Treaty of 1851 did more harm than good if its intent was to improve relations between the Indians and Great Father. Although the Crow and their neighbors must have welcomed the gifts of trade goods, the quantities involved were pitifully small. Agent Redfield complained to the commissioner of Indian affairs in 1858 that recipients often greeted the size of intended apportionments with scorn and derision. The invoice for Crow annuities in 1854, in fact, valued the goods at $3,320.62, or less than one dollar's worth of merchandise for each tribal member for that year.[48] The invoice for the 1857 annuities valued the merchandise distributed that year at only $2,665.36.[49] Even this low per capital figure assumes that all goods listed were actually distributed. It is anyone's guess what proportion of the tribe's annuity goods was siphoned off through collusion between agents and Company officials.

Then there is the matter of equitable apportionment of goods. William G. Hollins, who, as a Company employee, witnessed a number of annuity deliveries, informed the superintendent of Indian affairs in 1859 that in his experience never more than one-third of any tribe had ever participated in an annuity distribution. According to Hollins this inevitably bred dissatisfaction among those unable, for one reason or another, to share in the apportionment.[50] Another source of tension, one which was particularly galling to the Crow, had to do with misunderstandings over delivery points and, finally, there was widespread dissatisfaction regarding the kinds of merchandise included in shipments. The Crow, for example, would have preferred to receive fewer textiles and more lead, powder, and tobacco.[51] Crow complaints about annuities notwithstanding, their acceptance of free merchandise ushered in a new and insidious dependency: that of reliance on Great Father for subsistence. No matter that the quantities of goods were insignificant during these years, the annuity system set in motion a process that would end with the total dependency of the tribe on the Alien Culture for its very existence.

Excepting only the Atkinson expedition of 1825, the Indian Service was the only one of Great Father's agencies with a presence on the Northern Plains during the first half of the nineteenth century. During the third quarter of the century, another branch of the government, the army, joined the Indian Service in that vast region. The influx of travelers and settlers into the area after mid-century, coupled with the growing realization that the large Dakota nation constituted a threat to the security of whites in the region, dictated the presence of military forces. The army was therefore suddenly faced with responsibility for protecting the inhabitants of a region about which it had almost no knowledge.

The first army probe into Crow domain was led by a young, ambitious officer with a background in civil engineering, Lieutenant Gouverneur K. Warren. In early June of 1856, he was assigned the task of investigating the Upper Missouri River area for possible military installation sites. After examining lands in the general vicinity of Fort Pierre, he and his troops boarded a steamship provided by the Company and proceeded up river in search of suitable sites. The steamer on which they were traveling, however, was forced to turn back about sixty miles above Fort Union when it became apparent that the river was too shallow to proceed further. Lieutenant Warren and his contingent debarked at the trading post in late July to find that transportation for the return trip to Fort Pierre would not be available until September. He therefore decided to take advantage of the month's waiting period to make a trip up the Yellowstone River.[52]

Guided by Jim Bridger, Warren and his men left Fort Union on July 25 to make their way up the left bank of the river by wagon. Their progress was halted by rough terrain after a hundred or so miles, and the lieutenant established a base camp at that point. From here he took a detail of seven men up the valley on mules to the mouth of Powder River where astronomical readings were taken to fix its exact position. The return trip to base camp was uneventful, and once there Warren ordered his men to construct several bull boats. He and part of his contingent utilized these to float down the Yellowstone while the rest of his men drove the wagons back to Fort Union. Lieutenant Warren and party left the post on September 1 as planned but didn't reach Fort Pierre until October 2 because they stopped over at various locations along the river to sketch maps of the region and to take both temperature and barometric readings.[53]

That portion of Warren's report to the War Department which dealt with the Yellowstone Valley made it clear that his detour into that area was essentially taken for the purpose of assessing its worth as an avenue of transportation. He concluded that the Yellowstone River was navigable by steamboats of shallow draft at least as far as the mouth of Powder River. Relying mainly on observations made and recorded by William Clark a half century earlier but also partly on data obtained from fur traders, he expressed doubt that it was navigable for any great distance beyond that point. He went on to observe, however, that Company keel boats, drawing from fifteen to twenty inches of water, had for many years used the river as a waterway as far as the mouth of the Big Horn. As for using the valley of the Yellowstone as a wagon road, Warren could report from experience that it could be used as such for only the first hundred miles.[54] In his letter transmitting the report to his superiors, the lieutenant recommended that he be authorized to conduct a detailed examination of the Yellowstone drainage basin during the summer months of 1859 and 1860.[55]

The War Department approved Warren's recommendation but, as it turned out, the lieutenant didn't command the expedition. The explorer's father died early in 1859, and faced with the responsibility for raising his younger brothers and sisters, Warren applied for and received a teaching position at West Point. A newcomer to the frontier, Captain William F. Raynolds of the Corps of Engineers, was chosen as Warren's replacement. Great Father had obviously decided that the probability of war with the Dakota warranted a reconnaissance of Crow domain to identify transportation routes suitable for moving troops and military supplies. Raynolds was instructed to locate the most direct and feasible routes from Fort Laramie to the mouth of the Yellowstone, from Fort Laramie to Fort Benton and then on into the Bitterroot Valley, from the Yellowstone River to South Pass, and from the sources of Wind River to the Three Forks of the Missouri. His instructions also specified that the expedition assess the region's agricultural potential and its mineral resources. Raynolds was authorized to hire several topographers, a geologist, an astronomer, a naturalist, a meteorologist, and a physician.[56]

When Raynolds arrived at Fort Pierre on June 18, 1859 to launch the expedition, his professional roster was complete, along with a military escort of thirty men under the command of Lieutenant Caleb Smith. Lieutenant H.E. Maynadier accompanied Raynolds as his second-in-command. At the fort, Raynolds had the good fortune to hire Jim Bridger on as guide. He had the bad fortune to be joined by seven friends of

John B. Floyd, Secretary of War, who were tagging along as sightseers. Before leaving Fort Pierre, arrangements were made with the Company to transport part of the expedition's provisions and equipment to Fort Sarpy II.

Raynolds and his entourage left Fort Pierre on July 28, and after a grueling but uneventful march, arrived at the south bank of the Yellowstone River on August 15. Here, about nine miles below the Crow trading post, a base camp was set up to serve as headquarters for the expedition until such time as the Company's keel boats should arrive with their gear and supplies. When the boats finally did appear on August 26, it was learned that goods consigned to Raynolds had been indiscriminately packed with the 1859 annuities being transported to the post by Robert Meldrum under the supervision of Agent Schoonover. Captain Raynolds therefore decided to break camp and move on to the fort where the boats' contents could be sorted out as they were being unloaded.

A new camp was set up near the trading post on August 29, and learning that part of the Crow had assembled to receive annuities, Captain Raynolds made arrangements to hold a council with the tribe's head men on the following day. He opened the proceedings with greetings from Great Father and asked for permission to examine the tribe's lands. Raynolds promised that his party would exercise care not to disperse buffalo herds and said that it would kill only enough game to subsist the expedition. A Crow spokesman rose to say that relations between the whites and the Crow tribe had been consistently friendly over the years and that Raynolds and his men therefore had his permission to pass through tribal territory. He added that the expedition could rest easy in the knowledge that it would not be molested by the Crow as it went about its business. Robert Meldrum acted as interpreter for the council.

Meldrum performed another service for the expedition. He helped Raynolds draw a map of the country lying between the Yellowstone and North Platte Rivers. Armed with this knowledge, the expedition made its laborious way along the eastern flank of the Big Horn Mountains towards the North Platte River where, near the headquarters of the Upper Platte River Indian Agency, it arrived on October 8 to dig in for the winter. Agent Thomas Twiss suggested to Captain Raynolds that some buildings located not far from agency headquarters might be suitable winter quarters with only a few repairs. The buildings had been partially constructed years before by a party of Mormons who had intended them to serve as a waystation for Mormon immigrants. Necessary repairs were made in short order by the soldiers, and the expedition's personnel settled in for the winter. Procuring supplies from Fort Laramie, organizing data accumulated during the preceding summer, and feuding with the commander of his military escort, Lieutenant Caleb Smith, kept Raynolds occupied for most of the winter.

Problems developed between the two men almost as soon as the expedition arrived at the North Platte. First off, Smith's men got uproariously drunk at a nearby trading post. Raynolds, a religious man, was offended, and he chastised Smith for permitting such sinful behavior. The next day Smith refused to obey an order issued by Raynolds relative to the location of an overnight camping spot. Raynolds duly filed charges of insubordination against the commander of his military escort and arranged that he be replaced by a Lieutenant John Mullan. Smith was subsequently acquitted by a military tribunal on grounds that Corps of Engineer officers had no authority over line officers. By that time, of course, the expedition had been disbanded and Lieutenant Smith's role in the expedition terminated.

To expedite completion of the mission, Reynolds divided his command the following spring. He led one contingent due west from Deer Creek to arrive at the confluence of the Popo Agie and Wind Rivers on May 21. Lieutenant Maynadier, in command of the other contingent, took a more southerly course which provided him with an opportunity to explore the Sweetwater River and adjoining lands before veering north to join up with Captain Raynolds and his men on May 23. Reunion of the two groups was of short duration. They separated again the following day with Raynolds and his party headed for the Three Forks of Missouri via the headwaters of Wind River. Maynadier was ordered to take his men down the Wind/Big Horn River to the point where it disgorges from its lower canyon and to proceed from there in a westerly direction to rendezvous with Raynolds at the Three Forks on June 30.

The Raynolds group was guided by Jim Bridger, and, despite difficulties experienced in negotiating the continental divide, was able to make its way into Jackson Hole. From here Bridger led them to the Madison River which, of course, terminates at the Three Forks of the Missouri, where they arrived on June 20 to await the arrival of Lieutenant Maynadier. As instructed, the lieutenant had taken his party down the Wind/Big Horn River, but rather than following it all the way to the lower canyon had struck a northwesterly course at the mouth of Greybull River. This took his command across both Shoshone River and Clark's Fork to arrive at the Yellowstone River near the mouth of the Stillwater on June 23. Maynadier and his men then proceeded up Yellowstone Valley but had gotten only as far as Shields River by the rendezvous date. After leaving the valley at the Big Bend, they continued on a westerly course to the Gallatin River where they happened onto Raynolds and his detachment on July 3. Again, the reunion of the expedition's forces was of short duration.

Maynadier and his contingent returned to the Yellowstone River which they followed downstream to Fort Union. Captain Raynolds led his detachment down the Missouri River to Fort Benton where he divided his forces again. Lieutenant Mullan and a small contingent which included Jim Bridger struck out overland in the direction of Fort Union for the purpose of making an examination of the divide between the Missouri and Yellowstone Rivers. They arrived at the mouth of the Yellowstone on August 11. Raynolds acquired a keel boat at Fort Benton which he utilized to float his equipment and men down the Missouri to Fort Union. The boat docked at the trading post on August 7. Thus was the first formal examination and assessment of the Crow homeland by the Alien Culture completed.

The major impetus for Raynolds' reconnaissance of Crow territory was a desire on the part of the United States government to identify transportation routes suitable for moving troops and military supplies from one strategic point to another. The report filed by the expedition's commander makes clear that the best natural thoroughfare in the region was the Yellowstone River and its valley. The valley was described as being suitable for a railroad running all the way from Fort Union to the Big Bend and beyond, at least as far as the Three Forks of the Missouri. The river itself was deemed navigable by steamboats of shallow draft as far as the mouth of the Big Horn and perhaps on to the Big Bend. A caveat was included that the river's usefulness as a waterway might be limited by the strength of its current. The report maintained that it would be a relatively simple matter to connect Fort Laramie with the Yellowstone Valley. It pointed out that Sir George Gore had pioneered part of this route when he took his carts and wagons along the eastern flank of the Big Horn Mountains to his camp site on Tongue River. Few obstacles could be expected, therefore, in constructing a wagon road over that general route. Likewise, the report continued, construction of a road from the Yellowstone Valley to Fort Benton would present few difficulties.

On the other hand a transportation link between South Pass and the Yellowstone was deemed impracticable. Construction of a suitable wagon road northward through the Big Horn Basin would, according to the report, be prohibitively expensive due to the rough and broken terrain of that area. It pointed out that terrain between the headwaters of Wind River and the Three Forks region was even worse and that construction of a road between these two areas would therefore be impossible.

Actually, nothing in the report dealing with possible avenues of transportation would have come as a surprise to the Crow, or to trappers and traders for that matter. They all had for many years been using the routes recommended by the report. The expedition's assessment of natural resources, however, involved a fresh way of looking at the Crow homeland. White fur trappers and traders, no less than the Indians, had, perhaps subconsciously, appraised these lands in terms of their richness in resources which could be transformed into items of value through the application of technology possessed by the Indians. Raynolds, on the other hand, evaluated the economic potential of the Crow homeland in terms of resources which could be utilized to produce wealth only through the application of technologies more sophisticated than those possessed by the aborigines.

The Raynolds report was not at all sanguine about

the economic potential of Crow lands from that perspective. With regard to agricultural potential, it concluded that insufficient rainfall rendered the area virtually worthless in this regard, except for parts of the Yellowstone Valley. Most of the valley, as well as unspecified other parts of Crow domain, were portrayed as being suitable for livestock ranching by virtue of the presence of an abundance of nutritious grasses. In most other areas examined by the expedition, however, the sparse character of grasslands would dictate ranching operations based on small numbers of animals per acre. During the expedition's examination of Crow domain, Captain Raynolds had purposely minimized and downplayed the mineral potential of the lands under consideration. He was concerned that an accidental discovery would inevitably cause wholesale desertions within his staff and military escort. His report did, nonetheless, note that traces of color had been found at various sites, including some in the Big Horn Mountains. It also pointed out that the geology of much of the region included in the expedition's reconnaissance shared a number of similarities with that found in both the California and Colorado gold fields. The existence of large deposits of lignite were identified but doubt was expressed that they were of commercial quality.

If Sir George Gore personified one of the Alien Culture's least attractive attributes, unfettered exploitation of natural resources, the Raynold expedition reflected another of its salient features, that of technological sophistication. For example, with the ability to measure distances through the use of odometers, the capacity to estimate elevations from barometric readings and the skills needed to fix the relative location of topographic features through astronomical observations, Raynolds and his staff were able to construct the first reliable map of Crow

CAPTAIN WILLIAM F. RAYNOLDS
The Raynolds expedition of 1859–60, as a bearer of new technology, presaged the exploitation of many hiterto neglected natural resources in Crow domain.
Courtesy Library of Congress

country. The expedition, in other words, symbolized the technological sophistication necessary to exploit many hitherto neglected natural resources found in Crow domain.[57]

Bearers of these new approaches to creating wealth followed hard on the heels of the Raynolds expedition; whites entered the Northern Plains in unprecedented numbers during the decade of the 1860s. Once established on the old fur frontier, they imposed a new economic regimen on the region, replacing the hunting and gathering economic system of the aborigines. In the process, the Alien Culture eventually undermined the Indian way of life, and, in the end, destroyed the nexus of social, political, and economic relationships which had governed the region for millennia.

It was the lure of easy riches which attracted the first influx of white settlers. Following discoveries of gold in present Idaho, one John White found commercial deposits of that metal in July of 1862 near what is now Bannock City, Montana. Then, sometime during spring of the following year, a gold strike of major proportions was made in Alder Gulch, setting off a gold rush which in turn led to the founding of Virginia City, Montana.[58] A prospector called Tom Curry made the first gold discovery in Crow territory. He found color in the winter of 1863-64 at Emigrant Gulch, a few miles east of the Yellowstone River and about twenty miles south of present-day Livingston, Montana. Yellowstone City was founded several miles distant from the discovery site to service prospectors and miners working in that general area.[59]

A number of committees designed to provide sustenance for the new mining regions sprang up in short order. The closest of these to Crow territory was the agricultural community of Bozeman, situated some twenty miles west of the northwest corner of the Crow homeland. It was founded in 1864 by John Bozeman who at the time was scouting out an overland route to connect the Overland Trail with the Montana gold fields. The Bozeman farming community produced 20,000 bushels of wheat during the 1865 growing season. Reapers and threshers were introduced that same year along with a flour mill.[60]

The wagon road chosen by Bozeman was one which had been recommended by Captain Raynolds. It branched off from the Oregon Trail near Red Butte and ran in a northerly direction along the eastern flank of the Big Horn Mountains to the Big Horn River at a point a mile or so below where it leaves Big Horn Canyon. From here the Bozeman Road followed a northwesterly direction to follow Yellowstone valley up river to the Big Bend. Then, it left the valley to terminate twenty miles to the west at the town of Bozeman. An alternative route, a wagon road which ran from Red Butte through the Big Horn Basin to Bozeman, was established by Jim Bridger that same year.[61] Congress authorized yet another road in the general area, and in 1865 James A. Sawyers accordingly laid out a route for a wagon trail which ran from the mouth of the Niobrara River to Virginia City. There were already in existence, by the time gold was discovered in the region, two other routes which one could use to reach Montana mining areas. For those who found themselves in the Pacific Northwest regions when reports of gold discoveries in Montana began circulating, the Mullan Road, which ran from Walla Walla in Washington to Fort Benton, could be utilized. And, there was always, of course, the well-traveled Missouri River.[62]

In 1860 the Company extended its steamboat service to Fort Benton, and during the summer of 1862 more than 500 whites used this mode of transportation to reach the gold fields. In an attempt to make the Missouri River a safer avenue for the advance of miners and prospectors into Montana territory, Brigadier General Alfred A. Sully was ordered in 1864 to clear the waterway of Dakota warriors. At the head of 4,000 cavalry and 800 mounted infantry, he defeated a large band of Dakota warriors in the Battle of Killdeer Mountain in that same year.[63]

As the tentacles of the Alien Culture's transportation routes spread throughout the Northern Plains, Great Father extended and tightened his control over the region. The Territory of Montana with a population of perhaps 15,000 persons was formed on May 26, 1864 with Sidney Edgerton as its first governor. As governor, Edgerton also served as the territory's ex-officio superintendent of Indian affairs. In 1865 he returned to his home in the east on personal business. Thomas Francis Meagher, Edgerton's secretary, assumed the powers of governor and as such also exercised the powers of superintendent in the territory. A veteran of the Young Ireland movement in his native land, he had been banished to Tasmania in the year 1848. Escaping from exile in 1852, he eventually made his way to the United States where he became a journalist and, during the Civil War, a soldier of some note. He owed his appointment as secretary for Governor Edgerton to President Andrew Johnson.[64]

As ever-increasing numbers of white settlers were attracted to the Northern Plains, Great Father found it prudent to increase his presence there. As the Company, which for so many years had informally regulated relations between the Alien Culture and the Indians of the region, disintegrated after mid-century, the government gradually replaced the firm as the dominant outside force in the lives of the Crow and their neighbors. The first evidence of heightened interest was the attempt by the Indian Service to impose stability on the Indians of the Northern Plains through the Treaty of 1851. The treaty seems to have had no appreciable effect on intertribal relations, but it did mark the onset of a new form of Indian dependency by institutionalizing the distribution of free manufactured goods by the government. The most dramatic expression of Great Father's increased presence on the Northern Plains was the appearance of military expeditions he dispatched to gather data about the Indians, transportation routes, and economic potential. Discoveries of precious metals ended, once and forever, the relative isolation from unwanted Alien Culture forces and influences which had been enjoyed by the Crow and their Indian neighbors during the first half of the nineteenth century.

NOTES

1. Letter, J. Pilcher to W. Clark, September 15, 1838, LRUM, reel 884.
2. James H. Bradley, "Affairs at Fort Benton from 1831 to 1869," *Contributions to the Historical Society of Montana*, III (1900), 261.
3. Unless otherwise indicated, the account of life at Fort Sarpy is taken from James H. Chambers, "Original Journals of James H. Chambers, Fort Sarpy," *Contributions to the Historical Society of Montana*, X (1940), 99–183.
4. RICA, 1855, Senate Executive Document No. 1 (Serial 810), p. 394.
5. Rudolph Friederich Kurz, *Journal of Rudolph Friederich Kurz*, ed. J.N.B. Hewitt, Bureau of American Ethnology, Bulletin 115, (Washington: Government Printing Office, 1937), p. 205.
6. Clark C. Spence, "A Celtic Nimrod in the Old West," *Montana: The Magazine of Western History*, IX, No. 2 (Spring, 1959), 57–58, 61–62, 64; R.B. Marcy, *Thirty Years of Army Life on the Border* (New York: Harper and Brothers Publishers, 1866), p. 402.
7. Bradley, *op. cit.*, pp. 278–9.
8. Letter, R.W. McClelland to Commissioner of Indian Affairs, January 16, 1857, LRUM, reel 885.
9. Letter, A.J. Vaughan to A. Cumming, November 9, 1856, *ibid.*
10. *Explorer on the Northern Plains: Lieutenant Gouvernor K. Warren's Preliminary Report of Exploration in Nebraska and Dakota, in the Years 1855-56-57* (Washington: Government Printing Office, n.d.), pp. 18–19.

11. Letter, A.J. Vaughan to A. Cumming, December 25, 1856, LRUM, reel 885.
12. Chambers *op. cit.,* p. 146, Edwin Thompson Denig, *Of the Crow Nation,* ed. John C. Ewers (New York: AMS Press, 1980), pp. 24, 70-71.
13. The earliest reference to the new post found by the author is early February of 1858. See, Letter, A.H. Redfield to C.E. Mix, February 3, 1858, LRUM, reel 885.
14. Its existence on August 29, 1859 can be documented as can the fact of its abandonment sometime prior to July 20, 1860. See, W.F. Raynolds, *Report on the Exploration of the Yellowstone River* (Washington: Government Printing Office, 1868), pp. 50, 144.
15. Denig, *op. cit.,* pp. 68-71.
16. John E. Sunder, *The Fur Trade on the Upper Missouri* (Norman: University of Oklahoma Press, 1965), pp. 262-3.
17. Keith Algier, "Robert Meldrum and the Crow Peltry Trade," *Montana: The Magazine of Western History,* XXXVI, No. 3 (Summer, 1986), 44.
18. Letter, D.D. Mitchell to Commissioner of Indian Affairs, November 11, 1851, DRNR, reel 4.
19. *Ibid;* Hiram Martin Chittenden and Alfred Talbot Richardson, eds., *Life, Letters and Travels of Father De Smet* (New York: Arno Press, 1969), II, 673-4; Bradley, *op. cit.,* p. 266.
20. John C. Ewers, *The Blackfeet: Raiders on the Northwestern Plains* (Norman: University of Oklahoma Press, 1958), p. 206.
21. Chittenden and Richardson, *op. cit.,* II, 665-70.
22. *Ibid,* II, 682-3.
23. The treaty can be found in Charles J. Kappler, ed., *Indian Affairs: Law and Treaties* (Washington: Government Printing Office, 1904), II, 594-6; and in George E. Fay, ed., *Treaties, Land Cessions, and Other U.S. Congressional Documents Relative to American Indian Tribes: The Crow 1825-1912* (Greeley: Museum of Anthropology, 1982), pp. 5-8.
24. *Ibid.*
25. Letter, D.D. Mitchell to Commissioner of Indian Affairs, November 11, 1851, DRNR, reel 4.
26. Amendment, September 17, 1854, *ibid.*
27. Letter, D.D. Mitchell to Commissioner of Indian Affairs, November 11, 1851, *ibid.*
28. Charles Larpenteur, *Fifty Years a Fur Trader on the Upper Missouri: The Personal Narrative of Charles Larpenteur, 1833-1872,* ed. Elliott Coues (Minneapolis: Ross & Haines, Inc., 1962), pp. 420-1.
29. RCIA, 1853 Senate Executive Document No. 1 (Serial 690), p. 355; Letter, A Cumming to G.W. Manypenny, July 29, 1853, LRUM, reel 885.
30. Kappler, *loc. cit.*
31. RCIA, 1854, Senate Executive Document No. 1 (Serial 746), pp. 292-3.
32. Invoice, September 18, 1854, U.S. Department of Interior, Upper Missouri Agency Records, Small Collections 887, Folder 1, HSML.
33. Chambers, *op. cit.,* pp. 175-6; RCIA, 1856, Senate Executive Document No. 5 (Serial 875), pp. 631-2.
34. Letter, J.W. Denver to A. Cumming, May 30, 1857, LRUM, reel 885.
35. RCIA, 1857, Senate Executive Document No. 11 (Serial 919), p. 417.
36. Letter, A.H. Redfield to C.E. Mix, June 21, 1858, LRUM, reel 885.
37. RCIA, 1858, Senate Executive Document No. 1 (Serial 974), pp. 439-43.
38. Receipt for Goods, August 14, 1858, LRUM, reel 885.
39. Oswald F. Wagner, "Lutheran Zealots Among the Crows," *Montana: The Magazine of Western History,* XXII, No. 2 (Spring, 1972), 10.

40. *Ibid,* pp. 16–19; Raynolds, *op. cit.,* pp. 75–76.
41. *Ibid,* pp. 48–49.
42. Letter, T.S. Twiss to Commissioner of Indian Affairs, November 7, 1857, LRUP, reel 890. Twiss' career as Upper Platte agent is covered in Burton S. Hill, "Thomas S. Twiss, Indian Agent," *Great Plains Journal,* VI, No. 2 (Spring, 1967), pp. 85–96.
43. Letter, T.S. Twiss to Commissioner of Indian Affairs, February 2, 1859, LRUP, reel 890.
44. Letter, B.S. Schoonover to A.M. Robinson, July 12, 1860, LRUM, reel 885.
45. Letter, T.S. Twiss to J.C.R. Clark, December 13, 1860, LRUP, reel 890.
46. Letter, S.A. Latta to W.P. Dole, September 28, 1862, LRUM, reel 885.
47. Letter, S.A. Latta to W.P. Dole, March 2, 1864, LRUM, reel 885; Larpenteur, *op. cit.,* pp. 372–3.
48. Invoice, September 18, 1854, U.S. Department of Interior, Upper Missouri Records, Small Collections 887, Folder 1, HSML.
49. Receipt for Goods, August 14, 1858, LRUM, reel 885.
50. Letter, W.G. Hollins to A.M. Robinson, September 19, 1859, published in RCIA, 1859, Senate Executive Document No. 2 (Serial 1023), pp. 488–9.
51. Letter, A.J. Vaughan to A. Cumming, April 1, 1854, LRUM, reel 885.
52. *Explorer . . . Warren's, op. cit.,* pp. 14–15.
53. *Ibid,* pp. 15–16.
54. *Ibid,* pp. 37–38.
55. Letter, G.K. Warren to A.A. Humphreys, November 24, 1858, in *ibid,* pp. 9–11.
56. Unless otherwise indicated, the account of Captain Raynolds expedition is taken from Raynolds, *op. cit.*
57. The map has been published in Senate Executive Document No. 77 (Serial 1317), following page 174.
58. Clark C. Spence, *Territorial Politics and Government in Montana: 1864–89* (Urbana, Chicago, London: University of Illinois Press, 1975), pp. 6–7.
59. Merrill G. Burlingame, *The Montana Frontier* (Helena: State Publishing Company, 1942), p. 92.
60. *Ibid,* pp. 341–3.
61. *Ibid,* pp. 132–3.
62. Merrill G. Burlingame, *Historical Background for the Crow Indian Treaty of 1868,* unpublished manuscript, Small Collections No. 1045, Folder 6, HSML, p. 33.
63. RCIA, 1863, House Executive Document No. 1 (Serial 1182), p. 283; Robert G. Athearn, *Forts of the Upper Missouri* (Englewood Cliffs: Prentice-Hall, Inc., 1967), pp. 136–7.
64. Spence, *op. cit.,* pp. 34–35.

SIX

EVER-CONSTRICTING CIRCLES

The years immediately following the Treaty of 1851 were disastrous years for the Crow. The extent to which the tribe fell upon hard times during this period is suggested by an incident recounted in the Annual Report of the commissioner of Indian affairs for the year 1865. It seems that a party of Flathead Indians happened to stop over for a visit with a band of Crow warriors who were at the time camped near the confluence of Beaverhead Creek with Sun River. The visitors quickly learned from the camp's leader that he and his men had just been bested by a Dakota war party. The Crow chief was clearly in an agitated state as he went on to describe his tribe's life and death struggle with the Dakota. His greatest concern, he lamented, was that after six years of bitter warfare, he and his fellow tribesmen had become weakened to the point that they now faced the possibility of being enslaved by their long-time enemies.[1] The potential for a catastrophe of this magnitude had always existed, of course. Greatly outnumbered by two of its closest neighbors, the tribe had lived under the threat of domination by either the Dakota or Alliance Indians for generations. What had changed by 1865 was that a number of debilitating changes experienced during the decade of the 1850s, coupled with ever-increasing military pressure from its largest and most powerful neighbor, had operated to bring the tribe to its knees.

One phenomenon which weakened the tribe's

capacity to resist Dakota incursions after 1850 was a
paucity of able leaders. Long Hair died shortly after
mid-century and no leader of sufficient stature and
ability appeared to fill his moccasins.[2] The Treaty
Council held in 1851 undoubtedly contributed to the
leadership vacuum. Rotten Belly's successor to the
tribe's other major division, Grizzly Bear, was one of
two Crow leaders to place his mark on the Treaty of
1851. Along with several other Indian dignitaries, he
was escorted to Washington by the treaty commissioners to meet with Great Father. On the return trip
he disappeared under mysterious circumstances and
never did make it back to the tribe.[3]

The other Crow to place his mark on the treaty was
Big Robber. He had enjoyed little standing as a leader
prior to the treaty council but rather was elevated to
the status of chief by the commissioners simply for
the purpose of having a second representative of the
tribe approve the treaty. Rotten Tail, a renowned
warrior who had first come to prominence as leader
of the successful raid against the Small Robes band of
the Piegan tribe in 1845, complained to anyone who
would listen that he had been unjustly deprived of his
chieftainship by the treaty proceedings. Big Robber,
he claimed, enjoyed the status of chief only because
Robert Meldrum had found it convenient to settle for
the likes of Big Robber rather than taking the time to
search for a *bona fide* leader to represent the tribe at
the council. Rotten Tail had a point. During the years
following the treaty council, although he was widely
regarded as a chief, Big Robber and his followers
spent most of the year separated from the tribe,
begging and stealing from immigrants traveling the
Oregon Trail.[4]

Big Robber's withdrawal to the south had the effect
of fragmenting the tribe's traditional political structure. By the mid-1850s, his band was widely regarded

as a third major division within the tribe. It wintered on or near the headwaters of Powder River and spent the balance of the year in the North Platte River area. The largest of the three new divisions spent part of the year in or about the upper reaches of the Yellowstone River and the remainder of the year either in the Big Horn Basin or in Wind River Valley. It was led by Two Faces, a successful warrior who, as a young man, had participated in Rotten Belly's successful raid on a Cheyenne camp in 1833. The third major division restricted most of its activities to the lower Yellowstone Valley but occasionally ventured north to winter with the Assiniboine tribe. Bear's Head, another warrior of distinction, served as its chief. He had first come to prominence as Rotten Tail's second-in-command during the Little Robes massacre in 1845.[5]

There is evidence to suggest that political fragmentation went beyond the new tripartite structure. James Chambers' journal identifies twenty-five individuals, including Two Faces and Bear's Head, as being chiefs or leaders of one band or another. Assuming that the tribe was made up of thirteen clans and that each clan had its own chief, it is apparent that a number of warriors were exercising political power outside the tribe's traditional political structure. That this was indeed the case is confirmed by Robert Meldrum. In a conversation with Lewis Morgan in 1862, Meldrum told the noted ethnologist that although each clan had only one official chief, each also had a plethora of would-be leaders struggling to achieve power.[6] Even if Big Robber, Two Faces and Bear's Head were not also serving as chiefs of their respective clans, the total number of Crow chiefs should have been only sixteen, leaving at least nine ex officio leaders as identified by Chambers. It is likely that there were even more; not all elements of the tribe visited Fort Sarpy during the winter of 1856. Big Robber, for example, is not mentioned in the Chambers journal. The foregoing strongly suggests that Crow clans, no less than the tribe's larger political units, were experiencing political fragmentation during these years.[7]

Contemporaneous with disintegration of the tribe's political structure, there also was occurring a general demoralization in many areas of Crow life. Certainly pride of craftsmanship had declined by mid-century. A Fort Union employee named Friederich Kurz complained in 1851 that the Crow, who in past years had been notorious for the care they took in preparing buffalo robes for market, no longer took the time to properly dress their trade robes.[8] James Chambers made essentially the same complaint several years later when he groused that they spent altogether too much time hanging about the trading post making a general nuisance of themselves and far too little time collecting and preparing robes for market.[9]

An entry in Chambers' journal made at Fort Union on March 8, 1856 makes it abundantly clear that in the diarist's view, the tribe was in a debased and degraded state:

> . . . Crow Indians are a lousy, thieving, Beggardly set of rascals. They shot a Dutchman, kill'd a Boar cut up two carriages stole everything they could lay their hands on. Begged and Bothered Mr. Kipp to death got credits & never paid run everywhere through the Fort insulted and annoyed everyone . . . The Bucks are raping Squaws in broad daylight without regard to lookers on indeed they seem to prefer witnesses to the operation . . . Old Rips thieves and the elderly portion having run their course in these things, have now settled down to begging at which they excel all other tribes.[10]

While Chambers' journal makes it all too clear that he held the tribe in low esteem, his complaints in this instance were probably justified because they were substantiated by Captain Raynolds three years later when he observed that:

> They are importunate beggars and about camp they take the most disagreeable liberties, thronging into our tents, rolling their filthy bodies up in our blankets and prying into everything accessible. Their personal uncleanliness is disgusting and their bodies are covered with vermin. They have no idea about chastity, and greater general degradation could with difficulty be imagined.[11]

Raynolds' observations concerning cleanliness and general appearance stand in sharp contrast to the comment made by Charles Larpenteur in 1833 that the Crow were the finest appearing tribe of Indians in the mountains. An increase in those members of the tribe addicted to liquor may have been partly responsible for the obvious demoralization of the tribe, but there is little extant documentation to indicate that this was the case. The only suggestion that liquor may have played a role comes from Captain Raynolds who observed that even though the Crow had been exposed to little of "civilized life," they had nonetheless adopted all of its vices.[12] On the other hand James Chambers, who seems to have taken it upon himself to catalog all of the tribe's defects, makes no mention in his journal of liquor consumption on their part.

Perhaps it was the ravages of disease which brought about the tribe's obvious demoralization. Smallpox took some 400 men, women, and children in 1851 and a like number in 1855. The tribe was even harder hit by smallpox during the winter of 1856-57 when they lost nearly 1,000 to the malady.[13] As one might expect, then, the tribe's population decreased dramatically during the decade of the 1850s. Robert

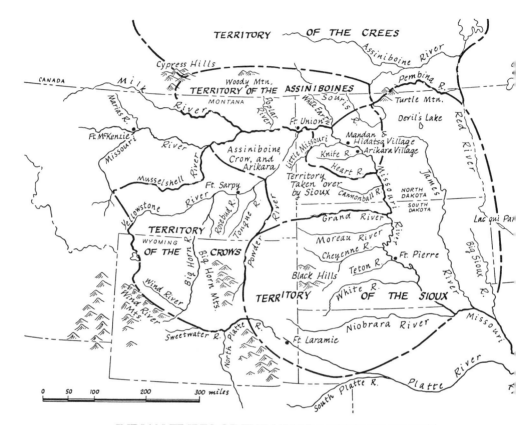

INDIAN TRIBES OF THE UPPER MISSOURI IN 1855

From *Five Indian Tribes of the Upper Missouri: Sioux, Arickaras, Assiniboine, Crees, Crows,* by Edwin Thompson Denig. Copyright ©1961 by The University of Oklahoma Press.

Meldrum estimated in 1862 that the tribe's numbers had declined to approximately 3,100 people.[14] Raynolds reckoned that their population stood at 3,000 in 1859.[15]

It was the great misfortune of the Crow that their demoralization and loss of numbers coincided with increased pressures brought to bear on their borders by the Dakota nation. Father de Smet's warning to the commissioner of Indian affairs in 1848 regarding diminution of buffalo herds on the Northern Plains along with the intertribal consequences of this phenomenon turned out to be all too true from the Crow point of view. Agent Alfred J. Vaughan noted in 1854 that Dakota lands along the Missouri River were rapidly becoming bereft of game animals of all kinds.[16] The following year he issued a warning to his superiors that many of the area's inhabitants would likely experience starvation for lack of game in the not too distant future.[17] Lands occupied by the Brule and Oglala tribes along the North Platte River likewise experienced depletion of game during these years. As early as 1850, these Indians were registering complaints with Indian Service officials that whites passing through the region were driving buffalo from their usual haunts. According to their agent, Thomas Twiss, the Dakota firmly believed buffalo would never return to an area in which they had scented whites.[18] The Crow homeland, in contrast, still served as home to myriad of game animals, including large numbers of buffalo.

Another factor which made lands along the North Platte River increasingly unattractive to the Dakota was the growing presence of the Alien Culture. The Brule and Oglala both found the existence of Fort Laramie in their midst so obnoxious that they petitioned Thomas Fitzpatrick for its removal in 1853.[19] Two years later relations between the garrison and the Indians took a decidedly violent turn when an inexperienced officer, Lieutenant John Grattan, led a small force out of the post to investigate the loss of a cow by a Mormon immigrant train. Learning that a Minneconjou warrior living in a Brule camp nearby had slaughtered the animal, Lieutenant Grattan tried to arrest the culprit over the objections of his Brule hosts. In the confusion that followed, Grattan and his entire force of twenty-nine men were either killed or mortally wounded.[20]

In retaliation the army placed General William S. Harney at the head of a 600-man fighting force created to punish the miscreants and restore stability to that part of the frontier. Harney marched his troops out of Fort Kearney in late summer of 1855, and on September 2 the detachment came upon and attacked a Brule camp at Ash Hollow in present-day Nebraska. Eighty-five inhabitants of the camp, including some women and children, were killed in the fray. Following the battle, Harney marched his victorious troops to Fort Laramie where he assembled neighboring tribes to issue the warning that they would suffer the same consequences as those who had died at Ash Hollow if they didn't behave themselves.[21]

From Fort Laramie Harney led his men to the Missouri River where they arrived without further incident. The army had recently purchased Fort Pierre from the Company for the purpose of establishing a military presence in Dakota territory, and the expedition's personnel spent the winter of 1855-56 in the new garrison. In early March, Harney met in council with upwards of 3,000 Dakota warriors. After warning them that swift and sure retribution could be expected for misconduct on their part, Harney negotiated a treaty dated March 6, 1856 with those assembled. In it the Indians promised to behave themselves in return for annual gifts of supplies and agricultural equipment. Fort Pierre was abandoned in late 1856 for a new post, Fort Randall, located near the mouth of Niobrara River.[22] The decade of the 1850s also witnessed the infiltration of white settlers along the Missouri into the present states of South Dakota and Nebraska. There were sufficiently large numbers of whites in the area by 1855 to justify creation of Nebraska Territory in that year.[23]

Of the Dakota tribes which continued to inhabit lands bordering the Missouri River, the Uncpapa and Blackfoot Sioux tribes proved to be the most troublesome for both the Crow and for whites who resided in that region. During the decade of the 1850s, the collective animus of the two tribes was most often focused on Company trading posts and personnel. In the year 1855 alone, Company employees were subjected to at least three serious attacks by them. On May 6, seven Fort Union employees who were transporting supplies from Fort Union to Fort Sarpy were attacked. On July 3, four employees from the same post were ambushed while conducting a buffalo hunt, and on August 23, a boat transporting supplies up the Yellowstone River for the Crow trade was attacked.[24] By the year 1856 Edwin Denig was of the opinion that a state of war existed between these tribes and the United States. He also believed that the Dakota nation had replaced the tribes of the Alliance as the Indians most feared by whites.[25]

These same Indians seem also to have replaced the Alliance as the Crow's most serious competitors for control of the Yellowstone Valley during the 1850s. Agent Vaughan reported to Alfred Cumming in 1854 that both the Uncpapa and Blackfoot Sioux were being exceptionally troublesome to the Crow.[26] The agent complained the following year that these tribes not only prevented Crow annuities from being delivered but that they also interfered with the tribe's access to their usual trading facilities. Captain William F. Raynolds reported that he had been given to understand during his short stay with the tribe at Fort Sarpy II in 1859 that the Crow regarded the Dakota as their most formidable and dangerous enemy.[27] James Chambers was of the opinion that the Crow were deathly afraid of their truculent neighbors to the east.[28]

SIOUX RECONNOITERING

By the middle of the nineteenth century, Dakota, or Sioux, warriors had replaced
Alliance warriors as the overriding security concern of the Crow.

Courtesy Walters Art Gallery, Baltimore   *A. Jacob Miller*

The danger of being overrun by their larger and
more powerful neighbors increased in 1855 when
some elements of both the Oglala and Brule tribes
abandoned the North Platte River area for a new
home in Powder River country. There is evidence
which indicates that this move was instigated by
Agent Twiss. Captain Raynolds later accused him of
masterminding a campaign to persuade his charges to
relieve the Crow of this portion of their bountiful

hunting grounds. Twiss admitted to the commissioner of Indian affairs in 1860 that he had in fact suggested to his Indians that they make the migration into Crow territory, but explained that he had done so in a last-ditch effort to bring peace to the area. His strategy, as he explained it, was to persuade them to occupy Crow lands in numbers large enough to convince their traditional enemies that suing for peace was the only means available to them for preserving their rich hunting grounds. Whether or not the commissioner accepted this bit of convoluted logic is not revealed by the record.[29]

What can be said with some certainty about the situation is that the Brule and Oglala migration brought about, or at least facilitated, a consolidation of Dakota forces opposed to the Crow. In 1855, not long after the migration was completed, 3,000 Dakota warriors, including those who had recently moved from the North Platte area, held a council on the headwaters of Grand River to organize resistance to white encroachment on their lands and to deal with the issue of Indian tribes they considered to be too tolerant of whites. Agent Vaughan was of the opinion that a consensus was reached among the Dakota at this meeting that whites had to be excluded from their lands at all costs. Vaughan also believed that the Dakota left the council unalterably inimical to all Indian tribes friendly to representatives of the Alien Culture.[30] A second general council of Dakota tribes dedicated to dealing with white interference in their affairs was held in the same general area during the summer of 1856. Several months later Lieutenant Gouverneur Warren happened to have a conversation with one of the participants in the council, Bear's Rib, an Oglala chief who informed the lieutenant that it was the consensus of those present that extinction of the Dakota nation was inevitable if whites were not soon expelled from the area. As a consequence, the various tribes which took part in the deliberations had agreed to fight the whites and their allies to the death, if necessary. The Oglala chief instructed Warren to tell Great Father that this declaration of war specifically also applied to the Crow tribe.[31]

It is appropriate to note at this point that relations between the Crow and the various Dakota tribes were not uniformly adversarial during these years. The winter of 1851-52, for example, was marked by a short period of peace between an unidentified Dakota tribe and the Crow.[32] Then in 1855, approximately 200 lodges of Crow conducted their fall hunt with a band of Minneconjou. The two tribes remained together after the hunt to spend the succeeding winter on the headwaters of Powder River.[33] However, peaceful interludes between the Crow and the Dakota were certainly the exceptions rather than the rule. During the second half of the decade, in fact, violent encounters between the two peoples reached new heights of intensity.

The Crow, perhaps in retaliation for Oglala and Brule intrusions onto their hunting grounds engineered by Twiss, took the fight to those Dakota who had opted to remain in the North Platte area. In early July of 1857, Agent Twiss complained to his superiors that the Crow had staged so many raids against the Indians in his jurisdiction, that more than 200 lodges had been forced to abandon the North Platte region.[34] The agent lodged similar complaints about the activities of Crow warriors in subsequent years. The last of these is dated January 4, 1860. In it Twiss charged a band of Crow warriors with attacking a Dakota camp which happened to be wintering on the headwaters of Powder River, forcing a retreat of the entire camp to his agency for protection. He added that the Crow had kept the country admin-

DODGING AN ARROW

During the late 1850s and early 1860s, the Crow tribe found itself locked in a
bitter struggle with the Dakota over hunting grounds.

Courtesy Walters Art Gallery, Baltimore   *A. Jacob Miller*

istered by his agency in a state of turmoil for almost
three years.[35] This aggressive behavior on the part of
the Crow strongly suggests that they were holding
their own against the much larger Dakota nation until
at least the end of 1859.

The numerical disparity between the Crow and their antagonists was striking. Estimates of the combined populations of the Teton and Yankton divisions made during the 1850s ranged from 12,000 to 30,000 as compared with 3,000 or so Crow.[36] Furthermore, Dakota forces were sometimes augmented with Northern Cheyenne and Arapaho warriors, in conformance with the alliance dedicated to displacing the Crow from their rich hunting grounds dating back to the 1840s. During the summer of 1857, a number of Cheyenne lodges conducted a hunt with some Dakota bands, and by 1859 were active participants in what seemed to the Crow to be a war of extermination against them[37] That the Arapaho were also present in Crow territory by 1859 was confirmed by one of Captain Raynolds' men who came upon an Arapaho village of 180 lodges camped on Powder River in September.[38]

Tribal elders among the Crow were well aware that the tribe's survival was threatened by Dakota truculence. At the 1854 annuities distribution at Fort Sarpy, Agent Vaughan received complaints from several leading men of the tribe that their territorial boundaries as established by the Treaty of 1851 were being violated with impunity by the several Dakota tribes. The Crow grumbled to the agent that they could not be expected to conform to the treaty's provisions under these circumstances. Vaughan explained that Great Father certainly didn't expect them to sit quietly in their tipis and be killed like so many buffalo. The Crow should therefore, he advised them, feel free to defend themselves against all intruders.[39] Captain Raynolds also received bitter complaints from tribal leaders with whom he met at Fort Sarpy II regarding the dangers posed to the tribe by Dakota intransigence. The Crow pointed out to him that their small size often rendered them helpless

CROW INDIAN ON THE LOOKOUT

Despite vigilance, the tribe found itself unable to preserve its territorial integrity in the face of Dakota truculence.

Courtesy of Walters Art Gallery, Baltimore   *A. Jacob Miller*

in the face of the almost constant warfare waged against them by a larger and more powerful enemy. Raynolds was of the opinion that although the tribe rarely failed to hold its own in engagements with its enemies, its numerical inferiority doomed its members to eventual extermination.[40] Edward Denig had made essentially the same prediction in 1856.[41]

Plenty Coups remembered that at the height of the Dakota wars, the tribe dispersed to its borders to inform intruders that although Crow boundaries would be defended to the death, all neighboring tribes were welcome to enter Crow lands on a temporary basis for hunting purposes.[42] The Dakota and their allies had more in mind than simply using Crow lands, however. At a council of Cheyenne leaders convened by the army in 1866,, several of the chiefs who participated therein frankly conceded that they and the Dakota had found the rich hunting lands of the Crow simply too tempting to pass up.[43] The crucial period of the struggle over Crow territory seems to have been the years from 1860 to 1862. Captain Raynolds was of the opinion, based on his first-hand knowledge of the area, that in 1859 the tribe still controlled the lands lying between the North Platte and Yellowstone Rivers as far east as Powder River.[44] By the summer of 1862, the Crow had been forced to abandon all of their lands south of the Yellowstone and east of the Big Horn, to the Dakota and their allies.[45]

The overwhelming numerical superiority enjoyed by enemies arrayed against the Crow during these years undoubtedly was a factor in the successful displacement of the tribe from so much of its rich hunting grounds. However, the ten-to-one advantage enjoyed by its enemies to the east was only one of several factors responsible for the catastrophe. The closing of Fort Sarpy II probably was a contributing factor in that it ended the tribe's convenient access to arms and ammunition. Certainly the demoralization of the tribe as described by both Chambers and Raynolds weakened its ability to successfully resist an invasion by a larger and better armed enemy, but it was the galvanization of Dakota military prowess against the Crow that proved to be the single most important factor in the loss of so much of their territory. After all, the Dakota, even without their allies, had for several generations possessed sufficient numbers to overrun the Crow. They had lacked only the will to marshal their combined forces against a smaller and weaker enemy. It was a desperation born of diminishing buffalo herds coupled with the identification of the Crow as a convenient surrogate for the hated whites which provided the cohesion necessary to drive the tribe from its prime buffalo lands.[46]

Cooperative and concerted action on the part of the Dakota nation and its allies against the Crow is clearly reflected in a pictographic history of the Oglala tribe drawn by a warrior named Bad Heart Bull. The intensity of the struggle is suggested by the circumstance that virtually all of his drawings for the late 1850s and early 1860s depict battles with the Crow. The participation of a broad array of tribes in this struggle is suggested by the inclusion of battles in the pictographic history of those years in which not only the Oglala participated but the Uncpapa, Minneconjou, Sans Arc, Brule, Cheyenne, and Arapaho tribes as well.[47]

The numbers of Dakota warriors arrayed against the Crow increased in 1862. During late summer of that year, certain elements of the Santee division of the nation living on the Redwood Reservation located in Minnesota rebelled against reservation life by burning agency buildings and killing some 200 neighboring white settlers. The governor of Minnesota called up the state militia, and it subsequently carried out a successful campaign of retribution against the rebellious Indians. Many Santee, in the face of avenging troops, fled westward to join their brethren, the Teton and Yankton Dakota. This not only increased the numerical advantage enjoyed by the Dakota; the Santee brought with them a virulent hatred for whites and their Indian allies which added fuel to the fires of hatred already burning in the breasts of Teton and Yankton warriors.[48]

Attacks against the Crow continued even after they had abandoned their superb hunting grounds. In 1865 Agent Mahlon Wilkinson informed the commissioner of Indian affairs that not only did the tribe refuse to visit lands south of the Yellowstone River, but that some of its members found it necessary to remain constantly on the move to avoid their Dakota antagonists, even as far north as Milk River.[49] Father de Smet, en route to Fort Benton via the Missouri River in 1865, witnessed one occasion in which the Crow were unsuccessful in evading the enemy. The cleric's steamboat was forced to put in at the mouth of Milk River because of low water, and, while camped there, he and his fellow passengers were joined by a band of Crow. Several days later, a war party of 600 Dakota attacked the camp, wounding several Crow warriors. De Smet was acquainted with the Dakota chiefs who led the raid, and he held a council with them to intercede on behalf of both whites and Indians in the camp. The attackers subsequently went on their way without inflicting further harm.[50]

That the beleaguered Crow did not experience extinction as predicted by Denig and Raynolds was at least partly due to certain changes which occurred within the Alliance during these same years. Population estimates for the four tribes ranged from 8,000 to 12,000. Collectively, then, the Alliance enjoyed a numerical superiority of more than two to one over their closest neighbor to the south. During the early years of the 1850s, relations between the two long-standing enemies were characterized by the usual round of horse thefts, clashes by small war parties, and raids of retribution. But in the last half of the decade, the incidence of warfare diminished. One factor in this welcome change was demographic in character. The Piegan Tribe abandoned the Three Forks area during the 1850s to inhabit lands north of the Missouri River between the deltas of Judith and Milk Rivers. This, at the very least, reduced the chances of violent encounters occasioned by casual contacts.[52]

Indian Service officials attributed the more peaceable behavior of the Alliance after mid-century to a treaty negotiated with them in 1855. For some years following the Treaty Council of 1851, tribes of the Alliance had agitated for a treaty of their own, pointing out that they were the only tribe in the region lacking a treaty arrangement with Great Father. Finally, on October 15, 1855, all four Alliance tribes accepted a treaty which, among other things, called on them to maintain peaceful relations with their neighbors in return for receiving annuities worth $20,000. The treaty identified the Musselshell River as the southern boundary of Alliance territory and set aside the Three Forks region as common hunting grounds.[53] Agent Alfred Vaughan claimed in 1857 that since implementation of the Treaty of 1855, the tribes of the Alliance had become the most peaceful in the entire region.[54]

Even if true, far more important from the Crow perspective was a realignment of loyalties within the Alliance. Strains first appeared in 1851 when the Atsina made peace with an Alliance enemy of long standing, the Assiniboine tribe.[55] Two years later an incident which involved the killing of an Atsina woman by some warriors of the Blackfoot tribe increased tension among long-time allies.[56] The Crow tried to take advantage of this rift by dispatching a peace delegation to the Atsina in 1854. Included in the deputation was a woman of Atsina heritage who had been captured by the Crow at a young age. Because she displayed a disposition to follow typically male pursuits, her adoptive father encouraged proficiency in the martial arts.[57] James Beckwourth referred to her as Pine Leaf and thought her every bit as good a warrior as most of her male contemporaries.[58] In any event as the peace commission of which she was a member approached its destination, it was attacked by Atsina warriors and all five members of the delegation were killed.[59]

This incident brought an end to Crow peace overtures for the time being, but tension between the Atsina and the other three Alliance tribes continued unabated. It had been apparent to the commissioners who negotiated the Treaty of 1855 that all was not well within the Alliance at that time, and in the years which followed, the Atsina put more and more distance between themselves and their former comrades-in-arms. Disintegration of the Alliance culminated in 1862 with the outbreak of warfare between the Atsina and the Piegan tribes. Feelings ran so high for a time that the Atsina were afraid to leave their homeland even to visit Fort Benton. It isn't clear which tribe initiated peace negotiations during these years, but the Crow and the Atsina did finally bury the hatchet and, by the close of the year 1862, were exchanging visits and fighting common enemies.[60]

Also helpful to the Crow during this critical period was their ability to improve relations with the Piegan tribe. Peace prevailed between the two tribes for a short period in 1857, and another peace was negotiated the following year. William Hamilton was a guest in a Piegan camp when Rotten Tail and some of his warriors appeared as peace emissaries in October of 1858.[61] Two Leggings later claimed that this period of amity ended when a band of Piegan warriors staged a horse-stealing raid on a Crow village. At least one more peace was negotiated by the two tribes. Henry W. Reed, agent for the Blackfoot Reservation, happened to be in Fort Benton when a party of several hundred Crow were visiting a Piegan camp nearby in late 1862. Despite having just fought each other in several bloody engagements, another truce was worked out between the two tribes.[62] Peace with the Piegan was clearly a desirable situation for the Crow if for no other reason than that Fort Benton offered the only trading facilities available to the tribe in this part of the country. However desirable peace between the two old adversaries might have been, it was a sometime phenomenon; by 1864 they were once again at each other's throats.[63]

Intermittent though they proved to be, these periods of peace coupled with the more permanent peace with the Atsina tribe contributed to the ability of the Crow to dodge the bullet of Dakota intransigence. The Crow had undoubtedly found themselves between a rock and a hard place as they tried to retreat across the Yellowstone River into Alliance territory. The steady barrage of hammer-like blows being administered by the Dakota may very well have destroyed the Crow had not the anvil formed by Alliance enmity been destroyed by internal problems.

As it was, the Dakota ended up in control of the prime buffalo hunting grounds which lay to the east of the Big Horn Mountains. The mouth of Powder River seems to have served as a focal point for

Dakota activities in their newly acquired lands, sometimes hosting as many as 600 lodges of warriors. By the early 1860s this area had come to serve as a rendezvous for the most dissatisfied and truculent of the Dakota bands.[64] It was from here that a prominent Oglala warrior called Red Cloud mounted a campaign to form a confederation uniting all the Northern Plains tribes against the presence of whites on Indian lands.[65] There is no extant evidence to indicate that the Crow, so recently displaced from their own lands by Red Cloud's people, took his entreaties seriously.

There are indications, however, that the Crow were growing increasingly restive about the large number of whites settling on neighboring lands. By 1865 Montana territory contained a non-Indian population of approximately 15,000. It must, in fact, have seemed to Indians of the region that whites had inexhaustible numbers. What the Crow may or may not have known was that whites would turn out to be a much more formidable foe than even the Dakota. Their superiority in numbers, coupled with an infinitely higher level of technology, would in the end provide the Alien Culture with the means to over-whelm and engulf the tribe. At least one Crow leader seems to have been aware of the seriousness of the threat to the Crow way of life posed by white interlopers. Red Bear, identified by George Catlin in 1832 as a distinguished warrior, had emerged as chief of one of the tribe's three major divisions by the time of Captain Raynolds' visit to Crow domain in 1859. It was Red Bear, in fact, who granted the expedition permission to explore Crow territory. In granting access to his homeland, however, he added a caveat to the effect that whites would not be allowed to build permanent dwellings thereon.[66] Later that same year, Red Bear and his men stole 200 horses from the Fort Benton trading post and a few days later harassed nine

Company employees engaged in chopping wood for the post.[67]

Red Bear may have understood that discoveries of precious metals on Crow domain would draw an influx of white settlers. In 1863 he and his followers tried to convince a party of miners from Bannock City that prospecting on Crow lands would not be worth the candle. James Stuart, a prospector with previous mining experience in California, organized and led a combination prospecting and colonizing party of fourteen men into the heart of Crow territory during spring of that year. Stuart and his men were camped near the mouth of Clark's Fork in late April when Red Bear and thirty Crow warriors approached, indicating that they wanted to do some trading. Once in camp the Indians behaved in a threatening and insolent manner, and insisted on spending the night with their reluctant hosts.[68]

The whites spent a restless, sleepless night awaiting an attack by their guests. The expected assault did not materialize, but, as the miners loaded their pack animals the next morning, the intruders forced them to trade some of their possessions for Indian goods of little or no value. Having had quite enough, Stuart gave a pre-arranged signal for his men to defend themselves. They grabbed loaded rifles and began firing, driving the Crow warriors from the campsite.

The prospecting party then proceeded down the valley of the Yellowstone to the delta of Big Horn River where they tested its gold potential by conducting extensive panning operations. They found nothing even approaching commercial quantities of the metal, but nonetheless laid out a townsite of 320 acres, which Stuart named Big Horn City. All the while keeping their eyes peeled for evidence of gold deposits, the party moved up the Big Horn River to the point where it debouches from its lower canyon.

Another camp was established here to serve as a base for another round of prospecting and panning. Several hours after nightfall on May 13, the camp was roused by a volley of rifle shots from, as it turned out, the same band of warriors which had harassed them at the mouth of Clark's Fork. A quick count by Stuart revealed that two of his men had been killed and five wounded. The survivors braced themselves for another assault, but it never came. At sunrise the prospectors were relieved to see that their attackers had moved on.

Shaken, Stuart and his men held a council to decide on a course of future action. A consensus was quickly reached that the area in which their camp was located was far too dangerous. Further discussion revealed that a majority of the party believed that it would be foolhardy to retrace their route back to Bannock City. It was therefore decided to make a beeline for the Oregon Trail. Dogged by Red Bear and his warriors for most of the way, the prospectors felt fortunate to safely reach their destination on May 28. The dispirited party eventually made its way to Fort Bridger, where its members were able to make arrangements for a safe return to Bannock City.

At least one other Crow leader turned against whites during these years. The small detachment sent overland from Fort Benton to Fort Union by Captain Raynolds during the summer of 1860 under Lieutenant John Mullan was camped along the banks of Big Dry Sandy Creek, when 250 Crow warriors, led by Great Bear, charged the camp in what appears to have been an attempt to stampede the contingent's horses. Mullan had only a few men, and the threatening, bellicose behavior of the intruders suggested to him that they had in mind annihilating his small command. Luckily for the lieutenant and his detachment, they had Jim Bridger along with them as

guide. The venerable mountain man stepped forward
and indicated that he wanted to hold a council. The
Crow leader informed Mullan through Bridger that he
no longer considered whites to be friends of the tribe.
For one thing, he charged, Great Father's decision to
divert the 1860 annuities to the Upper Platte Agency
had cheated the tribe out of its treaty goods for that
year. For another, he continued, the closing of Fort
Sarpy II by the Company had deprived the Crow of
access to trade goods, pointing out that Dakota
occupation of the lower Yellowstone River region
effectively precluded Crow access to trade goods at
Fort Union. In the end, though, the soldiers were
allowed to continue on their way.[69]

Had the Crow fully realized just how committed
whites were to displacing them from their lands, they
probably would have reacted to the presence of an
ever-increasing number of settlers even more violently
than they in fact did. The new territory of Montana
had barely been constituted when its Assembly, in
1864, passed a resolution which called for the
expropriation of all Crow lands.[70] Acting Governor
Meagher followed a slightly different approach. He
had in mind negotiating a treaty in which the tribe
would give up all its lands lying within the boundaries
of the new territory. Runners were sent out in
December of 1865 to find and invite tribal leaders to
a treaty council, but Meagher's emissaries were unable
to locate any Crow at all.[71] Although nothing came of
these early attempts to open up Crow lands for white
settlement, that attempts to do so were made at all
indicates that the whites were no less intent on taking
over the Crow homeland than were the Dakota and
their allies.

One of the interesting consequences of the struggle
between the Dakota and the Crow was a reconsolidation within the tribe's internal structure. As the Crow

retreated from their lands east of the Big Horn River and south of the Yellowstone, many found sanctuary in the homeland of their new allies, the Atsina tribe. As early as June, 1862, a large band of Crow was camped at the mouth of Milk River awaiting arrival of their annuities for that year. Another band of Crow spent part of the summer of 1862 in the vicinity of the confluence of the Missouri and Musselshell Rivers.[72] Robert Meldrum, the tribe's favorite white, was posted to Fort Charles, situated on the Missouri River about seventy-five miles below the mouth of Milk River, that same year. One can speculate that this was a strategy on the part of the Company to monopolize Crow trade in that area.[73] In subsequent years a number of observers commented on the Crow presence in Atsina territory.[74] In some instances Crow bands were reported to be camped with their former adversaries.[75]

By 1862 other bands of Crow had fled to mountainous areas far to the west of Atsina domain in an effort to avoid Dakota war parties.[76] In subsequent years these Crow bands could be found frequenting Fort Benton, the Gallatin River area, the upper reaches of Yellowstone Valley, and the newly-established town of Bozeman.[77] What happened, then, during this cataclysmic period was that in addition to driving the Crow from that part of their homeland situated east of the Big Horn River and south of the Yellowstone, the Dakota had also unwittingly brought about a reconsolidation of the tribe from three major divisions back into two, albeit with different names from those used in former times. As late as 1850, one division of the tribe was known as the Sapsuckers and the other as the Crow people, according to Thaddeus Culbertson who almost certainly based his nomenclature on information obtained from Company employees at Fort Union.[78] Indian Service officials were referring to the two branches as the River Crow (Dung on the Banks, Black Lodges) and the Mountain Crow (Main Body, Many Lodges) in 1865.[79] It has heretofore been assumed that these designations dated back to the early part of the nineteenth century. The culprit here seems to have been Lieutenant James Bradley, who, writing in 1876, described the tribe as having been in a united state until the time of Rotten Belly and Long Hair. According to Bradley, an intense rivalry which developed between the two chiefs split the tribe into the Mountain and River Crow divisions.[80] It is likely that the tribe was already divided into two branches at least as early as the time of Larocque's visit in 1805.[81]

The new appellations reflected the geographic circumstances of the two divisions following the tribe's retreat in the face of Dakota military prowess. One division, the River Crow, evolved out of the concentration of Crow which found itself living in the general area of the upper Missouri River after 1862. The other designation, Mountain Crow, was used to describe those of the tribe who ended up hiding from their Dakota enemies in the fortress-like mountains that formed the northwest corner of their territory. All of this begs the question of whether the designations of Mountain Crow and River Crow described two new major groupings or whether they were simply new names used for the original divisions. Unfortunately, there is insufficient extant evidence to provide a definitive answer for the question.

Leadership of the Mountain Crow seems to have first devolved upon Red Bear. Certainly he was the most visible of the Crow leaders operating in the mountains during this period.[82] After his death, sometime prior to 1865, leadership in the Mountain Crow became fragmented.[83] Plenty Coups remembered that when he was a young man, the Mountain

Crow were led by Thin Behind, Blackfoot (Sits-in-the-Middle-of-the-Land), Iron Bull, and Long Horse.[84] Thin Behind's prominence was evanescent, but the other three would all play important roles in the tribe's affairs well into the 1870s. Long Horse, like Red Bear before him, was a warrior of some renown. Iron Bull and Blackfoot, on the other hand, owed their power and prominence in tribal affairs to quite different attributes.

Blackfoot was a mountain of a man, well over six feet in height, and although overweight, was well proportioned. Despite his prepossessing physical appearance, he was not a particularly good warrior. His emergence as a tribal leader was due rather to his skills as an orator.[85] In the many treaty councils in which the Crow would participate during the late 1860s and early 1870s, Blackfoot assumed the role of the tribe's chief debater and negotiator with representatives of the Alien Culture. Iron Bull's reputation as a warrior also left something to be desired. His status and power in the tribe were due to his liberality, hospitality, and ability to get along with whites.[86] Rotten Tail and Horse Guard were the two leading men of the River Crow branch of the tribe. Horse Guard, no less than Rotten Tail, was noted for his abillities as a warrior. Thaddeus Culbertson described him in 1850 as a warrior who had achieved great distinction despite being only thirty years of age. Culbertson also noted that in physical appearance he had the characteristics of a white man.[87]

By far the most profound change in the Crow tribe's situation in the years immediately following mid-century was the loss of its buffalo-rich lands south of the Yellowstone River and east of the Big Horn River. Internal problems undoubtedly contributed to the tribe's inability to protect its traditional homeland. However, the major factor in the loss of such a large chunk of the tribe's territory almost certainly had to do with the emergence of a consensus among the tribes of the Dakota nation and their allies that the Crow were convenient surrogate enemies for the detested whites, and that their lands, therefore, were fair game. Crow domain was made all the more attractive to their long-time enemies by the disappearance of buffalo in their own lands. Driven out of the better part of their territory, some Crow retreated northward to take refuge with their erstwhile enemies, the Atsina. The rest of the tribe found itself squeezed into the northwest corner of its homeland and onto adjoining lands on the north and west. At the same time that the Crow were being displaced from their rich hunting grounds, they were gaining new neighbors who, in the end, would constitute a threat not only to what remained of their lands but to their very way of life as well.

NOTES

1. RCIA, 1865, House Executive Document No. 1 (Serial 1248), p. 423.
2. Edwin Thompson Denig, *Of the Crow Nation*, ed. John C. Ewers (New York: AMS Press, 1980), p. 63.
3. Vine Deloria, Jr. and Raymond De Mallie, eds., *Proceedings of the Great Peace Commission of 1867-1868* (Washington: The Institute for the Development of Indian Law, 1975), pp. 87, 90.
4. Rudolph Friederich Kurz, *Journal of Rudolph Friederich Kurz*, ed. J.N.B. Hewitt, Bureau of American Ethnology, Bulletin 115 (Washington: Government Printing Office, 1937), pp. 240-2; Denig, *op. cit.*, pp. 63-64.
5. *Ibid*, p. 24; Denton R. Bedford, "The Fight at the Mountain on Both Sides," *Indian Historian*, VIII, No. 2 (Fall, 1975), p. 18. Captain Raynolds found that the tribe was still divided into three major parts in 1859. W.F. Raynolds, *Report on the Exploration of the Yellowstone River* (Washington: Government Printing Office, 1868), p. 17.
6. Lewis Henry Morgan, *The Indian Journals, 1859-62* (Ann Arbor: The University of Michigan Press, 1959), p. 168; Denig, *op. cit.*, pp. 55-56.
7. James H. Chambers, "Original Journals of James H. Chambers, Fort Sarpy," *Contributions to the Historical Society of Montana*, X (1940), *passim*.
8. Kurz, *op. cit.*, p. 250.
9. Chambers, *op. cit.*, pp. 159-60.

10. *Ibid*, pp. 158-9.
11. Raynolds, *op. cit.*, p. 48.
12. *Ibid*, p. 17.
13. RCIA, 1853, Senate Executive Document No. 1 (Serial 690), p. 354; Chambers, *op. cit.*, p. 147; Raynolds, *op. cit.*, p. 51; *Explorer on the Northern Plains: Lieutenant Gouvernor K. Warren's Preliminary Report of Explorations in Nebraska and Dakota, in the Years, 1855-56-57* (Washington: U.S. Government Printing Office, n.d.), p. 51.
14. Morgan, *op. cit.*, p. 171.
15. Raynolds, *loc. cit.*
16. Letter, A.J. Vaughan to A. Cumming, April 1, 1854, LRUM, reel 885.
17. Letter, A.J. Vaughan to A. Cumming, February 11, 1855, LRUM, reel 885.
18. RCIA, 1859, Senate Executive Document No. 2 (Serial 1023), p. 497; Letter, T.S. Twiss to Commissioner of Indian Affairs, August 16, 1859, LRUP, reel 890.
19. RCIA, 1853, Senate Executive Document No. 1 (Serial 690), pp. 366-7.
20. Robert G. Athearn, *Forts of the Upper Missouri* (Englewood Cliffs: Prentice Hall, Inc., 1967), p. 33.
21. *Ibid*, pp. 38-39.
22. *Ibid*, pp. 40-50.
23. Dorothy Weyer Creigh, *Nebraska: A Bicentennial History* (New York: W.W. Norton & Company, Inc., 1977), p. 48.
24. Chambers, *op. cit.*, pp. 123-4; RCIA, 1855, Senate Executive Document No. 1 (Serial 810), p. 394.
25. Edwin Denig, *Five Indian Tribes of the Upper Missouri*, ed. John C. Ewers (Norman: University of Oklahoma Press, 1961), p. 27.
26. Letter, A.J. Vaughan to A. Cumming, July 3, 1854, LRUM, reel 885.
27. Raynolds, *loc. cit.*
28. Chambers, *op. cit.*, pp. 100-101.
29. Letter, T.S. Twiss to A.B. Greenwood, May 23, 1860, LRUP, reel 890.
30. Letter, A.J. Vaughan to A. Cumming, May 19, 1855, LRUM, reel 885.
31. *Explorer . . . Warren's*, *op. cit.*, pp. 20-21, 52.
32. Garrick Mallery, *Pictographs of the North American Indians: A Preliminary Paper*, Fourth Annual Report of the Bureau of Ethnology, 1882-83 (Washington: Government Printing Office, 1886), pp. 120-1; Garrick Mallery, *Picture Writing of the American Indians*, Tenth Annual Report of the Bureau of Ethnology, 1888-89 (Washington: Government Printing Office, 1893), p. 283.
33. Chambers, *op. cit.*, p. 136; Letter, T.S. Twiss to A. Cumming, December 25, 1855, LRUP, reel 889. For an explanation and an assessment of this phenomenon, see Kingsley M. Bray, "Long Horn's Peace: A New View of Sioux-Crow Relations, 1851-58," *Nebraska History*, LXVI, No. 1 (Spring, 1985), 28-47.
34. Letter, T.S. Twiss to A. Cumming, July 6, 1857, LRUP, reel 890.
35. Letter, T.S. Twiss to A.B. Greenwood, January 4, 1860, LRUP, reel 890.
36. *Explorer . . . Warren's*, *op. cit.*, p. 48; Denig, *Five Tribes*, pp. 14-15; Thaddeus A. Culbertson, *Journal of an Expedition to the Mauvaises Terres and the Upper Missouri in 1850*, ed. John Francis McDermott, Bureau of American Ethnology, Bulletin 147 (Washington: Government Printing Office, 1952), p. 137.
37. F.V. Hayden, *On the Ethnography and Philology of the Indian Tribes of the Missouri Valley; With a Map and Plates*, Transactions of the American Philosophical Society, XII (New Series) (Philadelphia: Blanchard and Lea, 1862), 278.

38. Raynolds, *op. cit.*, p. 130.
39. RCIA, 1854, Senate Executive Document No. 1 (Serial 746), p. 293.
40. Raynolds, *op. cit.*, p. 51.
41. Denig, *Crow Nation*, p. 71.
42. Frank B. Linderman, *Plenty Coups, Chief of the Crows* (Lincoln: University of Nebraska Press, 1962), p. 48. Plenty Coups was born at mid-century and was therefore but a child at the time. He went on to become a prominent warrior and a leading man of the tribe.
43. Margaret Irvin Sullivant Carrington, *Ab-sa-ro-ka, Land of Massacre, being the Experiences of an Officer's Wife on the Plains; with an Outline of Indian Operations and Conferences from 1865-1878 by Henry B. Carrington* (5th ed.: Ann Arbor: University Microfilm International, 1979), p. 17.
44. Raynolds, *op. cit.*, pp. 16-17.
45. RCIA, 1862, Senate Executive Document No. 1 (Serial 1157), p. 337; Letter, J. Pattie to G. Blunt, July 21, 1862, LRUM, reel 885.
46. Raynolds observed in 1859 that Crow territory comprised the best buffalo hunting grounds in the West. Raynolds, *op. cit.*, p. 17. Denig wrote in 1856 that Crow lands lying east of the Big Horn Mountains constituted the best game country in the world. Denig, *Crow Nation*, p. 21.
47. Helen H. Blish, *A Pictographic History of the Oglala Sioux* (Lincoln: University of Nebraska Press, 1967), pp. 117-8, 120-4, 126-8, 130, 132, 134-43, 146-68, 172-81, 185.
48. RCIA, 1863, House Document No. 1 (Serial 1182), p. 140.
49. Letter, M. Wilkinson to N. Edmunds, September 1, 1865, LRUM, reel 886.
50. Hiram Martin Chittenden and Alfred Talbot Richardson, eds., *Life, Letters and Travels of Father De Smet* (New York: Arno Press, 1969), II, 791.
51. Culbertson, *op. cit.*, p. 137; RCIA, 1853, Senate Executive Document No. 1 (Serial 690), p. 356; RCIA, 1858, Senate Executive Document No. 1 (Serial 974), p. 432.
52. Hayden, *op. cit.*, p. 249; John C. Ewers, *Blackfeet Indians* (New York and London: Garland Publishing Inc., 1974), pp. 87-89; RCIA, 1857, Senate Executive Document No. 11 (Serial 919), p. 410.
53. John C. Ewers, *The Blackfeet: Raiders on the Northwestern Plains* (Norman: University of Oklahoma Press, 1958), pp. 217-21.
54. RCIA, 1857, Senate Executive Document No. 1 (Serial 919), p. 410.
55. Ewers, *Blackfeet Indians*, p. 83.
56. RCIA, 1853, Senate Executive Document No. 1 (Serial 690), p. 460.
57. Denig, *Crow Nation*, p. 65.
58. James P. Beckwourth, *The Life and Adventures of James P. Beckwourth*, ed. Delmont R. Oswald (Lincoln: University of Nebraska Press, 1972), pp. 202-3, 211-2, 215, 271.
59. Denig, *Crow Nation*, p. 68.
60. Ewers, *Blackfeet Indians*, pp. 140, 142; Robert Vaughn, *Then and Now or, Thirty-Six Years in the Rockies* (Minneapolis: Tribune Printing Company, 1900), p. 137; RCIA, 1864, House Executive Document No. 1 (Serial 1220), p. 173.
61. William T. Hamilton, "A Trading Expedition Among the Indians in 1858," *Contributions to the Historical Society of Montana*, III (1900), 64-65.
62. Peter Nabokov, *Two Leggings: The Making of a Crow Warrior* (New York: Thomas Y. Crowell Publishers, 1967), p. 33; RCIA, 1862, House Executive Document No. 1 (Serial 1157), p. 323.
63. RCIA, 1864, House Executive Document No. 1 (Serial 1220), p. 173; RCIA, 1865, House Executive Document No. 1 (Serial 1248), p. 698.

64. *Ibid,* p. 446.
65. Granville Stuart, *Forty Years on the Frontier,* ed. Paul C. Phillips (Cleveland: The Arthur H. Clark Company, 1925), II, 60.
66. Raynolds, *op. cit.,* p. 51.
67. Vaughn, *op. cit.,* p. 134-5.
68. Unless otherwise indicated, the account of the Stuart party's adventures with Red Bear's band is taken from James Stuart, "The Yellowstone Expedition of 1863," *Contributions to the Historical Society of Montana,* I (1876), 149-233.
69. Raynolds, *op. cit.,* pp. 166-7. This is the only reference to Great Bear found by the author.
70. Memorial of the Legislative Assembly of Montana, House Miscellaneous Document No. 43 (Serial 1385).
71. Letter, T.F. Meagher to S. Edgerton, December 14, 1865, LRMS, reel 488.
72. RCIA, 1863, House Executive Document No. 1 (Serial 1182), p. 282.
73. Eli W. McNeal, *William T. Wheeler Papers,* Manuscript Collection No. 65, Folder 9, HSML; Morgan, *op. cit.,* p. 172.
74. For examples, see RCIA, 1864, House Executive Document No. 1 (Serial 1220), pp. 173, 415; Letter, M. Wilkinson to N. Edmunds, September 1, 1865, LRUM, reel 886; Letter, S.A. Latta to W.P. Dole, August 27, 1863, LRUM, reel 885.
75. Chittenden and Richardson, *op. cit.,* II, 791-2; Letter, H.V. Reed to W.P. Dole, n.d., LRUM, reel 885.
76. RCIA, 1862, House Executive Document No. 1 (Serial 1157), pp. 337-9.
77. *Ibid,* p. 323; Peter Ronan, "Discovery of Alder Gulch," *Contributions to the Historical Society of Montana,* III (1900), 145-7; Letter, S.A. Latta to W.P. Dole, March 3, 1864, LRUM, reel 885; E.S. Topping, *The Chronicles of the Yellowstone* (Minneapolis: Ross & Haines, Inc., 1968), p. 37; Thomas B. Marquis, *Memoirs of a White Crow Indian* (Lincoln: University of Nebraska Press, 1974), p. 14.
78. Culbertson, *op. cit.,* p. 137.
79. For examples, see Letter, M. Wilkinson to N. Edmunds, September 1, 1865, LRUM, reel 886; Letter, O. Guernsey to D.N. Cooley, July 19, 1866, *ibid;* RCIA, 1866, House Executive Document No. 1 (Serial 1284), p. 175.
80. James H. Bradley, "Indian Traditions," *Contributions to the Historical Society of Montana,* IX (1923), 312; James H. Bradley, *The March of the Montana Column: A Prelude to the Custer Disaster,* ed. Edgar I. Stewart (Norman: University of Oklahoma Press, 1961), pp. 82-83. Robert H. Lowie and Edward S. Curtis, both of whom conducted research on Crow culture during the early years of the twentieth century, came away from their studies believing that the separation of the tribe into the Mountain and River Crow divisions occurred at least as early as the Atkinson expedition of 1825. See Edward S. Curtis, *The North American Indian,* ed. Frederick Webb Hodge (New York and London: Johnson Reprint Corporation, 1970), IV, 8, 41, 43; Robert H. Lowie, *The Crow Indians* (New York: Farrar & Rinehart, Incorporated, 1935), p. 4; Robert H. Lowie, *Social Life of the Crow Indians* (New York: American Museum of Natural History, 1912), pp. 184-85.
81. Charles MacKenzie, "The Mississouri [sic] Indians: A Narrative of Four Trading Expeditions to the Mississouri [sic], 1804-1805-1806," in Louis Francois Rodrique Masson, *Les Bourgeois de la Compagnie du Nord-Oest* (New York: Antiquarian Press, Ltd., 1960), I, 345.
82. Red Bear was identified by Two Leggings as leader of the Mountain Crow. Nabokov, *op. cit.,* p. 2.

83. Red Bear was killed by the Dakota in a battle which took place on Pryor Creek. Edward S. Curtis was told by one of his informants that the battle occurred in 1862, Curtis, *op. cit.*, IV, 199. But the chief could not have died that early because it was he who led the band which harassed the James Stuart party in 1863.
84. Linderman, *op. cit.*, p. 50.
85. Edwin James Stanley, *Rambles in Wonderland* (New York and London: Garland Publishing Inc., 1978), p. 28.
86. Curtis, *op. cit.*, IV, 51–52.
87. Culbertson, *op. cit.*, p. 106.

SEVEN

GREAT FATHER TO THE RESCUE

Contacts between the Crow and representatives of the U.S. Government prior to 1865 were sporadic and of a character that resulted in few substantive changes in the pattern of tribal life. From the late 1860s forward, however, Crow destiny would become increasingly bound with and dependent upon Great Father, his institutions and his functionaries. Most decisions about the tribe's future would, in fact, be made on an impersonal basis by individuals living and working some 2,000 miles distant from the tribe's homeland. America's Indian policy assumed many faces during the early years of the new republic, but generally speaking, decisions affecting the nation's aboriginal inhabitants were predicated on the imperative that Indians lands somehow be made available for white settlement. The only question, really, was how such transfers could be most efficaciously implemented. Some decision makers believed that force, used either to exterminate the Indian or persuade him to abandon his lands to whites, should prevail. Others favored the more peaceful method of "civilizing" the Indians so that they could eventually be incorporated into white society, thus obviating the need for tribal territories.

One of Great Father's immediate Indian concerns after 1865 had to do with what most of his policy makers regarded as Dakota malevolence. From the government's point of view, the Dakota nation represented an obstacle not only to white settlement on Dakota lands but also an obstruction to the development of mining in Montana Territory. The immigrant route to Montana's mines pioneered by John Bozeman took settlers through lands controlled by one or another of the Dakota tribes or by the Crow. The Bozeman Trail, therefore, would be central to Great Father's Indian policy during the last half of the decade of the 1860s as it applied to the Dakota and the Crow. In an effort to secure the country through which the road ran, Brigadier General Patrick E. Connor was given command of 2,500 troops with orders to clear the Powder River country of the Dakota and their allies. Connor mounted a three-pronged campaign which began in late July of 1865 but which ended in abject failure a few months later. Logistical problems, lack of effective coordination between the three columns, low morale, and inclement weather plagued Connor and his troops all the way. The only discernible consequence of the campaign was construction of the first military installation in that vicinity, Fort Connor. The new post was erected on Powder River near the mouth of Dry Creek to serve mainly as a storage depot. It was, of course, abandoned when the general and his troops withdrew from the area.[1]

The military approach to the Dakota problem was undoubtedly discredited by the abortive Connor campaign, but in any event, it had already been decided that the fundamental assumptions of the nation's Indian policy should be reviewed. The Doolittle Commission was created by the Congress in March of 1865 and given a mandate to examine the general condition of the nation's Indian population as a prelude to a general reform in the conduct of Indian affairs.[2] Congress also authorized Governor Newton Edmunds of Dakota territory to form a commission for the purpose of entreating the Dakota tribes for peace. During the autumn of 1865, the Edmunds Commission ascended the Missouri River to negotiate nine treaties with various Dakota bands. As it turned out, however, few if any of the Indians who accepted the treaties had ever been involved in depredations committed against whites on either the Bozeman or Oregon Trails. The apparent success of Edmunds and his commissioners nonetheless lent credibility to those policy makers who favored a non-violent approach to resolving the nation's Indian problem.[3]

The Edmunds Commission divided itself for the following year. One team was led by its chairman, and it also   ascended the Missouri River. This time out Edmunds had in mind negotiating rights-of-way for a proposed wagon road which would run all the way from St. Paul, Minnesota to the Montana mines.[4] The commissioners embarked at Fort Union in early July of 1866 to find a band of River Crow awaiting their arrival, having been transported to the post by steamer from the mouth of Musselshell River.[5] Pierre Shane, an ex-employee of the Company, had been commissioned to bring the remainder of the tribe in. He found them near Fort Benton and persuaded upwards of five-hundred Mountain Crow to accompany him to Fort Union for the treaty council. They arrived on July 16 and representatives of both divisions of the tribe entered into negotiations with the treaty commissioners on the following morning. Out of these discussions came a treaty dated July 18, 1866 which granted a right-of-way ten miles in width, extending from the mouth of the Yellowstone to the Big Bend of that river in return for annuities in the amount of $25,000. Similar rights-of-way were negotiated with the Arikara, Atsina, Mandan, and Assiniboine tribes.[6]

The other division of the commission journeyed to Fort Laramie, where its members hoped to make

peace with those tribes of the Dakota nation which
had not signed treaties during the previous year. They
were met at the post by E.B. Taylor of the Indian
Service, and he thereupon assumed leadership of this
branch of the commission. Colonel Henry E.
Maynadier, who had served as second-in-command of
the Raynolds' expedition, but who was at this time
serving as commandant of Fort Laramie, was added to
the commission. The council convened on June 5 with
representatives of the Brule and Oglala tribes,
including Red Cloud, present. Taylor told the Indians
that Great Father hadn't the slightest interest in
acquiring any land from them, but rather wanted only
to arrange for use of the Bozeman Trail by white
settlers en route to the gold fields of Montana. After
a short session on the following day, Taylor, at the
request of Red Cloud and other Dakota leaders,
agreed to postpone the deliberations long enough to
allow certain other Dakota leaders who were camped
at that time near White River to complete their
journey to the peace council.[7]

That the proponents for a peaceful approach to the
Indian problem had not yet prevailed in their attempt
to dictate Indian policy is indicated by the arrival of
the 18th Infantry at Fort Laramie on June 16. Its
commander, Colonel Henry B. Carrington, had the
misfortune to lead his troops into the post while the
peace council was in session. The arrival of
Carrington and his men was interpreted by Red Cloud
and several other Dakota leaders as a sure sign that
Great Father intended to apply force to the Bozeman
Trail situation regardless of the outcome of Taylor's
negotiations. The Oglala leader and others consequently departed the council in a huff. Undeterred
by the absence of those elements of the Dakota nation
most adamant about excluding whites from their
lands, Taylor continued deliberating with the

remaining Dakota leaders. In the end he was able to negotiate a treaty which granted a right-of-way for the Bozeman Trail.[8]

Having wreaked havoc on Taylor's treaty deliberations, Colonel Carrington marched his troops out of Fort Laramie on June 17 in the direction of Powder River country. His strategy for making that area safe for travel involved the erection of strategically located military posts along the migrant road. The first stage of the plan, as implemented, was to refurbish Fort Connor and, at the same time, change its name to Fort Reno. Carrington next constructed a post near the forks of Piney Creek about sixty-five miles north of Fort Reno. He called the new installation Fort Phil Kearny and established his headquarters there. Construction of a third post was initiated in August under the supervision of Lieutenant Colonel N.C. Kinney. Located about two miles north of the debouchment of the river from Big Horn Canyon, it was given the name of Fort C.F. Smith, after General Charles F. Smith, a division commander for U.S. Grant during the Civil War.[9]

Fort C.F. Smith was similar in appearance to the numerous trading posts operated by the Company along the banks of the Yellowstone. A stockade twelve feet in height enclosed a square measuring approximately 200 feet on each side. All walls except the north one were fashioned of pine logs. The north wall contained the only entrance to the post and was constructed of a mixture of adobe and stone. The interior walls of the south and west sides of the enclosure were lined with log huts utilized as living quarters for the new garrison. Other buildings inside the stockade served as store houses and a commissary.[10]

Lieutenant Colonel Kinney's command consisted of 3 officers, 2 surgeons, and 179 enlisted men. Kinney,

who had served with distinction with the 18th
Infantry during the Civil War, stayed on as commandant of the post until June 12, 1867 when he was
transferred to Fort Phil Kearny.[11] He was replaced by
Lieutenant Colonel Luther P. Bradley, who, like his
predecessor, had performed meritorious service
during the Civil War. In fact he had been breveted to
the rank of brigadier general for gallantry during the
Battle of Chickamagua. Bradley brought to his new
command two more companies of infantry.[12] He was
in turn replaced by Captain Andrew S. Burt in June
of 1868. Burt had begun his service during the Civil
War as an enlisted man but had received a battlefield
commission in May of 1861. He was later made a
Brevet Major for gallant service in the Atlanta
campaign.[13]

The garrison also included a number of non-military
personnel. Six civilians were employed in September
of 1866. A year later their numbers had increased to
thirty-six.[14] Among the non-military personnel who
served at the post during its short life were a number
of whites already well known to the Crow. The two
most prominent of these were Jim Bridger and James
Beckwourth. The latter, it will be remembered, left
Crow country in 1837. His return in 1866 was the
mountain man's first visit to Crow country in almost
thirty years. In the interim Beckwourth, among other
things, had participated in the Santa Fe trade, farmed
in California, operated a mercantile establishment in
Denver, and acted as guide for the infamous Colonel
John M. Chivington in 1864 at the Sand Creek
massacre. He was hired on as a guide by Carrington at
Fort Laramie during the colonel's short stay at that
post during the summer of 1866.[15]

Less notorious were Pierre Shane, Mitch Boyer,
Thomas Leforge, and John Richard, Jr. All except
Leforge were sons of white fathers and Dakota

women, and were therefore fluent in the Dakota language. Shane, as previously indicated, had served for many years with the Company. He was married to a woman from one of the Alliance tribes and had a son who was married to a member of the Crow tribe.[16] Boyer, another ex-employee of the Company, had served with Patrick Connor in the general's disastrous Powder River campaign in 1865. The veteran frontiersman had a reputation for being a good worker and an expert guide, but was also known to be a hard drinker.[17] Richard was the son of John Baptiste Richard, a frontier entrepreneur who had operated trading posts, ferries, and toll bridges along the North Platte River since the 1830s. John, Jr. had a reputation for being knowledgeable about the Dakota but was thought by some to have a perfidious side to his nature.[18] Leforge was a relative newcomer to the northern frontier. He had come to Montana with his family in 1864 in search of gold but after failing to prosper in the mines had settled down in Bozeman to farm for a time. Here he became acquainted with the Crow, and finding their way of life agreeable, had married into the tribe.[19]

Two whites not previously known to the Crow would prove to be popular with most members of the tribe. John W. Smith and A.C. Leighton as post sutlers would give the Mountain Crow convenient access to trading facilities for the first time in six or seven years. The two men had formed a partnership in 1865 to service Fort Connor as sutlers and were later granted a license to operate a trading post at Fort C.F. Smith.[20] The existence of trading facilities at the new post, located just outside the gate, was probably responsible for the appearance of sixty Mountain Crow families within weeks after construction work on the post was initiated. One of their number, White Mouth, complained upon arrival that for many years past he had "been like a crazy man" for lack of trading opportunities.[21] Large numbers of other Mountain Crow drifted in over the next two or three weeks to establish camps in the general vicinity of the fort. The River Crow, for the most part, remained in the Milk River region with their new friends, the Atsina. One River Crow band did, however, join the Mountain Crow in their camp along the Big Horn River during early spring of 1867. Led by Wolf Bow, it would remain with the Mountain Crow until Fort C.F. Smith was abandoned.[22]

The Mountain Crow conducted their fall hunt in the Yellowstone Valley and then settled in for the winter near the fort, resuming a pattern of life similar to that followed during the years when the Company operated its Yellowstone posts.[23] The Dakota and their allies seem never to have been far from the post during the several months of its construction. In late August the troopers learned that a large contingent of Dakota warriors was camped on Tongue River. Warriors from that camp, and perhaps from other camps as well, apparently had in mind halting, or at least slowing, construction of the new fort. Beginning on September 2, work parties which found it necessary to perform duties at some distance removed from the installation were often fired upon, wagon trains bringing supplies and equipment to the new post were attacked, and mail parties were subjected to harassment. During the month of September, two men from the fort were killed by enemy warriors, and several more were wounded. However, construction continued apace, and the Indians withdrew, or at least ended their harassing tactics, in late October.[24] By the end of 1866, Dakota animus had obviously shifted away from Fort C.F. Smith to focus on its sister post, Fort Phil Kearny. On the morning of December 21, a combined force of Cheyenne and Dakota warriors lured a detachment of eighty men commanded by Captain William J. Fetterman into an ambush several miles north and west of the fort. All, including the contingent's commanding officer, were killed. What became known to whites as the Fetterman Massacre was a decisive victory for the Indians in the struggle for effective control of the Bozeman Trail.[25]

Dakota intransigence, strangely enough, didn't extend to the Crow. Members of the tribe consequently felt free to roam over and camp in areas which they had not visited for years. During the spring of 1867, for example, large numbers of Crow visited and camped near Fort Phil Kearny.[26] Furthermore, it was not at all unusual for the Crow to exchange visits with their enemies of long standing, both for social and trading purposes.[27] On at least one occasion, a band of Crow joined a war party organized by Dakota and Cheyenne warriors for the purpose of raiding a Shoshone camp.[28]

The sudden change in Crow-Dakota relations from implacable hostility to peaceful co-existence was undoubtedly due to the appearance of three military garrisons on the Bozeman Trail. The posts manifestly constituted a threat to the continued exercise of Dakota power in the region and therefore begged for eradication at the earliest possible moment. Red Cloud redoubled his efforts to form an alliance of Plains Indians, friend and foe alike, for the purpose of expelling all whites from the area.[29] Thomas Leforge happened to be present in a Crow camp when a delegation of Dakota warriors made an abortive attempt to enlist Crow aid in their crusade against whites. The guests were honored with a feast, after which they took turns haranguing their hosts about the importance of Crow participation in the effort to oust all whites. The major argument advanced on this occasion, according to Leforge, was that the Crow would be looked upon as traitors by other tribes if they did not join Red Cloud's movement.[30]

The army was aware of Dakota efforts to woo the Crow away from support of the whites, and was therefore concerned that the tribe might make common cause with its former enemy. Even before construction of Fort C.F. Smith was completed, Jim Bridger was dispatched to a large Crow camp located on Clark's Fork for the purpose of sounding out tribal leaders on just where their loyalties lay. Bridger reported back that he had discussed the matter with Blackfoot and Rotten Tail, both of whom admitted that friendly visits had recently been exchanged with their erstwhile enemies and that they indeed had been asked to fight alongside the Dakota against the whites. Both chiefs reassured Bridger, however, that although a few of their young men were in favor of joining Red Cloud's crusade, the vast majority of the Crow were dead set against aligning themselves with those who had only recently deprived them of a large chunk of their homeland.[31]

On September 29, 1866 James Beckwourth was sent to Iron Bull's camp, at the time also located on Clark's Fork, to shore up support for the white cause and to organize a detachment of Crow warriors for the purpose of renewing hostilities against the Dakota. But shortly after he arrived, he experienced a severe nose bleed and died shortly thereafter. Colonel Kinney didn't learn of the venerable mountain man's death until October 30. He had counted heavily on Beckwourth's presence to keep the tribe in line, and, in an alternative effort to cement friendly relations, convened a council with Crow leaders on October 31. Lieutenant George Templeton, Kinney's adjutant, attended the council and came away from the meeting with the distinct impression that the Crow were disappointed that Great Father's soldiers at the post had not yet taken the field against the Dakota. Templeton was persuaded that if military action in some form was not soon taken against the hostiles, the Crow would in fact go over to the Dakota cause.[32]

The humiliation experienced by Great Father's forces in the Fetterman debacle undoubtedly lowered whatever respect the Crow might have had for white warriors and must have weakened their resolve to withstand the blandishments of Red Cloud and his followers. Lieutenant Templeton was of the opinion that the outcome of the battle had convinced them that Great Father should abandon his recently-constructed forts. Perhaps in an attempt to buy their loyalty, Colonel Kinney hired Iron Bull and several other prominent members of the tribe to serve the army as scouts and spies in early January of 1867.[33]

The number of hostile Indians in the vicinity of the fort increased markedly in early 1867. Kinney reported to his superiors at Fort Phil Kearny in February that he had been informed by various Crow that at least 2,700 lodges of Dakota, Cheyenne, and Arapaho had congregated in the general vicinity of his post.[34] He also reported that, although the Crow still seemed to be friendly, a new source of alienation from the white cause had surfaced not long after news of the Fetterman incident began to circulate. According to the colonel, a number of Crow leaders had approached him in January of 1867 to complain that the tribe had never received annuities promised them for signing the treaty negotiated with them at Fort Union in July of 1866.[35]

Colonel Kinney was concerned enough about the complaint to appeal to higher authority for help. On February 8, he wrote the governor of Montana Territory to enlist his aid in satisfying Crow demands on this score. Otherwise, he warned the governor, the Crow could very well join the hostile tribes.[36] A few weeks later he likewise informed General Henry Wessells, who had by this time replaced Colonel Carrington as commanding officer of Fort Phil Kearny, that the Crow were becoming ever more insistent that the government live up to its treaty obligations.[37] General Wessells referred the matter to the commissioner of Indian affairs and also to his superior, General C.O. Augur, asking that they bring pressures to bear on the Indian Service to honor its treaty commitments with the Crow.[38] Kinney needn't have bothered; the treaty had never been placed before the Senate for ratification. It had instead been tabled by the commissioner of Indian affairs because the unsettled and chaotic situation in the area included in the proposed right-of-way rendered the treaty useless.[39]

Great Father's failure to fulfill the treaty's provisions did not in fact result in Crow disaffection from his troops in the area. Lieutenant Templeton was of the opinion by late March that their attitudes toward Fort C.F. Smith and its troops had improved dramatically. He attributed this welcome change to a realization on their part that Fort Phil Kearny had recently been reinforced with four companies of infantry and two companies of cavalry. That this new respect was not shared by the entire tribe, though, is indicated by a tale carried to Kinney by Wolf Bow. The River Crow chief claimed that an unidentified band of Crow planned to defect to the enemy as soon as the post's sutlers received their next shipment of goods. The plan, according to Wolf Bow, was that the dissidents would acquire powder and lead needed by the Dakota before leaving to join them.[40]

Throughout the summer months post personnel heard rumors that an attack on Fort C.F. Smith was imminent.[41] In an effort to neutralize the Dakota, Kinney sent Pierre Shane and Mitch Boyer out to surrounding hostile camps for the purpose of convincing the Indians that they should remain peaceful. John Richard, who in the past had been closely identified with the Oglala, was employed by the army to live with that tribe as a spy to report on their activities and movements. To make matters even grimmer, Colonel Kinney learned on July 15 that 600 Dakota warriors were being hosted by Long Horse in his camp.[42]

This was the situation when Colonel Luther P. Bradley replaced Kinney as commanding officer of Fort C.F. Smith on July 23, 1867. Four days after assuming command, Bradley wrote a report to the commandant at Fort Phil Kearny in which he outlined his assessment of the state of affairs in his new command. He expressed strong doubts about the loyalty of the Crow, pointing out that although tribal leaders professed friendship for whites, the insolence and threatening behavior of some younger warriors suggested to him that they secretly subscribed to the Dakota cause. He went on to say that, in his opinion, even supposedly friendly Crow engaged in trading ammunition secured from the post trader to enemy warriors. He ended his report by repeating the persistent rumor that his post was about to come under attack.[43]

When the long-expected attack finally came, it was anti-climactic in nature. On August 1 a civilian hay-cutting detail of nine men working for post sutler Leighton came under fire from a combined force of Dakota, Cheyenne, and Arapaho warriors. Twenty-one army personnel under Lieutenant Sigismund Sternberg had accompanied the detail as a military escort. As protection against attack, the small party had erected a crude stockade of logs and brush when they arrived, and as soon as the firing started, soldiers and hay cutters alike, made a beeline for the enclosure. Once inside, the defenders organized themselves to repel their attackers. Armed with Spencer breech-loading rifles brought to the post by Colonel Bradley only a week earlier they were able to hold the hostile warriors at bay.[44]

Sometime in late afternoon, the defenders selected one of their number to carry a message to the fort, about nine miles distant, asking for reinforcements. The messenger somehow made it through enemy lines, and Colonel Bradley dispatched twenty men to the aid of the besieged. The rescue party proved inadequate for the task; an additional eighty men armed with a howitzer were required to effect a successful rescue operation. A casualty count later revealed that one hay cutter had been killed and another wounded. Lieutenant Sternberg was also killed in the engagement, and one sergeant as well as two privates were wounded. Estimates of the number of assailants ranged from 500 to 800; estimates of enemy casualties ran from eight to twenty-five. The Crow were not directly involved in the incident, but it is more than likely that they were given advance notice that the attack was coming. With the exception of Iron Bull and a few of his followers, those camped in the vicinity of the post had hurriedly struck their tipis on July 30 and dispersed.[45]

In the meantime events in Washington were moving toward a resolution of the struggle between those who favored a peaceful approach to settlement of the Indian problem and those who advocated the use of force.[46] The Fetterman incident had added fuel to the fires of debate on Indian policy. The army stepped up its campaign to place the Bureau of Indian Affairs under its aegis, and it drew up plans for a punitive expedition against the miscreants. Peace advocates, led by Acting Commissioner of Indian Affairs Lewis V. Bogy, blamed Indian intransigence on the unwarranted

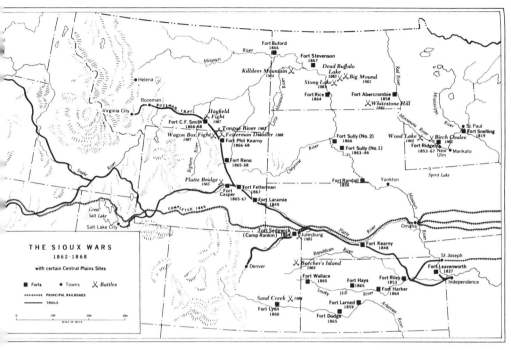

THE SIOUX WARS OF 1862-1868

Reprinted, by permission of the author, Robert M. Utley, *The Indian Frontier of the American West, 1846–1890*, University of New Mexico Press, 1984.

presence of troops on Indian lands. The political system took the path of least resistance and created a presidential commission in February of 1867 with a mandate to identify the causes of the Fetterman debacle and to ponder the battle's broader policy implications. General Alfred B. Sully was named chairman of the commission which also included Generals J.B. Sanborn and N.B. Buford as well as Colonel E.S. Parker, a Seneca Indian with close ties to General Grant. Two civilians, Judge J.F. Kinney and G.P. Beauvois, were also named to the body.[47]

After holding inconclusive meetings in the city of

Omaha and in Forts McPherson, Sedgwick, and Laramie, the commission split up. Sully and Parker, in company with Father de Smet, journeyed up the Missouri River where they held a series of inconclusive talks with several bands of Dakota Indians.[48] Judge Kinney was sent to Fort Phil Kearny to wean the Crow away from any attachment they might be forming with hostile Indians in the vicinity. He arrived at the fort on July 31 and found a small band of Crow Indians under White Mouth camped nearby. Runners were sent to Crow camps located on Tongue River to issue an invitation to come in for a council.[49] In addition, Colonel Kinney escorted a number of tribal leaders to Fort Phil Kearny on June 11 for that purpose.[50] Judge Kinney distributed six wagon loads of merchandise to the Indians before commencing deliberations, but whether they were distributed as gifts or as trade goods is a matter of controversy.

John W. Smith, sutler at Fort C.F. Smith, later wrote a letter to the editor of the Omaha Herald in which he charged Kinney with fraud in his dealings with the Crow. Smith contended that the sutler on that occasion had sold them goods which had been furnished him by the government for free distribution.[51] There may have been some foundation to Smith's charges. William Murphy, an enlisted man at Fort Phil Kearny who claimed to have witnessed the proceedings, later remembered that the Crow had paid dearly for their gifts with products of the chase. He also remembered that the six wagons in which Kinney had transported merchandise for the Indians left the fort full of furs.[52] Whatever the disposition of gifts intended for the Crow, Kinney's meeting with them came to nothing. The commission's report of the meeting stated only that the Indians with whom the judge had met expected to be protected by the government, if for no other reason than that the lands now occupied by the Dakota had been stolen from them. A *New York Times* summary of the meeting reported that the Crow had demanded that all whites be removed from Powder River country.[53]

The Fetterman Commission duly filed a general report in which it recommended that the government cease waging war with the Indians, set aside lands for their exclusive use, and create a legal mechanism with powers to adjudicate Indian complaints lodged against whites or their political system.[54] Its findings were generally congruent with those of the Doolittle Commission which had likewise completed its deliberations and had filed a report with the Congress on January 26, 1867. The two reports, along with increased Indian truculence in many parts of the West, were influential in the passage of legislation by Congress on June 20 which created the United States Peace Commission. The new body was authorized to conduct all future negotiations with Indian tribes and to establish reservations for all non-reservation Indians. Reservations were to serve a dual purpose; they would at the same time remove Indians from the paths of white settlement and provide settings in which the aborigines could be "civilized" for eventual incorporation into white society. To appease those who favored a policy which relied on force, the legislation also gave the president authority to use the army when peaceful methods proved ineffective.[55]

The commission was made up of four civilians named by Congress and three military men to be chosen by the president. Commissioner of Indian Affairs Nathaniel B. Taylor was identified as chairman by the enabling legislation which also named Samuel F. Tappan, a notorious do-gooder from Boston, Senator John B. Henderson of Missouri, and John B. Sanford, an attorney who had also served on the Fetterman Commission, as the other civilian members. President Johnson chose Generals William T. Sherman, Alfred H. Terry, and William S. Harney to complete the make-up of the new commission.[56]

The United States Peace Commission held its first meeting on August 7 in Omaha, Nebraska. It was decided there that two councils should be held. One was scheduled for the month of September and would treat with those Indians living north of the Platte River. The other was to be held during the month of October and would deal with those tribes living south of the river. The commissioners then chartered a steamship which carried them up the Missouri River to scout out possible reservation sites and to notify Indians of that area that they were expected at a council to be held at Fort Laramie in September. Returning to Omaha too late to make the September meeting, the commissioners postponed it until November and journeyed to Medicine Creek near Fort Larned where they held their scheduled meeting with the southern tribes in late October. After negotiating a treaty there, the commissioners, with the exception of General Sherman who was recalled to Washington to serve as a witness in Andrew Johnson's impeachment trial, made their way to Fort Laramie for the November council.[57]

Dr. H.M. Matthews was given the job of escorting the Crow delegation to Fort Laramie.[58] Matthews was unndoubtedly already well known to the tribe because he had served as a contract surgeon at Fort C.F. Smith from its founding until June 11, 1867 when he was transferred to Fort Phil Kearny.[59] Among assigned duties at his new posting, he assisted Judge Kinney in his deliberations with the Crow. Matthews returned to Fort C.F. Smith on September 12 as a Special Indian Agent. Mitch Boyer had previously been sent out to inform Crow leaders that they were expected at Fort Laramie in September to take part in a general peace council. A dozen or so principal men of the tribe had come in with Boyer on September 11 to inform Colonel Kinney that they didn't intend to make the long journey to meet with Great Father's representatives. On September 21 Matthews met with Long Horse and some of his followers, but the meeting ended in an atmosphere of mutual recriminations with Long Horse angrily leaving the meeting with his followers in tow. Dr. Matthews didn't give up. He held a council on October 11, with Blackfoot and several other tribal leaders, and after distributing gifts among them, received their assurances that they would make the trip. Two days later they all set out for the council site with a military escort provided by Colonel Bradley.[60]

When the United States Peace Commission arrived at Fort Laramie on November 9, its members found only a few Indians assembled there to participate in the scheduled proceedings. Conspicuous by their absence were the Dakota leaders most active in opposing the army's presence in the Bozeman Trail posts. Red Cloud had sent word to the commission that peace was possible only with the actual removal of the offending posts.[61]

The commission nonetheless held deliberations with the Crow delegation, which had been awaiting its arrival for several days. At ten o'clock on the morning of November 12, the Crow envoys were seated by rank on benches facing the commissioners who had already arranged themselves in a semicircle. Dr. Matthews introduced each Crow delegate, and Chairman Taylor then formally opened the proceedings with a statement that he had been sent to talk to the Crow in appreciation for their continued fidelity to the government. He went on to say that Great Father was aware that miners and other whites had in the past encroached upon Crow territory and that he wanted to set aside part of their traditional homeland for the exclusive and permanent use of the tribe. Payment would, of course, be made for any lands given up, and they would retain the right to hunt on all such lands. Taylor concluded his remarks with a statement to the effect that Great Father was prepared to provide the Crow with a saw mill, dwellings, cattle, farm implements, and teachers to assist them in making the transition from hunting to farming.[62]

The Crow delegation then huddled for a brief consultation, and then their first speaker, Bear's Tooth, took the floor. After vigorously shaking hands with each commissioner, he began by complaining about how poor he was and about what a difficult journey it had been from the Yellowstone River to Fort Laramie. Bear's Tooth then confirmed that he understood the remarks made by Chairman Taylor and then broke into a passionate plea for removal of the Bozeman Trail forts. His outburst was followed by a litany of charges levied against the Alien Culture, including the disappearance of Grizzly Bear following his visit to Washington in 1851, the pistol whipping of Crow participants at the treaty council of 1825, and the physical abuse experienced by the speaker from army personnel stationed at Fort C.F. Smith. He ended his diatribe with a flat rejection of Taylor's suggestion that the tribe give up buffalo hunting for farming.

Next, Blackfoot rose to shake hands with the commissioners. He prefaced his presentation with a reiteration of Bear Tooth's complaints about the hardships the Crow delegates had experienced on their trip to the council grounds and then, discarding his buffalo robe, placed it upon Chairman Taylor's shoulders. By this action, he explained, the two men became brothers. Blackfoot began his oration with the observation that reservation life would be incompatible with traditional Crow ways. He recommended that Great Father purchase rifles and horses for the tribe rather than spending the money necessary to create a reservation. Like Bear's Tooth, Blackfoot had a list of complaints to lodge against whites. Mainly he was upset that their political system had not lived up to the Treaty of 1851, despite the constancy of Crow friendship. He repeated Bear Tooth's query about the whereabouts of Grizzly Bear, and ended his speech with an impassioned plea for the removal of soldiers from the area and for the right of the tribe to continue its nomadic way of life.

Wolf Bow, the River Crow leader, was the third and final spokesman for the Crow delegation. He made a short and direct statement that the Crow had always been friendly with whites and that the government should therefore withdraw its troops and allow the tribe to continue its traditional ways. Similarities of themes in the presentations of the three chiefs was more than simple coincidence. Blackfoot had held a series of meetings on the trek to Fort Laramie in which he had achieved a consensus among the delegates on points to be emphasized with the commissioners. The council adjourned after Wolf Bow's presentation with an understanding that the principals would reconvene the following morning at ten o'clock.

Chairman Taylor opened the second day's proceedings by thanking the Crow representatives for the tribe's fast friendship with whites and for exercising restraint in not avenging themselves for mistreatment received at the hands of whites. To clear up the mystery of the missing chief, he explained that Grizzly Bear had been treated well on his visit to Great Father in Washington but that he had mysteriously disappeared on the return trip up the Missouri River. As compensation, the family of the missing chief would be given two horses. Taylor then got to the heart of the matter at hand by observing that however much the tribe might prefer to continue its traditional way of life, it must accept life on a reservation if for no other reason than that buffalo herds were rapidly disappearing. He then addressed himself to the concern expressed the previous day about the presence of white soldiers along the Bozeman Trail. He promised that Great Father would make a decision regarding the continued existence of the three posts by the following spring at the very latest.

Blackfoot rose to offer another defense of the Crow way of life by pointing out that the tribe's lands still contained an abundance of game. The Crow chief again reminded the commissioners that Great Father had not complied with all the provisions of the Treaty of 1851 and that it was therefore unrealistic that he should expect the tribe to sign yet another treaty. Wolf Bow followed Blackfoot, taking the floor to inform the commissioners that the Bozeman Trail was not really needed by white settlers because they could get to the gold fields of Montana by way of the Missouri River. He concluded his remarks with a request that the Crow be allowed to continue their nomadic existence.

Chairman Taylor then presented a treaty for acceptance by the Crow chiefs. They unanimously rejected the treaty until such time as the Bozeman Trail forts were abandoned and until the Dakota tribes had agreed to similar treaties. The commissioners gave up at this point and announced that the matter would be deferred until the following spring. If the council proceedings accomplished nothing else, they at least revealed that even if the Dakota had been unsuccessful in persuading the Crow to join a military alliance, the tribe was nonetheless committed to the proposition that Great Father's military presence was obnoxious and should therefore be removed. Why, the tribe was willing, in fact insistent upon, giving up the enhanced security so obviously offered by the existence of the posts is suggested in a letter written to Dr. Matthews by Colonel Bradley on January 10, 1868. Referring to food shortages being experienced by the Mountain Crow, Bradley observed that he had been informed by individuals long familiar with the area in which Fort C.F. Smith was located, that buffalo had greatly diminished in numbers there since establishment of the post.[63]

Before Matthews left Fort Laramie with his Crow charges, he received a formal appointment as agent for "the Crow Indians and other tribes inhabiting the vicinity of Fort Phil Kearny and Fort C.F. Smith."[64] Charged with responsibility for assembling not only the Crow for the spring council but the hostile Dakota tribes as well, Dr. Matthews convened a council at Fort Phil Kearny on January 2, 1868. Attended by Crow, Dakota, Cheyenne, and Arapaho warriors, the Indians were informed by the agent that because Great Father loved them, he wanted to negotiate a lasting peace in the region. Matthews warned, however, that if the council scheduled for the coming spring at Fort Laramie failed, Great Father might become angry enough to punish them.[65]

When asked by Matthews why Red Cloud was not in attendance, Dakota delegates told him that they had been sent to the meeting by Red Cloud just as Matthews had been sent by Great Father, and that when Great Father personally attended a meeting then so would Red Cloud. Following this exchange a Dakota chief rose to insist that all whites be removed from Dakota lands, charging that they were responsible not only for driving off buffalo herds but also for the persistence of intertribal warfare in the region. A Cheyenne chief got up to observe that he had heard a rumor that the Bozeman posts were to be abandoned and asked for confirmation from Matthews on this point. Blackfoot then rose to remind the agent that the Crow had always been friendly with whites and that they therefore wanted Great Father to give them lots of ammunition. Matthews then took the floor to conclude the conference by refusing to confirm or deny the rumor about removal of the forts. He could only promise, he said, that the peace commission would meet with them in the spring for the purpose of negotiating a treaty which would be satisfactory to all parties.[66]

Distribution of gifts clearly played a role in Dr. Matthews' strategy to get the Indians to the council site. He, for one thing, distributed gifts to the warriors who attended the aforementioned conference.[67] A week later John Richard was dispatched to Bozeman from Fort C.F. Smith to buy food for distribution to the Crow.[68] Commissioner Taylor directed a letter to the agent on March 11, 1868 in which he confirmed to Matthews that the Bozeman posts were to be closed and that council proceedings would therefore open on about May 11. He also advised Matthews that the distribution of lead and powder had been authorized for those who attended. The agent was informed that he could promise his charges that they would be given clothing upon their arrival at Fort Laramie.[69]

When Dr. Matthews and the Crow delegation arrived at Fort Laramie in early May, they found a number of Dakota, Cheyenne, and Arapaho delegates already present, but they learned that those present did not include Red Cloud. He and other holdouts had notified officials at Fort Laramie that they would not even consider a treaty until the Bozeman posts were actually abandoned. Again disappointed, the commissioners nevertheless treated with those Indians who were present. A treaty was signed by eleven Crow leaders on May 7 after only minimal discussion.[70] Representatives from the Oglala, Miniconjou, Yanktonai, Cheyenne, and Arapaho tribes signed similar treaties during the next three weeks. The military installations along the Bozeman Trail were then closed down, and Red Cloud and his followers signed appropriate treaties in early November.[71]

The Crow Treaty of 1868 was an expression of the peace advocates' approach to resolving the nation's Indian problem. It set aside a tract of land for the exclusive use of the tribe where, free from the distracting influences of whites and other Indians, its members could be introduced and converted to the Alien Culture's style of life. The reservation created by the treaty included all lands west of the 107th degree longitude lying between the southern border of present Montana and the Yellowstone River, encompassing approximately eight million acres. Acceptance of the treaty by the Crow legally extinguished all claims they may have had to any other lands, except that they retained the right to hunt on any unoccupied lands owned by the federal government.[72]

To initiate the transformation of the Crow from buffalo hunters into farmers, all heads of families were made eligible by the treaty to receive 320 acres of land for their exclusive use, along with seeds and agricultural implements in the amount of $100.00 for the first year and $25.00 for each of three additional years, as well as a one-time gift of a cow and two oxen. All other family members over the age of eighteen were in like manner authorized to select eighty acres for his or her exclusive use. A reservation farmer was to be furnished the tribe to instruct neophyte cultivators in proper agricultural procedures and methods. To maintain agricultural implements in good working order, a blacksmith was to be provided for each 100 persons cultivating the soil. As an added incentive the treaty promised $500.00 in gifts for each of three years to the ten new farmers who, in the judgment of their agent, grew the best crops during any given year. To process expected wheat harvests, a grist mill was authorized.

Of course it wasn't to be expected that the tribe would be able to raise enough foodstuffs to sustain itself during the first few years of transition from hunting and gathering to farming. Sustenance, therefore, in the form of rations amounting to one pound of meat and one pound of flour per day for each tribal member over the age of four, was to be provided by the government during each of the first four years of reservation life. In addition, to ease what would obviously be a difficult transition, the government obligated itself to annually provide every male over the age of fourteen with a woolen suit, a pair of pantaloons, a flannel shirt and one pair of woolen socks for a period of thirty years. Each female over the age of twelve was likewise promised a flannel shirt, a pair of woolen hose and twelve yards each of calico and cotton cloth. Sufficient flannel and cotton goods to make each child in the tribe a suit were also to be furnished on an annual basis. To complete the civilizing process envisioned by the peace advocates, the treaty specified that a teacher would be provided for every thirty children who could be induced or compelled to attend school. The government additionally promised to provide a physician, carpenter, miller, and an engineer for the reservation.

The Crow who placed their mark on the Treaty of 1868 were, with only one exception, of the Mountain Crow division of the tribe. Wolf Bow was the only representative of the River Crow division to assent to the document. Blackfoot's name appears thereon, but those of Long Horse and Iron Bull do not. Although it referred to the Crow tribe, the treaty would eventually be interpreted by the Indian Service as applying only to the Mountain Crow branch of the tribe. The River Crow were not completely neglected in the flurry of treaty making during the year 1868, however. W.J. Cullen, a seasoned Indian Service official, was appointed Special Agent for Montana in April of that year and given instructions to negotiate treaties with those tribes living along the Missouri River not already committed to reservation life.[73]

Cullen first journeyed to Fort Hawley where he arrived on July 7. The special agent held deliberations with the Atsina and completed treaty negotiations with them on July 13. He then turned his attention to the River Crow, some of whom also happened to be present at the post. He concluded a treaty with them on July 15 which created a reservation for their use in the Milk River region. Under the terms of the treaty, the River Crow were to be afforded the same opportunities to become "civilized" as the Mountain Crow.[74] However, the treaty was never submitted to the Senate for ratification, probably because Acting Commissioner of Indian Affairs Charles E. Mix believed that Cullen had exceeded his authority in negotiating with the River Crow.[75] The treaty with the Mountain Crow, on the other hand, was duly ratified by the Senate on July 25, 1868 and was accepted by President Johnson several weeks later, setting the stage for a new phase of Crow life.[76]

The citizens and officials of Montana Territory were less solicitous about the tribe's welfare, and the more economic potential white citizens of the territory saw in Crow lands, the less solicitous they became. Although the prospecting party led by James Stuart had failed to find gold in commercial quantities, it had in fact found color in some streams. Furthermore, harassment by Red Bear and his warriors had prevented the prospectors from exhausting all possibilities. The discovery of commercial quantities of the metal at Emigrant Gulch in 1865 undoubtedly heightened interest in the general area of the new reservation. In the first several months of Fort C.F. Smith's existence, four separate prospecting parties visited the post. The leader of the first of these told Lieutenant George Templeton that he and his men had found color in almost every stream or river they prospected but never enough to make mining operations profitable.[77]

The search for gold on or near the newly created reservation eventually played out for lack of significant discoveries, but there occurred an incident in 1866 which portended a more permanent form of economic activity for southwestern Montana. One Nelson Story, a native of Ohio, arrived in Bozeman in December of that year with a herd of 600 longhorn cattle. Story had come west in 1857 as an employee of a freighting contractor who was transporting merchandise to Salt Lake City. The Ohio lad fell ill at Fort Laramie on September 3, and had to leave the wagon train. Following his recovery, Story made his way to Denver where he engaged in the freighting business for several years. In 1863 he moved to Montana Territory and enjoyed some success in the mines at Alder Gulch.[78] Pocketing his mining profits, he went to Texas where he bought a herd of longhorns which would form the nucleus of what would turn out to be a most successful ranching operation. On the cattle drive from Texas back to Montana in 1866, Story and his men were detained at Fort Phil Kearny by Colonel Carrington for their own safety. Displaying the single-mindedness and daring that would characterize his subsequent career in Montana Territory, the entrepreneur ignored

Carrington's orders and slipped away to brave the threatening Dakota tribes. By traveling only at night, he was able to drive his herd safely through hostile territory to reach Bozeman in December.[79]

Although cattle had been raised in Montana on a small scale since about 1850, the introduction of Story's longhorns marked the beginning of the livestock industry in the territory. The *Montana Post* of Helena carried an article on July 28, 1866 which identified lands of the upper Yellowstone Valley as some of the best grazing and agricultural lands in Montana Territory. Story obviously agreed, because he turned his animals loose to graze along the banks of the Yellowstone in the general vicinity of Shields River. The freighter-cum-cowboy-cum-entrepreneur wasn't alone in coveting lands included in the new Crow reservation. The *Montana Post* acted as spokesman for those in the territory who resented the federal government's action in carving out such large amounts of Montana lands for Indian reservations. On July 21, 1866 the paper recommended that the nonsense of trying to civilize the Indian be replaced by a more aggressive national policy. An article in the January 26, 1867 issue called for an end to the "sickly sentimentalism" that had governed Indian policy in the past. A more realistic policy, it continued, would be to "wipe them out." Less harsh but equally insistent on Indian removal from the scene was the suggestion made in the December 21 edition that the Indian posed a barrier to the advance of civilization in the territory, and that he should therefore leave or suffer the consequences.[80]

Acting Governor Meagher continued to serve as point man in the struggle to force the Crow and other tribes in the territory to give way in the face of advancing white settlers. He recommended to the commissioner of Indian affairs in February of 1866 that treaty negotiations be scheduled for the River Crow with an eye to persuading them to renounce any claim or rights they might have on either the Musselshell or Yellowstone River Valleys.[81] Meagher, a month or so later, suggested to the commissioner that the Mountain Crow should also be called to a council for the purpose of persuading them to cede their lands to the government in return for the "usual guarantees of liberality."[82] His appeals to the federal government for help in removing Montana's Indians from the path of white settlement having fallen upon deaf ears, he settled on an approach to ridding the territory of its Indian population more in keeping with his military background. In October of 1866 Governor Meagher issued a call for volunteers to retaliate against Indians who reportedly were committing depredations in the vicinity of Bozeman. However, citizen apathy coupled with a shortage of funds temporarily thwarted his attempts to take the field against the territory's Indian population.[83]

Several months later John Bozeman provided the acting governor with a better excuse for the use of force against Montana's aboriginal population. On March 25 of 1867, Bozeman wrote to Meagher warning that the town of Bozeman and environs faced possible destruction if Indian depredations in the area were not soon met with force.[84] Meagher had lost his post as acting governor for a short time in late 1866 and early 1867. A new governor, Green Clay Smith, had been appointed governor in October of 1866 to replace Sidney Edgerton who had failed to return from the east. Smith in turn visited Washington early in 1867, once again leaving Meagher as acting governor.[85] In any event Meagher notified General Grant of the dangers faced by the community of Bozeman and requested military aid. Before a reply could be received, Bozeman and one Thomas Cover were attacked by a small band of Piegan while en route from Bozeman to Fort C.F. Smith. Cover survived the attack but Bozeman did not. When the acting governor received word of the incident, he immediately telegraphed the War Department requesting authorization to form a volunteer force of 800 men to take the field against hostile Indian warriors pending the arrival of regular troops. On May 7 General William Sherman wired Meagher that he was authorized to organize the force he had requested if the Indians in fact endangered settlers' lives.[86]

Several weeks later John Richard and Mitch Boyer arrived in Bozeman with the rumor that Fort C.F. Smith was in imminent danger of attack from hostile Indians in the area. Meagher dispatched fifty volunteers to rescue the fort, but when they arrived there on June 14, they learned that they were neither needed nor wanted. Colonel Kinney wouldn't allow them to cross the Big Horn River much less enter the fort.[87] At about this same time, the volunteer militia built two forts of their own. One was located eight miles east of Bozeman and the other at the confluence of the Shields and Yellowstone Rivers. However, the driving force behind the volunteer militia was removed shortly after the posts were completed. Acting Governor Meagher died in a drowning accident at Fort Benton in July.[88]

During its short existence the Montana militia engaged in no major battles with the territory's Indian population. The closest it came to actual fighting was in July when a small Piegan horse-stealing party wandered close enough to the recently-constructed post near Bozeman to be seen. Two Indians were killed in the encounter and a third captured. Meagher's military enterprise was probably doomed from the start. Tom Leforge served in a volunteer company for a time, and, according to him, volunteers were never issued arms of equipment of any kind. The militiamen, again according to Leforge, were mainly unruly ruffians and misfits. Desertions were common, and discipline was entirely lacking The men of one company in fact drowned their captain.[89] Meagher's militia seems to have created a greater problem for the army than for the Indians. General Alfred Terry was sent to investigate the operation, and finding no justification for the militia's existence, ordered it disbanded. Governor Green Clay Smith, on September 28, did so.[90] Looking back on the situation, it would appear that although the Indian population of Montana was never seriously threatened by Meagher's troops, it wasn't for lack of trying.

Great Father's growing interest in the Northern Plains was given physical expression after 1865 by a sudden extension of his military arm into the region and by a flurry of diplomatic activity on the part of the Indian Service. The rash of treaties negotiated with the Crow and their neighbors were clearly designed to make most of the lands still held by Indians available to white settlers. This approach to resolving the nation's Indian problem was a victory for those who advocated a peaceful solution, and the treaties therefore were blueprints for making the Indians disappear by making them over in the image of the Alien Culture. Construction of the Bozeman Trail forts was by way of clearing the path for development and expansion of mining in newly-created Montana Territory. The projection of military force into the area had a calming effect on Crow-Dakota relations, but at the same time a much more tenacious and dangerous foe was entering the region in unprecedented numbers.

NOTES

1. Robert M. Utley, *Frontiersmen in Blue: 1848–1865* (Lincoln and London: University of Nebraska Press, 1981), pp. 323–30.
2. Francis Paul Prucha, *The Great Father: The United States Government and the American Indians* (Lincoln and London: University of Nebraska Press, 1984), I, 485–6.
3. James C. Olson, *Red Cloud and the Sioux Problem* (Lincoln: University of Nebraska Press, 1965), pp. 13–14.
4. RCIA, 1866, House Executive Document No. 1 (Serial 1284), pp. 13–14.
5. Letter, N. Edmunds to D.N. Cooley, July 14, 1866, LRUM, reel 886; RCIA, 1867, House Executive Document No. 1, Part 2 (Serial 1326), p. 254. Shane's name was also spelled Chiene, Chienne, Chien, and Chene.
6. Letter, O. Guernsey to D.N. Cooley, July 19, 1866, LRUM, reel 886;RCIA, 1866, *op. cit.*, p. 172.
7. Olson, *op. cit.*, pp. 34–35.
8. Robert M. Utley, *Frontier Regulars: The United States Army and the Indian: 1866–1891* (New York: Macmillan Publishing Co., Inc.; London: Collier Macmillan Publishing Co., 1973), p. 99.
9. *Ibid*, p. 100.
10. Descriptions of the post can be found in James D. Lockwood, *Life and Adventures of a Drummer-Boy* (Albany: John Skinner, 1893), p. 154; Jerome A. Greene, ed., "We do not know what the Government Intends to do . . . . Lieutenant Palmer Writes from the Brozeman Trail," *Montana: The Magazine of Western History*, XXVIII, No. 3 (July, 1978), 21; Robert Beebe David, *Finn Burnett, Frontiersman* (Glendale: The Arthur H. Clark Company, 1937), p. 122.
11. RCFS, June, 1867; Francis B. Heitman, *Historical Register and Dictionary of the United States Army: From its Organization, September 29, 1779 to March 2, 1903* (Urbana: The University of Illinois Press, 1965), I, 602.
12. *Ibid*, I, 239; *RCFS*, July, 1867.
13. Heitman, *op. cit.*, I, 267; *RCFS*, June, 1868.
14. RCFS, September, 1866, September, 1867.
15. Elinor Wilson, *Jim Beckwourth: Black Mountain Man and War Chief of the Crows* (Norman: University of Oklahoma Press, 1972), pp. 92, 96, 147, 172, 174–5, 181.
16. Thomas B. Marquis, *Memoirs of a White Crow Indian* (Lincoln: University of Nebraska Press, 1974), p. 48.
17. *Ibid*, p. 15; "Captain H.E. Palmer's Account of the Connor Expedition," in Leroy R. Hafen and Ann W. Hafen eds., *Powder River Campaigns and Sawyer's Expedition of 1865*, XII of the Far West and the Rockies Historical Series (Glendale: The Arthur H. Clark Company, 1961), pp. 109–10. Boyer's name was also spelled Bouyer, Bouyier, Bouier.
18. Donald F. Danker, "The Violent Deaths of Yellow Bear and John Richard, Jr.," *Nebraska History*, LXIII, No. 2 (Summer, 1982), 138.
19. Marquis, *op. cit.*, pp. 4, 14, 36.
20. John S. Gray, "The Frontier Fortunes of John W. Smith," *Annals of Wyoming*, LI, No. 2 (Fall, 1979), 40–41.
21. George M. Templeton, *Diaries, 1866–1868* (typescript), Graff 4099, Folder 22, The Newberry Library, pp. 36–37.
22. *Ibid*, pp. 66–67.
23. *Ibid*, pp. 54–56; RCFS, December, 1866.
24. Templeton, *op. cit.*, pp. 36, 40–48; RCFS, September, October, 1866.

25. Robert M. Utley, *Frontier Regulars,* pp. 104–6.
26. William Murphy, "The Forgotten Battalion," *Annals of Wyoming,* VII, No. 2 (October, 1930), 396; Alson B. Ostrander, *An Army Boy of the Sixties,* ed. Howard R. Driggs (Yonkers-on-Hudson: World Book Company, 1936), p. 199.
27. For examples, see Letter, T.B. Burrows to T. Smith, July 16, 1867, RWLR; David, *op. cit.,* p. 166; Templeton, *op. cit.,* pp. 59–60, 68.
28. *Ibid,* p. 90.
29. Margaret Irvin Sullivant Carrington, *Ab-sa-ro-ka, Land of Massacre, being the Experiences of an Officer's Wife on the Plains; with an Outline of Indian Operations and Conferences from 1865–1878 by Henry B. Carrington* (5th ed.: Ann Arbor: University Microfilms International, 1979), p. 131.
30. Thomas Marquis, *Custer, Cavalry and Crows: The Story of William White as Told to Thomas Marquis* (Fort Collins: The Old Army Press, 1975), pp. 63–64.
31. Carrington, *op. cit.,* p. 130.
32. Templeton, *op. cit.,* pp. 47, 50–51.
33. *Ibid,* pp. 58–59; Letter, J.V.D. Reeves to E.W. Smith, December 24, 1867, LRUM, reel 887.
34. Merrill J. Mattes, *Indians, Infants and Infantry: Andrew and Elizabeth Burt on the Frontier* (Denver: The Old West Publishing Company, 1960), p. 129.
35. Letter, N.C. Kinney to T.L. Burt, February 9, 1867, RWLR.
36. Letter, N.C. Kinney to Governor of Montana, February 8, 1867, General Correspondence, 1864–1888, Executive Office, Record Series 40, Box 1, Folder 3, HSML.
37. Letter, N.C. Kinney to H.W. Wessells, February 24, 1867, LRUM, reel 887.
38. Letter, N.C. Kinney to Commissioner of Indian Affairs, March 15, 1867, *ibid;* Letter, C.C. Augur to Commissioner of Indian Affairs, April 6, 1867, *ibid.*
39. TCG, 39th Congress, 2nd Session, reel 36, p. 1797.
40. Templeton, *op. cit.,* pp. 68–69.
41. Letter, N.C. Kinney to T.L. Breck, March 1, 1867, RWLR; Letter, T.B. Burrows to Assistant Adjutant General, July 12, 1867, *ibid.*
42. Letter, A. Sully to E.S. Parker, November 30, 1869; LRMS, reel 489; Templeton, *op. cit.,* pp. 78–79.
43. Letter, L.P. Bradley to J. Smith, July 27, 1867, RWLR.
44. For contemporary accounts of the battle, consult Letter, T.B. Burrows to G.M. Templeton, August 3, 1867, RWLR; Templeton, *op. cit.,* p. 81; RCFS, August, 1867. For an authoritative secondary source, see Jerome A. Greene, "The Hayfield Fight: A Reappraisal of a Neglected Action," *Montana: The Magazine of Western History,* XXII, No. 4 (October, 1972), 30–43.
45. Templeton, *op. cit.,* pp. 81–82.
46. Olson, *op. cit.,* pp. 51–53.
47. Kinney, who incidentally was not related to Colonel Kinney, at the time was serving as post sutler at Fort Phil Kearny, and Beauvois was a St. Louis businessman with many years of trading experience among the Dakota.
48. Letter, P.J. de Smet to N.G. Taylor, June 1, 1867, LRUM, reel 887.
49. *Indian Hostilities,* Senate Executive Document No. 13 (Serial 1308), pp. 126–8.

50. General Order No. 15, June 11, 1867, RWDS; Templeton, *op. cit.*, p. 76.

51. *New York Times*, September 24, 1867, p. 1.

52. Murphy, *op. cit.*, p. 396.

53. RCIA, 1867, House Executive Document No. 1, Part 2 (Serial 1326), p. 3; *New York Times*, October 8, 1867, p. 5.

54. Olson, *op. cit.*, p. 56.

55. Prucha, *op. cit.*, I, 488–90.

56. *Ibid.*

57. Olson, *op. cit.*, pp. 66–68.

58. Matthews was a native of Monmouth, Illinois. Greene, *op. cit.*, p. 26.

59. RCFS, August, September, 1867.

60. Templeton, *op. cit.*, pp. 84–88.

61. Olson, *op. cit.*, p. 68.

62. This account of the Treaty Council of 1867, is, unless otherwise indicated, taken from Louis L. Simonin, *The Rocky Mountain West in 1867* (Lincoln: University of Nebraska Press, 1966), pp. 93–116. A heavily edited account of the proceedings can be found in Vine Deloria and Raymond De Mallie, eds., *Proceedings of the Great Peace Commission of 1867–1868* (Washington: The Institute for the Development of Indian Law, 1975), pp. 86–92.

63. Letter, L.P. Bradley to H.M. Matthews, January 10, 1868, LRMS, reel 488.

64. Letter, N.G. Taylor to H.M. Matthews, November 15, 1867, ROLS, reel 85.

65. George P. Belden, *Belden, the White Chief; or Twelve Years Among the Wild Indians of the Plains,* ed. James S. Brisbin (Athens: Ohio University Press, 1944), pp. 388–93.

66. Greene, *op. cit.*, pp. 27–29.

67. *Ibid.*

68. Special Order No. 15, January 10, 1868, RWDS.

69. Letter, N.G. Taylor to H.M. Matthews, March 11, 1868, ROLS, reel 86.

70. Deloria, *op. cit.*, p. 112.

71. Olson, *op. cit.*, pp. 74–75, 81.

72. The treaty has been reproduced in George E. Fay, ed., *Treaties, Land Cessions, and Other U.S. Congressional Documents Relative to American Indian Tribes, 1825–1912* (Greeley: Museum of Anthropology, 1982), pp. 9–15 and in Charles J. Kappler, ed., *Indian Affairs: Laws and Treaties* (2nd ed.: Washington: Government Printing Office, 1904), II, 1008–11.

73. Letter, C.E. Mix to W.J. Cullen, April 30, 1868, ROLS, reel 86. Cullen had previously served as Superintendent of Indian Affairs for the state of Minnesota. Roy W. Meyer, *History of the Santee Sioux* (Lincoln: University of Nebraska Press, 1967), p. 100.

74. Letter, W.J. Cullen to C.E. Mix, July 18, 1868, LRMS, reel 488; Fay, *op. cit.*, pp. 15–19.

75. Letter, C.E. Mix to W.T. Otto, September 8, 1868, LRMS, reel 488.

76. Fay, *op. cit.*, p. 14.

77. Templeton, *op. cit.*, pp. 35, 39, 47, 49.

78. Percival G. Lowe, *Five Years a Dragon, and Other Adventures on the Great Plains* (Norman: University of Oklahoma Press, 1965), p. 248; Letter, N. Story to E.A. Brininstool, October 5, 1920, Thomas Le Forge MS Collection, B-L522-th, Archives, American Heritage Center, University of Wyoming.

79. Merrill G. Burlingame, *The Montana Frontier* (Helena: State Publishing Company, 1942), p. 266.

80. Merrill G. Burlingame, *Historical Background for the Crow Indian Treaty of 1868,* unpublished manuscript, Small Collections No. 1045, Folder 6, HSML, pp. 48, 62–63.

81. Letter, T.F. Meagher to Commissioner of Indian Affairs, February 13, 1866, LRMS, reel 488.
82. Letter, T.F. Meagher to Commissioner of Indian Affairs, April 20, 1866, *ibid.*
83. James L. Thane, Jr. "The Montana Indian War of 1867," *Arizona and the West,* X, No. 2 (Summer, 1968), 154.
84. Robert G. Athearn, *Thomas Francis Meagher: An Irish Revolutionary in America* (Boulder: University of Colorado, 1949), p. 157.
85. Clark C. Spence, *Territorial Politics and Government in Montana: 1864-89* (Urbana, Chicago, London: University of Illinois Press, 1975), pp. 43, 51.
86. Athearn, *Thomas Francis Meagher,* p. 161.
87. Templeton, *op. cit.,* pp. 76-77; Stuart, *op. cit.,* II, 64-65.
88. Spence, *op. cit.,* p. 53.
89. Marquis, *Memoirs,* pp. 16-20.
90. Thane, *op. cit.,* pp. 167-8.

EIGHT

THE NEW TRADING POST ON MISSION CREEK

The reservation phase of Crow history set in motion by the Treaty of 1868 was grounded on the premise that the Crow could be made over in the image of whites. It seemed such a simple matter, really. All the Indians had to do was give up their traditional nomadic life in favor of a sedentary existence and redirect their energies away from the chase to the plow. Then, by transmitting the Alien Culture's basic skills, values, and ideas to the tribe's young through education, the next generation would be prepared to enter the mainstream of white society. But the Crow would prove to be less than enthusiastic about losing their identity. In fact they would resist attempts to alter their style of life at almost every turn. The early years of reservation existence would therefore largely be the story of Crow efforts to maintain their traditional ways within limitations imposed upon them by the reservation and to nullify those provisions of the treaty designed to effect the intended metamorphosis from Indian into white.

The tribe began reservation life in an atmosphere of reform in the conduct of Indian affairs. One of the more notable legislative responses to calls for reform was creation of the Board of Indian Commissioners by Congress, with the support of President Grant, on March 24, 1869. Created mainly to monitor the purchase and disbursement of goods intended for Indians, the board's first appointments suggested that the president believed the nation's Indian population would benefit from a dose of Christian charity. Most appointees were wealthy philanthropists with long histories of involvement in church-related activities. Mountain man Robert Campbell was included in Grant's initial appointments, but it isn't clear whether he was chosen for his Christian philanthropy or for his years of experience among the Indians.[1]

President Grant's choice for commissioner of Indian affairs was probably met with mixed feelings by reformers. He chose Ely S. Parker whose appointment must have been welcomed by some because, as a member of the Seneca tribe, he was of Indian heritage. On the other hand Parker would have been suspect in the eyes of other reformers because he came to the job with a military background, including a stint as Grant's aide-de-camp during the Civil War. Peace advocates must have likewise had ambivalent feelings about the president's approach to staffing Indian agencies. At the request of a group of prominent Quakers, he agreed to appoint a number of individuals of that denomination as agents. and by the summer of 1869, Quakers were serving as agents in Nebraska, Kansas, and Indian Territory. For this reason, what in the past had been referred to as the Peace Policy, was sometimes referred to as the Quaker Policy. But then a number of agencies during the early years of Grant's administration were staffed with army officers. At first blush this practice would appear to have been in direct contravention to the Peace Policy. As it turned out, though, such appointments were made simply to provide postings for the plethora of officers left over from the Civil War.[2]

Military officers rather than Quakers were chosen to staff Indian Service posts in Montana Territory. Accordingly, Civil War veteran, Captain Erskine M. Camp, was appointed as agent for Crow reservation in June of 1869.[3] At the same time the territorial governor was relieved of his responsibilities for Indian matters with the creation of a new office, Superintendent for Indian Affairs for Montana Territory. General Alfred A. Sully, an officer of broad experience on the Indian frontier, was named to this post.[4] A civilian, Leander M. Black, was designated as Special Indian Agent by Commissioner Parker to oversee the purchase and shipment of the 1869 annuity goods destined for the Crow tribe. A native of Crab Orchard, Kentucky, Black had emigrated to the gold fields of Colorado in 1862. Apparently unsuccessful in the mines, he turned to other pursuits in the new settlement of Denver. Here he made a small fortune fulfilling contracts to furnish hay and grain to the army.[5] Black was not without experience on the Indian frontier. He had served General Connor as a freighting contractor on that officer's ill-fated Powder River campaign in 1865.[6]

Sully, Black, and Camp traveled by rail to Sioux City, Iowa together, interrupting their journey in Chicago long enough to purchase a saw mill for the agency. Captain Camp left his traveling companions at Sioux City. Here he boarded the steamboat, *Fanny Baker*, to accompany annuity goods destined for the Crow. The general and Black continued by rail to Corinne, Utah where they made arrangements to tranship the machinery destined for the agency by wagon train to Bozeman.[7] They hired a coach to take them to the same destination, arriving there in late July. Sully then made his way to Helena to take up his new duties there, after appointing Black as temporary agent for the Crow reservation pending Camp's arrival with the annuity goods. General Sully later awarded Black a contract to construct buildings, which would make up the agency compound, on Mission Creek, ten miles or so west of the Big Bend of the Yellowstone and not far from the south bank of the

river.[8] The creek actually was named after the fact by
employees of the agency who, in the past, had
associated Indian agencies with Christian missions.[9]
Sully chose the location, justifying his selection on its
proximity to Fort Ellis, an abundance of good grazing
lands, and plentiful supplies of timber.[10]

Agent Camp, meanwhile, had experienced delay
after delay in his voyage up the Missouri River. His
progress had been slowed by orders given him by
Sully to distribute the annuities for several other
tribes being carried by the *Fanny Baker*. His progress
was stopped cold some fifty miles below the mouth of
Milk River by unseasonably low water.[11] Superintendent Sully made arrangements for a wagon train to
haul the merchandise from that point to the newly-
constructed agency where goods and agent arrived on
November 20.[12] The agency complex of buildings was
named Fort Parker in honor of the commissioner of
Indian affairs. Situated on a bench adjacent to
Mission Creek, it comprised buildings built to serve
as warehouses, offices, a trading post, and housing, all
enclosed by a stockade which measured 10 feet in
height and 200 feet on each side. Two blockhouses
were set on opposite corners.[13] The Crow must have
assumed that all buildings constructed by whites
conformed to this familiar configuration.

Agent Camp hired a storekeeper, a herder, a
messenger, and three laborers to assist him in
implementing the Treaty of 1868. If he did genuinely
try to fulfill his obligations as an agent in this regard,
he was singularly unsuccessful. Agricultural activities
during his tenure were limited to breaking four acres
of ground for the cultivation of vegetables,
undoubtedly for consumption by agency employees. If
he tried to implement the treaty's educational provision, his efforts came to naught. The agent
complained in his first and only annual report that in

his experience the obstacles in teaching "the arts of civilization" to his charges were well nigh insurmountable.[14] Actually, Camp seems to have been a poor choice as agent. J.W. Frost, an agency employee, directed a complaint to Commissioner Parker about Camp's performance as agent less than a month after the captain assumed his new duties. Frost charged him with having fraudulently taken robes and furs from the Crow and for having lost their confidence as a result of his intemperate habits. Instructed by Parker to investigate Frost's charges, Sully reported back that he had been unable to corroborate Camp's culpability in the matter of the peltries but did confirm that the captain, indeed, did have a drinking problem.[15]

Camp's service as agent lasted for only a year, but when he was terminated on September 23, 1870, it was not for malfeasance; rather he was routinely released in compliance with legislation passed by Congress which ended the use of army officers in the Indian Service.[16] Fellows D. Pease, originally of Pennsylvania, was chosen to serve as the tribe's second agent. He had come to the frontier as a freighter with the Harney expedition of 1856 and later served as sutler for Fort Pierre, where he was accused of illegally selling guns and ammunition to Indians. Eventually cleared of the charges by a commission created by General Sully, he gave up his license as sutler and entered the fur trade in 1865.[17] His first official connection with the Indian Service occurred in 1869 when Sully appointed him temporary agent for the Blackfoot reservation until such time as an army officer could be found for the post. Pease enjoyed a special place among the Crow as a white because he was married to a member of the tribe.[18] The same legislation that barred Camp from continuing as agent also deprived Sully of his post as Superintendent of Indian Affairs for Montana Territory. He was replaced by Jasper A. Viall of Keokuk, Iowa on October 13, 1870.[19]

Pease seems not to have taken his responsibilities as agent any more seriously than had his predecessor. He maintained a home in Bozeman where he spent most of his time. Furthermore, he was frequently absent from the territory. Granted a leave of absence for ninety days on May 17, 1871 he received a sixty-day leave on February 20, 1872, which was later extended to May 1.[20] Bozeman's daily newspaper, the *Avant Courier*, reported on October 31, 1872 that Pease had recently returned from a trip to the east.[21] There is nothing in the record to indicate that he received official sanction for this absence. The peripatetic agent began to agitate for additional leave early the next year to take care of personal business. Unsuccessful in receiving approval in this instance, he asked for emergency leave several months later to attend to pressing needs of his ailing father in Pennsylvania. Granted approval in late April, he was absent from his post on that occasion until June 27.[22]

The only provision of the treaty to be implemented by Pease was Article X; it dealt with agency personnel. He immediately hired a farmer, a miller, two blacksmiths, an engineer, a physician, and a carpenter as authorized. The new agent also added six unauthorized laborers to the four previously hired by Camp.[23] A fire which destroyed some agency buildings in October of 1872 necessitated the hiring of an additional carpenter and seven more laborers.[24] Examination of the backgrounds of agency personnel during the Pease years suggests that for the most part they were human detritus left over from earlier times and deposited along the banks of the Yellowstone by an advancing frontier. Pease was not the only refugee from the fur trade. Pierre Shane served as agency interpreter and Mitch Boyer worked as a sometime laborer. The frontier army was also represented. Dr. Francis Geisdorff, who had served as a contract surgeon at Fort C.F. Smith, was hired as agency physician. Barney Bravo, employed as a laborer, had been stationed at both Fort Phil Kearny and Fort C.F. Smith and had done time in the stockade for desertion at his last posting. Unemployed miners comprised the majority of the labor force at any given time.[25]

Pease, Geisdorff, and Boyer were all married to Crow women. Thomas Leforge, who had also married into the tribe and who occasionally worked as a laborer at the agency, maintained that numerous whites other than agency employees consorted with Crow women in and about the agency. According to Leforge, agency life was attractive to some whites from the standpoint that it placed almost no demands on the individual. Necessities of life could be satisfied through annuities and subsistence goods furnished by the government to consorts. The only work which need be performed was hunting and trapping for peltries, and this only if one wanted to purchase luxuries.[26] Agency laborers were paid $50.00 per month and provided with room and board.[27] The labor force was characterized by frequent turnovers in personnel. During the month of January, 1873, for instance, there occurred a turnover of one-half of the laborers employed by the agency.[28] The type of individuals hired by Pease, many of them married to Crow women, undoubtedly contributed to the high rate of turnover. Another factor was that the miners and prospectors employed as laborers customarily left the agency at the first hint of a new strike anywhere in the general area.

The high attrition rate of agency workers probably had little or no effect on the agency's operations because it is obvious that at any given time the agency was overstaffed. Late in the year 1871, Acting Commissioner of Indian Affairs H.R. Clum complained to Superintendent Viall that Pease was spending $6,000.00 more in pay for laborers than authorized by the Treaty of 1868 and that his expenditures should be reduced accordingly. Clum undoubtedly had a point. Thomas Leforge recalled in his memoirs that he and several other laborers were sent by Pease into the mountains one autumn to cut logs. Leforge and his fellow workers took their families and a large store of provisions with them and remained in the mountains until the following spring, dancing and feasting but without felling a single tree. When Pease criticized them on their return for doing nothing all winter, Leforge reminded him that they had undoubtedly been as productive as he, Pease, had been.[29]

In late January of 1873, the agent's cavalier attitude toward his job was brought to an abrupt halt by a personnel change in the office of superintendent. Jasper Viall was replaced by a Methodist Episcopalian minister named James A. Wright of Ottumwa, Iowa.[30] Pease must have had advance warning that his administration of the agency would in the future be subjected to more intense scrutiny than had been the case under either Sully or Viall. In early January he requested copies of Rules and Regulations of the Office of Indian Affairs and a few weeks later asked that a copy of the Indian Appropriations Act of 1872 be furnished him from the office of the commissioner of Indian affairs.[31] And, as it turned out, Pease had good reason to be concerned because Wright brought a reforming zeal to the job never displayed by either of the two previous occupants of the office.

Even before he left Iowa to assume his new duties in Montana Territory, Wright made recommendations to the Board of Indian Commissioners regarding the suppression of liquor traffic in the area to be placed under his jurisdiction, along with suggestions for new procedures in the letting of contracts for annuity goods.[32] Immediately upon his arrival in Helena, Wright requested, unsuccessfully as it turned out, permission to consult personally with the commissioner of Indian affairs regarding his duties as superintendent.[33] And, after only two months on the job, he provided the commissioner with a pessimistic assessment of the state of Indian affairs in the territory. His most serious indictment of the system had to do with the character of employees in the several Montana agencies. Wright contended that most lacked the morality and integrity necessary to set proper examples for the Indian. His remedy for what he regarded as a calamitous situation was to replace existing agents with men of strong Christian commitment.[34]

The new superintendent's program to reform Crow Agency was initiated in early March. Pease was reminded by Wright that some of his employees were living with Crow women without benefit of clergy and decreed that all such must marry within thirty days or remove themselves from agency premises. He, in addition, instructed Pease to rid his agency of all unemployed whites being subsisted with Crow rations. On April 25, a Methodist minister from Bozeman, Matthew Bird, legalized living arrangements for all but one of the offenders. William Parker, a Catholic, refused to be married in a Protestant ceremony and was subsequently fired by Pease.[35]

The termination of Pease as agent, as had been the case with Camp, came about as a result of policy changes in staffing procedures. Article VI of the 1873 Appropriations Act abolished the post of Montana Superintendent of Indian Affairs. Consistent with President Grant's new policy of staffing agencies in

Montana with Methodist clergymen, Pease was relieved of his duties as agent for the Crow reservation and was succeeded in that office by ex-Superintendent Wright on September 20, 1873.[36] Wright continued at least one tradition established by his predecessor. When the minister took over his new office, the agency had a total of sixteen employees. A year later, this number had been increased to twenty-five. Most of the increase was justified by a need for more laborers to complete repair of agency buildings destroyed by the fire which had occurred during the tenure of Pease.[37]

In other ways Wright's administration of the agency stands in sharp contrast to that of Pease. Wright, his wife, son, daughter, and son-in-law took up residence at the agency. Furthermore, the minister actively tried to create an environment on the reservation consistent with its mission as a "civilizing" force. Within weeks of taking over as agent, he organized a Methodist church for employees. Services included psalm singing by Wright's daughter accompanied by Mrs. Wright on an organ the family had brought from Iowa. A few Indians occasionally attended services, but only, at least in Thomas Leforge's opinion, to listen to the music.[38] Temperance was imposed on employees by dictum and supported through the founding of an agency chapter of the International Order of Good Templars, a society founded in 1851 to fight the evils of alcohol.[39] The lodge also served as a focus for employee social activities. In 1874 it sponsored the agency's Independence Day celebration which began at dawn with the firing of a howitzer. Later in the morning, employees assembled for a prayer offered by Wright, followed by the singing of *America*. The Declaration of Independence was then read by a visitor from neighboring Fort Ellis, after which Wright and several prominent citizens from Bozeman delivered patriotic speeches and offered toasts to the Republic. The day's festivities ended with rousing cheers to the Fourth of July given by all present.[40]

Wright, as agent, continued the campaign to rid the agency of undesirable whites he had inaugurated while superintendent. He enjoyed no more success in this enterprise as agent than he had as superintendent. Frustrated, he appealed to Commissioner E.B. Smith in May of 1874 for guidance, complaining that unemployed whites living with, but not married to, Crow women had refused to obey his orders to leave the reservation. Smith responded that as commissioner he had authority to order the removal from reservations of any individuals whose presence was detrimental to the welfare of Indians. He asked for the names of offenders so that he could initiate legal proceedings against them.[41] Wright subsequently wrote two more letters of complaint to Smith but never did furnish names as requested.[42] The exchange of letters on this subject ended in late September with a query from Acting Commissioner H.R. Clum in which he testily asked for the names of those individuals Wright wished to ban from the agency.[43]

Wright's frustration in dealing with this intractable problem may have contributed to his decision to leave the agency after less than a year's service. In a letter written in early June of 1874, but not posted until September, he resigned his position, citing problems created by "vile loafers, Blacklegs, and cutthroats."[44] Dr. Wright claimed, in fact, that he had uncovered a plot to murder him and his entire family while they slept. It is likely that other factors were also operative in his decision to give up the position. He was not a popular man. Nelson Story, perhaps Bozeman's most prominent citizen, thought him incompetent, and Territorial Governor B.F. Potts confided to Secretary of the Interior Columbus Delano that Wright was a

CROW LEADERS IN TRADITIONAL DRESS
The figure in the center is Blackfoot, flanked by Long Horse on his right and by
White Calf on his left.
Courtesy National Museum of the American Indian,
Smithsonian Institution

timid old fool who should retire to his farm in Iowa and that he not only lacked business acumen but that he, in addition, tended to heed bad counsel over good.[45] Potts also maintained that the Crow had never become reconciled to him as their agent. There appears to have been substance to at least the latter charge. In October, 1873 Blackfoot registered a complaint with the commissioner of Indian affairs to the effect that as agent, Wright was parsimonious in his dealings with the tribe. And in a letter to President Grant several months later, the chief referred to the agent as "your strange man."[46]

Furthermore, Wright's lack of administrative skills was a source of annoyance to his superiors. He was barraged with angry letters complaining about his careless handwriting, frequent lapses in reporting employee statistics, and irregularities in supply orders.[47] The number and frequency of recriminations from Washington may have contributed to his decision to resign. Whatever the reasons, his resignation was accepted on October 9, 1874 to be effective upon arrival of his successor.[48] Wright had already accepted a lateral transfer to Fort Hall in Idaho Territory and had asked that he be allowed to make the move before winter weather made travel difficult. However, his replacement, Dexter E. Clapp, didn't arrive at Crow Agency until December 6, and the hapless minister was forced to move his family to Idaho in the dead of winter.[49]

Clapp, the fourth Crow agent in five years, was, like Wright before him, a nominee of the Methodist Episcopal Church.[50] He came from quite a different background than had his predecessor, though. His past experience included service in the Union Army during the Civil War. Clapp joined the 148th New York Infantry on September 1, 1862 with the rank of captain and during the course of the war advanced to the rank of brigadier general.[51] Clapp's tenure as Crow agent lasted until October 23, 1876.[52]

A concern shared by all four agents was the ambiguous status of the River Crow branch of the tribe. The Treaty of 1868, in the view of the Indian Service, had been negotiated exclusively with the Mountain Crow. It wasn't quite that simple, of course. Wolf Bow, a River Crow leader, had also placed his mark on the treaty. The situation was further complicated by the treaty which had been negotiated by W.J. Cullen with the River Crow in July of 1868 but never ratified by the Senate. As a stop-gap measure, pending final resolution of the problem, the River Crow were assigned to the Milk River Reservation, recently established for the Atsina and Assiniboine tribes. Fort Browning agency was located on Milk River approximately seventy miles north of its confluence with the Missouri River.[53] Wolf Bow's band, however, remained with the Mountain Crow and was consequently informally attached to Fort Parker.[54]

Conditions at Milk River turned out to be less than ideal for the River Crow. Relations between the Assiniboine and Crow tribes had, over the years, ranged from outright hostility to tentative amity. Under reservation circumstances a competition soon developed between the two for the friendship of the Atsina tribe. A rash of marriages between the Assiniboine and Atsina operated to the detriment of the River Crow in this regard.[55] Then there was an outbreak of the dreaded smallpox disease on the reservation in September of 1869. Fortunately for the River Crow, they happened to be camped about twenty-five miles away at the time. When news of the disease reached them, they scattered westward into the Judith Basin. The River Crow were not so lucky in the next epidemic. Smallpox broke out in a large

River Crow camp located on the Musselshell River during the following summer, and they again dispersed. Twenty-two lodges returned to the agency, forty lodges fled to Fort Parker and the remainder again retreated to the Judith Basin.

Milk River Reservation became even less hospitable during the summer of 1871 when large numbers of Yankton and Yanktonai Dakota attached themselves to the agency. At about the same time, another heredity enemy of the Crow, the Arapaho, entered the reservation in large numbers.[56] Overcrowding prompted the Indian Service to close Fort Browning and replace it with two new agencies in 1873. Fort Peck, located near the mouth of Milk River, was given responsibility for the Dakota and Arapaho Indians as well as for a few of the Assiniboine. Fort Belknap agency, constructed near present Harlem, Montana, assumed control over the Atsina tribe and those Assiniboine not administered by Fort Peck.[57] These changes left the River Crow without an administrative home.

The obvious solution to the River Crow problem was to place them on the Mountain Crow reservation. And, in fact, attempts were made soon after the founding of Fort Parker to effect a union of the two tribal divisions. Superintendent Sully informed Commissioner Parker in late 1869 that the River Crow had been on the verge of joining the Mountain Crow when the outbreak of smallpox on Milk River Reservation prompted Sully to delay the union as a measure to protect the Mountain Crow from the epidemic. Sully was being overly optimistic about the ease with which unification could be accomplished. There were, as it turned out, a number of factors involved in the situation which militated against union. One of the major complicating factors was the failure of the Indian Service to make alternative arrangements for the River Crow after their treaty failed to be ratified. That nothing was done in this regard meant, among other things, that no funds were authorized for that branch of the tribe's subsistence nor for their annuities. This oversight was remedied in 1871 when $30,000 annually was authorized for those purposes.[58]

Another obstacle to unification was the considerable amount of tension which had built up over the years between the two divisions of the tribe. The Mountain Crow, for instance, had come to believe that their brethren had on occasion been too friendly with several of the Dakota tribes.[59] For their part the River Crow felt that the Mountain Crow treated them with contempt as inferiors. Several of their number complained to Agent Wright in 1873 that the Mountain Crow often teased them about being poor, and that on a recent occasion had referred to their habitations as ghost lodges.[60] By all accounts the River Crow were indeed in more impecunious circumstances than their fellow tribesmen.[61]

Competition between agents over control of the River Crow added to the difficulties of unification. In 1871 Superintendent Viall made an administrative decision which in effect dictated that the River Crow would continue to be administered at Fort Browning Agency when he issued instructions that their annuities would henceforth be shipped to that entity.[62] Agent Pease subsequently complained that although the River Crow had been formally detached from his agency, large numbers of them still insisted on being subsisted from his stores.[63] A.J. Simmons, agent at Fort Browning, on the other hand, assured Viall that the River Crow preferred to continue to receive their goods at his agency.[64] James Wright in his role as superintendent decided in early 1873 that they should be administered from Crow Agency in the hope that they would move away from the whiskey merchants who plied their trade in such large numbers in the Milk River area. In late March of that year, he issued orders that their annuity goods should henceforth be shipped to Pease for distribution.[65]

Formal administrative transfer was effected in early August, and Agent Simmons at Fort Peck was at the same time ordered to turn over all River Crow records to Agent Pease.[66] William Fanton, agent at Fort Belknap, was likewise notified that no River Crow were to be subsisted at his agency.[67] It was one thing to make administrative decisions concerning the legal abode of the Indians but quite another to effect the change. In December, several months after he assumed his duties as Crow agent, Wright dispatched an employee, Tom Stewart, to River Crow camps in the Judith Basin with instructions that they were to come in immediately to pick up their annuities. Agent Fanton learned of Stewart's presence in their camps and hastened to the Judith Basin to inform the interloper that he would be clapped into irons if he persisted in his efforts to lure the Indians to Crow Agency. A standoff ensued but Fanton eventually backed off. In the end River Crow leaders asked that the goods be brought to their camp on the grounds that their horses were too poor to make a trip to the agency. Several months later, Wright dutifully sent the agency farmer, R.W. Cross, to the Judith Basin with annuity goods and rations for ninety-five lodges.[68]

That the River Crow were being difficult about attaching themselves to Crow Agency is attested by a recommendation made by Wright in August of 1874 that he be given authorization to purchase one horse, saddle, and breech-loading rifle for each of the River Crow head men. He justified the expenditure on grounds that the intended gifts were necessary to wean the River crow away from whiskey traders on the Upper Missouri.[69] Authority was granted several weeks before Wright left his post, and distribution of the gifts was presumably made by his successor.[70] Clapp later reported that about one-third of the River Crow arrived at his agency in April, 1875 to receive subsistence supplies and that they continued to drift in until August, when, for the first time, the entire River Crow division was present on the reservation.

The majority of that branch of the tribe seems to have eventually united with the Mountain Crow and, in time, came to regard Crow Agency as their connection to Great Father. William White, who married a Crow woman and lived with the tribe for a time during the late 1870s, observed in his memoirs that by 1878, the two divisions were conducting tribal ceremonies together and intermarrying freely.[71] George Frost, who assumed the office of Crow Agent during the summer of 1877, observed that although he had to send runners out to bring them in to the agency when their presence was required, the River Crow seemed to regard Crow reservation as their home. In a census of the tribe he conducted in 1878, Frost made no distinction between individuals belonging to the River and Mountain Crow divisions. But in that same year, an unidentified number of River Crow were reported to have attached themselves to the Fort Belknap Agency.[72] It is likely that these were eventually absorbed into the Atsina tribe.

Both major divisions of the tribe tenaciously clung to traditional Crow ways in the face of government efforts to convert them to Alien Culture ways. It wasn't that they avoided the mechanism designed to supervise their metamorphosis; it was, rather, that their notion of Crow agency's functions was quite different from those envisioned by the Indian Service. After all, not only did the agency have the same appearance as the trading posts operated for them by the Company for so many years, it also offered trading facilities.

The dynamics and circumstances of hunting buffalo changed substantially at about the time the tribe entered upon reservation life. In the past, firearms had played only a minor role in the chase. Muzzle-loaders, the only type of gun available to them prior to the 1870s, had been found ineffective in killing buffalo by mounted hunters because the guns were virtually impossible to reload while riding pell-mell into stampeding buffalo herds. The bow and arrow were therefore used in buffalo hunts until introduction of breech-loading rifles.[73] It isn't clear when the Crow acquired the new weapons but probably not in large numbers until after 1870. In late May of that year, Iron Bull complained to Agent Camp that although they had been promised access to breech-loaders at the Treaty Council of 1868, the trader at Fort Parker consistently refused to make them available to the tribe.[74] By July of 1872, however, the new weapons were being used by some tribal members in buffalo hunts and by early 1873, the agency trading post was selling breech-loaders to all who could afford them[75] At the beginning of the year 1874, the Mountain Crow reportedly had 600 of the new weapons and the River Crow had about half that number.[76]

An even more fundamental change in buffalo hunting had occurred in the decade before the tribe began life on the reservation. Traditional Crow hunting grounds, up until the late 1850s, had stretched from Powder River on the east to the Absaroka Mountains on the west and from the Yellowstone River on the north to the North Platte River on the south. By 1862 they had lost all of their lands situated south of the Yellowstone and east of the Big Horn to the Dakota. In addition, by that same date, the Crow were sharing their hunting grounds in both the Big Horn Basin and in Wind River Valley with the Shoshone. To partially make up for these losses, they had appropriated for themselves some of the Alliance hunting grounds lying between the Yellowstone and the Missouri Rivers. The River Crow occasionally even ventured north of the Missouri on their hunts.[77]

The tribe continued to conduct summer hunts for lodge skins and winter hunts for trade robes. The Mountain Crow usually conducted their summer hunts in the upper part of Yellowstone Valley, sometimes in the company of the Nez Perce, the Bannocks, or the Flatheads. On at least one occasion, the Dakota drove the Mountain Crow from the Upper Yellowstone, and in this instance, they retreated to the Three Forks area to complete their summer hunt. On other occasions shortages of buffalo forced them to go north of the Yellowstone to the Musselshell River or even into the Judith Basin.[78] The River Crow often conducted their summer hunts west of Milk River in the Bear Paw Mountain area or in Judith Basin during the early 1870s.[79] Both tribal divisions often conducted their winter hunts in Judith Basin, sometimes together. During the winter of 1873–74, for example, several bands of River Crow shared camps with the Mountain Crow for limited periods of time, and at the end of the hunt all moved on to the main Mountain Crow camp where a celebration to commemorate a successful hunt was held.[80] During the winter of 1876–77, the two branches of the tribe left the agency together to conduct a joint winter hunt in Musselshell Valley.[81]

William White accompanied a joint Mountain and River Crow summer hunt in 1877. Approximately 400 lodges of men, women and children, followed by a herd of 10,000 horses and many dogs, left the agency on May 23. Each family traveled with all its worldly possessions: lodges, utensils of all kinds, robes, food, extra clothing, bedding, and personal trinkets. The column proceeded at a leisurely pace. The length of time spent at any one camp site depended on the amount of pasturage available and on the quantity of game in the vicinity. White was struck by the fact that the Indians seemed to regard the camping spot that they occupied at any given time as home. While males hunted, their mates were busy tanning hides, picking berries, and processing meat for future use. The column halted a few miles short of the mouth of the Big Horn in mid-June to construct rafts for transporting personal possessions to the north bank of the Yellowstone. Most males and females forded the river on horseback; others, mostly the very young and the infirm, were placed on rafts. The crossing consumed three full days, and once on the north bank the party struck out in an easterly direction, still hunting and picking berries as they went. They arrived at Big Porcupine Creek on July 17, and then proceeded on to the Big Bend of the Musselshell for more hunting. The column then set out for the agency where it arrived in early August.[82]

Creation of the reservation system in Montana Territory was accompanied by a proliferation of trading opportunities for Indians of the region. In addition to agency trading posts on each reservation, there were sutlers at army posts as well as private traders licensed by the federal government to conduct business with certain tribes in specified geographic areas. A diary of events kept by an employee of a trading post situated near the mouth of the Musselshell reveals that this particular installation was located there to service the River Crow and Atsina tribes.[83] Buffalo robes, as had been the case at

Company posts, were the basic medium of exchange. One robe brought three cups of coffee, six of sugar, or ten of flour at the post.[84]

Trading licenses for agency trading posts were issued by agents, subject to approval by the commissioner of Indian affairs. Superintendent Sully took it upon himself to issue a license in favor of Leander M. Black for Crow Agency several months before the agency was built. Informed by Commissioner Parker that only agents had authority to issue licenses, Sully nullified the one he had issued to Black. Black was in due course issued a proper license by Camp, and it was subsequently approved by Commissioner Parker on January 27, 1870.[85] Two years later Black sold the trading post to Nelson Story and C.W. Hoffman for $32,000. Pease subsequently issued a license to the partnership, and it was approved on August 24, 1872.[86] In early 1874, Story and Hoffman transferred ownership to Story's brother, Elias, who continued operation of the enterprise until the termination of Dexter Clapp's tenure as agent on October 26, 1876.[87]

The trading post was a two-room structure located inside the walls of the stockade. One room served as a storeroom and the other was, of course, used to accommodate customers. The wall separating the two rooms had a large rectangular opening through which trades were conducted. Gifts to patrons always preceded actual trading. Children were treated to candy, women were customarily given handkerchiefs or thread, and men received ammunition or hunting knives. The standard medium of exchange was the buffalo robe which was worth five dollars in merchandise.[88] The Crow trade was substantial. In 1875 it amounted to $70,000 worth of robes and other peltries. It was, in fact, lucrative enough to create an environment of intense competition between the agency trader and others in the general area. Black complained to Commissioner Parker on December 11, 1869 that the sutler at Fort Ellis was luring the Crow to the fort to trade at his shop. Sully was ordered to investigate the matter and reported back that he had instructed the commanding officer at the post to put an end to the practice.[89]

Sully's actions in this regard did not, however, secure a monopoly on the Crow trade for Black. Soon after completion of the agency compound, a trading house was established at the present site of Livingston, Montana on the north bank of the Yellowstone. Called Benson's Landing, it conducted business in direct competition with the agency trader.[90] Other competition came from individuals granted special licenses to trade with Indians on a transient basis. Other operators simply traded with the Indians illegally.[91] Proprietors of agency posts operated at a disadvantage in one respect. Traders with places of business outside reservation boundaries could legally dispense alcoholic beverages, whereas agency traders could not. Some unscrupulous traders without licenses sold liquor to both Indians and whites. Pease seems not to have been overly concerned about the liquor trade, but his successor was obsessed with keeping alcohol away from the Indians under his jurisdiction. Wright deluged Commissioner Smith with letters complaining about the activities of liquor dealers operating in the immediate vicinity of the reservation. But the main object of his ire was the trading post at Benson's Landing, which, he claimed, attracted ''all the bummers and thieves in the country.''[92] The temperance-minded agent maintained that it not only enticed his Indians to cross the river to purchase liquor, but also interfered with agency operations. His employees, Wright complained, frequently returned from Benson's Landing too drunk to properly perform assigned duties and, even worse, set bad examples for the Indians. His recommendations to suppress the liquor traffic included the passage of laws which would outlaw all trading posts not on reservation property, and the designation of Fort Benton, the source of most illegal liquor in the territory, as an Indian reservation. His patience obviously exhausted, Commissioner Smith informed Wright that there already existed sufficient laws to end the Indian liquor trade. The problem was, he patiently explained, that the Indian Service lacked the resources to enforce them.[93]

Agent Wright had tried, actually, to beef up his capacity to deal with illicit liquor sales soon after he took over as agent by requesting authorization to hire detectives who would have authority to monitor the activities of liquor dealers. He was turned down for lack of funds, but his successor was assigned the services of one Charles D. Hand for this purpose in June of 1875.[94] Hand served only until October of the same year when he was replaced by Frank Murray.[95] The use of detectives obviously did little to solve the problem; in March of 1876, Clapp complained to his superiors that liquor sales to his charges continued unabated.[96] The fuss about the activities of liquor dealers raised by both agents suggests that liquor was an ongoing problem for the tribe during the decade of the 1870s, particularly for the River Crow.

In addition to selling liquor, non-agency traders employed a variety of other strategies to attract the Crow trade away from the agency store. The trading post at Benson's Landing frequently held feasts for prospective patrons, for example. Some traders simply played upon the superstitious nature of the Indians to secure their business. A trader operating in the Milk River area once told some River Crow headed for Crow agency that if they used the trading facilities there, he would cause their arms to shrink and wither away. On another occasion he tried to keep them at his post by warning them that if they left the vicinity he would cause it to snow so hard that their horses would be unable to find pasturage.[97] Agency traders, for their part, used ploys of their own to retain the tribe's trade. Thomas Leforge was hired by Nelson Story on several occasions to live in Crow camps for the purpose of steering its inhabitants to the agency store. He was instructed by Story to make certain that if any of his Crow friends should insist on trading at other posts, Leforge was to see that only inferior robes went to competitors.[98]

The tribe found the agency useful for purposes other than as convenient trading grounds. One which had not been performed by Company posts was to care for those unable to participate in the chase. The old and the infirm, beginning in the winter of 1869–70, were routinely left at the agency to be fed and housed by the agent.[99] One of the major uses of the installation was as a distribution center for gifts lavished on the tribe in quantities that would have made even Robert Meldrum blanch. Congress appropriated $39,030 for the first installment of annuities intended for the Mountain Crow.[100] Superintendent Sully made a special trip to Fort Parker from Helena to witness Agent Camp's distribution of the goods on November 20, 1869.[101] The superintendent quickly learned that a considerable number of the intended recipients were reluctant to accept their due. It seems that the tribe had been hunting buffalo in company with some members of the Flathead tribe when summoned to the agency to pick up their annuities. Their hunting companions had convinced some of the Mountain Crow that acceptance of goods would later be used by Great Father as justification for taking the remainder of their lands. Another complicating factor was the presence of Wolf Bow and his band of River Crow; some Mountain Crow objected to their inclusion as recipients on the grounds that the Treaty of 1868 didn't apply to the River Crow branch of the tribe. It also became painfully apparent to both Sully and Camp that there was almost unanimous dissatisfaction with the kinds of goods included in the shipment. Many insisted that they had been promised at the Treaty Council of 1868 that their annuities would include guns, ammunition, and blankets. They made it abundantly clear to Sully that they had little or no use for the clothing which constituted the bulk of the gifts. The superintendent was able to overcome objections to receiving the distribution only by sweetening the pot with $4,500 worth of blankets, tobacco, knives, and ammunition purchased in Bozeman.[102]

The make-up of subsequent annuity shipments was partially altered to more closely suit the needs of recipients. The 1875 annuities included 192 axes, 475 blankets, 400 pounds of tobacco, 559 skinning knives, 326 mirrors, and 2,002 rounds of ammunition. The bulk of the shipment, though, still consisted of clothing.[103] Most clothing distributed over the years was sold to the agency trader or to other whites. The Indians found their own apparel much more durable and comfortable than that which came from Great Father.[104] Cooking utensils were sometimes included in annuity distributions but, according to both Pease and Wright, they were too small for Crow cooking methods, and, anyway, were for the most part defective in one way or another.[105] Blackfoot probably spoke for the entire tribe when he complained to a member of the Board of Indian Commissioners in August, 1873 that the Crow had sold their lands for stockings and shirts that fell to pieces when first worn and for kettles that didn't hold water. He claimed that the tribe annually gave robes to whites worth more than the annuity goods received. He went on to observe that the Crow really only wanted blankets, elk teeth, beads, eagle feathers, panther and otter skins, breech-loading guns, ammunition, and horses. So much for being made over in the image of whites.[106]

Unreliable transportation facilities made for unreliable and irregular distribution dates. In no instance during the years from 1869 to 1876 did the goods arrive by September 1 as prescribed by the treaty. The nomadic character of Crow life contributed to difficulties in establishing predictable and regular distribution patterns. The circumstances of the 1873 annuities distributions is instructive in this regard. The shipment of annuity goods didn't arrive at the agency until late December, and Agent Wright subsequently set January 1, 1874 as the distribution date. Only one-half of the Mountain Crow and none of the River Crow were present at the agency on that date. Others sent word that they were too busy with their winter hunt to come in and asked the agent to hold their gifts until such time as they were able to return to the agency.[107] Two weeks later, forty-four lodges drifted in, and in early March twenty more lodges came in. At this point Wright estimated that only forty lodges under Blackfoot had not yet received their annuities. Blackfoot and his people finally picked up their goods in early May, but the chief had seventy-five lodges with him rather than the expected forty.[108]

Article IX of the Treaty of 1868 specified that an army officer be present at all distributions of annuity goods.[109] Lieutenant L.C. Forsythe of Fort Ellis witnessed the distribution of the annuities for 1875 on April 24, 1876, and his report of the proceedings provides a convenient window through which the mechanics of an annuity distribution can be viewed. There were in attendance twenty bands of Mountain Crow, and representatives of each were arranged in a large semicircle just outside the agency stockade. Lieutenant Forsythe, Agent Clapp, and an interpreter consulted with the twenty chiefs to ascertain the number of lodges each represented. The three officials then returned to the agency compound to supervise the division of three-fifths of the goods into twenty piles in proportion to the number of lodges in each band. Piles were identified with a card bearing the appropriate leader's name. Each pile was then loaded onto a wagon for delivery outside the compound to tribal leaders who, in turn, distributed what they had been given to the families in their respective bands. Lieutenant Forsythe then queried each leader to confirm that the distribution had been equitable. The remaining two-fifths of the shipment was set aside for distribution to those elements of the tribe not present.[110]

Gatherings of the tribe to receive annuities customarily assumed a festive air. The division of the 1871 annuities which took place in late March of 1872, for example, was preceded by a long oration given by Iron Bull. Following the distribution of merchandise, tribal leaders bestowed gifts of robes on agency officials. Next, a scalp dance in celebration of a recent victory over the Dakota was presented by both male and female participants. This concluded, there suddenly appeared about thirty warriors mounted on horses captured in the same battle. The victorious braves proceeded to leisurely trace a large circle in single file, each recounting his role in the battle. The Indians afterward broke up into small groups to gossip and smoke. Then, as if by a pre-arranged signal, they all rose to attend horse races which were being organized nearby.[111]

The distribution of subsistence stores, or rations, got off to a rocky start because the 1869–70 appropriations bill inadvertently failed to include subsistence funds for the Crow. Commissioner Parker apprised General Sully of the omission in late July of 1869 and suggested that commissary stores at Forts Benton and Buford be drawn upon to feed the Crow until appropriations for the following year were authorized.[112] Sully replied that insufficient stores were available at Fort Benton and that, because navigation on the Missouri had ended and would not be resumed until the following spring, it would be impossible to transport stores from Fort Buford to the agency. He added that the Crow were aware that the treaty called for one pound each of flour and meat and that if it wasn't soon forthcoming, there would be serious trouble with the tribe.[113] Parker informed Sully by telegram that he had approval to purchase $10,000 worth of meat and flour locally. Over the course of the next twelve months, the superintendent was authorized to purchase an additional $30,000 worth of foodstuffs for the tribe.[114]

The distribution of rations was regularized by the appropriations bill of 1870–71. In addition to authorizing funds to purchase annuities for the tribe, it also approved the expenditure of $131,000 for meat and flour.[115] Within only a few years, subsistence supplies distributed to the tribe also included foods other than meat and flour. By the year 1874, coffee, sugar, beans, baking soda, and salt were also being furnished to tribal members.[116] Distribution procedures were by necessity geared to the rhythm of buffalo hunts. The pattern of ration allotments for 1874 was probably typical. During the first part of the year, Agent Wright issued food to an average of 1,300 Indians, most of whom had camped near the agency to dress robes acquired during the tribe's winter hunt.[117] Early in February some small parties rejoined the chase, slightly reducing the number of rations issued. They returned in late March with a number of other lodges whose occupants had been out all winter. During the month of April, Wright issued rations at an average of 2,000 per day.[118] About the middle of May, most left to conduct their summer hunt. The majority returned to the agency in late August, and from then until late October Wright subsisted an average of 1,300 daily. From late October until the end of the year, only 300 received rations while the majority of the tribe participated in the winter hunt. A chit system was employed by the agent to assure fairness in the division of foodstuffs.[119]

When first introduced, rations were for the most part unappreciated by most members of the tribe. Beef was eaten only when buffalo meat was not available, and bacon was used only to obtain the grease it contained. This was used for frying buffalo meat and for tanning buffalo robes. Flour issues were valued more for the sacks than the contents, which were either sold for a pittance or thrown away. Sacks were used to make clothing or, more often, to line the interiors of tipis.[120] Within a relatively short period of time, however, government rations had become an integral component of Crow life. In a treaty council held at the agency during the summer of 1873, Iron Bull complained that his people had not asked for rations but that they had now become accustomed to receiving them and did not want to give them up.[121] Gifts of foodstuffs, of course, were not essential to the tribe's survival so long as buffalo continued to roam the reservation and adjacent areas. By 1880, though, there was but little game left within a hundred miles of the reservation.[122] In 1881 almost no buffalo could be found in areas south of the

Yellowstone River, and by 1887, there were few buffalo to be found any place in Montana Territory.[123]

This, of course, left the tribe dependent for its survival on its ability to exploit the reservation's natural resources and on the good will of Great Father. Rations were still being issued at the time of the disappearance of the buffalo, but the capacity of the Crow to extract subsistence from their lands hadn't progressed nearly as rapidly as had been anticipated by the policy makers who drafted the Treaty of 1868. In fact it hadn't progressed at all. A few tribal members applied for their allotments of 320 acres as allowed by the Treaty of 1868, but in almost all cases, these were spouses of whites.[124] And, although a few crops were raised on lands adjacent to the agency complex, most agricultural labor was performed by the agency farmer and agency laborers. Wolf Bow and several others tried their hands at establishing farms of their own, but none seemed to last long.[125] As of the summer of 1879 there were only thirty-seven acres under cultivation on the entire reservation, including lands being cultivated by the agency farmer.[126]

Thomas Leforge was married to one of the Crow women who filed for her allotment, and he was persuaded by Agent Wright to settle down to work the land. Leforge explained his eventual abandonment of the farm to the circumstance that "trapping and hunting were too good to be bothering the land."[127] This mind set probably helps to explain why so few male Crow could be induced to take up farming. It also appears that Great Father did not always scrupulously fulfill his part of the bargain. Agent Pease informed Wright during the spring of 1873 that the Indians refused to farm because they had not been given tools, cattle, and wagons as called for by the treaty.[128]

The other integral component of the Peace Policy, education, fared no better during the first decade of the tribe's reservation experience than efforts to induce the Crow to abandon the chase for farming. Captain Camp made no effort to implement the education provision of the treaty, and, although Fellows Pease did hire a teacher, little progress was made in educating Crow children during his tenure as agent.[129] James Wright seems to have taken his responsibilities as educator somewhat more seriously than had his predecessors. He was aware that the time-honored rhythm of buffalo hunts during early summer and again during late fall interfered with regular school attendance. To house students whose parents left the agency on these occasions, he founded a boarding school on October 27, 1873 with two matrons to care for boarding students. A Bozeman minister named Matthew Bird was hired as a full-time teacher.[130] The results must have been disappointing to Agent Wright. He could persuade only eight children to become boarding students, and one of these was kidnapped and returned to her camp. After four months the student population was comprised of seven Indian boarding students and fourteen day students made up of white children and children of Crow mothers and white fathers.[131]

Wright blamed Crow resistance to having their children attend school on parents' fears of being ridiculed by friends, and on a conviction that an education would strip offspring of their Crow heritage. Other factors which limited enrollments were parental objections to cutting children's hair and a refusal on the part of many tribal members to believe that their children could benefit in any way from an education.[132] To boost enrollment the agent recommended in May of 1874 that each Crow band be obligated to furnish a specified number of students to the school each year, but nothing came of his plan. None of Wright's immediate successors was able to improve on his record as an educator of the tribe's young.[133]

Attempts by Great Father to "civilize" his Crow children have to be considered an abysmal failure. The extent to which the tribe had preserved its traditional ways after more than a decade of reservation life is suggested by the following description of the Crow included by Agent A.R. Kellar in his annual report for 1879:

> When the grass begins to grow in the spring they all sigh for the excitement of the chase, strike their tents, and, like a grand army, move out upon the broad prairies to engage in their summer hunt, which they keep up until midsummer, when they return to the agency, dress their hides, make their lodges, and remain until fall, when robes are good, when they go out to kill the buffalo and secure robes and dry the meat, which constitutes their stock in trade. So soon as this hunt is concluded, which usually runs to the middle of January, they return to the agency, tan their robes, draw their annuities, and enjoy themselves singing and dancing, with a hilarity unknown to any other people on the continent.[134]

The reservation, then, failed abysmally as a mechanism for transforming Crow males from hunters into farmers. Not the least reason for its failure in this regard was that reservation life too closely approximated pre-reservation conditions. The tribe consequently found it a simple matter to continue its buffalo-hunting, berry-picking, nomadic ways. It didn't help matters any that agency personnel were something less than ideal choices for the successful operation of such an enterprise. Another factor was that the Indians regarded the agency as a new version of the trading post system maintained by the Company along the banks of the Yellowstone. It wasn't so much that the agency complex had the appearance of a Company post; it also satisfied Crow needs for manufactured goods. The agency differed from a typical trading post mainly in the circumstance of providing some goods free of charge. Gifts distributed to the Indians, especially foodstuffs, in such large quantities, represented a giant step down the road to total dependency on the federal government. The reservation turned out to be no more successful in passing along the values, beliefs, and life style of the Alien Culture to the tribe's young than in weaning their fathers from the chase. One of the few successes of the system was the reunification of the tribe. And, of course, it was responsible for opening up part of the tribe's traditional homeland to white settlement, as calculated.

NOTES

1. Francis Paul Prucha, *The Great Father: The United States Government and the American Indians* (Lincoln and London: University of Nebraska Press, 1984), I, 503, 506-7.
2. *Ibid,* I, 512-3.
3. Letter, E.S. Parker to E.M. Camp, June 2, 1869, ROLS, reel 90.
4. Letter, E.S. Parker to A. Sully, June 1, 1869, *ibid.*
5. Letter, E.S. Parker to L.M. Black, May 11, 1869, *ibid; Bozeman Chronicle,* August 10, 1954, p. 2c.
6. "Captain Palmer's Account of the Connor Expedition," in Leroy R. Hafen and Ann W. Hafen, eds., *Powder River Campaigns and Sawyer's Expedition of 1865,* XII of The Far West and the Rockies Historical Series 1826–1875 (Glendale: The Arthur H. Clark Company, 1961), p. 105.
7. RCIA, 1870, House Executive Document No. 1 (Serial 1449), p. 661.
8. Letter, A. Sully to E.S. Parker, August 4, 1869, LRMS, reel 489; Letter, A. Sully to E.S. Parker, September 1, 1869, *ibid.*
9. Thomas B. Marquis, *Memoirs of a White Crow Indian* (Lincoln: University of Nebraska Press, 1974), p. 32.
10. Letter, A. Sully to E.S. Parker, September 21, 1869, LRMS, reel 489; RCIA, 1869, House Executive Document No. 1 (Serial 1414), p. 733.
11. Letter, E.M. Camp to E.S. Parker, September 18, 1869, LRMS, reel 489.

12. RCIA, 1870, House Executive Document No. 1 (Serial 1449), p. 661.
13. Marquis, *op. cit.,* pp. 71–72.
14. RCIA, 1870, House Executive Document No. 1 (Serial 1449), p. 662.
15. Letter, J.W. Frost to E.S. Parker, December 15, 1869, LRMS, reel 489; Letter, A. Sully to E.S. Parker, January 16, 1870, LRMS, reel 490.
16. Special Order No. 253, October 23, 1870, LRMS, reel 490.
17. Robert G. Athearn, *Forts of the Upper Missouri* (Englewood Cliffs: Prentice Hall, Inc., 1967), p. 172.
18. Tom Stout, ed., *Montana: Its Story and Biography* (Chicago and New York: The American Historical Society, 1921), III, 1051.
19. Letter, J.A. Viall to E.S. Parker, October 15, 1870, LRMS, reel 490.
20. Letter, H.R. Clum to J.A. Viall, May 17, 1871, ROLS, reel 102; Letter, J.A. Viall to F.D. Pease, February 20, 1872, RMSI, reel 1.
21. *Avant Courier,* October 31, 1872.
22. Letter, F.D. Pease to J.A. Wright, January 22, 1873, RMSI, reel 1; Letter, F.D. Pease to J.A. Wright, April 14, 1873, *ibid; Avant Courier,* June 27, 1873.
23. Letter, J.A. Viall to E.S. Parker, December 6, 1871, LRMS, reel 491.
24. Letter, F.D. Pease to J.A. Viall, October 31, 1872, RMSI, reel 1.
25. Letter, F.D. Pease to J.A. Viall, December 6, 1871, LRMS, reel 492; RCFS, July 1867, September, 1867.
26. Marquis, *op. cit.,* pp. 44, 58.
27. Letter, A. Sully to E.S. Parker, February 15, 1870, LRMS, reel 490.
28. Letter, F.D. Pease to J.A. Wright, March 24, 1873, RMSI, reel 1.
29. Marquis, *op. cit.,* pp. 58–60.
30. Letter, F.A. Walker to J.A. Wright, December 23, 1872, ROLS, reel 110.
31. Letter, H.R. Clum to F.D. Pease, January 10, 1873, ROLS, reel 110; Letter, H.R. Clum to F.D. Pease, January 31, 1873, *ibid.*
32. Letter, J.A. Wright to B.R. Cowan, January 4, 1873, LRMS, reel 496.
33. Letter, J.A. Wright to Commissioner of Indian Affairs, January 27, 1873, *ibid.*
34. Letter, J.A. Wright to Commissioner of Indian Affairs, March 11, 1873, *ibid.*
35. Letter, F.D. Pease to J.A. Wright, April 30, 1873, RMSI, reel 1.
36. Letter, E.P. Smith to F.D. Pease, September 3, 1873, ROLS, reel 114; Letter, J.A. Wright to E.P. Smith, September 20, 1873, LRMS, reel 497.
37. Report of Employees for Fourth Quarter, 1874, LRMS, reel 500; Letter, J.A. Wright to E.P. Smith, September 20, 1873, LRMS, reel 497.
38. Marquis, *op. cit.,* pp. 38–39.
39. Letter, J.A. Wright to E.P. Smith, June 2, 1874, LRMS, reel 500; RCIA, 1874, House Executive Document No. 1 (Serial 1639), p. 570.
40. *Avant Courier,* July 10, 1874.
41. Letter, E.P. Smith to J.A. Wright, June 19, 1874, ROLS, reel 118.
42. Letter, J.A. Wright to E.P. Smith, July 14, 1874, LRMS, reel 500; Letter, J.A. Wright to E.P. Smith, September 8, 1874, *ibid.*
43. Letter, H.R. Clum to J.A. Wright, September 23, 1874, ROLS, reel 120.
44. Letter, J.A. Wright to E.P. Smith, June 2, 1874, LRMS, reel 500.
45. Letter, B.F. Potts to C. Delano, July 11, 1874, *ibid;* Letter, B.F. Potts to C. Delano, July 1, 1873, LRMS, reel 495. Potts was a native of Ohio; an attorney by training and a politician by choice. He served under General Sherman on his March to the Sea, and by the end of the war had attained the rank of brigadier general. He was appointed governor of Montana Territory by President Grant on August 29, 1870. Clark C. Spence, *Territorial Politics and Government in Montana: 1864–89* (Urbana, Chicago, London: University of Illinois Press, 1975), pp. 74–75.

46. Council, October 29, 1873, LRMS, reel 495; (F.D. Pease for) Blackfoot to Great Father, December 5, 1873, LRMS, reel 500.
47. For representative examples, see Letter, E.P. Smith to J.A. Wright, January 22, 1873, ROLS, reel 116; Letter, H.R. Clum to J.A. Wright, August 28, 1874, ROLS, reel 120; Letter, H.R. Clum to J.A. Wright, September 15, 1874, ibid; Letter, H.R. Clum to J.A. Wright, October 1, 1874, ibid.
48. Letter, E.P. Smith to J.A. Wright, October 9, 1874, ROLS, reel 120.
49. Letter, J.A. Wright to E.P. Smith, November 30, 1874, LRMS, reel 500; Letter, J.A. Wright to E.P. Smith, December 7, 1874, ibid. Wright served as agent at Fort Hall until May 4, 1875. Letter, H.R. Clum to J.A. Wright, June 22, 1875, ROLS, reel 124.
50. Clapp was a resident of Methodist Mission House in New York City at the time he posted his bond. Letter, D.E. Clapp to E.P. Smith, October 29, 1874, LRMS, reel 498.
51. Francis B. Heitman, *Historical Register and Dictionary of the United States Army: From its Organization, September 29, 1779 to March 2, 1903* (Urbana: University of Illinois Press, 1965), I, 302.
52. Letter, L.H. Carpenter to J.Q. Smith, October 26, 1876, LRMS, reel 504.
53. Letter, W.J. Cullen to N.G. Taylor, October 22, 1868, LRMS, reel 488; RCIA, 1868, House Executive Document No. 1 (Serial 1366), p. 689.
54. RCIA, 1873, House Executive Document No. 1 (Serial 1601), p. 616.
55. RCIA, 1869, House Executive Document No. 1 (Serial 1414), pp. 741-2.
56. RCIA, 1871, House Executive Document No. 1 (Serial 1505), pp. 846-7.
57. RCIA, 1874, House Executive Document No. 1 (Serial 1639), p. 360.
58. TCG, 41st Congress, 3rd Session, p. 1564, *Laws,* p. 386, reel 45.
59. RCIA, 1869, House Executive Document No. 1 (Serial 1414), p. 732; RCIA, 1870, House Executive Document No. 1 (Serial 1449), p. 656.
60. Letter, J.A. Wright to E.P. Smith, August 21, 1873, LRMS, reel 497; Letter, R.W. Cross to J.A. Wright, April 5, 1874, LRMS, reel 500.
61. Peter Koch, "Life at Muscleshell in 1869 and 1870," *Contributions to the Historical Society of Montana,* II (1898), 296; Letter, A. Sully to E.S. Parker, April 1, 1870, LRMS, reel 490; Letter, P.F. Sheridan to E.O. Townsend, August 1, 1870, ibid; Letter, T. Stewart to J.A. Wright, January 27, 1874, LRMS, reel 500.
62. Letter, J.A. Viall to H.R. Clum, November 19, 1871, LRMS, reel 491.
63. RCIA, 1872, House Executive Document No. 1 (Serial 1560), p. 662.
64. Letter, A.J. Simmons to J.A. Viall, August 1, 1872, LRMS, reel 498.
65. Letter, J.A. Wright to Commissioner of Indian Affairs, March 13, 1873, LRMS, reel 496.
66. Letter, H.R. Clum to F.D. Pease, August 19, 1873, ROLS, reel 113; Letter, E.P. Smith to J.A. Wright, September 6, 1873, ibid.
67. Letter, H.R. Clum to W. Fanton, December 15, 1873, ROLS, reel 115.
68. Letter, T. Stewart to J.A. Wright, January 27, 1874, LRMS, reel 500; Letter, R.W. Cross to J.A. Wright, April 5, 1874, ibid.
69. Letter, J.A. Wright to E.P. Smith, August 25, 1874, ibid.
70. Letter, C. Delano to Commissioner of Indian Affairs, November 14, 1874, LRMS, reel 499.
71. Thomas Marquis, *Custer, Cavalry & Crows: The Story of William White as Told to Thomas Marquis* (Fort Collins: The Old Army Press, 1975), p. 149.
72. RCIA, 1878, House Executive Document No. 1 (Serial 1850), pp. 473, 580; Roll of Indians, June 30, 1878, LRMS, reel 506.
73. Frank B. Linderman, *Plenty Coups, Chief of the Crow* (Lincoln: University of Nebraska Press, 1962), p. 17.

74. Letter, E.M. Camp to E.S. Parker, May 24, 1870, LRMS, reel 490.
75. Letter, Nelson Story & Co. to Z.H. Daniels, June 12, 1873, LRMS, reel 497; *Fourth Annual Report of the Board of Indian Commissioners to the President of the United States, 1872* (Washington: Government Printing Office, 1872), p. 72.
76. Letter, N.B. Sweitzer to Assistant Adjutant General, January 5, 1874, LRMS, reel 500.
77. *Ibid.*
78. Letter, A. Sully to Commissioner of Indian Affairs, August 14, 1870, LRMS, reel 490.
79. John C. Ewers, *Blackfeet Indians* (New York and London: Garland Publishing, Inc., 1974), pp. 146-7.
80. *Diary*, Hans Peter Koch Reminiscences, Small Collections No. 950, Folder 1, HSML; Letter, R.W. Cross to J.A. Wright, April 5, 1874, LRMS, reel 500.
81. *Avant Courier*, October 13, 1876.
82. Marquis, *Custer, Cavalry*, pp. 118-20, 126-7, 131.
83. Elers Koch, ed., *Journal of Peter Koch: 1869-70*, Sources of Northwest History No. 5 (Missoula: State University of Montana, n.d.), pp. 3-14. Koch was born in Denmark in 1844 and immigrated to the United States in 1865. He moved to the frontier in 1869 to work in this post. He went on to become a prominent businessman in Bozeman.
84. Koch, *Life at*, p. 297.
85. Letter, E.S. Parker to A. Sully, July 19, 1869, ROLS, reel 91; E.S. Parker to A. Sully, January 27, 1870, ROLS, reel 94.
86. Letter, H.R. Clum to J.A. Viall, August 24, 1872, ROLS, reel 108.
87. Letter, H.R. Clum to D.E. Clapp, July 20, 1875, ROLS, reel 126.
88. Marquis, *Memoirs*, pp. 63-64.
89. Letter, W.F. Cady to A. Sully, December 30, 1869, ROLS, reel 94; Letter, A. Sully to Commissioner of Indian Affairs, January 14, 1870, LRMS, reel 490.
90. Marquis, *Memoirs*, pp. 41-42.
91. Report: Doane and Pease, Appendix F, February 19, 1874, LRMS, reel 498.
92. Letter, J.A. Wright to E.P. Smith, October 12, 1874, LRMS, reel 500.
93. Letter, J.A. Wright to E.P. Smith, September 19, 1873, LRMS, reel 497; Letter, J.A. Wright to E.P. Smith, October 16, 1873, *ibid;* Letter, J.A. Wright to E.P. Smith, April 18, 1874, LRMS, reel 500; Letter, J.A. Wright to E.P. Smith, May 20, 1873, *ibid;* Letter, J.A. Wright to E.P. Smith, October 12, 1874, *ibid;* Letter, E.P. Smith to J.A. Wright, June 6, 1874, ROLS, reel 118.
94. Letter, J.A. Wright to E.P. Smith, September 2, 1873, LRMS, reel 497; Letter, E.P. Smith to J.A. Wright, September 25, 1873, ROLS, reel 114; Letter, E.P. Smith to D.E. Clapp, June 30, 1875, ROLS, reel 124.
95. Letter, E.P. Smith to D.E. Clapp, November 9, 1875, ROLS, reel 129. For an account of Murray's activities for the first half of 1876, see Letter, F.M. Murray to E.C. Watkins, August 14, 1876, LRMS, reel 505.
96. Letter, D.E. Clapp to J.Q. Smith, March 6, 1876, LRMS, reel 504.
97. Letter, R.W. Cross to J.A. Wright, April 5, 1874, LRMS, reel 500.
98. Marquis, *Memoirs*, pp. 60-63.
99. Letter, A. Sully to E.S. Parker, January 8, 1870, LRMS, reel 490.
100. *Appropriations for Crow Indians*, House Executive Document No. 42 (Serial 1372).
101. RCIA, 1870, House Executive Document No. 1 (Serial 1449), p. 661.

102. *Ibid,* p. 662; Letter, A. Sully to E.S. Parker, December 8, 1869, LRMS, reel 489.
103. Letter, L.C. Forsythe to Post Adjutant, April 28, 1876, LRMS, reel 505.
104. Report: Doane and Pease, February 19, 1874, LRMS, reel 498.
105. RCIA, 1871, House Executive Document No. 1 (Serial 1505), p. 804; Letter, J.A. Wright to E.P. Smith, May 21, 1874, LRMS, reel 500.
106. *Fifth Annual Report of the Board of Indian Commissioners to the President of the United States: 1873* (Washington: Government Printing Office, 1874), p. 117.
107. Letter, N.B. Sweitzer to Assistant Adjutant General, January 5, 1874, LRMS, reel 500; Letter, J.A. Wright to E.P. Smith, January 6, 1874, *ibid.*
108. Letter, J.A. Wright to E.P. Smith, January 25, 1874, *ibid;* Letter, J.A. Wright to E.P. Smith, March 14, 1874, *ibid;* Letter, J.A. Wright to E.P. Smith, May 15, 1874, *ibid.*
109. George E. Fay, ed., *Treaties, Land Cessions, and other U.S. Congressional Documents Relative to American Indian Tribes: The Crow 1825-1912* (Greeley: Museum of Anthropology, 1982), p. 12; Charles J. Kappler, *Indian Affairs: Laws and Treaties* (2nd ed.: Washington: Government Printing Office, 1904), II, 1011.
110. Letter, L.C. Forsythe to Post Adjutant, April 28, 1876, LRMS, reel 505.
111. *Avant Courier,* April 4, 1872.
112. Letter, E.S. Parker to A. Sully, July 29, 1869, ROLS, reel 91; TCR, 41st Congress, 1st Session, *Laws,* p. 42, reel 41.
113. Letter, A. Sully to E.S. Parker, August 13, 1869, LRMS, reel 489.
114. Letter, E.S. Parker to A. Sully, August 13, 1869, ROLS, reel 91; Letter, E.S. Parker to A. Sully, March 11, 1870, ROLS, reel 93; Letter, W.F. Cady to A. Sully, August 8, 1870, ROLS, reel 97; Letter, W.F. Cady to A. Sully, September 9, 1870, *ibid.*
115. TCG, 41st Congress, 2nd Session, *Laws,* p. 730, reel 44.
116. Letter, T. Cree to E.P. Smith, March 6, 1874, LRMS, reel 498.
117. Letter, J.A. Wright to E.P. Smith, January 14, 1874, LRMS, reel 500.
118. Letter, J.A. Wright to E.P. Smith, April 20, 1874, *ibid;* Letter, J.A. Wright to E.P. Smith, May 15, 1874, *ibid.*
119. Letter, J.A. Wright to E.P. Smith, August 22, 1874, *ibid;* Letter, J.A. Wright to E.P. Smith, December 7, 1874, LRMS, reel 503.
120. Marquis, *Custer, Cavalry,* p. 117; Marquis, *Memoirs,* p. 56.
121. *Fifth Annual Report, op. cit.,* p. 110.
122. RCIA, 1880, House Executive Document No. 1 (Serial 1959), p. 110.
123. *The Extermination of the American Bison,* House Miscellaneous Document No. 600, Part 2 (Serial 2582), pp. 508-11.
124. Letter, J.A. Wright to E.P. Smith, October 30, 1874, LRMS, reel 500.
125. RCIA, 1871, House Executive Document No. 1 (Serial 1505), p. 808.
126. RCIA, 1879, House Executive Document No. 1 (Serial 1910), p. 199. For references to farming operations on the reservation during the late 1870s, see RCIA, 1877, House Executive Document No. 1 (Serial 1800), p. 529; RCIA, 1878, House Executive Document No. 1 (Serial 1850), p. 581.
127. Marquis, *Memoirs,* p. 50.
128. Letter, F.D. Pease to J.A. Wright, April 4, 1873, LRMS, reel 496. As late as 1969, 82% of the tribe's landowners leased their lands to others for agricultural purposes. Genevieve De Hoyos and Arturo De Hoyos, *The Crow Indian Reservation of Montana* (Provo: Brigham Young Press, 1969), p. 3.

129. See, *Fourth Annual Report, op. cit.,* p. 74, for a pessimistic assessment made during the summer of 1872 by Felix R. Brunot of the Board of Indian Commissioners regarding the agency school's performance up to that time. The first teacher hired by Pease died on January 6, 1871 and was replaced on April 25, 1871. RCIA, 1871, House Executive Document No. 1 (Serial 1505), p. 808.
130. RCIA, 1874, House Executive Document No. 1 (Serial 1639), p. 569.
131. Letter, J.A. Wright to E.P. Smith, February 21, 1874, LRMS, reel 500.
132. RCIA, 1873, House Executive Document No. 1 (Serial 1601), pp. 616-7.
133. Letter, J.A. Wright to E.P. Smith, May 28, 1874, LRMS, reel 500. For assessments of agency school activities, consult RCIA, 1876, House Executive Document No. 1 (Serial 1749), p. 492; RCIA, 1877, House Executive Document No. 1 (Serial 1800), p. 530; RCIA, 1878, House Executive Document No. 1 (Serial 1850), p. 582; RCIA, 1879, House Executive Document No. 1 (Serial 1910), p. 199.
134. *Ibid,* p. 198.

NINE

DECEPTION AND VENALITY ALONG MISSION CREEK

Settlers in Montana were forced to accept the existence of Crow reservation when the Treaty of 1868 was ratified by the Senate, but that they didn't do so gracefully is suggested by early attempts by territorial officials, especially those of Acting Governor Meagher, to do away with the reservation. A letter written to the editor of the *Nation* in 1879 by Peter Koch probably reflected the attitudes of most residents of the territory toward the tribe and its reservation. In Koch's estimation federal policies designed to "civilize" the Crow were not only misguided but poorly administered as well. He cited frequent changes in agency personnel, the dishonesty of agents, and bureaucratic red tape as obstacles to realization of the treaty's goals.[1] What bothered Koch most, though, was the size of the reservation. He pointed out that it contained twenty square miles for each man, woman, and child in the tribe and that this was far too large for the Indians' needs. His specific objection in this regard was that the Indians didn't effectively utilize the lands set aside for them. He was convinced that they used the reservation only for hunting and as a distribution point for annuities and subsistence supplies. These lands could be put to far better uses by whites, he insisted, because they had the vision, talent, and drive to exploit the agricultural, timber, and mineral resources of the area. Anyway, Koch complained, the vast extent of the reservation militated against the government's much

publicized goal of persuading the Indians to abandon
their hunting and gathering style of life for that of a
farmer. Its size gave the tribe every opportunity to
continue its nomadic way of life. Furthermore, Koch
observed, Crow lands included the single best natural
route for a railroad into the region, making it unlikely
that the territory would acquire a much needed rail
connection with the east anytime soon.[2]

The Yellowstone Valley was regarded by one
prominent livestock man as a grazing area without
parallel anyplace in the territory.[3] Nelson Story
obviously agreed with this assessment. He illegally ran
both horses and cattle on reservation lands in the
valley for many years.[4] Other settlers cast covetous
eyes on reservation lands known or thought to have
mining potential. Deposits of both gold and silver
were discovered on the headwaters of Clark's Fork in
1870, and about 150 prospectors illegally entered that
area to work the new finds.[5] It was widely believed
that there existed rich deposits of iron and copper in
the Stillwater River region, and it was known that
numerous deposits of coal were scattered throughout
the reservation.[6] Agent Pease noted in his first annual
report that the size of the reservation made it
impossible for him to exclude prospectors from the
lands, and recommended that the Crow be persuaded
to sell that portion of their territory which contained
mineral deposits to the government.[7]

Governor Benjamin Potts shared Peter Koch's
concern that Crow lands might prove to be an
obstacle to the extension of rail service to the
territory. The governor was absolutely convinced that
Montana's economic future was dependent upon a
railway connection with the nation's eastern states.
Such a link had been in the works since 1864 when
the Northern Pacific Railroad was granted a charter to
construct a rail line connecting Puget Sound with

Lake Superior. Construction was delayed until 1869 for lack of funds, but in that year the Philadelphia banking firm of Jay Cooke and Co. committed its financial resources to the enterprise. By early 1872 the firm's track-laying crews were rapidly approaching the Missouri River from the east, and although the projected route through Montana Territory had not been announced, Potts had learned that it would traverse Yellowstone Valley. His anxiety about the railroad's progress stemmed from the company's charter, which called for grants of land extending for twenty miles on either side of the road bed, some of which had already been set aside for the Crow tribe.[8]

Montana's delegate to the House of Representatives, William H. Clagett, no less than Potts, believed that completion of the projected railroad was vital to the territory's economic well-being. On March 12, 1872 he introduced a resolution in the House which would authorize the Secretary of Interior to negotiate with the Crow for surrender of their reservation or such part of it as might be desirable. The bill was duly referred to the Committee on Indian Affairs and was subsequently passed by both the House and the Senate. It was approved and signed into law by the president on March 3, 1873.[9]

In the meantime Superintendent Viall had instructed Pease to convene the Crow for a council to ascertain the tribe's attitude toward negotiating a treaty which would change their reservation's boundaries. Pease reported back in early July of 1872 that the Indians might be interested in negotiating a new treaty but that they insisted on first consulting with Great Father in person.[10] Several weeks after Pease held his meeting with the tribe, Felix Brunot of the Board of Indian Commissioners, traveled to Montana Territory and while there decided to visit Crow Agency to sound out tribal leaders on this matter. When Brunot arrived on July 17, he learned that Pease had sent runners out to bring tribal leaders in for a council. Long Horse and three minor leaders came in on July 19. However, the chief refused to talk about anything except the tribe's problems with the Dakota. The commissioner waited for either Blackfoot or Iron Bull to come in, but when neither had made an appearance by July 27, he left without having learned much of anything about the matter at hand. His formal report of the visit did note, however, that mining operations on the reservation, coupled with the likelihood that a railroad would soon be constructed along the northern boundary of the reservation, made it imperative that negotiations be conducted to secure Crow relinquishment of a portion of their reservation.[11]

Within a month of Brunot's departure from Montana Territory, Superintendent Viall informed the commissioner of Indian affairs that the Crow were growing increasingly restive about the presence of miners on the reservation. The tribe was, he believed, ready to accept a new treaty which would cede to the federal government those lands on which mines were already located. Viall urgently recommended that Pease be allowed to consult with Great Father on the matter. Viall's recommendation was turned down for lack of funds.[12]

Once the bill authorizing negotiations had been signed, Felix Brunot was designated by the secretary of the interior to head a treaty commission which would hold its deliberations at the agency. Superintendent James Wright and General E. Whittlesey were named to assist Brunot, and Thomas K. Cree of the Indian Service was chosen to act as secretary for the proceedings. Brunot's instructions specified that he negotiate surrender of only so much of reservation lands as were necessary to accommodate the prior rights of miners and provide a suitable right-of-way for the proposed railroad.[13]

The treaty commissioners arrived at the agency on July 31, 1873 to find that most tribal leaders had not yet appeared.[14] When the stragglers finally did arrive on August 8, Brunot was informed that both Blackfoot and Iron Bull were ill. The proceedings were therefore delayed until August 11. Brunot opened the council with a statement that Crow reservation boundaries were no longer viable, citing the existence of mining settlements in Emigrant Gulch and suggesting that because this area was mountainous and therefore of no practical use to the Crow, they might consider selling it to Great Father. He then observed that an "iron road" was being built along the north bank of the Yellowstone River, and that although it would benefit the tribe by ensuring timely deliveries of annuity goods, it would also inevitably attract more whites into the area. He suggested that the tribe might therefore want to consider selling off a strip of reservation land along its northern border.[15]

Blackfoot responded with a recitation of instances in which the Crow had exhibited friendship for whites and then sharply criticized Great Father for not keeping intruders, both whites and Indians, off reservation lands as promised in the Treaty of 1868. Commissioner Brunot closed the session with a suggestion that the Indians consider and discuss among themselves the matter of selling a portion of their lands and return to the council on the following morning with their decision.

Following some verbal sparring between Brunot and Blackfoot about past indignities suffered by the Crow at the hands of whites, the commissioner formally opened the second session with a suggestion that the tribe give up its reservation. Specifically, he proposed a total withdrawal of the tribe from its lands in exchange for a new reservation in the Judith Basin. Admitting that the new reservation would be smaller, he suggested that Great Father might set up a one million dollar trust fund from which the tribe would receive fifty thousand dollars annually in interest payments. Blackfoot responded to Brunot's offer by ticking off a number of advantages that their current reservation lands had over the Judith Basin and ended his speech with a flat rejection of the new proposal. Wolf Bow chimed in at this point with an offer to sell the western part of the reservation for 1,500 breech-loading guns. Brunot then adjourned the gathering with a request that they consider his latest offer and give him their decision at the next session.

Blackfoot took the floor before Brunot had an opportunity to formally open the third meeting and asked the commissioner to explain the contents of the Treaty of 1868 to him. Brunot proceeded to read the treaty, explaining what each provision meant as he went along. About halfway through the presentation, Blackfoot interrupted the commissioner to brand the treaty as a document full of lies. Brunot discontinued his word-for-word approach and quickly summarized the remaining provisions. Blackfoot then assumed a more conciliatory tone, explaining that Brunot's rendering of the treaty's contents didn't square with what they had been told at the treaty councils of 1867 and 1868. After reminding the participants that although it was their decision to accept or reject his offer, Brunot advised them to accept it, pointing out the probability that white settlers would soon occupy the Judith Basin. He closed the session with a hint that if his offer was accepted, a trip to visit Great Father would be arranged for tribal leaders.

The fourth session opened with Brunot explaining the terms of a new treaty which would exchange the tribe's present reservation for a new one in Judith

Basin. Blackfoot rose to point out that the Judith Basin was already being used, not only by white trappers and hunters, but by Indians from other tribes as well. Therefore, he proposed that the tribe remain on the present reservation and agree to sell the mountains in the western part of the reservation, retaining only the valleys. And, because the proposed rail line might not be built for some time, he suggested that the matter of selling a strip of land across the northern border of the reservation be deferred until some later date. The commissioner rejected the chief's offer out of hand, noting that whites who wished to utilize the resources of mountainous areas would by necessity have to use adjoining valleys for access roads. Furthermore, he warned, by selling the mountainous areas the tribe would lose access to timber and lose control over major watersheds. Brunot then confirmed that upon acceptance of the treaty, arrangements would indeed by made to take tribal leaders to meet with Great Father. The treaty was then read for formal consideration by the tribe.

Blackfoot, obviously still dissatisfied with the proposal, tried a new tack. Citing the relatively small size of Judith Basin, he offered to accept the new treaty provided that it be amended to include all lands between the basin and the north bank of Yellowstone River. The Commissioner demurred. He explained that the one million dollar trust fund was meant to compensate the Crow for the difference in size involved in the exchange of lands and that the provision setting up the trust would have to be deleted if additional lands were included in the trade. Then, clearly having lost patience with the Indians, Brunot announced that he had no more to say on the subject and that if the tribe wanted to accept the new treaty, they could convene the next morning to sign it. If not he would return to Washington. The following morning, tribal leaders, including Blackfoot, returned to the council to accept the treaty. A British adventurer, the Earl of Dunraven, visited the agency the following year, and, based on conversations he had with some of the principals, concluded that the Indians had signed the treaty only because they felt they had no other choice.[16] Brunot justified his departure from the instructions provided him by Secretary Delano on three considerations. First, he found that the topography of the mining area didn't lend itself to a convenient dividing line between lands occupied by miners and the remainder of the reservation. The second justification advanced had to do with the proposed rail line. His thinking here was that the railroad would inevitably attract large numbers of settlers into areas immediately adjoining the reservation, creating great potential for conflict between Indian and white. Finally, the commissioner noted that the proposed fifty thousand dollar annual payment to the tribe would allow the government to reduce the amount of money appropriated for the tribe's subsistence. He pointed out that, although the treaty obligation to provide rations would expire at the end of the 1873 fiscal year, the tribe had made no progress in becoming self-sufficient and would therefore require some sort of support for the foreseeable future.[17]

Brunot kept his promise to arrange for tribal leaders to journey to Washington. The practice of bringing Indian leaders to the seat of government was rooted in the distant past. Spain, France, and England had all made it a point to expose aborigines in their colonies to the resources and power of their respective political systems as a means of shoring up allegiances of subjected peoples. The goal of the United States in its use of this practice was to awe tribal leaders into peaceable behavior.[18] In the case of the Crow visit to the nation's capitol, there seems to have been little reason to fear an outbreak of Crow hostility, and the visit may therefore have been arranged simply to honor Brunot's pledge. Fellows D. Pease was commissioned to shepherd fourteen Crow, including Blackfoot, Iron Bull, and Long Horse, to the seat of the Alien Culture's political system, where they arrived on October 20, 1873. Bernard Bravo and one S.B. Shively went along as interpreters. C.W. Hoffman, the agency trader in partnership with Nelson Story, made the trip at his own expense.[19]

The entire contingent met with Secretary Delano, Felix Brunot, and Commissioner of Indian Affairs E.P. Smith on October 21. Blackfoot, as usual, acted as spokesman. The chief reminded his hosts that the Crow, unlike most Indian tribes, had been consistently friendly with whites and went on to claim that they therefore deserved better treatment than that afforded them by the new treaty. He complained that Judith Basin contained insufficient pasture, timber, and water for the tribe's needs and repeated the proposal he had made at the council that all lands lying between the Yellowstone River and Judith Basin be added to the new reservation. Long Horse seconded Blackfoot's remarks. Delano ignored the objections to the treaty which had just been raised and terminated the meeting with the observation that although he didn't really understand the purpose of the Indians' visit to Washington, he would arrange for a meeting with the president.[20]

President Grant met with the delegation for a short time on October 29. He asked the tribe's leaders to maintain peaceful relations with their neighbors, encouraged them to initiate farming operations, and urged that the tribe's young be persuaded to take advantage of the educational opportunities being offered them. The visit ended with an exchange of gifts. Grant was given a buffalo robe by Blackfoot, and the president, in turn, presented his Indian guests with pipes. Blackfoot was most dissatisfied with the delegation's encounter with Great Father. He later grumbled that the president had obviously been less than interested in talking with the Crow and blamed the delegation's inability to make the tribe's opposition to the proposed treaty known to Grant on the temerity of the two interpreters.[21] After the meeting with President Grant, the delegation adjourned to the office of Commissioner Smith where Blackfoot, with vociferous support from both Iron Bull and Long Horse, once again pressed for inclusion of additional lands in the proposed new reservation. Smith refused to consider the matter because the treaty had already been submitted to the Senate for ratification. He did indicate, however, that if and when the treaty was approved, he would consider adding the Musselshell Valley. Blackfoot raised the issue of spending money for the delegation on its return trip. He asked for one hundred dollars for each delegate and, after some wrangling with the commissioner, agreed to settle for fifty dollars per delegate.[22]

Two days later Pease and his charges embarked on the long journey home. He found it necessary to stop over in New York City for a week. He justified the delay on the grounds that several Indians had taken ill on the trip from Washington.[23] The party checked into a hotel where it remained until November 8. Great Father unknowingly provided a variety of entertainment for the Indians: meals served in rooms, baths, cigars, carriage rides, and a boat trip to Long Island.[24] The Crow may not have had as much fun in New York, though, as in the nation's capital where Pease had arranged for visits to brothels.[25] The trip from New York City to the reservation was interrupted for several days more in St. Louis where, according to Pease, Iron Bull fell ill. The delegation, traveling by rail, arrived at Corinne, Utah on November 26, and from there they caught a stage-coach to Bozeman.[26]

Shortly after his return Pease was designated by the Indian Service, along with Lieutenant G.C. Doane of Fort Ellis, to visit the lands to be included in the proposed new Crow reservation. Their purpose was to prepare a report on the general characteristics of the area. The two were also instructed to select a site for a new agency.[27] Although told to include a variety of prominent Crow leaders in his party, Pease was able to persuade only Pretty Lodge, a River Crow, to accompany him. Blackfoot not only refused to take part in the enterprise, he also informed Pease that he would never move to the new reservation.[28] Accompanied by only one member of the tribe, then, Pease and Doane set out from the agency on December 23 and returned on January 30. A report of their findings was filed with the Indian Service in Washington on February 19, 1874. It confirmed that there were no permanent settlements in the lands included in the proposed reservation and observed that, although the basin was prime buffalo country, it lacked sufficient water for successful agricultural operations.[29]

The treaty creating the new reservation was submitted to the Congress on January 17, 1874, and the lands affected by the treaty were withdrawn from sale and settlement by Executive Order of January 31, 1874.[30] However, the treaty was never ratified and, in fact, failed to reach the floor of the Senate. On March 25, 1874 the lands in question were restored to the public domain by Executive Order of that date with a notation that the Crow had refused to move to their new reservation and that Congress had failed to ratify the new treaty.[31] It seems more than likely that the financial failure of Jay Cooke & Co. in late 1873, along with the consequent cessation of work on the Northern Pacific Railroad, had at least as much to do with the government's action in returning the lands to the status quo as did the reasons cited.

The status quo included dissatisfaction in some quarters with the location of the old agency. James Wright had begun agitating for a new agency site while still serving as superintendent and continued to do so after assuming the post of Crow agent. In his first annual report, for instance, he recommended that the agency be moved at the earliest possible moment because of its proximity to liquor dealers. He added that the Indians would prefer an agency site closer to their hunting grounds. In letters written to the commissioner of Indian affairs on the subject, he expressed his concern about the influence of traders at Benson's Landing and complained about the physical shortcomings of the existing site.[32]

Finally, in late October of 1874, Smith instructed the agent to scout out and recommend a new site.[33] By this time Wright's resignation had been accepted, and the search for a new site had to be deferred pending arrival of his successor, Dexter Clapp. Clapp set out on December 16 to scout lands lying east of the existing agency. He subsequently recommended that the new agency be constructed at the junction of the Stillwater and Rosebud Rivers, approximately sixty miles east of the old agency and twenty miles south of Yellowstone River. Clapp justified his choice on the availability of good agricultural lands, its distance from the pernicious influences of liquor shops, and the absence of the strong winds which made life miserable for inhabitants of the old agency.[34] Commissioner Smith approved the location on March 22, 1875, and at the same time authorized the expenditure of fifteen thousand dollars toward construction of a new agency compound. Work on agency buildings commenced on June 1 and was completed in early November. When completed, the new agency complex was very much like the Mission Creek Agency in appearance.[35]

If the Indians were consulted on the suitability of the new agency, their views on the matter seem not to have been heeded. Captain George L. Tyler of Fort Ellis reported to his superiors shortly after construction was commenced that the Crow were dissatisfied with the new location. First and foremost, he maintained, they were concerned that the presence of the agency and its personnel would drive the buffalo away from what the tribe regarded as prime hunting grounds. Another objection voiced by some tribal members, according to Tyler, was that the projected new site typically received inordinate amounts of snow, reducing the amount of pasturage available for their horses. And then there was the matter of a Crow burial ground being located nearby.[36] Clapp admitted that there was some resistance to the move on the part of a few Crow, but claimed that whatever dissatisfaction existed had been implanted in the minds of tribal members by those who wanted to protect the illicit liquor trade at Benson's Landing.[37]

Clapp may have misrepresented the facts. His successor, George W. Frost, observed in his first annual report that the agency:

> . . . could scarcely, all things considered, have been located in a more unfavorable position. Just as good water could have been found, much better soil and more arable pasture and hay land could have been secured in many parts of the reservation. In winter the snow covers the ground, feed is scarce for the animals belonging to the agency, and for the ponies of the Indians while in many parts of the large reservation but

> little snow remains on the ground . . . The
> present site has not one advantage over the old
> agency, and it has a great many disadvantages
> that were not found there.[38]

Governor Potts was of the opinion that the Crow were adamantly opposed to the move and that, moreover, the new location posed security problems for agency personnel.[39] Suggesting collusion between the Crow agent and the agency trader, Captain D.W. Benham of Fort Ellis believed that the move had been instigated by Nelson Story as a strategy to secure a monopoly on Crow trade against the trading posts located at Benson's Landing. An article which appeared in the April 30 edition of the *Avant Courier* lends credence to Benham's conjecture. It noted that the majority of Crow trade was being conducted in four trading houses located on the north bank of the Yellowstone.[40]

At about the same time that Agent Clapp began construction of the new agency complex, he took steps to further isolate the new site from outside influences. On June 23 he recommended that a strip of land twenty miles in width, bounded on the south by the Yellowstone River, on the west by Big Timber Creek and by a projection of the existing boundary on the east be added to the reservation on its northern border. Justification for the addition of more lands was identical with one which Wright had advanced for moving the agency; the Indians needed to be isolated from the whiskey dealers who were at the time already moving their operations to locations along the north bank of the Yellowstone as a strategy to get as close as possible to the site of the projected new agency.[41] President Grant issued an Executive Order on November 20, 1875 approving Clapp's recommendation by withdrawing the lands in question and adding them to the reservation.[42]

News of the Crow reservation expansion raised a fire storm of protest from almost every quarter. Territorial Representative Martin Maginnis objected to the addition on the grounds that it was nothing more nor less than yet another attempt by Nelson Story to assure a trade monopoly with the tribe.[43] Governor Potts complained to Secretary Delano that the Crow reservation was already the nation's largest in proportion to the tribe's population. In this same complaint the governor raised the question of why, if the agency's location in fact placed the Indians in the clutches of liquor dealers, the recent relocation hadn't placed the agency far enough away from the reservation's northern border to preclude this problem. Opposition from the town of Bozeman was also made evident. Meetings were held to organize methods for opposing the expansion, and a petition signed by sixty-six citizens of the town was submitted to the president in which he was asked to rescind his recent order.[44] Governor Potts was notified in March of the following year that representations from the Territorial Legislative Assembly against the extension, coupled with the Bozeman petition, had prompted President Grant to rescind his order and restore the lands to the public domain. The president passed along a suggestion that the territory enact legislation to suppress illegal liquor sales.[45]

If the charges levied by Captains Tyler and Denham as well as by Representative Maginnis that movement of the agency and extension of the reservation were effected at the instigation of Nelson Story, there obviously had occurred, at least in these instances, collusion between Story and both Wright and Clapp. There is, in fact, evidence that collusion between Indian Service officials and certain favored residents of Bozeman was a common practice in the management of Crow Agency. The first beneficiary of this

larcenous symbiosis was Leander M. Black, the
reservation's first trader and builder of the original
agency complex. In addition to receiving the contract
for constructing Crow Agency, he was granted a
contract by Commissioner Parker to transport annuity
goods from Corinne, Utah to the several agencies
located in Montana Territory for fiscal year
1870–71.[46] Large scale peculation, however, focused
mainly on Crow subsistence supplies. The $130,000
annually appropriated for this purpose was obviously
viewed by some as a new form of bonanza in an
economic environment depressed by a decline in gold
mining. Black, in partnership with Nelson Story,
enjoyed a monopoly in the sale of subsistence supplies
to the tribe until the summer of 1871.[47] The two men
also furnished foodstuffs to other agencies in the
territory.[48]

Black's good fortune in these matters seems to have
stemmed from his relationship with Ely S. Parker.
That a special relationship did exist between the two
men is suggested by Black's practice of communi-
cating directly with the commissioner about affairs on
Crow reservation even after his appointment as
temporary agent was terminated in November of
1869. Black wrote the commissioner on numerous
occasions to provide instructions on the payment of
certain vouchers and to request information on the
distribution of the 1870 annuities, as well as on other
matters.[49] Black certainly wasn't above using his
connections with Parker to further his aims and
ambitions. Agent M.M. McCauley of the Blackfoot
Reservation complained to Parker that Black tried to
induce him, McCauley, to falsify vouchers in the
amount of $45,000 with a promise that if the agent
did so, he could expect to keep his job as long as
Grant was president. The entrepreneur allegedly cited
his friendship with Parker as proof that he could
deliver on his promise.[50]

Commissioner Parker had a personal connection with Crow Agency in the person of his brother, Isaac Newton Parker. Like his illustrious brother, Isaac had served in the Union Army during the Civil War, but unlike Ely, hadn't risen above the non-commissioned officer rank. In fact, despite a good education, he hadn't done much of anything with his life. Regarded as something of a black sheep, he became a source of acute embarrassment to his family in 1855 as the result of a scandalous involvement with a married woman in Hartford, Connecticut.[51] The commissioner was probably responsible for his employment at the agency on September 7, 1870, as its first teacher. If Isaac Parker was in fact employed by the agency at the behest of his powerful brother, it may have been to satisfy Ely Parker's desire to place someone at the agency to watch over whatever pecuniary interests he might have had there. Or, more likely, Isaac's presence at the agency was arranged merely as a convenience to the Parker family.[52]

There is no hard evidence that Alfred Sully personally profited from Black's Crow Agency dealings, but it must be remembered that in his role as superintendent, Sully would have had to recommend all supply contracts and approve all vouchers issued to Black. That Sully may indeed have been involved in illegal goings on is suggested by an observation made by General P.H. Sheridan to General W.T. Sherman that irregularities had occurred in Sully's conduct of Indian affairs in Montana.[53] There is, however, irrefutable evidence that Superintendent Viall acted in collusion with Black. For one thing, Black acted as one of two sureties on Viall's $100,000 bond for faithful performance of his duties as superintendent.[54] In a blatant instance of conflict of interest, Viall recommended on May 11, 1871, that Black be given a contract to supply all Indian agencies in Montana Territory for fiscal year 1871-72. Parker approved Viall's recommendation on June 1.[55] Two days later, however, H.R. Clum of the Indian Service notified Viall that Parker's approval had been revoked and that new contracts would be let based on competitive bids.[56] This sudden reversal of policy coincided with a campaign on the part of William Welsh to root out corruption in the Indian Service. Welsh had been named as the first chairman of the Board of Indian Commissioners but had resigned from that post as a protest against the board's lack of power. He thereafter made efforts to reform the Indian Service as a private citizen.[57]

Welsh started at the top, charging Parker with irregularities in connection with a contract he had let to James Bosler of Carlisle, Pennsylvania in June of 1870 for subsistence supplies to be furnished various tribes living along the Missouri River.[58] Welsh's charges prompted an investigation of Parker's tenure in office by the House Committee on Appropriations beginning on January 18, 1871. The investigating committee cleared the commissioner of any intent to defraud but did criticize Parker's role in the affair on the grounds of neglect of duty, irregularities, and incompetence. The committee recommended passage of legislation that would give the Board of Indian Commissioners supervision over all expenditures made by the Indian Service. In the past the board had been authorized to check only vouchers dealing with annuities. Enabling legislation was included in the Indian Appropriations Act of March 3, 1871. Parker resigned from his office effective on July 31, 1871, complaining that the new procedure would unnecessarily complicate the commissioner's job.[59]

Neither Black nor Story was a successful bidder in the letting of contracts for Crow subsistence supplies for fiscal year 1871–72. Higgins and Hagadorn, a commercial firm in Helena, won the right to furnish beef to the reservation, and a Hiram Faris received the contract to provide flour and other foodstuffs for the tribe's sustenance.[60] That Black was still somehow involved in furnishing supplies to the tribe, however, is suggested by reports carried in the *Avant Courier* that he made deliveries of flour to the agency in December of 1871 and again during the following month.[61]

The occasion of letting contracts for the 1872–73 supplies resulted in a break of relations between Black and Viall. The bids were opened at Helena in early July under the supervision of B.R. Cowan, Assistant Secretary of the Interior.[62] The contract for all foodstuffs except beef was awarded to John T. Baldwin of Council Bluffs, Iowa. Nelson Story was the successful bidder for beef.[63] Black, perhaps angry because his bid for flour was rejected, withdrew his name as surety on Viall's performance bond on July 6. A few weeks later, the *Avant Courier* which was owned by Black and can therefore be assumed to have reflected his views, excoriated Viall as the head of what the article called the Iowa Indian Ring and went on to accuse the superintendent of fraudulently granting a contract for foodstuffs to his fellow Iowan, John Baldwin.[64]

Viall probably had little or nothing to do with the decision to let the contract to Baldwin. A man of questionable ethics and morality, the latter was a long-time associate of General Grenville Dodge, a civil war veteran, builder of railroads, and crony of President Grant. Dodge and Baldwin had formed a banking and real estate business in Council Bluffs during the 1850s, and the two men continued their business relationship into the 1870s. Their joint ventures included the furnishing of Indian supplies to various Indian tribes.[65] Dodge received contracts for supplying Indian goods amounting to $537,966.81 in his own name during fiscal year 1872–73.[66] That he was involved in Baldwin's Crow contract is indicated by his actions in presenting vouchers in Baldwin's name to the Office of the Commissioner of Indian Affairs for payment.[67] Dodge was called before Congress in 1874 to explain certain irregularities in his dealings with the Indian Service and admitted that he had in the past received contracts on bids which turned out to be higher than bids submitted by others, and that he had on at least one occasion been allowed by Commissioner E.P. Smith to substitute corn for flour at highly inflated prices.[68]

Leander Black, this time in partnership with Nelson Story, emerged with a pecuniary interest in the 1872–73 subsistence supplies for the Crow. According to Felix Brunot, Nelson Story purchased the contract from Baldwin.[69] Black's participation in the enterprise can be deduced from a notation which appeared on vouchers for Crow supplies that he had been granted Baldwin's power of attorney.[70] By the summer of 1872, Black was widely regarded as one of Bozeman's most substantial and wealthy citizens. Not only did he own the *Avant Courier*, he also served as president of the First National Bank of Bozeman. In addition the entrepreneur operated both retail and wholesale commercial establishments, a freighting firm, a livery stable, a saloon, and a hotel. In keeping with his role as merchant prince of Bozeman, he customarily traveled around town in a Concord coach drawn by spirited, prancing horses equipped with gold-plated harness. The prince and his family took temporary leave of Montana Territory in late autumn of 1872 to take up residence in the nation's capital.[71]

Jasper Viall left the territory at about the same time as the Blacks. Charges of malfeasance on the part of the superintendent had surfaced early in 1871. Blackfoot Agent, M.M. McCauley, accused Viall of improprieties in the distribution of annuities, and these accusations were brought to the attention of the House of Representatives on March 14, 1871. However, no action was taken by that body.[72] Felix Brunot had been asked to look into the accusations while he was in Montana Territory during the summer of 1872. The commissioner reported that although he had talked to a number of Montanans who were not only willing but anxious to charge Viall with fraud, evidence was lacking to substantiate the charges.[73] Viall's tenure as superintendent was ended neither by Leander Black's campaign to discredit him nor by charges of irregularities in the performance of his duties. Viall was fired for political reasons. Governor Potts, angry because the superintendent refused to get rid of an agent who happened to belong to the wrong political party, wrote to Secretary Delano on November 14 accusing Viall of employing political enemies of the administration. Viall was called to Washington on November 28 and after a meeting with Delano, resigned effective on December 10.[74]

The office of superintendent was partially removed from temptation at about the time that James Wright took over the post. Contracts for subsistence goods to be distributed in Montana were let in New York City rather than in Helena, beginning in 1873. But on at least one occasion during Wright's term as superintendent, he was guilty of nepotism. Shortly after he assumed office, he granted trading licenses to his son-in-law, Robert Cross, in partnership with Nelson Story, for a trading post in Judith Basin and another at the confluence of the Big Horn and Yellowstone Rivers. The *Avant Courier* was suspicious of the Superintendent Wright from the very beginning, noting that Wright's home was in Iowa and expressing hope that he was not part of the Iowa Ring.[75] The paper may have been expressing a valid concern. Wright's cover letter submitting his hundred thousand dollar performance bond was written on stationery bearing the letterhead of the Pacific National Bank of Council Bluffs. Grenville Dodge and John T. Baldwin were identified on the letterhead as being president and vice-president, respectively, of the firm.[76] Apart from the above-cited instance of nepotism, however, there is no extant evidence that Wright abused his position as superintendent.

At the agency level Fellows D. Pease had the longest tenure during the reservation's first decade of operation. It seems reasonable to conclude that General Sully was responsible for his appointment. Their relationship went back at least as far as 1865 when Pease was cleared of illegal trading charges by a military commission which reported directly to the general. During the summer of 1868, Pease was appointed temporary agent of the Blackfoot Agency by Sully, pending arrival of the army officer chosen to administer the agency. And at the time that a successor to Captain Camp was being considered, the superintendent recommended that a civilian with broad experience on the frontier and among the Indians be appointed. Pease certainly fit this description.[77]

At the very least Pease was guilty of practicing nepotism in his administration of the agency. Two of his cousins, S.B. Bowen and Z.H Daniels, both served at one time or another as agency farmer, and as such, both administered the agency during the agent's many absences.[78] Pease also appears to have been guilty of petty theft. Thomas Cree, who served as secretary for the Brunot Commission in 1873, reported to the commissioner of Indian affairs that Pease routinely drew rations from Crow subsistence supplies to feed agency employees. For the period which began on August 1 and ended on August 10, 1873, he drew 200 pounds of flour, 35 pounds of corn meal, 200 pounds of beef, 45 pounds of bacon, 22 pounds of coffee, 33 pounds of sugar, 20 pounds of hominy, 30 pounds of beans, 10 pounds of apples, 8 pounds of salt and 4 pounds of soap for this purpose. According to Cree, Agent Pease turned only part of this over to the agency cook; he sold the remainder on the open market. Worse, Pease collected five dollars per month from each employee for board.[79] G.G. Holloway, a miner in Emigrant Gulch, registered a complaint with Secretary Delano in 1873 that the Crow agent was involved in much more serious improprieties in his administration of the reservation. Holloway complimented Pease on his management of the Indians under his jurisdiction but was concerned that the agent's relationship with contractors might sometime in the future bring about a breakdown in peaceful relations between the tribe and white settlers. Specifically, he accused Agent Pease of collusion with contractors in depriving the Indians of goods promised them in the Treaty of 1868. The miner's fear was that the Crow might take out their frustration in not receiving expected goods on their white neighbors.[80]

There are indications that contractor Leander Black enjoyed a special relationship with Pease. Black's *Avant Courier* carried several laudatory articles about the agent which congratulated him for his deft management of the Crow, praised his honest nature, and expressed gratitude for his relationship with Bozeman residents.[81] That Pease may have reciprocated with pecuniary favoritism is suggested by instructions the agent received from Commissioner F.A. Walker in late 1871 that he was to discontinue making purchases for the Indians from the agency trader. Black, of course, still had an interest in the agency trading post at that time.[82]

A better case can be made for collusion between Pease and Nelson Story. On July 13, 1873 Story delivered thirty-seven hundred pounds of flour to the agency which had been purchased by Pease on an exigency basis.[83] In the view of Indian Service officials in Washington, Story was paid an exorbitant amount for the shipment. When called upon to explain the inflated price paid for the flour, Pease lamely explained that he had no reason to believe that any other contractor would have given him a lower price.[84] On another occasion Pease was called upon to justify a voucher issued to Story for delivery of 180 head of cattle. The issue which had been raised by auditors in this regard was that the average weight specified in the voucher was 250 pounds per animal in excess of that specified in previous vouchers. The explanation offered by the agent on this occasion was that these particular cattle had been grazed in the Yellowstone Valley and were for this reason of an unusually large size.[85]

Furthermore, the vast majority of services contracted to be performed for the agency during the tenure of Pease were with either Story or his partner in the agency trading post, Charles W. Hoffman. These services included sawing firewood, constructing a warehouse, and transporting goods to the agency.[86] Goods purchased from Story included horses, seeds, farm implements, tea, hominy, cornmeal, and beans.[87] Pease also purchased gifts from the agency trader consisting of both food and dry goods which were furnished the Indians who attended the treaty council conducted by Felix Brunot in 1873. Charles Hoffman also supplied gifts for the Indians on that occasion. Hoffman was favored by Pease in other ways as well. He was, for instance, granted a contract to build twenty-five small log houses for the agency at a cost of eleven thousand dollars.[88]

Despite what appear to have been improprieties on his part, Pease completed his services as Crow agent in the good graces of the Indian Service. Not only was he designated to accompany tribal leaders to Washington after the treaty council held during the summer of 1873, he was also given responsibility for making a feasibility study for the proposed new reservation. He seems to have had the support of Governor Potts, who, when he learned that Pease might be replaced, recommended to Secretary Delano that he be retained in office because of his ability to maintain peaceful relations between Indians and settlers.[89] James Wright didn't share the governor's high regard for Pease. In his letter of resignation from the post of agent, he specifically recommended that Pease not be re-appointed.[90]

Given the animus he felt toward his predecessor, it is interesting that Wright's administration of Crow Agency so closely paralleled, in some respects, that of Pease. The minister's eighteen-year-old son was employed by the agency as a laborer, and Robert Cross, the agent's son-in-law, held the post of agency farmer,[91] Wright followed the practice initiated by Pease of diverting Indian subsistence supplies to his employees, one of whom complained to Representative Maginnis that the agent, despite having criticized Pease for charging his employees for board, was collecting ten dollars per month from every employee for this service. Furthermore, continued the complaint, the boarding plan under Pease had been optional, whereas it was mandatory under his successor.[92] When questioned about this practice, Wright admitted that he did distribute Indian rations to agency employees but that he drew only single rations for each, whereas his predecessor had drawn double rations. He justified his charges for food furnished employees on a need to pay the agency cook out of his own pocket.[93]

The most telling similarity in the two men's administration of the agency was the virtual monopoly enjoyed by Nelson Story in furnishing goods, services, and supplies contracted locally. During Wright's term of service as agent, all extant vouchers issued by the agency for such expenses were in favor of Nelson Story with only one exception. This was a voucher in favor of his brother, Elias, for cutting hay.[94] All purchases of foodstuffs by Wright on an exigency basis were also made from Story. Short of flour, coffee, and sugar in early May of 1874, the agent purchased $13,243.70 worth of those commodities from the contractor.[95] Wright made a series of additional exigency purchases from Story beginning in late June and ending in September, 1874. These included flour, coffee, sugar, hominy, rice, and potatoes, and totaled $17,187.58. Perhaps because he regarded the purchase of exigency supplies in the amount of $30,000 in only four months excessive, the commissioner of Indian affairs notified the agent in October that he was to purchase no more foodstuffs without express permission from higher authority.[96]

There is in fact a great deal of additional evidence which appears to link Agent Wright with contractor Story. Horace Countryman, who served as agency miller for a time, charged in 1878 that Wright and Story conspired to divert Crow annuity goods and subsistence supplies to a trading post that the contractor operated with C.W. Hoffman in the Judith Basin. Countryman claimed to have first-hand knowledge of a large quantity of bacon taken from an agency storeroom and transported to the trading house in November 1873.[97] William Carr, a teamster for Nelson Story, claimed that he saw Story, Robert Cross, Peter Koch, and Wright loading a wagon with sugar and coffee at the agency destined for the same trading post. On another occasion Carr helped Story drive unbranded cattle to the agency where the two largest cattle were weighed to determine an average weight. The entire herd was then driven, uncounted, into a corral which contained unbranded agency stock. Carr subsequently told Wright that Story had chosen unrepresentative animals to weigh and that he had failed to take an accurate count of his herd before placing it in the corral. The agent thanked the teamster and said that he would look into the matter. In the nine days that Carr was present at the agency on this occasion, Wright did nothing to rectify the situation.[98]

James Wright, like Pease before him, closed out his term as agent for Crow Reservation in good standing with the Indian Service. He went on to Fort Hall where he served as agent from January of 1874 until June 22, 1875 when he returned to his farm, and perhaps to his parish, in Iowa. He surfaced again in 1882 when he was appointed Special Agent to perform unspecified duties as an inspector for the Indian Service.[99] Dexter E. Clapp didn't fare as well as his predecessors. His years as agent were marred by charges of fraud which were aired in the House of Representatives, a major investigation of his relationship with Story, and an inquiry into the financial aspects of his tenure as agent by the Senate. Clapp came under suspicion soon after he took over as agent. On April 15, 1875, one J.M. Yandell wrote a letter to the secretary of the interior in which he accused Clapp and Story of stealing both annuity and subsistence supplies destined for consumption by the Crow. Yandell charged that clothing included in shipments of annuity goods was sold by the two men to merchants in Bozeman and in other Montana towns. With regard to subsistence supplies, he claimed to have personal knowledge that Story, in collusion with the Fort Peck agent, W.W. Alderson, diverted 189 barrels of sugar intended for the Dakota to the Crow Agency. Clapp issued a voucher to Story for the merchandise, but rather than distributing it to the Crow, allowed the contractor to retain the sugar. It was later sold to merchants throughout western Montana, according to Yandell.[100] Commissioner E.P. Smith detailed Inspector E.C. Watkins to investigate Yandell's charges.[101] The Indian Appropriations bill of 1873 had carried an amendment which authorized the president to name five inspectors with summary powers to investigate reports of fraud in the Indian Service.[102] Watkins spent several days at the agency in late September of 1875 investigating the complaint, but no charges were brought against either man as a result of his inquiries.[103]

This didn't end Clapp's problems nor those of contractor Story for that matter. In February of the following year, Captain Edward Ball of Fort Ellis submitted a report to Commissioner Smith in which he charged that the two had conspired to defraud the government. Called to the agency for the purpose of inspecting a shipment of mess pork being delivered by Story as specified by law, Ball claimed that the contractor had offered him a thousand dollars to certify that the average weight of the barrels was 450 pounds rather than their actual average weight of 279 pounds. Story reputedly also suggested to Ball that with his cooperation they, along with Agent Clapp, could make a great deal of money from future shipments of Crow subsistence goods. Ball reported that he peremptorily refused to be party to Story's scheme. The officer's inspection of the merchandise in question revealed that it consisted mainly of heads, shoulders, backs, and inedible trimmings, and, as a result, Ball rejected the entire shipment. Story also delivered a shipment of flour on the same day. Established procedures for inspecting flour involved random sampling of the shipment and, if up to specifications, stamping each sack. Ball found that Story had double sacked the flour and concluded that the contractor had in mind removing the outer, stamped sacks and running the shipment through the inspection process again.[104]

Commissioner Smith didn't take immediate action on Ball's charges, but at the local level Story and Clapp were summoned before a federal grand jury sitting in Virginia City to answer the charges which had been made by Captain Ball. The grand jury adjourned on April 11 without bringing indictments against them. The presiding judge, H.N. Blake, made it clear in dismissing the jury that he was dissatisfied with its deliberations and intimated that he believed it had been tampered with in an effort to protect Story and Clapp against indictment.[105]

In late August the Indian Service finally got around to investigating the charges which had been levied by Ball. Inspector E.C. Kemble was dispatched to the agency with instructions which referred to the grand jury hearing and informed the inspector that Story and Clapp had publicly imputed malicious intent on Ball's part. Kemble was also apprised of a rivalry which had developed between Leander Black and Story over Crow subsistence contracts after the former had returned to Bozeman from Washington in August of 1874.[106] The inspector didn't arrive at the agency until October 1, 1876. He reported back to the commissioner of Indian affairs on November 10 that his investigation of the affair had led him to the conclusion that the charges which had been made by Captain Ball were indeed true and that he, Kemble, had, in addition, turned up evidence that Clapp and Story had conspired to submit vouchers for flour and meat never delivered.[107] Kemble informed the commissioner that he had summarily relieved Clapp of his office on October 26 and that he had later discharged all agency employees.[108]

Story later admitted to Indian Service officials that the barrels containing mess pork had originally held inferior cuts of meat but that he had discovered the unsuitable character of the shipment only on the way to the agency. The objectionable pieces were removed, he averred, and replaced with suitable cuts before delivery. As for the double-sacked flour, the contractor readily acknowledged that he was guilty as charged but explained that he routinely double-sacked flour to preclude leakage in shipment. Regarding the allegation that he had offered Captain Ball a bribe, Story pointed out that the small amount he would have gained by falsifying the weight simply wouldn't have been worth the risk involved. With regard to the false vouchers purportedly issued to him by Agent Clapp, Story categorically denied their existence. Finally, Story attacked Ball's character, portraying him as an inveterate gambler and drinker.[109] Clapp, for his part, directed an angry letter to Commissioner J.Q. Smith protesting his innocence on all counts and accusing Inspector Kemble himself, of being part of an "Indian Ring" which was, according to the ex-agent, protected by President Grant.[110]

There may have been more to the imbroglio over Crow subsistence supplies than meets the eye. Governor Potts was of the opinion that Leander Black was behind Kemble's investigation of Ball's charges. According to the governor, Black and Story had for several years been trying to discredit each other with the Indian Service. Then, when the grand jury failed to indict Story and Clapp, Black used his influence in high places to set in motion an official inquiry into the matter.[111] The bad blood between Story and Black referred to by Potts first surfaced shortly after Black's return to Bozeman in late summer of 1874. In its

September 4 edition, Black's newspaper, the *Avant Courier*, published an article which denounced James Wright for his management of the agency and strongly hinted at malfeasance on Story's part in his dealings with the agency.[112] Two weeks later the newspaper accused the two men of acting in collusion to charge the government fraudulently high prices for beef furnished to the Crow.[113]

It isn't possible, given the availability of pertinent evidence, to sort out the charges and counter charges levied by the various participants in this sordid affair. But there is sufficient evidence to characterize the business of supplying the Crow tribe with annuities and rations as a frontier quick step performed against a backdrop of funhouse mirrors and punctuated by puffs of blue smoke which obscured the more blatant instances of larceny. The purported beneficiaries, the Crow, paid the fiddler for this dance macabre in the currencies of insufficient foodstuffs and shoddy merchandise.

Nor is there any way from a vantage point so far removed in time from the events in question, to determine how much of the resources intended for the tribe were siphoned off by Indian Service officials and contractors. That it was considerable can perhaps be inferred from the subsequent careers of the Bozeman participants. Nelson Story, for instance, became one of the wealthiest individuals in Montana. His holdings included a bank, wheat farms, livestock ranches, and mercantile establishments. In his declining years, he divided his time between Bozeman and Los Angeles, California, where he maintained a palatial residence. Story's sometime partner, C.W. Hoffman, became involved in coal mining, merchandising, and stock raising. In addition, he served as president of the Bozeman National Bank for a number of years.[114] Fellows D. Pease did well for himself in the years following his service as Crow agent. He held interests in silver mines located on Clark's Fork as well as in a number of coal mines. Pease also owned a large livestock ranch in Yellowstone Valley. That he was successfully involved in local politics is indicated by his service as a delegate to Montana's Constitutional Convention held in 1883. Of the principal players, only L.M. Black's career ended badly. Things started to go wrong for him in 1878 when his First National Bank of Bozeman failed, forcing him to sell all of his property in Bozeman. He subsequently moved to Butte, where he died of peritonitis on June 18, 1881.[115]

White settlers in Montana Territory were of two minds about having the Crow as neighbors. The vast majority seemed to regard their reservation as a nuisance and an obstacle to progress. Some, in fact, wanted it moved so that its lands could be made available for economic development. In response to this sentiment, a new treaty was negotiated with the tribe which, had it been ratified by the Senate, would have exchanged the reservation for inferior lands to the north. That the Crow agreed, however reluctantly, to the treaty is a reflection of the degree to which they had become dependent upon Great Father for subsistence, indeed for their very survival. A small minority of the tribe's neighbors were in favor of the reservation because they had found pecuniary advantage in its proximity to Bozeman. This privileged few included agency traders and contractors who furnished supplies to the Indians in accordance with the Treaty of 1868. Indian Service officials responsible for administering the treaty, from agents up to the highest ranks of the bureaucracy, also found ways to profit from the reservation system. It seems that no one connected with the distribution of government goods to the Indians was immune from corruption whether soldier, freighter, rancher, merchant, or minister.

NOTES

1. P. Koch, "The Crow Indians and Their Neighbors," *Nation,* XXVIII (February 13, 1879), 116-7.
2. *Ibid.*
3. E.S. Topping, *The Chronicles of the Yellowstone* (Minneapolis: Ross & Haines, Inc., 1968), pp. 4-5.
4. Letter, G.W. Frost to E.P. Smith, September 28, 1877, LRMS, reel 506.
5. Letter, J.A. Viall to E.S. Parker, May 6, 1871, LRMS, reel 491.
6. Topping, *op. cit.,* pp. 238-9.
7. RCIA, 1871, House Executive Document No. 1 (Serial 1505), p. 805.
8. RCIA, 1872, House Executive Document No. 1 (Serial 1560), pp. 462, 662; Clark C. Spence, *Territorial Politics and Government in Montana: 1864-89* (Urbana, Chicago, London: University of Illinois Press, 1975), P. 117.
9. TCG, 42nd Congress, 2nd Session, p. 1586, reel 48; TCG, 42nd Congress, 3rd Session, pp. 1309, 1343, 2126, 2205, 2209, reel 49.
10. RCIA, 1872, House Executive Document No. 1 (Serial 1560), p. 662; Letter, F.D. Pease to Commissioner of Indian Affairs, July 12, 1872, RMSI, reel 1.
11. *Fourth Annual Report of the Board of Indian Commissioners to the President of the United States: 1872* (Washington: Government Printing Office, 1872), pp. 71-75.
12. Letter, J.A. Viall to F.A. Walker, September 26, 1872, LRMS, reel 493; Letter, H.R. Clum to J.A. Viall, October 18, 1872, ROLS, reel 110.
13. Letter, C. Delano to Commissioner of Indian Affairs, May 14, 1873, LRMS, reel 495; C. Delano to Commissioner of Indian Affairs, July 12, 1873, *ibid;* Letter, E.P. Smith to F.R. Brunot, May 31, 1873, ROLS, reel 112.
14. Letter, T. Cree to E.P. Smith, August 1, 1873, LRMS, reel 494.
15. This account of the proceedings is, unless otherwise indicated, taken from *Fifth Annual Report of the Board of Indian Commissioners to the President of the United States: 1873* (Washington: Government Printing Office, 1874), pp. 93-124.
16. Earl of Dunraven, *The Great Divide: Travels in the Upper Yellowstone in the Summer of 1874* (Lincoln: University of Nebraska Press, 1967), p. 67.
17. Letter, F.R. Brunot to C. Delano, November 19, 1873, LRMS, reel 494.
18. Herman J. Viola, *Diplomats in Buckskins: A History of Indian Delegations in Washington City* (Washington: Smithsonian Institution Press, 1981), pp. 13-21, 24.
19. Letter, F.D. Pease to E.P. Smith, October 20, 1873, LRMS, reel 495.
20. Report of Council with Delegation of Crow Indians from Montana, October 21, 1873, *ibid.*
21. Letter (F.D. Pease for) Blackfoot to Great Father, December 5, 1873, LRMS, reel 500.
22. Council Held in Office of Commissioner Affairs with Delegation of Crow Indians, October 29, 1873, LRMS, reel 495.

23. Letter, F.D. Pease to Commissioner of Indian Affairs, November 1, 1873, *ibid.*
24. Voucher, Grand Central Hotel, November 8, 1873, *ibid.*
25. Letter, F.D. Pease to B.F. Beveridge, April 11, 1874, LRMS, reel 500.
26. Letter, F.D. Pease to E.P. Smith, November 26, 1873, LRMS, reel 495.
27. Letter, E.P. Smith to F.D. Pease, November 12, 1873, ROLS, reel 114.
28. Letter, B.F. Potts to C. Delano, March 14, 1874, LRMS, reel 500; Letter, J.A. Wright to E.P. Smith, December 31, 1873, *ibid.*
29. Report: G.C. Doane and F.D. Pease, February 19, 1874, LRMS, reel 498.
30. TCR, 43rd Congress, 1st Session, Vol. II, Part 1, p. 957, reel 1.
31. Charles C. Royce, *Indian Land Cessions in the United States,* Eighteenth Annual Report of the Bureau of American Ethnology, (Washington: Government Printing Office, 1899), II, 864; George E. Fay, ed., *Treaties, Land Cessions, and other U.S. Congressional Documents Relative to American Indian Tribes: The Crow, 1825-1912* (Greeley: Museum of Anthropology, 1982), pp. 27-28.
32. RCIA, 1874, House Executive Document No. 1 (Serial 1639), p. 569; Letter, J.A. Wright to E.P. Smith, June 24, 1874, LRMS, reel 500; Letter, J.A. Wright to E.P. Smith, October 5, 1874, *ibid.*
33. Letter, E.P. Smith to J.A. Wright, October 21, 1874, ROLS, reel 120.
34. Letter, D.E. Clapp to Commissioner of Indian Affairs, December 22, 1874, LRMS, reel 501. Thomas Leforge claimed that he and Mitch Boyer selected the new site. Thomas B. Marquis, *Memoirs of a White Crow Indian* (Lincoln: University of Nebraska Press, 1974), p. 110.
35. RCIA, 1875, House Executive Document No. 1 (Serial 1680), p. 804; James H. Bradley, *The March of the Montana Column: A Prelude to the Custer Disaster* (Norman: University of Oklahoma Press, 1961), p. 38. The new agency was used for only ten years. The tribe accepted a new treaty in June of 1880 in which they ceded more than a million and a half acres, including the site of the old agency, back to the government in return for twenty-five annual payments of $30,000. The treaty was ratified by Congress and approved by the president on April 11, 1882. A new agency was constructed in 1884 near its present location, approximately fifteen miles south of Hardin, Montana. RCIA, 1880, House Executive Document No. 1 (Serial 1959), p. 115; RCIA, 1882, House Executive Document No. 1 (Serial 2100), p. 54; RCIA, 1884, House Executive Document No. 1 (Serial 2287), p. 153.
36. Memorandum, G.L. Taylor to D.W. Benham, appended to Letter, D.W. Benham to Assistant Adjutant General, June 29, 1875, LRMS, reel 503.
37. RCIA, 1875, House Executive Document No. 1 (Serial 1680), p. 805.
38. RCIA, 1877, House Executive Document No. 1 (Serial 1800), pp. 528-9.
39. Letter, B.F. Potts to B.R. Cowen, August 20, 1875, LRMS, reel 502.
40. Letter, D.E., Benham to Acting Assistant Adjutant General, July 8, 1875, LRMS, reel 501; *Avant Courier,* April 30, 1875.
41. Letter, D.E. Clapp to E.P. Smith, June 23, 1875, LRMS, reel 501.
42. Letter, E.P. Smith to D.E. Clapp, October 25, 1875, ROLS, reel 126. A copy of the Executive Order can be found in Faye, *op. cit.,* p. 29 and in RCIA, 1877, House Executive Document No. 1 (Serial 1800), p. 639.
43. Letter, M. Maginnis to C. Delano, September 27, 1875, LRMS, reel 502.
44. Letter, B.F. Potts to C. Delano, September 27, 1875, *ibid; Avant Courier,* November 12, 1875; Petition to President Grant, n.d., LRMS, reel 505.
45. Letter, Secretary of the Interior to B.F. Potts, March 9, 1876, General Correspondence, 1864-1888, Executive Office, Record Series 40, Box 1, Folder 14, HSML. The recision has been published in Faye, *op. cit.,* p. 29.

46. Letter, E.S. Parker to L.M. Black, August 30, 1870, ROLS, reel 95.
47. All vouchers for Crow subsistence supplies approved by both Viall and Sully until this date were in favor of either Story or Black. See *passim,* LRMS, reels 490, 491, 492.
48. For examples, see Letter, Lewis Johnson and Co. to Commissioner of Indian Affairs, August 10, 1871, LRMS, reel 491; Letter, E.S. Parker to Mssrs. Rittenhouse, Fowler and Co., April 22, 1870, ROLS, reel 95; Letter, E.S. Parker to H.C. Swain, October 21, 1870, ROLS, reel 97.
49. For examples, see Letter, L.M. Black to E.S. Parker, March 4, 1870, LRMS, reel 490; Letter, L.M. Black to E.S. Parker, September 29, 1870, *ibid;* Letter, L.M. Black to E.S. Parker, March 2, 1870, *ibid;* Letter, L.M. Black to E.S. Parker, March 4, 1870, *ibid.*
50. Letter, M.M. McCauley to E.S. Parker, February 13, 1871, LRMS, reel 491.
51. William H. Armstrong, *Warrior in Two Camps: Ely S. Parker, Union General and Seneca Chief* (Syracuse: Syracuse University Press, 1978), pp. 56–57, 82.
52. Letter, W.F. Cady to E.M. Camp, September 7, 1870, ROLS, reel 98; Letter, F.D. Pease to J.A. Viall, January 5, 1871, RMSI, reel 1; RCIA, 1871, House Executive Document No. 1 (Serial 1505), p. 808.
53. Letter, P.H. Sheridan to W.T. Sherman, n.d., LRMS, reel 490.
54. Letter, L.M. Black to Commissioner of Indian Affairs, July 6, 1872, LRMS, reel 491. The other surety was C.K. Peck, owner of Northwest Transportation Co. Letter, J.A. Viall to F.A. Walker, October 5, 1872, LRMS, reel 493.
55. Letter, J.A. Viall to E.S. Parker, May 11, 1871, LRMS, reel 491; Letter, E.S. Parker to J.A. Viall, June 1, 1871, ROLS, reel 101.
56. Letter, H.R. Clum to J.A. Viall, June 3, 1871, *ibid.*
57. Francis Paul Prucha, *The Great Father: The United States Government and the American Indians* (Lincoln and London: University of Nebraska Press, 1984), I, 508.
58. *Ibid,* p. 520; *New York Times,* January 31, 1871, p. 8. Bosler was a native of Carlisle, Pennsylvania. He had in the past supplied army posts along the Missouri River with supplies.
59. Armstrong, *op. cit.,* pp. 152–61.
60. Letter, J.A. Viall to Commissioner of Indian Affairs, August 1, 1871, LRMS, reel 491.
61. *Avant Courier,* December 14, 1871, January 18, 1872.
62. Letter, F.A. Walker to B.R. Cowan, July 6, 1872, ROLS, reel 107.
63. Letter, F.A. Walker to J.A. Viall, July 24, 1872, *ibid.*
64. Letter, L.M. Black to Commissioner of Indian Affairs, July 6, 1872, LRMS, reel 492; *Avant Courier,* July 25, 1872.
65. Stanley P. Hirshson, *Grenville M. Dodge: Soldier, Politician, Railroad Pioneer* (Bloomington and London: Indiana University Press, 1967), pp. 28–30, 52, 59–60, 176–7.
66. *Ibid,* p. 186.
67. For examples, see Letter, E.P. Smith to J.A. Wright, May 9, 1873, ROLS, reel 111; Letter, H.R. Clum to G.M. Dodge, August 21, 1872, ROLS, reel 113.
68. Hirshson, *op. cit.,* pp. 197–8.
69. Letter, F.R. Brunot to C. Delano, August 28, 1873, LRMS, reel 494.
70. See *passim,* LRMS, reel 492.
71. *Avant Courier,* September 13, 1871, October 11, 1871, June 6, 1872, November 14, 1872.

72. TCG, 42nd Congress, 1st Session, pp. 108, reel 46; Spence, *op. cit.,* p. 82.
73. *Fourth Annual Report, op. cit.,* p. 69.
74. *Ibid,* p. 83; Letter, C. Delano to Commissioner of Indian Affairs, December 10, 1872, LRMS, reel 492.
75. *Avant Courier,* August 22, 1873.
76. Letter, J.A. Wright to C. Delano, December 25, 1872, LRMS, reel 496.
77. Letter, A. Sully to E.S. Parker, January 15, 1870, LRMS, reel 490.
78. Letter, F.D. Pease to J.A. Wright, April 29, 1873, RMSI, reel 1; Letter, H.R. Clum to J.A. Viall, August 26, 1872, ROLS, reel 108; *Avant Courier,* April 4, 1872.
79. Letter, T. Cree to E.P. Smith, March 6, 1874, LRMS, reel 498.
80. Letter, G.G. Holloway to C. Delano, April 15, 1873, LRMS, reel 495.
81. *Avant Courier,* May 2, 1873, September 19, 1873.
82. Letter, F.A. Walker to F.D. Pease, December 19, 1871, ROLS, reel 105.
83. Supplies could be purchased by agents on the open market locally in cases of *bona fide* exigencies. Letter, E.S. Parker to J.A. Viall, November 16, 1870, ROLS, reel 97.
84. Letter, F.D. Pease to Commissioner of Indian Affairs, December 8, 1873, LRMS, reel 495; Letter, E.P. Smith to F.D. Pease, December 27, 1873, ROLS, reel 115.
85. Letter, Second Auditor to Commissioner of Indian Affairs, December 7, 1872, LRMS, reel 492; Letter, F.D. Pease to Commissioner of Indian Affairs, December 28, 1872, RMSI, reel 1.
86. Letter, F.D. Pease to J.A. Viall, November 22, 1872, LRMS, reel 493; Voucher: Nelson Story, December 1, 1872, LRMS, reel 494; Voucher: Nelson Story, January 25, 1873, *ibid.*
87. See *passim,* LRMS, reels 494, 495, 496, 497, 499, 500.
88. Voucher: C.W. Hoffman, August 16, 1873, LRMS, reel 495; F.D. Pease to J.A. Viall, April 14, 1871, LRMS, reel 491.
89. Letter, B.F. Potts to C. Delano, May 2, 1873, LRMS, reel 495.
90. Letter, J.A. Wright to E.P. Smith, June 2, 1874, LRMS, reel 500.
91. Letter, J.A. Wright to E.P. Smith, November 7, 1874, *ibid.*
92. Letter, Anonymous to M. McGinnis, February 28, 1874, Martin Maginnis Papers, Manuscript Collection No. 50, Box 1, Folder 16, HSML.
93. Letter, E.P. Smith to J.A. Wright, May 30, 1874, ROLS, reel 116; Letter, J.A. Wright to E.P. Smith, April 6, 1874, LRMS, Reel 500; Letter, J.A. Wright to E.P. Smith, June 30, 1874, *ibid.*
94. Letter, E.P. Smith to J.A. Wright, November 13, 1874, ROLS, reel 421; *passim,* LRMS, reels 498, 499, 500, 502.
95. Special Requisition, May 4, 1874, LRMS, reel 500.
96. Letter, E.P. Smith to J.A. Wright, October 28, 1874, ROLS, reel 121.
97. "Brisbin's Report of Indian Frauds Made to General Sheridan (draft), December 21, 1878," James S. Brisbin Papers, Manuscript Collection No. 39, Box 1, Folder 12, HSML, pp. 7–8. Major Brisbin seems to have been collecting evidence which would discredit the Indian Service. It isn't known if the draft was re-written and eventually mailed to General Sheridan.
98. *Ibid,* pp. 14–17.
99. Letter, H.R. Clum to J.A. Wright, June 22, 1875, ROLS, reel 124; Paul Stuart, *The Indian Office: The Growth and Development of an American Institution, 1865–1900* (Ann Arbor: UMI Research Press, 1978, 1979), p. 84.
100. Letter, J.M. Yandell to C. Delano, April 1, 1875, LRMS, reel 503. Alderson was a resident of Bozeman.

101. Letter, E.P. Smith to E.C. Watkins, July 10, 1875, ROLS, reel 127; Letter, E.P. Smith to E.C. Watkins, July 12, 1875, *ibid.*
102. Prucha, *op. cit.,* I, 590.
103. *Avant Courier,* October 1, 1875.
104. Ball's report, dated February 18, 1876, has been published in *Avant Courier,* July 28, 1876.
105. *Avant Courier,* April 14, 1876; Letter, S.A. Galpin to E.C. Kemble, August 30, 1876, ROLS, reel 132.
106. *Ibid.*
107. Letter, D.E. Clapp to Commissioner of Indian Affairs, n.d., LRMS, reel 506; *In the Matter of the Investigation Into the Affairs at the Crow Agency and the Conduct of the Late Agent, Mr. Clapp, and Nelson Story,* p. 2. A bound copy of this document can be found in the Montana Historical Society Library, call number 970.5/stz.
108. Letter, L.H. Carpenter to J.Q. Smith, October 26, 1876, LRMS, reel 504; *Avant Courier,* November 23, 1876.
109. *In the Matter of, op. cit.,* pp. 4-5, 8-12.
110. Letter, D.E. Clapp to J.Q. Smith, n.d., LRMS, reel 506.
111. Letter, B.F. Potts to E. Merritt, October 9, 1876, published in *In the Matter of, op. cit.,* pp. 16-17.
112. *Avant Courier,* September 4, 1874.
113. *Avant Courier,* September 18, 1874.
114. *Progressive Men of the State of Montana* (Chicago: A.W. Bower & Co., n.d.), pp. 248, 1256; Malcolm Story, *Bozeman's Early Businessmen,* typescript, Renne Library, Bozeman, Montana, No. 38.
115. *Bozeman Chronicle,* August 10, 1954, p. 2c.

TEN

THE DAKOTA AGAIN

The mutual hostility of Crow and Dakota warriors, briefly interrupted by the establishment of military posts along the Bozeman Trail, began to express itself again soon after suppression of the forts was announced. On June 7, 1868, for instance, the Crow raised a war party to avenge the death of one of their warriors at the hands of the Dakota.[1] For the greater part of the next decade, warfare would again characterize relations between the two long-time antagonists. Although Article II of the Crow Treaty of 1868 set aside lands for the absolute and undisturbed use by the tribe, many of the battles fought during these years would take place on these same reservation lands.[2] In fact the Crow would for a time be denied access to most of their reservation lands by the Dakota. All Dakota tribes accepted treaties in 1868 similar to the Crow treaty, but certain elements of the nation refused to submit to reservation life.

Referred to as non-treaty Indians by government officials, the dissidents roamed up and down the Yellowstone Valley, occasionally venturing north to the Missouri River. Adherents of Sitting Bull, a prominent leader of the Uncpapa tribe, formed the nucleus of the non-treaty Indians, but their numbers also included individuals from other Dakota tribes and from the Northern Cheyenne and Arapaho tribes as well. The population of the non-treaty Indians varied with the seasons. It was the practice of some dissidents to spend the winter months in one or

another of the Dakota reservations and then join
Sitting Bull when the weather moderated.[3]

Up until the summer of 1870, relations between the
Dakota and Crow were characterized by clashes
between small war parties alternating with periods of
peace during which the non-treaty Indians courted the
Crow in an attempt to persuade them to join their
movement to expel the whites. In most clashes the
Crow came off second best because, at least in their
opinion, Dakota warriors were better armed. Superintendent Sully apparently agreed with this assessment
because in the fall of 1869 he recommended, albeit
unsuccessfully, that a contingent of Crow warriors be
armed by the government to beef up the tribe's ability
to protect itself.[4] Relations with the Dakota took a
catastrophic turn for the Crow during the summer of
1870. In July of that year, a large band of enemy
warriors attacked a Crow camp of 160 lodges located
near the Little Big Horn River, well within the
confines of the reservation. The Crow suffered
thirteen casualties in the ensuing battle, and the entire
camp was forced to beat a hasty retreat. Some fled
northward to the Musselshell River; others fled
westward toward the agency, where they stopped only
long enough to complain to Agent Camp that they
had suffered defeat only because they had run out of
ammunition. From the agency they made their way to
the Three Forks area where they completed their
summer hunt.[5] This incident marked the end of Crow
control over that part of their reservation which was
situated east of the Big Horn River. They would only
infrequently pass beyond the river for the next half
decade or so.

Crow complaints about ammunition shortages
finally bore fruit during the summer of 1871. On
June 7 the secretary of war issued instructions to the
commander of Fort Ellis to furnish the tribe with

breech-loading rifles and appropriate ammunition. It
was also during the summer of 1871 that federal
officials decided that the Dakota posed a threat to the
well-being of white residents of the area. On July 24 a
party of non-treaty warriors, reputedly led by Sitting
Bull himself, raided several ranches in Gallatin Valley,
killing two settlers and running off 300 horses.[6]
Governor Potts subsequently informed Secretary
Delano that the Dakota intended to soon initiate full-
scale warfare against not only the Crow but against
white settlers in the Gallatin Valley as well.[7]
Superintendent Viall was of the opinion that Sitting
Bull had attracted perhaps a thousand lodges to his
camp at the mouth of Powder River that summer, and
it was Viall's judgment that the chief and his
followers also intended to block construction of the
proposed Northern Pacific Railroad.[8]

Secretary Delano thought the threat serious enough
to suggest to Viall that he visit the dissidents' camp
for the purpose of negotiating a peace treaty with
them. However, the army refused the superintendent's
request for a military escort to accompany him to
Sitting Bull's camp, and Viall accordingly decided
against making the effort.[9] A year later, a delegation
was named to meet in council with the non-treaty
Indians at the Fort Peck trading post to negotiate
their incorporation into the reservation system.
Assistant Secretary of the Interior B.R. Cowan was
appointed chairman of the commission with instructions that he make it clear to the Indians that the
government under no circumstances would change its
decision to support the building of a railroad through
Yellowstone Valley. It was thought unlikely that all of
the dissidents could be persuaded to accept reservation life, but Cowan was instructed to lure as many as
possible away from the Yellowstone and onto reservations through the distribution of gifts and
assurances of good treatment.[10]

The commissioner and his party arrived at Fort Peck to find few Indians in the vicinity. Runners were sent out and were able to persuade 453 lodges, including 69 lodges of Uncpapa, to come in. Sitting Bull declined to attend the council but sent his brother-in-law, Techanke, to observe the proceedings. Cowan refused to even discuss the railroad issue during the council proceedings, which he opened on August 21. The commissioner, in fact, tried to limit the council's agenda to the attractions of reservation life but found that the Indians wanted to discuss only their need for more arms and ammunition. Frustrated, Cowan ended the council without having accomplished anything of substance. In his report of the proceedings, he nonetheless recommended that a reservation be established for the non-treaty Indians at Fort Peck.[11]

Sitting Bull and his followers, in the meantime, had bigger fish to fry along the banks of the Yellowstone. On July 27, 1872, the day after Cowan arrived at Fort Peck, a Northern Pacific survey team, escorted by Major E.M. Baker and 187 men of the Seventh Infantry, left Fort Ellis to continue a survey conducted during the previous summer. The head surveyor was J.A. Haydon, and the survey team was under the general supervision of Major J.W. Barlow, Chief Engineer for the Military Division of the Missouri. The last stake of the 1871 survey was located on August 13 near the present site of Billings, Montana, and preparations were made to begin extension of the survey line.[12]

At three o'clock on the following morning, the command was awakened by a volley of rifle fire. A battalion of infantry was deployed to fire in the general direction from which the enemy fire had come. Desultory fire was exchanged until first light when two detachments of cavalry sallied forth to engage the attackers, clearing nearby bluffs of hostile warriors. By seven o'clock all immediate danger to the expedition had ended. Army casualties from the attack amounted to one dead and three wounded. One civilian had been mortally wounded. The Dakota left two dead bodies behind but got away with eight horses and fifteen cattle belonging to the surveyors and their escort. The party then proceeded to extend the survey line down the valley until August 20 when Haydon, despite assurances from Major Baker that the survey could be completed in safety, decided the risk of continuing was simply too great. Accordingly, the expedition broke camp that morning and struck out to the north for the valley of the Musselshell River where the survey party set out to lay a line from the Big Bend of that river back to Gallatin Valley.[13]

The retreat of the survey party was interpreted by the Crow as a failure of nerve on the part of Major Baker and his men. In a broader sense most tribal leaders viewed the incident as yet another expression of Great Father's inability to live up to his treaty obligation of ensuring the territorial integrity of their reservation.[14] Agent Pease was convinced that the impudence and impunity with which the Dakota and their allies violated Crow territory coupled with Baker's retreat had completely shaken the tribe's confidence in whites. According to Pease most members of the tribe had become convinced by the summer of 1872 that it was only their presence in the region which protected settlers in the Gallatin Valley from annihilation by the Dakota.[15]

Crow contempt for white military prowess was dramatically illustrated by an exchange which took place between Blackfoot and Felix Brunot during the council the latter held at the agency in 1873. One of the arguments advanced by the commissioner to convince the Indians that it would be to their advantage to exchange existing reservation lands for a new reserve in Judith Basin was that the proposed rail line would be inimical to the Crow way of life. He pointed out that although a railroad on the northern border of the reservation would assure faster delivery of annuity goods, it would also attract large numbers of whites to the general area of the reservation. And, he warned, construction of the railroad would proceed with the inevitability of a whirlwind. Blackfoot responded that in his opinion the Northern Pacific Railroad whirlwind was of little force. He reminded Brunot that the railroad's survey party, despite protection by a large military force, had been deflected from its course by a few Dakota warriors.[16] If the commissioner didn't understand that he had been deftly hoist on his own petard, he certainly should have.

As it turned out the attackers had not been in the area to block the survey party's advance down Yellowstone Valley. Techanke told B.R. Cowan that the non-treaty Indians had not congregated in the upper reaches of the valley that summer to interfere with the activities of railroad survey parties. Rather, they were organizing themselves to wage warfare against the Crow. A Minneconjou chief named Black Moon later confirmed to Agent A.J. Simmons that Sitting Bull's war party had indeed been looking for a battle with the Crow when they happened on the survey party.[17]

The traditional enmity of the Crow and Dakota peoples undoubtedly partially accounted for the violent tenor of their relations during the reservation period. But the frequency of warfare between the two groups may have owed something to a special animus for the Crow felt by Sitting Bull. According to Frank Grouard, an adoptive member of the renowned Uncpapa leader's band, Sitting Bull's pronounced limp was the result of an encounter with a Crow warrior. In one of the innumerable small engagements fought between Dakota and Crow during the early 1870s, Sitting Bull challenged a Crow war party's leader to a knife duel. The unidentified Crow, apparently fearful of losing the contest, grabbed a rifle from a bystander, and, taking hurried aim at his opponent, shot him in the left foot. Sitting Bull, enraged, charged his opponent and inflicted a mortal knife wound.[18] Another incident recounted by Grouard suggests that the Uncpapa chief did indeed feel a special animosity toward the tribe. Sometime during the summer of 1870, thirty-one Crow warriors on a horse-stealing expedition were approaching Sitting Bull's camp located near the mouth of Powder River when they were accidentally spotted by the chief and some of his warriors. The Dakota gave chase, and the Crow, outnumbered, were forced to take refuge in a natural fortification located nearby. Despite the advantage of superior numbers, the pursuers were unable to dislodge the intruders. As the second night of siege approached, Sitting Bull convened a war council and informed his followers that Dakota honor demanded that all members of the enemy party be immediately killed. Therefore, he proclaimed, he was going to lead a frontal assault on the fortification in a kill or be killed effort. His warriors were free to join him or not as they chose. Twenty minutes later, all thirty-one of the enemy had been killed and scalped.[19]

In any event the retreat of Baker and his troops seems to have emboldened the non-treaty Indians almost as much as it had galled the Crow. In late August, 1872, Pease informed Superintendent Viall that a large band of Dakota had established a camp on Clark's Fork, some twenty miles south of the Yellowstone. Using the camp as a base of operations,

Pease complained, the dissidents had become a source of more or less constant harassment, both for the Crow and for agency personnel.[20] On September 21 a war party of one hundred or more warriors suddenly appeared at the agency and proceeded to run off mules and horses belonging to the agency and its employees. During this same raid, the intruders killed a Bozeman resident and his family who happened to be in the vicinity.[21] The situation had become so threatening by the first week of October that the agent requested protection from Fort Ellis, citing the reluctance of his employees to venture beyond the walls of the agency stockade to perform assigned tasks.[22] The situation turned out to be less desperate than Pease had imagined; a shortage of buffalo in the upper Yellowstone Valley forced the hostile Indians to move north into the Dry Forks of the Missouri area for the winter.[23]

During the early part of 1873, conflicts were limited to the sort of minor skirmishes attendant to horse stealing raids.[24] Later, though, a large band of Mountain Crow under Blackfoot was camped on Pryor Creek in mid-July when they were discovered by a party of Dakota scouts. Aware that his camp's presence was known to the enemy, Blackfoot moved his people to a more defensible position near the mouth of the stream and prepared them for battle. And it was well that he took precautions. By sunrise of the following morning, the surrounding area was teeming with enemy warriors. The battle lasted until noon when the Dakota abandoned the field, retreating in confusion toward the Big Horn River. According to Tom Leforge who participated in the conflict, eight Crow warriors lost their lives in the encounter. The number of Dakota killed was not recorded.[25]

This singular victory by the Crow may have been attributable to a division of forces among the non-treaty Indians. At the time of the battle, a large contingent of Uncpapa and Sans Arc warriors was waiting at the mouth of Tongue River to greet Colonel David S. Stanley.[26] Colonel Stanley commanded a force of fifteen hundred men serving as a military escort for surveyors running a survey line up the valley of the Yellowstone for the Northern Pacific Railroad. Lieutenant Colonel George A. Custer (Son of the Morning Star) and his Seventh Cavalry were part of Stanley's command. Custer and his troopers engaged the Dakota warriors twice during the summer of 1873. The first battle took place near the mouth of Tongue River on August 4 and the second at the mouth of the Big Horn on August 11. In both instances the cavalry prevailed.[27]

Sitting Bull and his warriors soon regained the initiative, though. On September 3 a small raiding party made off with most of Crow agency's horses, killing and scalping two employees in the effort.[28] James Wright, only recently installed as agent, asked Commissioner Smith on September 20 to make arrangements with the secretary of war to detail one hundred troopers to the agency. Smith complied but was turned down by the army on the grounds that Montana Territory could not spare that many personnel for reservation duty.[29] All in all, by the end of the year, the non-treaty Indians had extended their control over all Crow reservation lands east of Clark's Fork, effectively depriving the tribe of more than half of the lands set aside for its exclusive use by the Treaty of 1868. By this time some members of the tribe had apparently despaired of surviving the unrelenting Dakota onslaught. Agent Wright notified his superiors in late 1873 that he had been informed by Iron Bull that a number of his followers were agitating for peace negotiations with the Dakota.[30]

The already troubled condition of the Yellowstone

Valley region was muddled and complicated by the actions of certain Bozeman citizens. Counting heavily on the proposed railroad to stimulate the economic development of Gallatin Valley, prominent citizens of the area were distressed when they learned in 1873 that the financial house backing the Northern Pacific Railroad, Jay Cooke & Co., had failed. Frustrated in their attempts to provide a rail link to markets for the valley's agricultural products, citizens of Bozeman clearly needed to come up with alternative transportation facilities. The most obvious solution was to use the Yellowstone and the Missouri River systems as waterways to the Northern Pacific's railhead at Bismarck and then tranship goods by rail from that point to markets in the eastern part of the nation. Even before it became general knowledge that construction on the railroad had been halted, Nelson Story, C.W. Hoffman and others, including a relative of Fellows D. Pease named S.B. Bowen, formed the Yellowstone Transportation Company for the dual purpose of building a wagon road to the head of navigation on the Yellowstone and raising money for the purchase of a steamboat. In late November the *Avant Courier* noted that the territory's representatives in the nation's capital were lobbying to secure appropriations for improving navigation on the river.[31]

It was known that the Yellowstone was navigable at least to the mouth of Powder River because steamboats had negotiated the river to that point during the summer of 1873 in support of Colonel Stanley's command. How much beyond this point steamships could pass was a matter of conjecture and would have to be determined before plans could be made for an alternate route to connect the Gallatin Valley with eastern markets. And then there was the matter of Dakota control over a substantial segment of the

river's course. The Indians' violent reaction to the
survey party escorted by Colonel Stanley's troops
augured ill for any attempt to establish communi-
cations systems of any kind through Dakota territory.
Pease, even before he turned his office over to James
Wright, was known to favor negotiating some kind of
settlement between the Dakota and Crow as a means
of restoring stability to the Yellowstone Valley.[32]
Several months after his official connection with
Crow reservation ended, he informed the commissioner of Indian affairs that the time was ripe for
negotiating a peace agreement with the non-treaty
Indians. Pease requested authorization to visit the
camps of hostile Indians to pursue this goal, but the
commissioner demurred on the grounds that there
was insufficient data available for him to make an
informed decision on the matter.[33]

Unresolved problems notwithstanding, representatives of the Yellowstone Transportation Company,
now calling itself the Yellowstone Transportation and
Prospecting Company, held a series of Bozeman
meetings in January of 1874 for the purpose of raising
money and men for an expedition to prospect for
gold and found a town at the head of navigation on
the Yellowstone.[34] Then, on January 8, J.L. Vernon,
an ex-school teacher from Bozeman, held a public
meeting of his own in which he called for volunteers
to join a prospecting party to search for gold in
Yellowstone Valley. He claimed to have been a
member of the survey party escorted by Colonel
Stanley in 1873 and maintained that in the course of
performing other duties he had happened upon large
deposits of gold in the vicinity of the Tongue River
delta.[35]

Organizers of the Yellowstone Expedition made it
abundantly clear that participants would be given
ample time to work the gold deposits discovered by

Vernon. It just happened that the Yellowstone's head of navigation was then believed to be the mouth of Tongue River. The final meeting sponsored by the organizers was held on January 17 when it was announced that the expedition would get underway on or about February 10. Another announcement was made that a number of small towns scattered throughout Gallatin Valley had donated arms, ammunition, and foodstuffs for the enterprise. Judge H.N. Maguire then took the podium to deliver a lecture on the history of gold prospecting in the lower Yellowstone Valley, culminating in Professor J.L. Vernon's recent discovery. The meeting closed with an announcement by Vernon that his proposed prospecting expedition had been called off and suggested that those who had planned to accompany him might want to join the company's expedition.[36]

Conclusive evidence is lacking to state categorically that the Yellowstone Transportation and Prospecting Company acted in collusion with Vernon for the purpose of attracting participants to the venture. But certainly the professor's report of gold discoveries in the very area where the organizers intended to found a town virtually guaranteed the organizers that the expedition would have sufficient fire power to make its way through what was known to be very hostile country. In any event 125 men with 20 wagons loaded with enough provisions for several months started down Yellowstone Valley in mid-February.[37] By the time the expedition reached the mouth of the Big Horn, its numbers, made up of wolfers, trappers, unemployed miners, and a few seasoned frontiersmen, had increased to 153.[38]

The column kept to the north bank of the river until it reached Big Porcupine Creek where terrain considerations forced it to cross the Yellowstone and leave its valley to follow a more southerly course.

Several days later, on March 26, a scouting party was attacked by a small band of hostiles. The scouts avoided taking any casualties, but on March 30 another scouting party was attacked and one W.A. Bostwick was seriously, but not mortally, wounded. That same night an attempt by a few warriors to stampede and make off with the participants' horses was foiled by alert guards. Continuing in a south-easterly direction, the expedition reached the Rosebud River on April 3 at a point about thirty miles above its mouth. Early next morning the camp was awakened by gunfire and found itself under attack by a sizeable war party made up of warriors from the Minneconjou and Two Kettles tribes. In the ensuing battle the whites suffered one casualty. Even though the attackers were eventually driven off, the expedition's members, apparently deciding that discretion was indeed the better part of valor, abandoned their goal of establishing a town at the mouth of Tongue River. The column changed its course to ascend the Rosebud River, reaching its major forks on April 8. Here they struck out in a westerly direction, intending to do some prospecting in the Wolf Mountain region. On April 12 the Dakota struck again, killing one.[39]

Again chastened, the Yellowstone Expedition set a course for the valley of the Little Big Horn where a meeting was held to consider a future course of action. Opinion was divided; some wanted to go south into Wyoming Territory to prospect for gold and others were in favor of returning to Bozeman. A consensus was eventually reached that they would find the Bozeman Trail and follow it to Goose Creek where a member of the party claimed to have found color several years before. On April 18, however, the column was again attacked, and, although no casualties were taken, the presence of hostile Indians coupled with bad weather, persuaded the majority of the participants that it would be futile to continue. Without having achieved either of its two stated goals, or much of anything for that matter, the expedition disintegrated, and its constituent parts straggled back to Bozeman. The fate of the expedition's abortive intrusion into Dakota territory can have done little to reassure the Crow with regard to their informal alliance with the Alien Culture. First, Major Baker's military contingent had retreated in the face of Dakota intransigence and now a large force of well-armed and well-provisioned civilians had met the enemy and been found wanting.

Government officials responsible for administering the Peace Policy were furious to learn of the activities of the Yellowstone Transportation and Prospecting Company. When Secretary of War Belknap heard that the expedition had entered territory controlled by hostile Indians, he dashed off an angry letter to Governor Potts pointing out that relations with the non-treaty Indians were complicated enough without an unwarranted intrusion into their lands by a large body of armed men. The governor's immediate superior, Secretary of the Interior Delano, informed him that he should have prevented the party's departure and strongly suggested that Potts had placed his territory at risk of a general Indian uprising by his failure to do so. In a letter written several days later, Secretary Delano instructed the governor to use every means at his disposal to preclude any further destabilization of an already precarious situation.[40] J.V. Bogert, a prominent Bozeman merchant and a stockholder in the Yellowstone Transportation and Prospecting Company, tried to mollify Delano in a letter written to the secretary on June 5. Bogert insisted that the expedition had not intended to violate the law and that any violence which may have occurred had been a matter of participants protecting themselves from

Indian attacks. The expedition, according to the merchant, was nothing more nor less than an act of desperation on the part of Gallatin Valley residents. They were simply trying to establish a water transportation link to Bismarck in a last ditch effort to secure an outlet for surplus agricultural products grown in the valley.[41]

After departure of the Yellowstone Expedition, but before its first engagement with hostile Indians, Agent Wright began to complain to his superiors about the untenable situation of his agency.[42] His pleas for military protection were granted on March 20 with the arrival of a detachment of twenty-five men and one officer from Fort Ellis. This force remained on duty until June 1, when it was replaced by a force of fourteen. The smaller guard unit remained on duty at the agency until September 6, when all troops were withdrawn.[43] Wright also requested that the Crow be provided with government issue arms and ammunition to improve their chances of withstanding an expected Dakota onslaught. Despite endorsement by Governor Potts, Wright's request was denied on the grounds that the tribe already possessed sufficient arms and ammunition to defend itself. Potts was cautioned by Secretary Delano to do everything in his power to prevent the Crow from provoking their enemies. Rumors persisted in Bozeman and around the agency that a few Crow leaders, including Long Horse, were interested in making peace with the dissident Dakota bands.[44]

Hostile Indians were spotted hanging about the agency grounds in early July of 1874. A week later a small party of warriors attacked a work party at the agency sawmill, but no casualties were inflicted in the action. The same evening, however, the Indians were able to steal several horses from the agency herd. Not long thereafter, Dakota warriors were also spotted in the Gallatin Valley. A daring raid on the Fort Ellis herd netted the visitors several army horses. Throughout the first two weeks of August, enemy warriors were seen skulking around the agency, but they inflicted no damage.[45]

The residents of Bozeman continued to constitute a nuisance factor in affairs of the Yellowstone Valley, but the major source of destabilization in the region during the year 1875 was the removal of the Crow Agency to a location within thirty miles of lands controlled by the Dakota dissidents and their allies. Whatever considerations were operative in deciding to move the agency complex to this particular site, the consequences of locating the administrative head-quarters for the Crow tribe to a spot so close to their traditional enemies can't have been among them. It isn't clear whether the non-treaty Indians saw the new agency as a challenge to their control over lands recently taken from the Crow or whether its new location simply made it more convenient for the dissidents to attack a symbol of the tribe's alliance with the hated whites. Or perhaps it was simply that the agency's livestock herds presented a target too tempting for them to resist. Governor Potts was of the opinion that the agency's new location promised to precipitate a general Indian war and therefore recommended that it be abandoned.[46] Officials at Fort Ellis concurred with the governor's interpretation of the situation as well as with his recommendation.[47]

The troubles began on July 2. Early that morning a party of agency employees which was felling timber to be used in constructing agency buildings was attacked by hostile Indians in full war regalia. One agency employee was killed in the fray, and seven head of stock were driven off by the attackers. Agent Clapp and several of his employees visited the battlefield the following day to recover the body, but could find only a piece of scalp.[48] Shortly after midnight on July 5, the same Indians mounted an attack on the agency compound itself. No casualties were suffered by agency employees in this encounter, but the raiders were able to make off with thirty-two head of stock. The rustlers remained in sight of the agency until the following evening, taunting the agent and daring him to come out and fight. Agent Clapp, no stranger to warfare, asked Governor Potts to endorse his request that Fort Ellis furnish the agency with at least one company of men.[49]

Captain D.W. Benham, acting commandant of Fort Ellis, undoubtedly felt that he needed all the troops at his disposal to deal with security problems closer to home. On July 7, in fact, he reported to officials at Fort Shaw that a body of hostile Indians was moving up the valley of the Yellowstone toward Bozeman. Benham went on to ask that a company of troops from Fort Shaw be detailed to Fort Ellis as reinforcements.[50] The rumored attack on Bozeman never did materialize, but one citizen of the municipality was killed by a band of Dakota near the mouth of Shields River in early July. Two other residents of the town were fired upon in the same area the next day.[51] Then, on July 10 a party of three whites was attacked just north of the new agency site, near the mouth of Stillwater River. One man was killed and another seriously wounded. The agency complex was again attacked on July 21 with the loss of one horse and forty-eight oxen, and less than a week later a wagon train enroute from Bozeman to the agency was attacked and an employee of Nelson Story was killed. By August 1, when two agency employees were waylaid and slain while on their way from the agency to the Yellowstone River, travel anyplace in the general area was life threatening to all save those in large, armed parties.[52]

Clapp sent a telegram to the commissioner of Indian affairs on August 6 in which he urgently asked for fifty cavalrymen to be used as escorts for workmen trying to complete agency buildings.[53] By the middle of August, though, the situation had eased, either because the Dakota had given up on trying to obstruct construction progress or because they had tired of the game. On August 13 Clapp notified the commissioner to disregard his previous communication on security problems because he had been able to get the situation in hand.[54] Clapp did eventually receive aid from Fort Ellis. On September 11 one officer and ten men were sent to the old agency to escort employees and their families to the new agency. But the agent was clearly disgusted with the army for its unwillingness to furnish protection for his agency during times of need. In his annual report for 1875, he complained that although his requests for protection had been denied for lack of sufficient personnel, Fort Ellis officials were at the same time dispatching forces into areas where there was little if any chance that hostile Indians would be encountered. The agent, in fact, charged the post's commanding officer with being deliberately uncooperative for reasons having to do with the army's opposition to moving the agency.[55]

Contemporaneous with construction of the new agency, certain Bozeman residents were involved in events which also had the effect of destabilizing Yellowstone Valley. The fiasco which had resulted from the abortive attempt to establish a town at the mouth of Tongue River in 1874 didn't deter some of the principals of that questionable venture from trying again. In the April 2, 1875, issue of the *Avant Courier*, E.B. Way, a leader of the ill-fated Yellowstone Expedition, ran a notice to the effect that a new expedition would get under way in early May to prospect for gold in Yellowstone Valley.[56]

The driving force behind the second attempt to connect the Gallatin Valley with markets in the east seems to have been Fellows Pease.[57] The question of where the head of navigation for the Yellowstone really lay was about to be answered by the army which planned to send a steamship up the river for that purpose as soon as weather permitted.[58] There remained unresolved the intransigence of the non-treaty Indians who still controlled most of the Yellowstone River and its valley downstream from Clark's Fork. In an attempt to resolve this problem, Pease, who was generally acknowledged to have more influence over the Crow than any other white, arranged for the tribe to meet him at the mouth of the Big Horn on June 15. He had in mind negotiating a truce between the Crow and the non-treaty Indians. Unfortunately, Pease and his expedition didn't get away from Bozeman until June 17 and thus missed the scheduled rendezvous with the Crow.[59] A large party of Crow had in the meantime moved down the Yellowstone in early June, and they arrived at the mouth of the Big Horn on June 14. Their presence was almost immediately discovered by dissident Indians, and a major battle ensued. After three days of intermittent fighting, the Crow were forced to withdraw to the Musselshell River.[60] The Crow got revenge for this defeat a month or so later. On July 25 a Crow war party surprised a Dakota band in the Judith Basin, and, after a short but fierce battle, killed eight of the enemy, forcing them to beat a hasty retreat. However, the tribe paid a high price for the victory because the renowned warrior, Long Horse, lost his life in the battle.[61]

Pease and his party, consisting of thirty-two men, arrived at the mouth of the Big Horn about a week after the first battle between the Crow and the Dakota. He now knew that the head of navigation lay

upstream from that point because the army survey of
the Yellowstone's navigability had been completed on
June 6. Lieutenant Colonel James W. Forsythe had
left Fort Buford on March 26 aboard the steamship
Josephine. Under the competent command of Grant
Marsh, the steamship reached the mouth of the Big
Horn on June 2. Marsh gingerly piloted his vessel up
that river for a distance of twelve miles before turning
back to re-enter the Yellowstone. Continuing up that
waterway, the *Josephine* was able to reach a point just
beyond Pompey's Pillar. Preparatory to reversing his
course, Captain Marsh debarked to carve "Josephine,
June 7, 1875" on a cottonwood tree located near the
river's north bank.[62] Pease and his party had espied
the message on their way down river and could thus
safely assume that a trading post located at the mouth
of the Big Horn River would be well within reach of
steamboat transportation.[63]

The expedition's leader remained only long enough
to choose a suitable site for a trading post and
supervise commencement of its construction. Three
days after his arrival, Pease and two companions
floated down the river bound for Chicago and New
York City, where they hoped to raise capital for the
new venture. As Fort Pease took shape, it looked very
much like Forts Raymond, Benton, and Cass, all
constructed in that general location earlier in the
century to exploit the peltry trade. Although deep in
hostile territory, the party encountered only minor
resistance to its presence, perhaps because most of the
dissident Indians were at the time harassing the
builders of the new Crow agency. Hostile warriors
were sighted soon after arrival, but attacks were
limited to one instance of firing from a distance and
intermittent harassment of woodcutting details and
small hunting parties. In early October even these
attacks ended and not a single hostile Indian was seen
for several months thereafter.[64]

Pease returned to Bozeman on October 12 without the capital he had hoped to raise in the east but announced that he would be making a visit to the fort in early November. That he failed to do so was probably due either to his failure to find adequate funding for the project or to the fact that his attention was diverted to other, more lucrative, enterprises. In December he made another trip east in search of financial backing, but on this outing Pease was trying to raise capital for his silver mines located in the Clark's Fork region.[65] This is not to say that plans to connect Bozeman with Bismarck by water had been abandoned. The October 8 edition of the *Avant Courier* announced that Nelson Story and other investors planned to purchase a steamship capable of navigating the Yellowstone River.[66] One of Story's partners, Achilles Lamme, a prosperous Bozeman businessman, left Bozeman in November to purchase such a vessel in Jeffersonville, Indiana.[67] Lamme was successful in his quest and piloted his new steamboat, the *Yellowstone*, up the Missouri River, intending to enter and traverse the Yellowstone to its head of navigation. However, at the mouth of the Yellowstone, he received news of unsettled conditions in Yellowstone Valley, and he decided to continue up the Missouri to Fort Benton. The *Yellowstone* was later commandeered by the army to support its campaign against the non-treaty Indians in 1876. The vessel was eventually returned to Lamme, but it was never utilized for its intended purpose of transporting agricultural products from Bozeman to the railhead in Bismarck.[68]

Meanwhile, the occupants of Fort Pease had fanned out into surrounding lands to hunt wolves, taking full advantage of the disappearance of hostile Indians. Small camps were established by the wolfers as far east as the Rosebud River and others as far south as the Little Big Horn. In mid-December their activities were interrupted by the return of hostile Indians. During the last two weeks of the year, the scattered camps were repeatedly attacked or harassed. One trapper was killed and another wounded, and, by the end of the year, all had retreated to the relative safety of the fort. An all-out attack on the post was expected, but hostilities during the month of January were limited to isolated attacks on small parties which found it necessary to venture outside the confines of the post. Five casualties were taken during the course of the month. In late January a band of over one hundred warriors approached the fort, but it turned out to be a Crow war party which had just success-fully ambushed a small band of Dakota warriors. The visitors were invited in and proceeded to entertain their hosts with a scalp dance. Following departure of the Crow, wolfing operations resumed, albeit pro-secuted by larger parties than during the first round of trapping. There was only minor interference from the Dakota until late February when seven wolfers left the post to examine previously baited carcasses. A war party stumbled upon a temporary camp which had been established by the trappers about nine miles distant from the fort, and, in the ensuing battle, one white was killed and all of the party's horses were stolen.[69]

The perception in Bozeman regarding the Fort Pease situation, fed by wolfers who had tired of the post and returned to town, was that its occupants were in imminent danger of being overrun by hostile Indians. On February 19, 1876, Major James S. Brisbin, recently appointed commandant of Fort Ellis, asked for and received permission from General Alfred Terry to mount a rescue operation for what was believed to be a beleaguered outpost. Brisbin led a force of two hundred troops and fifty civilians out of

Fort Ellis on February 22 and arrived at the fort on March 4. The expedition found nineteen men there and learned that there were no hostile Indians at all in the immediate vicinity.[70] Many of the wolfers were reluctant to leave, but the major insisted. The post was evacuated and abandoned on March 6, 1876.[71] It is obvious that the wolfers of Fort Pease were not really in need of rescue. Either Brisbin had over-reacted to the stories of their plight brought back to Bozeman by deserters from the post, or, as Dexter Clapp later charged, the major had mounted the expedition as a favor to Bozeman merchants who had furnished trade goods and supplies for the post and were looking for a convenient method of assuring the safe return of their merchandise.[72]

Given their efforts to block the access of railroad survey crews during the summer of 1873, the mild reaction of the non-treaty Indians to the building of Fort Pease is puzzling. They could easily have overrun the installation and dispersed its occupants. Perhaps they were not aware that it had been constructed as an initial stage in the formation of a transportation system intended to link western Montana with the eastern part of the United States.

The resurgence of Dakota hostility after removal of the Bozeman Trail forts set in motion a new round of Dakota aggrandizement at the expense of the Crow. Although involving only a small minority of the Dakota nation, the non-treaty Indians were able to drive the Crow tribe from most of the lands set aside for them by the Treaty of 1868. This must have given the Crow pause about the wisdom of their long-established policy of allying themselves with the whites. The army, for example, located only thirty miles or so from the reservation agency was either unable or unwilling to guarantee the tribe use of its reservation lands. In the one confrontation between troops from Fort Ellis and the renegades, the soldiers abandoned their line of march after only one inconclusive battle. Well-armed civilian expeditions fared little better. Unfortunately, the military capabilities of the tribe were in a state of decline. The ease with which the non-treaty Indians were able to conquer and occupy Crow territory suggests that the warrior ethic which had stood them in such good stead in the past was diminishing. The death of Long Horse in 1875 serves as a convenient watershed event for this phenomenon. What seems to have happened in this regard was that the Crow, despite their misgivings about the efficacy of the Alien Culture's military establishment, had gradually, and perhaps subconsciously, come to depend on external forces as guarantors of their security just as they had come to depend on external forces to satisfy their material needs and wants.

NOTES

1. George H. Templeton, *Diaries 1866–1868* (typescript), Graff 4099, Folder, 22, The Newberry Library, p. 101.
2. George E. Fay, ed., *Treaties, Land Cessions, and Other U.S. Congressional Documents Relative to American Indian Tribes: The Crow, 1825–1912* (Greeley: Museum of Anthropology, 1982), p. 107; Charles J. Kappler, *Indian Affairs: Laws and Treaties* (2nd ed.: Washington: Government Printing Office, 1904), II, 1008–11.
3. Robert M. Utley, *Frontier Regulars: The United States Army and the Indian* (New York: Macmillan Publishing Co., Inc.; London: Collier Macmillan Publishing Co., 1973), pp. 239–40.
4. Letter, A. Sully to E.S. Parker, November 3, 1869, RMSI, reel 1.
5. Letter, A. Sully to E.S. Parker, August 14, 1870, LRMS, reel 490; RCIA, 1870, House Executive Document No. 1 (Serial 449), pp. 662–3.
6. Letter, W.W. Belknap to Secretary of Interior, June 7, 1871, LRMS, reel 491; Letter, J.A. Viall to Commissioner of Indian Affairs, July 26, 1871, *ibid.*
7. Letter, B.F. Potts to C. Delano, August 2, 1871, *ibid.*
8. RCIA, 1871, House Executive Document No. 1 (Serial 1505), p. 802; Letter, J.A. Viall to Commissioner of Indian Affairs, August 21, 1871, LRMS, reel 491.

9. Letter, C. Delano to H.R. Clum, September 16, 1871, *ibid;* Letter, H.R. Clum to J.A. Viall, September 22, 1871, ROLS, reel 103.
10. Letter, F.A. Walker to B.R. Cowan, June 21, 1872, ROLS, reel 108.
11. RCIA, 1872, House Executive Document No. 1 (Serial 1560), pp. 840–4.
12. *Letter from the Secretary of War, December 14, 1872,* Senate Executive Document No. 16 (Serial 1545), pp. 1–6; Major Baker is better known for his involvement in the destruction and massacre of a Piegan village in 1870. See Wesley C. Wilson, "The U.S. Army and the Piegans—The Baker Massacre of 1870," *North Dakota History,* XXXII, No. 1 (January, 1965), pp. 40–57.
13. *Letter from, op. cit.,* pp. 6–19; Edward J. McClernand, "Service in Montana, 1870 and 1871," *Military Affairs,* XV, No. 4 (Winter, 1951), 197–8.
14. Letter, J.A. Viall to Commissioner of Indian Affairs, September 26, 1872, LRMS, reel 493.
15. RCIA, 1872, House Executive Document No. 1 (Serial 1560), p. 664.
16. *Fifth Annual Report of the Board of Indian Commissioners to the President of the United States* (Washington: Government Printing Office, 1874), p. 114.
17. Letter, A.J. Simmons to B.R. Cowan, December 8, 1872, LRMS, reel 495.
18. Joe De Barthe, *Life and Adventures of Frank Grouard,* ed. Edgar I. Stewart (Norman: University of Oklahoma Press, 1958), pp. 80–81.
19. *Ibid,* pp. 103–5.
20. Letter, F.D. Pease to J.A. Viall, August 31, 1872, RMSI, reel 1.
21. RCIA, 1872, House Executive Document No. 1 (Serial 1560), p. 658.
22. Letter, F.D. Pease to J.A. Viall, October 8, 1872, RMSI, reel 1.
23. Letter, H.C. Thum to N.J. Turner, January 16, 1873, LRMS, reel 496.
24. Letter, F.D. Pease to J.A. Wright, February 1, 1873, RMSI, reel 1.
25. For Blackfoot's account of the battle, see *Fifth Annual, op. cit.,* pp. 104–5; for Leforge's account, see Thomas B. Marquis, *Memoirs of a White Crow Indian* (Lincoln: University of Nebraska Press, 1974), pp. 88–96.
26. Letter, E. Collins to Acting Assistant Adjutant General, October 7, 1873, LRMS, reel 497.
27. Utley, *op. cit.,* pp. 242–3.
28. Letter, Z.H. Daniels to F.D. Pease, September 3, 1873, LRMS, reel 497.
29. Letter, J.A. Wright to E.P. Smith, September 20, 1873, *ibid.*
30. Letter, F.R. Brunot to C. Delano, November 19, 1873, LRMS, reel 494; Letter, J.A. Wright to E.P. Smith, December 31, 1873, LRMS, reel 500.
31. *Avant Courier,* July 4, 1873, November 21, 1873.
32. Letter, N.B. Sweitzer to Assistant Adjutant General, January 10, 1874, LRMS, reel 500.
33. Letter, F.D. Pease to E.P. Smith, December 9, 1873, LRMS, reel 495; Letter, E.P. Smith to F.D. Pease, December 24, 1873, ROLS, reel 116.
34. *Avant Courier,* January 16, 1874.
35. *Ibid,* January 9, 1874.
36. *Ibid,* January 23, 1874.
37. Letter, N.B. Sweitzer to Assistant Adjutant General, February 11, 1874, LRMS, reel 500.
38. *Avant Courier,* March 6, 1874.
39. This account of the expedition is taken from James S. Hutchins, "Poison in the Pemmican; The Yellowstone Wagon-Road and Prospecting Expedition of 1874," *Montana: The Magazine of Western History,* VIII, No. 3 (July, 1958), pp. 8–25. For first-hand accounts, consult Oliver Perry Hanna, *The*

Old Wild West; Being the Recollections of O.P. Hanna, Indian Fighter and Frontiersman (typescript), MS 322-A, Wyoming State Archives; Charles Avery, *Charles Avery Reminiscences* (typescript), Small Collections No. 372, HSML; Addison M. Quivey, "The Yellowstone Expedition of 1874," *Contributions to the Historical Society of Montana*, I (1876), 268-84.

40. Letter, W.W. Belknap to B.F. Potts, March 9, 1874, General Correspondence, 1864-1888, Executive Office, Box 1, Folder 12, Record Series 40, HSML; Letter, W.W. Belknap to B.F. Potts, March 13, 1874, *ibid.*

41. Letter, J.V. Bogert to Secretary of the Interior, June 5, 1874, LRMS, reel 498.

42. Letter, J.A. Wright to E.P. Smith, March 5, 1874, LRMS, reel 500; Letter, J.A. Wright to E.P. Smith, March 14, 1874, *ibid.*

43. RPFE, March, June, and September, 1874.

44. Letter, E.P. Smith to J.A. Wright, April 7, 1874, ROLS, reel 116; Letter, C. Delano to B.F. Potts, May 22, 1874, General Correspondence, 1864-1888, Executive Office, Record Series 40, Box 1, Folder 12, HSML; Letter, Assistant Adjutant General to N.B. Sweitzer, April 15, 1874, LRMS, reel 500; Letter, J.A. Wright to E.P. Smith, June 9, 1874, *ibid.*

45. Letter, J.A. Wright to E.P. Smith, July 14, 1874, LRMS, reel 500; Letter, J.A. Wright to E.P. Smith, August 17, 1874, *ibid.*

46. Letter, B.F. Potts to C. Delano, July 8, 1875, LRMS, reel 503.

47. Letter, D.W. Benham to Assistant Adjutant General, July 8, 1875, *ibid.*

48. Letter, D.E. Clapp to E.P. Smith, July 5, 1875, LRMS, reel 501.

49. *Ibid;* Letter, D.H. Carpenter to G.L. Tyler, July 7, 1875, LRMS, reel 503; Letter, D.E. Clapp to B.F. Potts, July 9, 1875, General Correspondence, 1864-1888, Executive Office, Record Series 40, Box 1, Folder 13, HSML.

50. Letter, D.W. Benham to Acting Assistant Adjutant General, July 7, 1875, LRMS, reel 503.

51. Letter, D.W. Benham to Acting Assistant Adjutant General, July 9, 1875, *ibid.*

52. Letter, D.E. Clapp to E.P. Smith, August 4, 1875, LRMS, reel 501.

53. Letter, D.E. Clapp to E.P. Smith, August 4, 1875, *ibid.*

54. Letter, D.E. Clapp to E.P. Smith, August 13, 1875, *ibid.*

55. RCIA, 1875, House Executive Document No. 1 (Serial 1680), p. 805.

56. *Avant Courier*, April 2, 1875.

57. Letter, D.E. Clapp to E.P. Smith, April 6, 1875, LRMS, reel 501.

58. *Avant Courier*, April 2, 1875.

59. *Ibid,* June 18, 1875.

60. Letter, G.L. Tyler to D.W. Benham, n.d., LRMS, reel 503.

61. Letter, G.L. Browning to Assistant Adjutant General, July 30, 1875, *ibid.*

62. William E. Lass, "Steamboats on the Yellowstone," *Montana: The Magazine of Western History*, XXV, No. 4 (Autumn, 1985), 27-28.

63. E.S. Topping, *The Chronicles of the Yellowstone* (Minneapolis: Ross & Haines, Inc., 1968), p. 136.

64. *Ibid,* pp. 138-41, 150-2.

65. *Avant Courier*, December 17, 1875.

66. *Ibid,* October 8, 1875.

67. *Ibid,* November 5, 1875.

68. Charles W. Bryan, Jr., "Dr. Lamme's Gallant Sidewheeler 'Yellowstone'," *Montana: The Magazine of Western History*, XV, No. 3 (July, 1965), 29-34.

69. Topping, *op. cit.*, pp. 152-5, 159-63, 164-8.

70. Letter, J.S. Brisbin to Assistant Adjutant General, March 21, 1876, LRMS, reel 505.

71. Topping, *op. cit.*, p. 168.

72. Letter, D.E. Clapp to J.Q. Smith, April 15, 1876, LRMS, reel 504.

ELEVEN

DENOUEMENT

While the occupants of Fort Pease were struggling, unsuccessfully as it turned out, to establish a foothold in Dakota country, events in the nation's capital were moving toward a resolution of the non-treaty Indian problem. Apparently tiring of the intractable nature of the dissidents, President Grant decided to dismantle his Peace Policy. Accordingly, Commissioner of Indian Affairs J.Q. Smith, on December 16, 1875, instructed agents of the several Dakota reservations to notify non-treaty Indians that any who had not submitted to reservation life by January 31, 1876, would be classified as hostile Indians subject to military action. On February 1 the army was given authority to deal with those who not had complied with the ultimatum.[1]

The army's plan was to conduct a winter campaign in the hope of engaging the non-treaty Indians before their numbers could be augmented by reservation Indians who customarily joined them as the rigors of winter weather abated. The specific strategy, as it evolved, was to converge on the dissidents from three directions. Lieutenant Colonel George Custer was to hit them from the east, General George Crook (Three Stars), was to strike from the south, and Colonel John Gibbon was assigned the task of patrolling Yellowstone Valley to cut off any possibility of escape to the north. Crook left Fort Fetterman at the head of 883 troops on March 1, but his campaign failed due to an unfortunate combination of mismanagement and inclement weather. After dispersing a small band of Cheyenne on March 17 which they found camped along Powder River, Crook and his men ignominiously returned to their home base on March 26.[2]

Colonel Gibbon's home base was Fort Shaw, and he left there on March 17 at the head of six companies of infantry. He was joined by four troops of cavalry from Fort Ellis under the command of Major Brisbin on April 7. The combined forces made up what came to be called the Montana Column. Gibbon and a small detachment left the column on April 9 to meet in council with Crow tribal leaders at their new agency. Colonel Gibbon informed the Crow that he had come to make war on their enemies and invited them to join in his effort to drive them from Crow lands. Responses made by Blackfoot, Iron Bull and other tribal leaders reflected a deep-seated skepticism about the army's will and ability to prevail against the non-treaty Indians. The council ended with acrimonious complaints about treatment the tribe had received from agents and particularly about the inadequacy of subsistence supplies being furnished. The following morning, however, twenty-three warriors volunteered their services. Tom Leforge and Barney Bravo were hired on as interpreters, and Mitch Boyer was employed as a guide.[3]

Gibbon, his staff, and the new detachment of scouts left the agency on April 11 to rejoin the Montana Column. Early on the morning of the thirteenth, the entire command, consisting of 27 officers, 426 enlisted men and 27 scouts, guides and interpreters, began its march down the north bank of the Yellowstone River. Lieutenant James Bradley was given command of the scouting detachment and almost immediately alienated his charges by insisting that they stand reveille every morning. Leforge warned the lieutenant that the Crow would likely refuse to serve unless he relented. The scouts took a more direct approach. They went over Bradley's head to Gibbon, who, after hearing their complaints, gently suggested to the young officer that he might find it prudent to bend the rules in this instance. Even after the reveille issue was resolved to their satisfaction, the Crow chafed under what they considered to be onerous restrictions to their freedom of movement. Leforge was of the opinion that the traditional individualism which characterized Crow life made it difficult for them to submit to any form of discipline, let alone the rigors of army discipline.[4]

The column reached Fort Pease on April 21 without having encountered enemy warriors. Soon after their arrival, Gibbon received a dispatch informing him that Crook planned to lead another column out of Fort Fetterman but that he would not be able to take the field until, at the earliest, the middle of May. The colonel received a second dispatch which notified him that Custer had been delayed and would likewise be unable to start his campaign until about May 15. Gibbon accordingly decided to remain at Fort Pease pending receipt of further orders.[5]

The Montana Column spent the better part of the next three weeks in camp. The scouting detachment, including Bravo and Leforge, camped apart from the troops, but relations between the two groups were cordial. In fact the Crow freely exchanged visits with the soldiers, often indulging in horseplay with them. The monotony of camp life was occasionally broken by the need to conduct routine scouting operations. Although these were nominally under the command of Lieutenant Bradley, it is clear that the scouting detachment considered itself to be an autonomous body. According to Leforge, they held councils before and after each mission to smoke and make plans for upcoming operations or to critique completed excursions. That there were hostile Indians in the immediate vicinity became all too apparent on May 3 when the scouts awoke to find that thirty-two of their horses had been stolen. Bradley attributed the theft to the relaxed discipline dictated by General Terry and noted that the Crow greeted the loss of their mounts with tears. Thomas Leforge interpreted their reaction as more of a feeling of outrage at having been humiliated in the presence of the soldiers than of sorrow at having lost the horses.[6]

On May 9 Gibbon was notified that the Dakota Column was enroute to the Yellowstone and was ordered to resume his march down the valley for the purpose of establishing contact with Custer and his troops. The column got underway the following morning. On May 15, while camped several miles west of the mouth of the Rosebud, four scouts who had taken it upon themselves to wander off for a horse-stealing expedition several days earlier, returned to report that they had discovered a large, fresh trail which seemed to lead toward Tongue River. Bradley asked for and received permission to lead a small detachment in that direction to determine if enemy warriors had established a camp on that river. At the head of twenty soldiers, his five Crow scouts, and Barney Bravo, he set out with three days rations. The Crow had become party to this enterprise only reluctantly, and when the route they had chosen turned out to be inordinately difficult, Bradley gave them a stiff rebuke and informed them that the scouting party was going to Tongue River if it took a month. According to the lieutenant, the trail became easier almost immediately. On the following afternoon a large cloud of smoke was spotted rising from the general direction of Tongue River. Bradley immediately called a halt and informed his small detachment that when darkness fell, they would approach the village on foot to determine the number of lodges it contained. The Crow opposed the plan on the grounds that so many men would almost certainly be discovered; they insisted that they be allowed to scout out the village alone. Bradley refused because he feared that the Crow would be unable to resist the temptation to steal enemy ponies. The impasse couldn't be resolved; Bradley had to return to camp and report the existence of the village to Gibbon without being able to pinpoint its precise location or specify its size.[7]

The report apparently was specific enough for Colonel Gibbon because he made preparations to attack the village on May 17. To do so, however, he had to get his troops and supplies to the south side of the Yellowstone, and he found that the river was too swollen to ford. He therefore canceled the assault. Bradley was under the impression that his scouts were upset with the decision. The Indian auxiliary troops, it seemed to him, had been itching for an opportunity to exact revenge for the loss of their horses. Leforge, on the other hand, believed that they were less anxious to fight the enemy than the lieutenant assumed they were. The Crow, the interpreter explained, had been expressing misgivings among themselves about the undertaking for some time because they knew from past experience that the camps of the dissident Indians were greatly augmented by reservation Indians during late spring.[8] In any event, rather than leading the column into battle, Bradley and his scouts were sent up the Yellowstone to meet and escort back to camp some couriers expected from Fort Ellis. The couriers bore a dispatch from General Alfred Terry informing Gibbon that Custer had been relieved of command of the Dakota Column in favor of Terry and that it would not be able to rendezvous with Gibbon's forces for another month. President Grant, apparently angry with Custer over his testimony to a congressional committee investigating corruption in the Grant administration, had ordered the flamboyant cavalry officer's removal from command of the Dakota Column.[9]

On May 20 Gibbon received intelligence from his scouts that a large war party of enemy warriors was moving up the Yellowstone between the Tongue and Rosebud Rivers. Concerned that a company of cavalry he had previously sent out to scout that general area might blunder into the war party, Gibbon quickly mobilized his troops for a relief mission. Having found neither war party nor scouting detail by the time he reached the mouth of the Rosebud, Gibbon decided to halt there and make camp for the night. The cavalry patrol showed up the following morning and reported that they had not encountered a single hostile Indian nor had they seen evidence that any had tried to cross the Yellowstone to its north bank. Gibbon decided to establish a new base camp near the site of his overnight camp.[10]

The Montana Column spent the next two weeks here, and this interlude was spent in much the same way as during the enforced stay at Fort Pease. Routine scouting parties were sent out, but for the most part, officers and men were free to follow their natural proclivities. Lieutenant Bradley visited the site of Fort Van Buren to satisfy his historical curiosity, but most of his comrades-in-arms played cards, fished, wrote letters, slept, or talked. The boredom of camp life was eased by merchants from Bozeman who risked the wrath of hostile Indians to bring down two boat loads of fresh vegetables, butter, meats, tobacco, and alcoholic beverages for sale to Gibbon's men.[11]

Not everyone enjoyed the respite. The first violent contact with enemy warriors occurred here when two troopers and a civilian packer left camp without permission and were killed. Tom Leforge and Mitch Boyer had a more peaceful encounter with the enemy. They spotted several Dakota warriors on the south bank of the river at some distance from camp and engaged them in conversation from across the river. Leforge and Boyer learned that an exceptionally large number of Dakota had abandoned their reservations that spring because the subsistence supplies being doled out were insufficient for the needs of many families. The dissidents claimed that they would much rather expend their energies and resources on hunting than on fighting. The enemy warriors ended the conversation with a bizarre request for ammunition. The veteran frontiersmen did not report the encounter to Bradley. In fact, according to Leforge, the scouts failed to report many things observed during the course of the expedition, particularly the many signs they saw which suggested that the enemy was present in larger numbers than assumed. They adopted this strategy out of fear that revelation of an enemy presence might result in needless and fruitless sallies, or worse, a disastrous defeat for the command.[12]

These fears were undoubtedly intensified on May 27 when, conducting a routine scouting assignment, Bradley and his scouts learned that the large camp they had previously discovered on Tongue River was now located on the Rosebud River only eighteen miles south of the column's camp. Lieutenant Bradley hurried back to report his find to Gibbon, fully expecting his commanding officer to order an immediate attack on the enemy. But he did not; the Montana Column remained in camp until June 5 when it packed up and marched down the Yellowstone to the mouth of Tongue River where it arrived on June 7. Early the following morning, Major Brisbin and two other officers along with two Crow scouts floated in a small boat downstream to the mouth of Powder River where they found the steamship *Far West* tied up to the bank. General Terry arrived shortly thereafter and sent a dispatch to Colonel Gibbon instructing him to proceed downriver for the purpose of effecting a rendezvous with the steamer. Gibbon got away from camp at about seven o'clock on the following morning to intercept the steamboat approximately eight miles downriver, linking the two commands on June 9, almost three months after the Montana Column began its march from Fort Shaw.[13]

A week or so earlier, Crook's column, which he dubbed the Big Horn and Yellowstone Expedition, had belatedly left Fort Fetterman. Crook headed north from the post with fifteen companies of cavalry and five companies of infantry, making a total of forty-seven officers and one thousand enlisted men. His command was accompanied by several journalists and, of course, included assorted scouts, guides, interpreters and teamsters. The notorious Calamity Jane was numbered among the latter group. General Crook had telegraphed the Crow and Shoshone agencies from Fort Fetterman to request that auxiliary forces from both tribes join him en route. When the Indians had not made an appearance by the time Crook and his men reached the site of Fort Reno on June 2, the general dispatched three of his scouts to Crow Agency for the purpose of raising a force of auxiliary troops if such was not already on its way. Frank Grouard, Baptiste Pourier, and Louis Richard were chosen for the mission.[14]

Crook continued to probe northward until he struck Tongue River near the point where it crosses the present border between Wyoming and Montana. Here, on June 6, he established a temporary camp. Two days later a courier arrived bearing a dispatch with news that the requested Shoshone auxiliaries

were on their way. On the evening of June 9,
occupants of the camp were startled by a barrage of
rifle fire from a nearby bluff. The attack resulted in
the wounding of two soldiers. Both cavalry and
infantry units were deployed against the snipers,
causing them to disappear into the surrounding
countryside. Several days later, the camp was moved
south a few miles to the forks of Goose Creek to
await arrival of the Indian auxiliary troops.[15]

Grouard and his companions found it unnecessary
to journey all the way to Crow Agency. About a week
after leaving Crook's column, they were camped near
the site of Fort C.F. Smith when their presence was
discovered by a band of Crow warriors. After being
escorted to the Indians' camp, the emissaries called a
council where it was explained to the Indians that
General Crook needed their help in a campaign he
intended to wage against the Dakota and their allies.
The Crow were less than enthusiastic about the
enterprise, but in the end fifty-nine warriors under
chiefs Old Crow, Good Heart, and Medicine Crow
agreed to participate in the campaign. Perhaps dis-
trustful of Grouard because of his past association
with the Dakota, the volunteers were reluctant to
enter Crook's camp when it was sighted on June 14.
Grouard therefore went on ahead into camp alone to
return shortly with Captain Andrew S. Burt, who was
well known to the tribe from his service at Fort C.F.
Smith. Assured by Burt that a battle with their
enemies was indeed imminent, the Crow contingent
proudly filed into Crook's camp in full war regalia.
Crook received intelligence from them regarding the
activities of the Montana Column. He also learned
that Sitting Bull's camp was located at the mouth of
Tongue River.[16]

The new arrivals quickly made themselves at home
by constructing temporary lodges of saplings covered

with branches. Camp fires were soon blazing, and, as the soldiers congregated in small groups to observe their new allies, the Crow cooked and devoured food furnished them by the army. A few hours later, eighty-six Shoshone warriors entered camp to a boisterous welcome from the Crow contingent. Once the Shoshone had settled in, General Crook held a war council against the backdrop of an enormous fire to explain to his Indian auxiliaries what he had in mind for them. Old Crow rose to speak for his warriors. He proclaimed that the Crow were present to reclaim lands, including those on which the camp was located, stolen from them by the Dakota. Also, he continued, the Crow would participate in the impending battle to gain revenge for horses stolen from them and for the many Crow women and children murdered by a black-hearted foe. He sat down after promising his followers that they would not only win their lands back but would also take many enemy women as slaves and would steal many enemy horses as well. When the council broke up, the Indians returned to their respective camps to prepare themselves for the coming battle. These preparations included ceremonies which were noisy enough to keep most of Crook's men in a state of wakefulness for the better part of the night.[17]

The day of June 16 was devoted to those more practical forms of combat preparation which precede most battles. The Big Horn and Yellowstone Expedition, weapons glinting in the bright sunlight and flanked on either side by Indian auxiliaries in full battle regalia, got underway early the next morning. Lieutenant John Bourke, General Crook's aide-de-camp, happened to be riding with the Crow auxiliaries when he noticed tears running down the face of one of his companions. Asked by Bourke why he was weeping, the warrior replied that one of his uncles had been killed by the Dakota some years before and that the tears were for this relative who could not be present to exact revenge.[18] Enroute to the lower reaches of Rosebud River, a large herd of buffalo was spotted. Both the Crow and Shoshone warriors immediately broke ranks and dashed pell-mell into the animals with their brilliantly colored war bonnets trailing in the wake of galloping mounts. The general was annoyed, fearing that the whooping and yelling of the hunters had nullified whatever element of surprise the column might have enjoyed to this point. He was undoubtedly even more annoyed that evening when he learned that his auxiliary troops had built fires on which to cook the fruits of their hunt despite express orders to the contrary.[19]

At the crack of dawn on June 17, Crook broke camp and set his column in motion down the headwaters of the Rosebud River. At about eight o'clock it passed the junction of the south branch of the river with its north fork and entered the valley of the main river. From this point the Rosebud runs in an easterly direction for about three miles before making a sharp bend to the north. The valley here is bounded on the south by high bluffs and on the north by a series of gently rising slopes which were later named Crook's Hill. Approximately one mile from the river's bank, the slopes of Crook's Hill suddenly steepen to form what is now called Conical Hill. Crook's Hill is bounded on the west by an intermittent stream, Kollmar Creek.[20]

Crook called a temporary halt about halfway down the valley and dispatched a contingent of auxiliaries, both Crow and Shoshone, to scout the valley beyond the point where it changes direction to the north. Some minutes after they disappeared from sight, the sound of gunfire was heard, followed by a reappearance of the auxiliary troops, gesticulating wildly and excitedly yelling, "Dakota! Dakota!" And Dakota and Northern Cheyenne warriors, led by Crazy Horse, were indeed in hot pursuit of the retreating scouting party. Those auxiliaries who had remained behind responded to this unexpected threat by promptly mounting a counter attack as the army frantically tried to organize itself for battle. There followed almost twenty minutes of close-in fighting during which Crazy Horse and his warriors lost their initial advantage of surprise. Meanwhile, other hostile forces had filtered down from the northwest to occupy Crook's Hill. By the time they were in place, Crook had completed deployment of his forces, and there ensued one of only a few pitched battles fought between the frontier army and Indian opponents.[21]

The Battle of the Rosebud was waged along a broad front of about three miles with most of the action occurring on Crook's Hill. After dispatching some cavalry units to secure his left flank and positioning other units on the high bluffs south of the river, General Crook reinforced the Crow and Shoshone vanguard holding off the enemy in the northeast section of the battlefield. Once the initial thrust of Crazy Horse and his men had been stalled and the attackers dispersed, General Crook ordered his infantry, supported by several companies of dis-mounted cavalry, to challenge the enemy's control of Crook's Hill. At the same time cavalry units charged both the right and left flanks of the hill, and within an hour the Dakota and their allies had been forced to retreat to the protective cover of Conical Hill. However, when the dust of battle had settled, Lieutenant Colonel W.B. Royall and five companies of cavalry, on Crook's left flank, found themselves isolated from the main body of troops by the valley of Kollmar Creek.[22]

The next phase of the battle began with a series of

isolated skirmishes along a broad front but culminated in an attack by a concentration of enemy
forces against Royall's position. Fearful that the
colonel and his men were in danger of being overrun,
Crook ordered his Indian auxiliaries in against the
attackers. Crow and Shoshone warriors rode down
into, and then swept up, the valley of the Kollmar to
hit the enemy. There followed another fierce hand-to-
hand battle, and, in the end, Royall was able to
redeploy his troops to a more defensible position. In
the confusion of battle, one of the colonel's troopers,
Sergeant Van Moll, found himself horseless in the
midst of a body of enemy warriors. An unlikely hero,
a small, deformed Crow called Humpy, dashed in
amongst the astonished Dakota and Northern
Cheyenne combatants to the sergeant's rescue. Van
Moll vaulted onto Humpy's pony behind the little
warrior, and the two rode off to the safety of their
own lines.[23]

Crook shored up and reformed his lines at midday.
With the battle seemingly at stasis, he detached eight
companies of cavalry under Captain Anson Mills with
orders to proceed down the valley of the Rosebud in
search of the enemy's village. Not long after the
detachment's departure, the enemy again concentrated
its forces against Colonel Royall. A courier was sent
after Mills to relay the general's orders that he and his
troopers were to rejoin the battle with an attack on
the enemy's rear flank. The captain left the valley of
the river to head directly for Conical Hill, where,
with a spirited cavalry charge, his forces surprised and
dispersed the enemy. Thus ended the Battle of the
Rosebud after almost six hours of more or less
continual fighting. Satisfied that his Indian opponents
had permanently abandoned the field to him, Crook,
early the next day, withdrew his men. He called for an
overnight camp on a tributary of Tongue River, but

the Crow auxiliaries chose to continue on in search of their own people. The next day Crook and his troops returned to the camp on Goose Creek to await the arrival of requested reinforcements.[24]

Plenty Coups, a participant in the battle, later remembered that he and his fellow tribesman had left Crook's command with ten scalps and a sense of pride in the belief that they had acquitted themselves in battle with both honor and bravery.[25] Frank Grouard believed that if the Crow and the Shoshone had not met the first charge of enemy warriors, at least half of Crook's command would have been wiped out at that point.[26] Crook's aide-de-camp, Lieutenant John Bourke, agreed that the Crow auxiliaries had fought well. He was of the opinion, in fact, that the relief of Colonel Royall and his stranded troops by Crow and Shoshone auxiliaries was the turning point in the battle.[27] Captain Gerhard Luke Kuhn, commanding officer of Company K of the Fourth Infantry, held an opposite opinion. He believed that the presence of Indian auxiliary forces hampered the effectiveness of his soldiers. The problem was that the soldiers found it difficult to distinguish "friendlies" from "hostiles," inhibiting the discharge of weapons.[28] One of the journalists who covered the campaign, John G. Finerty, wrote that the Crow were mostly braggarts in peace and laggards in war. His assessment of the tribe's military prowess may have been colored by the revulsion he experienced as he watched their mutilation and dismemberment of an enemy warrior's body.[29]

Given the length of the engagement and the number of participants, casualties were light. According to Plenty Coups, the Crow took eleven; one dead and ten wounded.[30] With regard to army casualties, Grouard reported that twenty-eight soldiers had been killed and fifty-six wounded.[31] Captain Kuhn counted only nine dead and twenty wounded, while Bourke believed that total casualties, killed and wounded, amounted to fifty-seven.[32] General Crook's official report listed ten of his men killed and twenty-one wounded. Crazy Horse later estimated his casualties in the battle at thirty-six killed and sixty-three wounded.[33]

Five days after the Battle of the Rosebud was fought, the Montana and Dakota Columns went their separate ways. General Terry remained aboard the *Far West*, while Custer led the Seventh Cavalry, which now included Mitch Boyer as guide and six Crow warriors as scouts, up the valley of the Rosebud to sweep the area south of the Yellowstone in search of a large Indian village thought to be someplace in that general vicinity. Colonel Gibbon returned his forces to patrol duty along the banks of the Yellowstone, closing off the possibility of escape for any of the enemy who might try to remove themselves from harm's way in the face of Custer's expected assault on their village. Gibbon was to proceed up river to the mouth of the Big Horn and then up the valley of that river to its confluence with the Little Big Horn.[34]

Custer and his troops encountered ever-increasing signs of recent Indian camp sites. On Saturday, June 24 his column intersected a wide fresh trail near present Busby, Montana, which appeared to head in the direction of the Little Big Horn. A halt was called here and a temporary camp established to await the return of three Crow scouts who had been sent ahead to scout out the area to the west. At about nine o'clock that evening, the three returned to report that although they had been unable to locate the dissidents' camp, they were satisfied that the trail they had been following did in fact lead to the Little Big Horn River. Custer responded to this intelligence by dispatching a larger scouting party under Lieutenant

Charles Varnum and which included Mitch Boyer, four Crow, and several Arikara Indians, with orders to pinpoint the camp's location. Two hours later the entire column was set in motion on a night march intended to place the Seventh Cavalry as close to the enemy as possible before daylight. Custer informed his officers that their troops would be allowed to rest for a full twenty-four hours before mounting an attack. The scouting party, in the meantime, had reached the divide which separates the valleys of the Rosebud and Little Big Horn Rivers at about two-thirty, and scrambled up to a lookout point called the Crow's Nest to await first light. Shortly after dawn broke, Lieutenant Varnum, who had dozed off, was awakened by his scouts to news that the valley of the Little Big Horn did indeed contain a large village of Indians.[35]

Although unable to see the village, Varnum sent two Arikara scouts back to intercept the column and inform Custer of the discovery. After receiving the message, Custer left his command to join the scouting party on Crow's Nest to see for himself. He couldn't really see enough to confirm the village's existence but was persuaded by Boyer that the guide had in fact seen the village clearly by dawn's early light, and that, furthermore, it was the largest congregation of Indians ever assembled in the region. When Lieutenant Colonel Custer rejoined the column, he was informed that enemy scouting parties had discovered the army's presence. It was perhaps for this reason that he changed his mind about giving his forces a day's rest, and instead issued an order to mount an immediate attack on the village. At about noon Major Frederick Benteen was detached with three troops of cavalry to scout the area south of the line of march, and Captain Thomas McDougall was detached with one troop of cavalry to support the slower-moving pack train.

Custer divided his forces again as the column approached what is today called Reno Creek. Shortly after two o'clock in the afternoon, Major Marcus Reno was ordered to advance down the valley of the Little Big Horn and to attack the village with three troops of cavalry. Custer then veered off to his right a bit to lead the remaining four troops of the Seventh Cavalry along the bluffs bordering the river's north bank into notorious oblivion.[36]

The Montana Column had meanwhile reached Fort Pease on June 23, and the *Far West*, carrying not only General Terry but Colonel Gibbon and Major Brisbin as well, arrived the next morning. Late that same afternoon the column, under the command of Brisbin, started up the east bank of the Big Horn, headed for the mouth of the Little Big Horn, to be followed by the *Far West*. Colonel Gibbon was feeling under the weather and therefore remained aboard the steamship. As Lieutenant Bradley and his scouting detail approached the rendezvous point early on the morning of June 26, they espied three Indians on the opposite bank of the Big Horn. Bradley sent several of his scouts down to river's edge to determine whether they were friendly or hostile. As he watched them conduct a conversation in sign language across the broad expanse of water, he was surprised to hear his men break out in a dolorous chant. When the scouts returned to report on what they had learned, the lieutenant learned that the three were Hairy Moccasin, White Man Runs Him, and Goes Ahead; three of six Crow scouts who had been detached to Custer's command at the mouth of the Rosebud. Bradley was told that Custer had engaged the enemy but that the Seventh Cavalry had been drawn toward a large village where the troopers were engulfed by over-whelming numbers of hostile Indians. At the time the three had left the battlefield, they averred, all but a few of Custer's men had been killed, including two Crow scouts, White Swan, and Half Yellow Face. The fate of Curley, the other Crow scout assigned to Custer, was unknown to them, but they assumed that he had also fallen in battle with Custer and his troopers.[37]

Bradley hurried back to the main body of the Montana Column to relay the bad tidings to Major Brisbin. The lieutenant's entire contingent of scouts had received the news of Custer's defeat with sobs, tears, and the wailing sounds of their mourning song. He therefore had allowed them to remain behind long enough to recover from the shock of learning that their long-time enemy had just administered a devastating defeat to the U.S. Army. Once Bradley was out of sight, however, the scouting detail, led by Barney Bravo, crossed the river to join their colleagues on the west bank, and then all high-tailed it to Crow Agency as fast as their mounts would carry them.[38]

As it turned out, Half Yellow Face and White Swan had survived the battle after all. What had happened was that they had become separated from their fellow scouts when Major Reno and his troops left the main column to attack the village. That they, along with a dozen or so Arikara scouts, accompanied the major is clear, but there is some controversy surrounding the circumstances under which the separation occurred. White Man Runs Him and Curley both later recalled that the two were ordered by Custer to ascend a nearby ridge to check on enemy movements, but that rather than reporting back they had joined Reno's forces.[39] Hairy Moccasin, on the other hand, remembered in 1911 that they had been assigned to Reno's contingent because they were familiar with the area.[40] Whatever the circumstances may have been, they were with Reno and his troopers when they collided with enemy forces not far from the southeastern corner of the village. In the confusion which followed, both the Arikara and Crow scouts followed the soldiers in their retreat into a grove of trees situated along the banks of the Little Big Horn. From here the survivors of the battle clambered up the bluffs on the north side of the river to what is today known as Reno's Hill, where they were rescued by the Montana Column the following day. According to Young Hawk, who was one of the Arikara scouts, White Swan took two wounds in the engagement, one in the arm and another in the leg.[41]

As for Curley, it seems that he, in company with Goes Ahead, White Man Runs Him, and Hairy Moccasin, remained with Custer's column for a time after Reno and his men were detached. At some point thereafter, Curley became separated from Custer and his forces. Apart from these two facts, though, there is little agreement in the various accounts which describe his role in the dramatic events which unfolded in the valley of the Little Big Horn on June 25, 1876. Curley's official rendering of these events took the form of an oral report he made to Lieutenant Bradley, through Tom Leforge, several days after the battle. In this account the scout said that he, Goes Ahead, White Man Runs Him, and Hairy Moccasin were some distance behind Custer's column when it was attacked. When the sounds of battle reached them, he left his companions and retreated to a hill nearby from which he watched the battle for a time. From this vantage point he spotted two Dakota ponies running loose and rode off to capture them. Finding that they slowed his progress in getting away from the battlefield, he abandoned them to make his way to the mouth of the Little Big Horn and the safety of the Montana Column.[42]

Widely regarded as the sole survivor of one of the

nation's most famous battles, Curley was asked to repeat his story on numerous occasions. In these subsequent accounts he arrogated to himself a more intimate and heroic role in the Battle of the Little Big Horn than reflected in his first telling of the events of that fateful day. In subsequent versions Curley claimed that he did not leave Custer's column before the fighting started as had the other three Crow scouts. Rather, he, in company with Mitch Boyer, stayed with Custer until after the battle began and he, Curley, left before it was over only because Boyer suggested to him that he should save himself.[43]

Statements made by Curley's fellow scouts only add confusion to an already confused picture. Goes Ahead, according to his wife, Pretty Shield, remembered that Curley had feigned illness to leave the column long before the engagement started. In an interview Goes Ahead gave in 1909, he refused to answer a question about Curley's departure from the column, but three years later he stated that his colleague had disappeared with an Arikara scout sometime before the engagement began.[44] White Man Runs Him couldn't remember seeing Curley at all after the column left Reno Creek.[45] An entirely different version of Curley's activities on that fateful day is provided by an Arikara scout named Red Star. He contended that Curley and an Arikara named Black Fox left the command together near Reno Creek to return to the Busby campsite. They had in mind, according to Red Star, stealing hard tack which had been cached there by some troopers.[46] Red Star's statement is partially confirmed by Private John Burkman, Custer's orderly, who happened to be with the column's pack train when the fighting started. He remembered that Curley and some Arikara scouts had approached the pack train sometime after he heard the first sounds of gunfire coming from the direction

CURLEY

Perhaps better known than any other Crow, his involvement in the Battle of the Little Big Horn is shrouded in controversy.

Courtesy National Anthropological Archives, Smithsonian Institution

of the Custer battlefield, but didn't comment on the scout's activities after that.[47]

It is likewise a matter of controversy as to when Hairy Moccasin, White Man Runs Him, and Goes Ahead left Custer and his troops, and what they did afterward. White Man Runs Him said in one interview that Boyer ordered them back to the pack train shortly before fighting broke out. On the way back they joined the soldiers defending Reno's Hill and remained there until nightfall. According to this account, they then left the defenders of the hill to make their way to the banks of the Big Horn, where they happened onto Bradley and his scouts.[48] On another occasion White Man Runs Him said that they ran into Benteen's troops, and after a short conversation with one of his troopers who spoke Crow, continued eastward and eventually circled around the battlefield to the Big Horn. Goes Ahead's version of the day's events generally conform to that of White Man Runs Him.[49] Hairy Moccasin, on the other hand, claimed that they did not leave the troopers until after fighting broke out. He went on to indicate that they later met the pack train but made no mention of their participation in the defense of Reno Hill.[50] Only marginally helpful in trying to trace their movements and activities is Red Star's account. The Arikara scout noted in this regard only that he and several other Arikara ran into the three someplace to the north of the pack train after the battle started.[51]

Mitch Boyer was the only member of the Crow contingent which served with Custer to lose his life in the battle. Boyer was experienced enough in the ways of Indian warfare to understand that Custer's chances of prevailing against the non-treaty Indians were remote. While approaching the village, two hours or so before hostilities began, he warned Custer that if they entered the village they would never come out.

WHITE MAN RUNS HIM

One of the six Crow scouts who, along with Curley, served with Custer and managed to survive the battle.

Courtesy National Anthropological Archives, Smithsonian Institution

In a conversation with a Private McGuire shortly before the fighting started, the frontiersman observed that there were far too many Indians ahead for the number of troops in Custer's command. He went on to express his fear that because he was so well known to the enemy, he would undoubtedly be a prime target in their eyes. When McGuire asked why, given his reservations about the impending battle, he simply didn't leave the column, Boyer replied that he had been drawing ten dollars per day for some time now and that he intended to stick it out until the bitter end.[52] Tom Leforge was later told by an unidentified informant that after Boyer had warned Custer about the odds facing him, Custer reminded him that he could honorably leave now that the village had been located. The guide retorted that he was capable of facing any situation that Custer's soldiers could handle.[53] Boyer's bravado cost him his life. His mutilated body was discovered along the banks of the Little Big Horn by soldiers of the Montana Column some twenty-four hours later.[54]

The enormity of Custer's defeat, coupled with Crow remembrances of the army's wretched performance against dissident Indians over the years, undoubtedly added to the tribe's anxiety and concern for its security. It is likely that the tearful reaction of Bradley's scouts to news of Custer's defeat was due, at least in part, to a fear that the tribe would now be in imminent danger of being overrun by its enemies. Within a week, though, Agent Clapp reported that tribal leaders had become convinced that the Battle of the Little Big Horn had given the dissidents quite enough fighting for the time being. It had been learned that as the Dakota and their allies left the battlefield area, they had abandoned their lodge poles, a certain indication that they intended to leave the scene of battle as quickly as possible. Some Crow, again according to Clapp, believed that the enemy had exhausted its supply of ammunition in the fray.[55]

And, although the Crow had no way of knowing this, the humiliation suffered by the army at the Battle of the Little Big Horn would harden its resolve to bring the non-treaty Indians to terms once and for all. After tidying up the battlefield, General Terry moved the Montana Column, reinforced by what remained of the Seventh Cavalry, down the Big Horn River to its mouth. Joined by fifty Crow scouts, he moved down the Yellowstone to the mouth of the Rosebud. Here the general received more reinforcements in the form of six companies of the Twenty-second Infantry under Lieutenant Colonel Elwell Otis and six companies of the Fifth Infantry commanded by Colonel Nelson A. Miles. On August 18 Terry set a course up the Rosebud with his combined forces in search of the enemy.[56]

General Crook remained at his camp on Goose Creek awaiting reinforcements, unaware of Custer's defeat until so notified by a courier from General Terry on July 10. Colonel Wesley Merritt joined Crook with the long-awaited reinforcements in the form of his Fifth Cavalry on August 3. Merritt's command included William F. Cody. Buffalo Bill had been performing with his Wild West troupe in Wilmington, Delaware when he learned that the Fifth Cavalry, with which he had served as chief scout from 1868 to 1871, had been ordered to take the field against the Dakota. He immediately disbanded his theatrical company and caught a train to Cheyenne where he was reinstated as chief scout for the regiment. Crook's reinforced command immediately headed north to join Terry on the Rosebud. The newly combined forces then followed a fresh trail to the mouth of Powder River where a temporary camp was established on August 17.[57]

While in camp here the Crow scouts, impatient with the army's inaction, abandoned the campaign.[58] Crook and Terry divided their forces in late August. Terry, chasing a rumor that hostile Indians had been spotted down river on the Yellowstone, pointed his troops in that direction; but not having found any dissidents by September 5, he called off the campaign. Crook, in the meantime, had followed an Indian trail eastward until it petered out, and then continued on to Slim Buttes in northwestern South Dakota where an advance party found a small Dakota camp. The camp was attacked and destroyed. Following the battle of Slim Buttes, Crook sent his troops into winter quarters, and he made his way to Fort Laramie where he held consultations with General Sheridan.[59]

Crook took the field again on November 14 with a new command assigned to him at Fort Fetterman. His scouts reported the existence of a Cheyenne village on a tributary of Powder River, and a large force of cavalry under Colonel Ranald S. Mackenzie was ordered to the attack on the morning of November 25. The inhabitants of the village offered stiff resistance but in the end were forced to disperse, leaving their village to be destroyed by Mackenzie's troopers. Continuing its march, Crook's forces reached the headwaters of the Little Missouri River where, in late December, a contingent of one hundred or more Crow joined the expedition only to be told that the campaign had just been called off.[60]

Those Crow scouts who served with either Terry or Crook during this phase of the campaign against the non-treaty Indians had every right to conclude that little, if anything, had changed with regard to the army's ability to deal with hostile Indians. Those who served with Colonel Nelson A. Miles, on the other hand, were treated to a more aggressive and effective form of campaigning. On August 28 he began con-

struction of a cantonment near the mouth of the
Tongue River to serve as winter quarters for his
troops and as a storage depot for supplies and
equipment. Informed in mid-October that Sitting
Bull's warriors were harassing supply trains enroute
to his cantonment, Miles marched his Fifth Infantry
out of the temporary post in search of the malefactors. He found them camped about twenty miles
north of the mouth of Powder River, and was invited
into the village to confer with Sitting Bull. Nothing
came of the meeting; Miles insisted that the Indians
retire to a reservation, and Sitting Bull insisted that
the soldiers vacate Dakota territory. There ensued a
two-day battle, in which the Indians suffered a
complete rout and were forced to abandon most of
their supplies and horses to the colonel's disciplined
infantry. A few drifted into a reservation located on
Cheyenne River, but Sitting Bull led most of his
Uncpapa band north out of harm's way. Others fled
southward to Crazy Horse's camp, which at the time
was located on Powder River.[61]

Despite uncommonly cold and disagreeable weather,
the persistent Miles spent the better part of the next
two months in pursuit of Sitting Bull and his followers. In November he sent a message to Thomas
Leforge, asking that he raise a contingent of Crow
scouts to once again assist the army in its campaign
against the Dakota and their allies. The veteran
frontiersman was able to raise a suitable contingent.
When they arrived at the cantonment, they were
assigned to a detachment being dispatched to hunt
down a band of hostile Cheyenne warriors, reported
to be someplace to the east of Tongue River. After a
fruitless search which took them as far as Heart River,
the expedition returned to the post. Following several
weeks of inactivity, an incident occurred which would
end the scouting party's association with Miles and

which may well have prolonged his campaign. On December 16, six chiefs from Crazy Horse's camp, recently moved from Powder River to the headwaters of the Tongue, were approaching the cantonment to discuss peace with Miles when they were spotted by Crow scouts returning from a buffalo hunt. Unaware of the party's peaceful intentions, the Crow staged an ambush. They killed five, and the survivor returned to his camp where he reported this bit of perfidy. Miles was furious; the entire Crow scouting contingent was sent packing.[62]

There followed a series of attacks on the cantonment by Crazy Horse and his warriors in what appears to have been an effort to draw Miles and his soldiers into an ambush. The colonel obliged in late December by leading seven companies of infantry up the valley of Tongue River. Early on the morning of January 8, Crazy Horse led an attack on the column. Miles was ready for him, however, and through effective utilization of artillery and intelligent deployment of troops was able to hold the attackers at bay until a blizzard forced the Indians to withdraw at midday. A week or so later, Sitting Bull visited Crazy Horse's village to announce that he was giving up the struggle and intended to soon move his forces out of the United States and into Canada. In late January, Crazy Horse abandoned his camp on Tongue River and moved to the valley of the Little Big Horn.[63]

The final phase of the army's war against the nontreaty Indians involved three approaches; peace missions to persuade as many dissidents as possible to submit to reservation life, a continuation of military pressure by Colonel Miles, and the establishment of permanent military installations in strategic locations. Utilizing friendly Indians such as Chief Spotted Tail of the Brule Tribe, the army spread the word that the government would no longer insist on unconditional

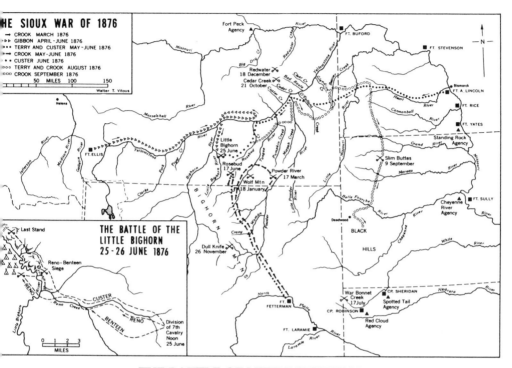

THE BATTLE OF LITTLE BIGHORN

Reprinted, by permission of the author, Robert M. Utley, *Frontier Regulars: The United States Army and the Indian, 1866–1891*, Macmillan Publishing Co., 1973.

surrender of the dissidents and that some reservations would be moved to more desirable locations. There followed a migration of non-treaty Indians to one or another of the Dakota reservations, culminating in the appearance of Crazy Horse at Red Cloud Agency on May 6. This left only some Minneconjou under Chief Lame Deer and the Uncpapa under Sitting Bull as fugitives in the eyes of the army. On May 7, 1877 Colonel Miles located Lame Deer's village on a tributary of the Rosebud and quickly mounted a surprise attack. The chief was killed in the battle

along with thirteen other warriors. The survivors fled
to the safety of neighboring hills and canyons.[64] Miles
spent most of the summer of 1877 tracking them
down and rounding up other small bands which for
one reason or another had not yet submitted to
reservation life. He was assisted in this effort by four
hundred auxiliary Crow troops.[65]

By summer's end the Crow could rest secure in the
knowledge that for the first time in several decades
they could hunt, move camp, or simply go about the
daily business of living without fear of attack. Plenty
Coups, reminiscing in the early 1920s about the
Battle of the Little Big Horn, observed that the white
soldiers had been unlucky but that in the end, they
had prevailed over the Dakota. From the Crow point
of view, in the chief's words, this meant that "We
could now sleep without expecting to be routed out
to fight, and this was the first time I had known such
a condition."[66] The tribe's security was enhanced
during the summer of 1877 with the construction of
Fort Keogh on the site of Miles' cantonment at the
mouth of the Tongue, and the building of Fort Custer
twelve miles north of Custer Battlefield.[67] Sitting Bull
returned to the United States in 1881, and on July 19
of that year surrendered to United States authorities
at Fort Buford.[68]

The Crow tribe was undoubtedly aware of the role
Colonel Miles had played in creating their new, secure
environment. Its members were given an opportunity
to express their gratitude to him during the spring of
1878. While en route to the site of Custer's last
battle, Miles and his retinue unexpectedly entered a
Crow camp situated near the mouth of the Big Horn
River. Crow leaders invited the soldiers to stop over
to commemorate the colonel's victory over the
Dakota. It took the camp several days to complete
preparations for the celebration, and on the afternoon

of the third day, Crook and his party were treated to what amounted to a military review. The festivities got underway with the firing of a rifle, whereupon a large body of warriors, each mounted on a prancing pony, moved from one end of the camp in a column of twos to pass in review before Miles and Chief Blackfoot. Miles was impressed with the precision with which the drill was carried out. He was even more impressed by the brilliant raiment of the participants; as near as he was able to make out, each outfit was unique. Once the body of warriors had all passed in review, they retired to a plain which adjoined the camp where a mock battle was staged for the enjoyment of the onlookers.[69]

The celebration held in honor of Miles was undoubtedly staged in affirmation of the tribe's decision, taken during the early years of the nineteenth century, to align itself with the whites. Great Father's decision to take the field against the Dakota owed little or nothing to a concern for Crow security, but it nonetheless had the effect of neutralizing the military power of the tribe's most dangerous enemies. Crow warriors weren't totally divorced from the campaign, but their participation was reluctant and marginal. It had become an article of faith among them that in the unlikely event that the frontier army should ever engage the Dakota and their allies in battle, it would be bested. In the end, though the army, smarting from its humiliating defeat along the banks of the Little Big Horn, was able to prevail in its face-off against the non-treaty Indians. This meant, from the Crow perspective, that they no longer had to live in a state of constant readiness against an attack by their enemies. It also, as it turned out, meant that the Crow male, as his role of warrior lapsed, would find himself deprived of his main reason for being. Likewise, as buffalo disappeared, he would soon lose his role as a provider. What was really happening, of course, was that the Crow way of life was rapidly drawing to a close.

NOTES

1. Francis Paul Prucha, *The Great Father: The United States Government and the American Indians* (Lincoln and London: University of Nebraska Press, 1984), I, 540.
2. Robert M. Utley, *Frontier Regulars: The United States Army and the Indian, 1866-1891* (New York: Macmillan Publishing Co., Inc.; London: Collier Macmillan Publishing Co., 1973), pp. 248–50.
3. James H. Bradley, *The March of the Montana Column: A Prelude to the Custer Disaster,* ed. Edgar I. Stewart (Norman: University of Oklahoma Press, 1961), pp. 37–48.
4. *Ibid,* pp. 48–51; Thomas B. Marquis, *Memoirs of a White Crow Indian* (Lincoln: University of Nebraska Press, 1974), pp. 210–1.
5. Bradley, *op. cit.,* pp. 63–68.
6. Marquis, *op. cit.,* pp. 212–3.
7. Bradley, *op. cit.,* pp. 93, 96–102.
8. *Ibid,* pp. 103–4; Marquis, *op. cit.,* p. 241.
9. Utley, *op. cit.,* p. 252; Bradley, *op. cit.,* pp. 108–9.
10. *Ibid,* pp. 109–12.
11. *Ibid,* pp. 113–4, 121–2.
12. Marquis, *op. cit.,* pp. 221–2.
13. Bradley, *op. cit.,* pp. 123–6, 132–7.
14. John Gregory Bourke, *On the Border with Crook* (Chicago: The Rio Grande Press, Inc., 1962), p. 291.
15. *Ibid,* pp. 294–7.
16. Joe DeBarthe, *Life and Adventures of Frank Grouard,* ed. Edgar I. Stewart (Norman: University of Oklahoma Press, 1958), pp. 214–21.
17. John F. Finerty, *War Path and Bivoac or the Conquest of the Sioux* (Norman: University of Oklahoma Press, 1961), pp. 66–68.
18. Bourke, *op. cit.,* pp. 308–10.
19. Finerty, *op. cit.,* pp. 76–80.
20. Neil C. Mangum, *Battle of the Rosebud: Prelude to the Little Big Horn* (El Segundo: Upton & Sons, 1987), pp. 52–53.
21. De Barthe, *op. cit.,* pp. 224–5; Frank B. Linderman, *Plenty Coups, Chief of the Crows* (Lincoln: University of Nebraska Press, 1962), pp. 165–6; Bourke, *op. cit.,* p. 311.
22. James H. Nottage, "The Big Horn and Yellowstone Expedition of 1876," *Annals of Wyoming,* XLV, No. 1 (Spring, 1973), 35; Finerty, *op. cit.,* pp. 84–85; De Barthe, *op. cit.,* pp. 225–6.
23. Bourke, *op. cit.,* pp. 312–3; Finerty, *op. cit.,* pp. 86–88.
24. De Barthe, *op. cit.,* pp. 228–9; Bourke, *op. cit.,* pp. 315–6.
25. Linderman, *op. cit.,* p. 171.
26. De Barthe, *op. cit.,* p. 224.
27. Bourke, *op. cit.,* p. 313.

28. Nottage, *loc. cit.*
29. Finerty, *op. cit.*, pp. 96–97.
30. Linderman, *op. cit.*, p. 171.
31. De Barthe, *op. cit.*, p. 233.
32. Nottage, *op. cit.*, p. 34; Bourke, *op. cit.*, p. 315.
33. Utley, *op. cit.*, p. 256.
34. Bradley, *op. cit.*, pp. 143–4.
35. Edgar I. Stewart, *Custer's Luck* (Norman: University of Oklahoma Press, 1955), pp. 252–6, 265–73.
36. *Ibid*, pp. 316–25; Utley, *op. cit.*, pp. 257–9.
37. Bradley, *op. cit.*, pp. 146–54.
38. *Ibid*, pp. 154–67; Thomas Marquis, *Custer, Cavalry & Crows: The Story of William White as Told to Thomas Marquis* (Fort Collins: The Old Army Press, 1975), p. 66.
39. Kenneth Hammer, ed., *Walter Camp's Notes on the Custer Fight* (Provo: Brigham Young Press, 1976), p. 166; W.A. Graham, *The Custer Myth: A Source Book of Custeriana* (New York: Bonanza Books, 1976), p. 13.
40. *Ibid*, p. 25; Hammer, *op. cit.*, pp. 176–7.
41. O.G. Libby, ed., *The Arikara Narrative of the Campaign Against the Hostile Dakotas, June 1876* (New York: Sol Lewis, 1973), pp. 95–101.
42. Marquis, *Memoirs*, pp. 249–50. We have only Leforge's recollection of Curley's conversation with the lieutenant. It is not mentioned in Bradley's journal, and if he made a formal report of the interview to his superiors, it has not surfaced.
43. For examples see Hammer, *op. cit.*, pp. 155–9; Graham, *op. cit.*, pp. 13–14, 18–19.
44. Frank B. Linderman, *Pretty Shield, Medicine Woman of the Crows* (Lincoln: University of Nebraska Press, 1972), pp. 232–3; Hammer, *op. cit.*, p. 174; Libby, *op. cit.*, p. 160.
45. Graham, *op. cit.*, pp. 15–16.
46. Libby, *op. cit.*, pp. 119–20.
47. Glendolin Damon Wagner, *Old Neutriment* (New York: Sol Lewis, 1973), pp. 158–9.
48. Graham, *op. cit.*, pp. 15–16.
49. Libby, *op. cit.*, pp. 159–60; Hammer, *op. cit.*, pp. 174–5.
50. *Ibid*, p. 177.
51. Libby, *op. cit.*, p. 120.
52. Hammer, *op. cit.*, p. 124.
53. Marquis, *Memoirs*, p. 249.
54. Stewart, *op. cit.*, pp. 469–70.
55. Letter, D.E. Clapp to J.Q. Smith, August 5, 1876, LRMS, reel 504.
56. Utley, *op. cit.*, pp. 267–9.
57. *Ibid*; Charles King, *Campaigning with Crook* (Norman: University of Oklahoma Press, 1964), pp. 104–6.
58. Marquis, *Memoirs*, p. 263.
59. Utley, *op. cit.*, pp. 269–71.
60. Bourke, *op. cit.*, pp. 392–5.
61. Utley, *op. cit.*, pp. 273–4.
62. Marquis, *Memoirs*, pp. 266–70; Marquis, *Custer, Cavalry*, p. 97.
63. Utley, *op. cit.*, pp. 276–8.
64. *Ibid*, pp. 279–81.
65. Letter, N.A. Miles to Assistant Adjutant General, July 14, 1877, LRMS, reel 507.
66. Linderman, *Plenty Coups*, pp. 176–7.

67. Richard Upton, ed., *Fort Custer on the Big Horn, 1877–1898: Its History and Personalities as Told by Its Contemporaries* (Glendale: The Arthur H. Clark Company, 1973), p. 18.
68. Utley, *op. cit.,* p. 288.
69. Nelson Appleton Miles, *Personal Recollections and Observations of General Nelson A. Miles* (New York: Da Capo Press, 1969), pp. 283–6.

BIBLIOGRAPHY

1 GOVERNMENT PUBLICATIONS
   BOARD OF INDIAN COMMISSIONERS. Annual Reports.
   COMMISSIONER OF INDIAN AFFAIRS. Annual Reports.
   CONGRESSIONAL GLOBE.
   CONGRESSIONAL RECORD.
   Culbertson, Thaddeus A., ed. John Francis McDermott. *Journal of an Expedition to the Mauvaises Terres and the Upper Missouri in 1850.* Bureau of American Ethnology Bulletin 147. Washington: Government Printing Office, 1952.
   Explorer of the Northern Plains; Lieutenant Gouverneur K. Warren's Preliminary Report of Exploration in Nebraska and Dakota, in the Years 1855-'56-'57. Washington: Government Printing Office, n.d.
   Hodge, Frederick Webb, *Handbook of American Indians North of Mexico.* Bureau of American Ethnology Bulletin 30. 2 vols.; Washington: Government Printing Office, 1912.
   Kappler, Charles J., *Indian Affairs: Laws and Treaties.* 2nd ed.; 2 vols.; Washington: Government Printing Office, 1904.
   Kurz, Rudolph Friederich, *Journal of Rudolph Friederich Kurz,* ed. J. N. B. Hewitt. Bureau of American Ethnology Bulletin 115. Washington: Government Printing Office, 1937.
   Mallery, Garrick, *Pictographs of the North American Indians; A Preliminary Paper.* Fourth Annual Report of the Bureau of Ethnology, 1882–83. Washington: Government Printing Office, 1886.
   ———, *Picture Writing of the American Indians.* Tenth Annual Report of the Bureau of Ethnology, 1888–89. Washington: Government Printing Office, 1893.
   Papers Relating to Talks and Councils Held with the Indians in Dakota and Montana Territories in the Years 1866–1869. Washington: Government Printing Office, 1868.
   Raynolds, W. F., *Report on the Exploration of the Yellowstone River.* Washington: Government Printing Office, 1868.
   Royce, Charles C., *Land Cessions in the United States.* Eighteenth Annual Report of the Bureau of Ethnology, 1896–97. 2 vols.; Washington: Government Printing Office, 1899.

UNITED STATES CONGRESS: SENATE
Joshua Pilcher's Report of December 1, 1831, Senate Document No. 90, Serial 213.
Indian Hostilities, Senate Executive Document No. 13, Serial 1308.
Letter from the Secretary of War, December 14, 1872, Senate Executive Document No. 16, Serial 1545.
UNITED STATES CONGRESS: HOUSE OF REPRESENTATIVES
Memorial of the Legislative Assembly of Montana, House Miscellaneous Document No. 43, Serial 1385.
Appropriations of Crow Indians, House Executive Document No. 42, Serial 1372.
The Extermination of the American Bison, House Miscellaneous Document No. 600, Part 2, Serial 2582.

2 NATIONAL ARCHIVES
Letters Received by the Office of Indian Affairs, Montana Superintendency, 1864–1880, microcopy 234, reels 488–508.
Letters Received by the Office of Indian Affairs, Upper Platte Agency, 1836–66, microcopy 234, reels 889–891.
Letters Received by the Office of Indian Affairs, Upper Missouri Agency, 1874–1881, microcopy 234, reels 883–888.
Records of the Montana Superintendency of Indian Affairs, 1867–1873, microcopy 883, reels 1–3.
Records of the Office of Indian Affairs: Letters Sent, microcopy 21, reels 85–134.
Documents Relating to the Negotiations of Ratified and Unratified Treaties with Various Tribes of Indians, 1801 to 1869, microcopy T-494.
Returns from U.S. Military Posts, 1800–1916, microcopy 6517, reels 347, 1190.

3 UNPUBLISHED MATERIAL
MISSOURI HISTORICAL SOCIETY
Fur Trade Envelopes
Kaskaskia Papers
Meriwether Lewis Collection
Pierre Chouteau Collection
Sublette Family Papers
ILLINOIS STATE HISTORICAL LIBRARY
Pierre Menard Collection

HISTORICAL SOCIETY OF MONTANA LIBRARY
William T. Wheeler Papers
Hans Peter Koch Papers
General Correspondence, 1864–1888, Executive
Office
James S. Brisbin Papers
U.S. Department of Interior, Upper Missouri Agency
Records
Martin Maginnis Papers
Charles Avery Reminiscences
Merrill G. Burlingame, *Historical Background for the
Crow Indian Treaty of 1868*
BANCROFT LIBRARY
Col. Robert Campbell's Narrative
THE NEWBERRY LIBRARY
George M. Templeton Papers, 1852–1858
RENNE LIBRARY, BOZEMAN, MONTANA
Bozeman's Early Business Men
AMERICAN HERITAGE CENTER, LARAMIE, WYOMING
Thomas Leforge Manuscript Collection
WYOMING STATE ARCHIVES
Records of the War Department Army Commands,
Deparent of the Platte, microcopy
MANUSCRIPTS
Medicine Crow, Joe, *The Effects of European Cultural
Contacts Upon the Economic, Social, and
Religious Life of the Crow Indians*. M. A.
Thesis, University of Southern California,
1938.
Stafford, John Wade, *Crow Culture Change: A
Geographical Analysis*, Ph.D. Thesis,
Michigan State University, 1971.
Whitner, Robert Lee, *The Methodist Episcopal
Church and Grant's Peace Plan: A Study of
the Methodist Agencies, 1870–1882*, Ph.D.
Thesis, University of Minnesota, 1959.

4 NEWSPAPERS
Avant Courier, Bozeman, Montana
Bozeman Chronicle
New York Times

5 BOOKS
Abel, Annie Heloise, ed., *Chardon's Journal at Fort Clark:
1834–1839*. Freeport: Books for Libraries Press, 1970.
———, ed., *Tabeau's Narrative of Loisel's Expedition to the
Upper Missouri*. Norman: University of Oklahoma
Press, 1939.

Alter, Cecil J., *James Bridger: Trapper, Frontiersman, Scout and Guide*. Salt Lake City: Shephard Book Co., 1925.

Armstrong, William H., *Warrior in Two Camps: Ely S. Parker, Union General and Seneca Chief*. Syracuse: Syracuse University Press, 1978.

Athearn, Robert G., *Forts of the Upper Missouri*. Englewood Cliffs: Prentice-Hall, Inc., 1967.

———, *Thomas Francis Meagher: An Irish Revolutionary in America*. Boulder: University of Colorado Press, 1949.

Beckwourth, James P., *The Life and Adventures of James P. Beckwourth as Told to Thomas P. Bonner*, ed. Delmont R. Oswald. Lincoln: University of Nebraska Press, 1972.

Belden, George P., *Belden, the White Chief: or, Twelve Years Among the Wild Indians of the Plains*. Athens: Ohio University Press, 1944.

Blish, Helen H., *A Pictographic History of the Oglala Sioux*. Lincoln: University of Nebraska Press, 1967.

Boller, Henry A., *Among the Indians: Four Years on the Upper Missouri, 1858–1862*. Lincoln and London: University of Nebraska Press, 1973.

Bolus, Malvina, ed., *People and Pelts: Selected Papers of the Second North American Fur Trade Conference*. Winnipeg: Peguis Publishers, 1972.

Bourke, John Gregory, *On the Border with Crook*. Chicago: The Rio Grande Press, 1962.

Brackenridge, Henry Marie, *Views of Louisiana: Together with a Journal of a Voyage up the Missouri in 1811*. Chicago: Quadrangle Books, Inc., 1962.

Bradley, James H., *The March of the Montana Column: A Prelude to the Custer Disaster*, ed. Edgar I. Stewart. Norman: University of Oklahoma Press, 1961.

Bradley Jr., Charles C., *A History of the Crow Indians*. Lodge Grass: Lodge Grass Schools, 1971.

Brown, Mark, *Plainsmen of the Yellowstone*. Lincoln: University of Nebraska Press, 1961.

Burlingame, Merrill G., *The Montana Frontier*. Helena: State Publishing Company, 1942.

Burpee, L. J., ed., *Journal of Laracque from the Assiniboine to the Yellowstone, 1805*. Publications of the Canadian Archives, No. 3. Ottowa: Government Printing Bureau, 1910.

Camp, Charles L., ed., *Essays for Henry Raup Warner*. San Francisco: California Historical Society, 1947.

———, *James Clyman, Frontiersman: The Adventures of a Trapper and Covered-wagon Emigrant as Told in His Own Reminiscences and Diaries*. Portland: Champoeg Press, 1960.

Carrington, Margaret Irvin Sullivant, *Ab-sa-ra-ka, Land of Massacre, Being the Experience of an Officer's Wife on the Plains: With an Outline of Indian Operations and Conferences from 1865–1878 by Henry B. Carrington.* 5th ed.; Ann Arbor: University of Microfilms International, 1979.

Carter, Harvey Lewis, *Dear Old Kit: The Historical Christopher Carson.* Norman: University of Oklahoma Press, 1968.

Catlin, George, *North American Indians: Being Letters and Notes on Their Manners, Customs and Conditions Written During Eight Year's Travel amongst the Wildest Tribes of Indians in North America.* 2 vols.; Edinburgh: John Grant, 1926.

Chittenden, Hiram Martin and Alfred Talbot Richardson, eds., *Life, Letters and Travels of Father De Smet.* 4 vols.; New York: Arno Press & New York Times, 1969.

Creigh, Dorothy Weyer, *Nebraska: A Centennial History.* New York: W.W. Norton & Company, Inc., 1977.

Curtis, Edward S. *The North American Indian.* 20 vols.; New York and London: Johnson Reprint Corporation, 1970.

David, Robert Beebe, *Finn Burnett: Frontiersman.* Glendale: The Arthur H. Clark Company, 1937.

Davis, Leslie B., ed., *Lifeways of Intermontane and Plains Montana Indians.* Occasional Papers of the Museum of the Rockies No. 1. Bozeman: Montana State University, n.d.

Dale, Harrison Clifford, ed., *The Ashley-Smith Explorations and the Discovery of a Central Route to the Pacific: 1822–29.* Cleveland: The Arthur H. Clark Company, 1918.

De Barthe, Joe, *Life and Adventures of Frank Grouard*, ed., Edgar I. Stewart. Norman: University of Oklahoma Press, 1958.

De Hoyos, Genevieve and Arturo De Hoyos, *The Crow Indian Reservation of Montana*, Provo: Brigham Young University Press, 1969.

Deloria, Jr., Vine and Raymond De Mallie, eds. *Proceedings of the Great Peace Commission of 1867–68,* Washington: The Institute for the Development of Indian Law, 1975.

Denig, Edwin Thompson, *Five Indian Tribes of the Upper Missouri*, ed. John C. Ewers. Norman: University of Oklahoma Press, 1961.

———, *Of the Crow Nation*, ed. John C. Ewers. New York: AMS Press, 1980.

Dunraven, Earl of, *The Great Divide: Travels on the Upper Yellowstone in the Summer of 1874.* Lincoln: University of Nebraska Press, 1967.

Ewers, John C., *Blackfeet Indians*. New York: Garland Publishing, Inc., 1974.

————, *The Blackfeet: Raiders on the Northwestern Plains*. Norman: University of Oklahoma Press, 1958.

Fay, George E., ed., *Treaties, Land Cessions, and Other U.S. Congressional Documents Relative to American Indian Tribes: The Crow, 1825–1912*. Greeley: Museum of Anthropology, 1982.

Ferguson, R. Brian, ed., *Warfare, Culture and Environment*. San Diego: Academic Press, 1984.

Ferris, W.A., *Life in the Rocky Mountains: A Diary of Wanderings on the Sources of the Rivers Missouri, Columbia, and Colorado from February, 1830, to November, 1835*, ed. Paul C. Phillips. Denver: Fred A. Rosenstock, The Old West Publishing Company, 1960.

Finerty, John F., *War Path and Bivouac or the Conquest of the Sioux*. Norman: University of Oklahoma Press, 1961.

Fremont, John Charles, *The Expeditions of John Charles Fremont*, eds. Donald Jackson and Mary Lee Spence. 2 vols.; Urbana, Chicago, and London: University of Illinois Press, 1970.

Frey, Rodney, *The World of the Crow: Indians as Driftwood Lodges*. Norman: University of Oklahoma Press, 1987.

Graham, W.A., *The Custer Myth: A Source Book of Custeriana*. New York: Bonanza Books, 1953.

Grinnell, George Bird, *The Fighting Cheyennes*. Norman: University of Oklahoma Press, 1966.

Hafen, Leroy R., and Ann Hafen, eds., *Powder River Campaigns and Sawyer's Expedition of 1865*. Vol. XII of the Far West and the Rockies Historical Series, 1820–1875. Glendale: The Arthur H. Clark Company, 1961.

Hamilton, W.T., *My Sixty Years on the Plains: Trapping, Trading, and Indian Fighting*. Norman: University of Oklahoma Press, 1960.

Hammer, Kenneth, ed., *Custer in '76: Walter Camp's Notes on the Custer Fight*. Provo: Brigham Young Press, 1976.

Hayden, F.V., *On the Ethnography and Philology of the Indian Tribes of the Missouri Valley; With a Map and Plates*. Transactions of the American Philosophical Society, Vol. XII (New Series). Philadelphia: Blanchard and Lea, 1862.

Heitman, Francis B., *Historical Register and Dictionary of the United States Army: From Its Organization, September 29, 1779 to March 2, 1903*. 2 vols.; Urbana: University of Illinois Press, 1965.

Henry, Alexander and David Thompson, *The Manuscript Journals of Alexander Henry and of David Thompson, 1799–1814,* ed. Elliott Coues. 2 vols.; Minneapolis: Ross and Haines, Inc., 1897.

Hirshson, Stanley P., *Grenville M. Dodge: Soldier, Politician, Railroad Pioneer.* Bloomington & London: Indiana University Press, 1967.

Hoxie, Frederick E., *The Crow.* New York and Philadelphia: Chelsea House Publishers, 1989.

Hurt, Wesley R., *Dakota Sioux Indians.* New York & London: Garland Publishing Inc., 1974.

Hyde, George E., *Red Cloud's Folk: A History of the Oglala Sioux.* Norman: University of Oklahoma Press, 1957.

———, *Spotted Tail's Folk: A History of the Brule Sioux.* Norman: University of Oklahoma Press, 1974.

Irving, Washington, *The Adventures of Captain Bonneville, U.S.A. in the Rocky Mountains and the Far West,* ed. Edgeley W. Todd. Norman: University of Oklahoma Press, 1961.

Jablow, Joseph, *The Cheyenne in Plains Indian Trade Relations, 1795–1840.* Monographs of the American Ethnological Society, Vol. XIX. New York: J.J. Augustin, 1951.

James, Thomas, *Three Years Among the Indians and the Mexicans,* ed. Milo Milton Quaife. New York: The Citadel Press, 1966.

Johansen, Dorothy O., ed., *Robert Newell's Memoranda: Travels in the Territory of Missouri, Travels to the Kayuse War; Together with a Report on the Indians South of the Columbia River.* Portland: Champoeg Press, 1959.

King, Charles, *Campaigning with Crook.* Norman: University of Oklahoma Press, 1964.

Koch, Elers, ed., *Journal of Peter Koch: 1869–1870.* Sources of Northwestern History No. 5. Missoula: State University of Montana, n.d.

Larpenteur, Charles, *Forty Years a Fur Trader on the Upper Missouri: The Personal Narrative of Charles Larpenteur, 1833–1872,* ed., Eliott Coues, Minneapolis: Ross & Haines, Inc., 1962.

Leonard, Zenas, *Zenas Leonard, Fur Trader,* ed. John C. Ewers. Norman: University of Oklahoma Press, 1959.

Libby, O.G., ed., *The Arikara Narrative of the Campaign Against the Hostile Dakotas, June, 1876.* New York: Sol Lewis, 1973.

Linderman, Frank B., *Plenty Coups, Chief of the Crows.* Lincoln: University of Nebraska Press, 1962.

———, *Pretty Shield, Medicine Woman of the Crows.* Lincoln: University of Nebraska Press, 1972.

Lockwood, James D., *Life and Adventures of a Drummer Boy.* Albany: John Skinner, 1873.

Lowe, Percival G., *Five Years a Dragoon: And Other Adventures on the Great Plains.* Norman: University of Oklahoma Press, 1965.

Lowie, Robert H., *The Crow Indians.* New York: Farrar & Rinehart, Incorporated, 1935.

———, *Indians of the Plains.* New York, Toronto, London: McGraw-Hill Book Company, Inc., 1954.

———, *The Material Culture of the Crow Indians.* New York: The American Museum of Natural History, 1922.

———, *Social Life of the Crow Indians.* New York: American Museum of Natural History, 1912.

———, *The Sun Dance of the Crow Indians.* New York: American Museum of Natural History, 1915.

Luttig, John C., *Journal of a Fur-Trading Expedition on the Upper Missouri, 1812–1813,* ed. Stella M. Drummond. New York: Argosy-Antiquarian Ltd., 1964.

McGinnis, Dale K. and Floyd W. Sharrock, *The Crow People.* Phoenix: Indian Tribal Series, 1972.

Mangum, Neil C., *Battle of the Rosebud: Prelude to the Little Big Horn.* El Segundo: Upton & Sons, 1987.

Marcy, R.B., *Thirty Years of Army Life on the Border.* New York: Harper and Brothers Publishers, 1866.

Marquis, Thomas, *Custer, Cavalry, & Crows: The Story of William White as Told to Thomas Marquis.* Fort Collins: The Old Army Press, 1975.

———, *Memoirs of a White Crow Indian.* Lincoln: University of Nebraska Press, 1974.

Masson, Louis Francois Rodrique, *Le Bourgeois de la Compagnie du Nord-Oest.* 2 vols.; New York: Antiquarian Press, Ltd., 1960.

Mattes, Merrill J., *Indians, Infants and Infantry: Andrew and Elizabeth Burt on the Frontier.* Denver: The Old West Publishing Company, 1960.

Maximilian, Alexander Philip, *Travels in the Interior of North America, 1832–1834.* 3 vols. in Reuben Gold Thwaites, ed., *Early Western Travels: 1748–1846.* Cleveland: The Arthur H. Clark Company, 1906.

Meek, Stephen Hall, *The Autobiography of a Mountain Man: 1805–1889.* Pasadena: Glen Dawson, 1948.

Meyer, Roy W., *History of the Santee Sioux.* Lincoln: University of Nebraska Press, 1967.

———, *The Village Indians of the Upper Missouri: The Mandans, Hidatsa, and Arikara.* Lincoln and London: University of Nebraska Press, 1977.

Miles, Nelson Appleton, *Personal Recollections and Observations of General Nelson A. Miles.* New York: Da Capa Press, 1969.

Morgan, Dale L., *Jedediah Smith and the Opening of the West.* Indianapolis and New York: The Bobbs-Merrill, Inc., 1953.

————, ed., *The World of William Ashley.* Denver: The Old West Publishing Company, 1964.

Morgan, Lewis Henry, *The Indian Journals, 1859–62.* Ann Arbor: The University of Michigan Press, 1959.

Moore, John H., *The Cheyenne Nation.* Lincoln and London: University of Nebraska Press, 1987.

Nabokov, Peter, *Two Leggings: The Making of a Crow Warrior.* New York: Thomas Y. Crowell Publishers, 1967.

Nasatir, A.P., ed., *Before Lewis and Clark: Documents Illustrating the History of the Missouri, 1785–1804.* 2 vols.; St. Louis: Historical Documents Foundation, 1952.

Oglesby, Richard Edward, *Manuel Lisa and the Opening of the Missouri Fur Trade.* Norman: University of Oklahoma Press, 1963.

Olson, James C., *Red Cloud and the Sioux Problem.* Lincoln: University of Nebraska Press, 1965.

Ostrander, Alson B., *An Army Boy of the Sixties,* ed. Edward R. Driggs. Yonkers-on-Hudson: World Book Company, 1936.

Plummer, Norman B., *Crow Indians.* New York & London: Garland Publishing, Inc., 1974.

Porter, Mae Reed and Odessa Davenport, *Scotsman in Buckskin: Sir William Drummond Stewart and the Rocky Mountain Fur Trade.* New York: Hastings House, 1963.

Point, Nicholas, *Wilderness Kingdom; Indian Life in the Rocky Mountains: 1840–1847.* New York, Chicago, San Francisco: Holt, Rinehart and Wilson, 1967.

Progressive Men of the State of Montana. Chicago: A.W. Bowen & Co., n.d.

Prucha, Francis Paul, *The Great Father: The United States Government and the American Indians.* 2 vols.; Lincoln and London: University of Nebraska Press, 1984.

Quaife, Milo Milton, ed., *Kit Carson's Autobiography.* Lincoln: University of Nebraska Press, 1966.

Russell, Osborne, *Osborne Russell's Journal of a Trapper,* ed. Aubrey L. Haines. Lincoln: University of Nebraska Press, 1959.

Ruxton, George Frederick, *Life in the Far West,* ed. Leroy R. Hafen. Norman: University of Oklahoma Press, 1964.

Schusky, Ernest L., *Political Organization of Native North Americans*. Washington: University Press of America, 1980.

Simonin, Louis L., *The Rocky Mountain West in 1867,* ed. William O. Clough. Lincoln: University of Nebraska Press, 1966.

Skarsten, M.O., *George Drouillard: Hunter and Interpreter for Lewis and Clark and Fur Trader, 1807–1810*. Glendale: The Arthur C. Clark Company, 1964.

Slattery, Charles Lewis, *Felix Reville Brunot*. New York: Longmans, Green, and Co., 1901.

Spence, Clark C., *Territorial Politics and Government in Montana: 1864–89*. Urbana, Chicago, London: University of Illinois Press, 1975.

Stanley, Edwin James, *Rambles in Wonderland*. New York and London: Garland Publishing, Inc., 1976.

Stewart, Edgar I., *Custer's Luck*. Norman: University of Oklahoma Press, 1955.

Stout, Tom, ed., *Montana: Its Story and Biography*. 3 vols.; Chicago and New York: The American Historical Society, 1921.

Stuart, Granville, *Forty Years on the Frontier*, ed. Paul C. Phillips. 2 vols.; Cleveland: The Arthur H. Clark Company, 1925.

Stuart, Paul, *The Indian Office: The Growth and Development of an American Institution, 1865–1900*. Ann Arbor: UMI Research Press, 1978, 1979.

Sullivan, Maurice S., *The Travels of Jedediah Smith: A Documentary Outline, Including the Journal of the Great American Pathfinder*. Santa Ana: The Fine Arts Press, 1934.

Sunder, John E., *The Fur Trade on the Upper Missouri, 1840–1865*. Norman: University of Oklahoma Press, 1965.

———, *Joshua Pilcher: Fur Trader and Indian Agent*. Norman: University of Oklahoma Press, 1968.

Thorpe, Raymond W. and Robert Bunker, *Crow Killer: The Saga of Liver-Eating Johnson*. Bloomington and London: Indiana University Press, 1969.

Thwaites, Reuben Gold, *Original Journals of the Lewis and Clark Expedition, 1804–1806*. 7 vols.; New York: Arno Press, 1969.

Topping, E.S., *The Chronicles of the Yellowstone*. Minneapolis: Ross & Haines, Inc., 1968.

Upton, Richard, ed., *Fort Custer on the Big Horn, 1877–1898: Its History and Personalities as Told by Its Contemporaries*. Glendale: The Arthur H. Clark Company, 1973.

Utley, Robert M., *Frontiersmen in Blue: 1848–1865*. Lincoln and London: University of Nebraska Press, 1981.
———, *Frontier Regulars: The United States Army and the Indian, 1866–1891*. New York: Macmillan Publishing Co., Inc.; London: Collier Macmillan Publishers, 1973.
———, *The Indian Frontier of the American West, 1846–1890*. Albuquerque: University of New Mexico Press, 1984.
Viola, Herman J., *Diplomats in Buckskins: A History of Indian Delegations in Washington City*. Washington: Smithsonian Institution Press, 1981.
Vaughn, Robert, *Then and Now, or Thirty-Six Years in the Rockies*. Minneapolis: Tribune Printing Company, 1900.
Victor, Frances Fuller, *The River of the West*. Oakland: Brooks-Sterling Company, 1974.
Voget, Fred W., *The Shoshoni-Crow Sundance*. Norman: University of Oklahoma Press, 1985.
Wagner, Glendolin Damon, *Old Neutriment*. New York: Sol Lewis, 1973.
——— and William A. Allen, *Blankets and Moccasins: Plenty Coups and His People, the Crows*. Caldwell: The Caxton Printers, Ltd., 1936.
Wildschut, William, *Crow Indian Medicine Bundles*. 2nd ed.; New York: Museum of the American Indian, 1975.
Wilson, Elinor, *Jim Beckwourth: Black Mountain Man and War Chief of the Crows*. Norman: University of Oklahoma Press, 1972.
Wishart, David J., *The Fur Trade of the American West 1807–1840: A Geographical Synthesis*. Lincoln and London: University of Nebraska Press, 1979.
Wood, W. Raymond and Thomas D. Theisson, eds., *Early Fur Trade on the Northern Plains*. Norman: University of Oklahoma Press, 1985.
Young, F.G., ed., *The Correspondence and Journals of Captain Nathaniel J. Wyeth*. New York: Arno Press, 1973.

5 ARTICLES

Algier, Keith, "Robert Meldrum and the Crow Peltry Trade," *Montana: The Magazine of Western History*, XXXVI, No. 3 (Summer, 1986), 36–47.
Bedford, Denton R., "The Fight at the Mountain on Both Sides," *Indian Historian*, VIII, No. 2 (Fall, 1975), 13–23.
"Biological Sketches of North Dakota Pioneers," *Collections of the State Historical Society of North Dakota*, VII (1924), 61–130.

Bolton, Herbert E., "New Light on Manuel Lisa and the Spanish Fur Trade," *Southwestern Historical Quarterly*, XVII (1913), 61–66.

Bradley, James H., "Affairs at Fort Benton from 1831 to 1869," *Contributions to the Historical Society of Montana*, III (1900), 201–87.

———, "Indian Traditions," *Contributions to the Historical Society of Montana*, IX (1923), 288–345.

Bray, Kingsley M., "Long Horn's Peace: A New View of Sioux-Crow Relations, 1851–1858," *Nebraska History*, LXVI, No. 1 (Spring, 1985), 28–47.

Bryan, Jr., Charles W., "Dr. Lamme's Gallant Sidewheeler Yellowstone," *Montana: The Magazine of Western History*, XV, No. 3, (July, 1965), 24–43.

Calloway, Colin G., "The Intertribal Balance of Power on the Great Plains," *Journal of American Studies*, XVI, No. 1 (1982), 25–47.

———, "The Only Way Open to Us: The Crow Struggle for Survival in the Nineteenth Century," *North Dakota History*, LIII, No. 3 (Summer, 1986), 24–34.

Chambers, James H., "Original Journals of James Chambers, Fort Sarpy," *Contributions to the Historical Society of Montana*, X (1940), 100–187.

Corson, Edward F., "A Final Note About Long Hair," *Archives of Dermatology*, LXXXIII, No. 2 (May, 1961), 852–3.

D'Elia, Donald J., "The Argument Over Civilian or Military Control," *The Historian*, XXIV, No. 2 (February, 1962), 207–25.

Danker, Donald F., "The Violent Deaths of Yellow Bear and John Richard Jr.," *Nebraska History*, LXIII, No. 2 (Summer, 1982), 137–51.

Davis, Leslie B., ed., "Symposium on the Crow-Hidatsa Separation," *Archaeology in Montana*, XX, No. 3 (September-December, 1979), 1–142.

Ewers, John C., "The Indian Trade of the Upper Missouri before Lewis and Clark: An Interpretation," *Bulletin of the Missouri Historical Society*, IV, No. 4, part 1 (July, 1954), 429–46.

———, "Intertribal Warfare as the Precursor of Indian-White Warfare on the Northern Plains," *Western Historical Quarterly*, VI, No. 4 (October, 1975), 397–410.

Gray, John S., "The Frontier Fortunes of John W. Smith," *Annals of Wyoming*, LI, No. 2 (Fall, 1979), 26–53.

Greene, Jerome A., ed., "We Do Not Know What the Government Intends to Do . . . . Lieutenant Palmer Writes from the Bozeman Trail," *Montana: The Magazine of Western History*, XXVIII, No. 3 (July, 1978), 16–35.

————, "The Hayfield Fight: A Reappraisal of a Neglected Action," *Montana: The Magazine of Western History,* XXII, No. 4 (October, 1972), 30–43.

Guthrie, Chester L. and Leo L. Gerald, "Upper Missouri Agency: An Account of the Indian Administration on the Frontier," *Pacific Historical Review,* X, No. 1 (March, 1941), 47–56.

Hamilton, William T., "A Trading Expedition Among the Indians in 1858," *Contributions to the Historical Society of Montana,* III (1900), 33–123.

Herdenreich, C. Adrian, "The Native American's Yellowstone," *Montana: The Magazine of Western History,* XXXV, No. 4 (October, 1985), 2–17.

Hill, Burton S., "Thomas A. Twiss, Indian Agent," *Great Plains Journal,* VI, No. 2 (Spring, 1967), 85–96.

Holmes, Reuben, "The Five Scalps," *Glimpses of the Past,* V, Nos. 1–3 (January-March, 1938), 1–54.

Humphreys, A. Glen, "The Crow Indian Treaties of 1868: An Example of Power Struggle and Confusion in United States Indian Policy," *Annals of Wyoming,* XLIII, No. 1 (Spring, 1971), 73–89.

Hutchins, James S., "Poison in the Pemmican: The Yellowstone Wagon-Road & Prospecting Expedition of 1874," *Montana: The Magazine of Western History,* VIII, No. 3 (July, 1958), 8–25.

"Investigations as to Causes of Indian Hostilities West of the Missouri River, 1824," *Annals of Wyoming,* XX, No. 3 (July, 1943), 198–220.

Jensen, Richard C., "A Description of the Fur Trade in 1831 by John Dougherty," *Nebraska History,* LVI, No. 1 (Spring, 1975), 109–20.

"The Journals of Charles Le Raye," *South Dakota Historical Collections,* V (1905), 150–80.

Koch, Peter, "Life at Muscleshell in 1869 and 1870," *Contributions to the Historical Society of Montana,* II (1898), 292–303.

————, "The Crow Indians and Their Neighbors," *Nation,* XXVIII (Feb. 13, 1879), 116–17.

————, "A Trading Expedition Among the Crow Indians, 1873–74," ed. Carl Cone, *Mississippi Valley Historical Review,* XXXI, No. 4 (December, 1944), 407–30.

Lass, William E., "Steamboats on the Yellowstone," *Montana: The Magazine of Western History,* XXXV, No. 4 (October, 1985), 26–41.

Lowie, Robert H., "Minor Ceremonies of the Crow Indians," *Anthropological Papers of the American Museum of Natural History,* XXXI, Part 5 (1924), 329–65.

McClernand, Edward J., "Service in Montana, 1870 and 1871," *Military Affairs*, XV, No. 4 (Winter, 1951), 192-8.

Mattison, Roy H., "The Indian Frontier on the Upper Missouri to 1865," *Nebraska History*, XXXIX, No. 3 (September, 1958), 241-66.

———, "The Upper Missouri Fur Trade: Its Methods of Operation," *Nebraska History*, XLII, No. 1 (March, 1961), 1-28.

Murphy, William, "The Forgotten Battalion," *Annals of Wyoming*, VII, No. 2 (October, 1930), 383-401.

Nasatir, Abraham P., "Notes and Documents: The International Significance of the Jones and Immell Massacre and of the Aricara Outbreak in 1823," *Pacific Northwest Quarterly*, XXX (1939), 77-108.

Nottage, James H., "The Big Horn and Yellowstone Expedition of 1876," *Annals of Wyoming*, XLV, No. 1 (Spring, 1973), 27-46.

Ouivey, Addison M., "The Yellowstone Expedition of 1874," *Contributions to the Historical Society of Montana*, I (1876), 268-84.

———, ed. "Bradley Manuscript: Book F," *Contributions to the Historical Society of Montana*, VIII (1917), 197-200.

Reid, Russell and Clell G. Gannon, eds., "Journal of the Atkinson-O'Fallon Expedition," *North Dakota Historical Quarterly*, IV (October, 1929), 5-56.

Ronan, Peter, "Discovery of Alder Gulch," *Contributions to the Historical Society of Montana*, III (1900), 143-52.

Rowe, David C., "Government Relations with the Fur Trappers of the Upper Missouri: 1820-1840," *North Dakota History*, XXXV, No. 2 (Spring, 1968), 481-505.

Schoenberger, Dale T., "Custer's Scouts," *Montana: The Magazine of Western History*, XVI, No. 2 (April, 1966), 40-49.

Schusky, Ernest L., "The Upper Missouri Indian Agency: 1819-1868," *Missouri Historical Review*, LXV, No. 3 (April, 1971), 249-69.

Sievers, Michael A., "The Administration of Indian Affairs on the Upper Missouri, 1858-1865," *North Dakota History*, XXXVIII, No. 3 (Summer, 1971), 367-94.

Simms, S.C., "Traditions of the Crows," *Field Columbian Museum, Anthropological Series*, II, No. 6 (1903), 281-316.

Spence, Clark C., "A Celtic Nimrod in the Old West," *Montana: The Magazine of Western History*, IX, No. 2 (Spring, 1959), 56-66.

Stuart, James, "The Yellowstone Expedition of 1863," *Contributions to the Historical Society of Montana*, I (1876), 149–233.

Thane, James L., Jr., "The Montana Indian War of 1867," *Arizona and the West*, X, No. 2 (Summer, 1968), 153–70.

"Trade and Intercourse," *Annals of Wyoming*, XV, No. 2 (April, 1943), 133–42.

Voget, Fred, "Crow Socio-Cultural Groups," *International Congress of Americanist Proceedings*, No. 29 (1952), 88–93.

Wagner, Oswald F., "Lutheran Zealots Among the Crows," *Montana: The Magazine of Western History*, XXII (April, 1972), 2–19.

Weist, Katherine M., "An Ethnohistorical Analysis of Crow Political Alliances," *The Western Canadian Journal of Anthropology*, VII, No. 4 (Winter, 1977), 34–54.

White, Richard, "The Winning of the West: The Expansion of the Western Sioux in the Eighteenth and Nineteenth Centuries," *The Journal of American History*, LXV, No. 2 (September, 1978), 319–43.

Wilson, Wesley C., "The U.S. Army and the Piegans—The Baker Massacre of 1870," *North Dakota History*, XXXII, No. 1 (January, 1965), 40–58.

INDEX

#2